social research

An International Quarterly
Vol 77 : No 4 : Winter 2010

EDITOR Arien Mack

EDITORIAL BOARD Arjun Appadurai, Ahmed Bawa, Alice Crary, Oz Frankel, Elzbieta Matynia, Corey Robin, Alan Ryan, Jamie Walkup

MANAGING EDITOR Cara Schlesinger

COPY EDITOR Bill Finan

MANAGING EDITORIAL ASSISTANTS Melynda Fuller, Kianoosh Hashemzadeh, and Lesley Steele

CONFERENCE COORDINATOR Roberta Sutton

ENDANGERED SCHOLARS WORLDWIDE RESEARCH ASSISTANT John Clegg

COVER Jamie Prokell

BUSINESS & EDITORIAL OFFICE

Social Research, The New School for Social Research, 80 Fifth Avenue– 7th Floor, New York, NY 10011. Email: socres@newschool.edu

SUBSCRIPTIONS

Print + Online: $54 per year individuals, $180 libraries and institutions. Print only: $50 individuals, $170 libraries and institutions. Online only: $44 individuals, $155 libraries and institutions.

Single print issues available through our office. Agency discounts available. Subscribe online at <www.socres.org> or contact our office.

Social Research is published quarterly by The New School for Social Research, a division of The New School, 66 West 12th Street, New York, NY 10011.

Contributions should be no more than 8,000 words and formatted according to MLA style. Please see our website at <www.socres.org> for complete submission guidelines. Articles published in *Social Research* may not be reprinted without permission.

Back issues, if available, may be ordered from our business and editorial office. Issues from 2002 to date are also available online through our website at <www.socres.org>. Reprints of other issues may be ordered from Periodicals Service Co., 11 Main St., Germantown, NY 12526. Microfilm or microfiche copies of complete volumes of Social Research may be ordered from Bell & Howell Information and Learning/ UMI, P.O. Box 1346, Ann Arbor, MI 48106.

Social Research is indexed in *ASSIA, Current Contents / Social & Behavioral Sciences, Public Affairs Information Service (PAIS), Research Alert, Social Sciences Citation Index, Social Scisearch,* and *United States Political Science Documents.*

Copyright 2011 by The New School. All rights reserved. ISSN 0037-783X.
ISBN 978-1-933481-23-4

Periodicals postage paid at New York, NY and at additional mailing offices.

Postmaster: Send address changes to *Social Research*, 80 Fifth Avenue, Room 715, New York, NY 10011.

Contents

From Impunity to Accountability: Africa's Development in the 21st Century

v Endangered Scholars Worldwide

xiii BEFEKADU DEGEFE AND BERHANU NEGA
Guest Editor's Introduction: Accountability for Development in Africa

1049 MARK HAUGAARD
Democracy, Political Power, and Accountability

1075 WILLIAM EASTERLY
Democratic Accountability in Development: The Double Standard

1105 PAUL COLLIER
The Political Economy of Natural Resources

1133 ROBERT H. BATES
Democracy in Africa: A Very Short History

1149 THANDIKA MKANDAWIRE
Aid, Accountability, and Democracy in Africa

1183 GEORGE B. N. AYITTEY
Traditional Institutions and the State of Accountability in Africa

1211 AGNÈS CALLAMARD
Accountability, Transparency, and Freedom of Expression in Africa

1241 CLEMENT EME ADIBE
Accountability in Africa and the International Community

1281 NICOLAS VAN DE WALLE AND KRISTIN MCKIE
Toward an Accountable Budget Process in Sub-Saharan Africa: Problems and Prospects

1311 MUENI WA MUIU
Colonial and Postcolonial State and Development in Africa

1339 MWANGI S. KIMENYI, JOHN MUKUM MBAKU, AND
NELIPHER MOYO
Reconstituting Africa's Failed States: The Case of Somalia

1367 KELECHI A. KALU
Nigeria: Learning from the Past to Meet the Challenges of the 21st Century

1401 BERHANU NEGA
No Shortcut to Stability: Democratic Accountability and Sustainable Development in Ethiopia

1447 INDEX, VOL. 77: 1-4

NOTES ON CONTRIBUTORS
Inside Back Cover

Endangered Scholars Worldwide

BELGIUM

According to the Network for Education and Academic Rights (NEAR), **MARIANNE MAECKELBERGH,** a U.S. scholar based in the Netherlands, has accused Belgian police of abusing her along with many other arrestees at a "No Borders" protest camp in Brussels. Maeckelbergh, an assistant professor of cultural anthropology at the University of Leiden, was reportedly arrested on October 1, 2010, while taking pictures of the arrest of activists at the protest camp. A statement by her publisher, Pluto Press, claims that "when Marianne began taking pictures, she was arrested. She was taken into police custody where she was violently dragged by her hair, chained to a radiator, hit, kicked, spat upon, and threatened with sexual assault by the police. She also witnessed the torture of another prisoner also chained to a radiator." She has since been released, but has yet to have her property, including her camera with photos, returned by the police. Maeckelbergh is the author of *The Will of the Many: How the Alterglobalisation Movement is Changing the Face of Democracy,* and focuses her academic research on the anthropology of globalization, democracy, and social movements. She was due to observe decision-making structures within the No Borders camps on October 2-3, but was arrested before this took place.

Appeals to:

Monsiuer Yves Leterme
Prime Minister
16 Rue de la Loi /Wetstraat
1000 Brussels
Belgium
sophie.pieters@premier.fed.be
(secretary to the Prime Minister)

Madame Annemie Turtelboom
Minister of the Interior
2 Rue de la Loi
1000 Brussels
Belgium
min.annemie.turtelboom@ibz.fgov.be
Fax : 02 504 85 00 – 02 504 85 80

Information current, to the best of our knowledge, as of January 30, 2011.

IRAN

AHMAD GHABEL, a prominent Iranian religious scholar, was arrested on September 8, 2010, and sentenced to three years' imprisonment, three years' exile from his city of residence, and a three-year ban on speeches. This is the maximum sentence for the crime of acting against national security. After spending almost four months in prison, Gabel was released on a $50,000 bail on January 4, 2011; the remainder of his sentence was converted into a fine of $4,000. He had previously been arrested in December 2009 and held for five months without charge in Vakilabad prison. According to the International Campaign for Human Rights in Iran, Ghabel was rearrested because, following his release, he gave reports and interviews regarding his detention and secret mass executions in Vakilabad prison. Gabel is currently awaiting the release of his appeal court's ruling.

We are sorry to announce that JA'FAR KAZEMI, a scholar featured in our previous issue, was executed on January 24, 2011. The execution took place without notification of his family or lawyer, and came shortly after he refused to give a television interview for the authorities. Kazemi was arrested in September 2009 and charged with *Moharebeh* (enmity against God) for his alleged contact with the banned organization the People's Mujahideen of Iran

Scholars featured in previous issues who remain in prison in Iran include EMADEDDIN BAGHI, a well-known Iranian scholar and human rights defender serving a total of seven years in prison on charges related to the formation of an organization to defend prisoners' rights and for recording an interview with a reformist cleric; MAJID TAVAKOLI, BAHAREH HEDAYAT, and MILAD ASADI, distinguished student activists sentenced to eight-and-a-half, nine-and-a-half, and seven years, respectively, for their involvement in 2009 anti-government protests; DR. MOSTAFA ALAVI, an Iranian doctor and researcher sentenced to 15 years' imprisonment in August 2008 for "plotting against the regime"; DRS. ARASH and KAMIER ALAEI, two AIDS researchers who were sentenced to three and six years, respectively, in January 2009 for "seeking to overthrow the government"; and BEHROOZ JAVID-TEHRANI, a student activist and prisoners' rights campaigner sentenced to seven years in jail in 2005. All of these individuals are at risk of torture and need your support.

Appeals to:

His Excellency Ayatollah Sayed
'Ali Khamenei
Leader of the Islamic Republic
The Office of the Supreme Leader
Islamic Republic Street–
Shahid Keshvar Doust Street
Tehran
Islamic Republic of Iran
E-mail: info@leader.ir
Salutation: Your Excellency

Ayatollah Mahmoud Hashemi Shahroudi
Head of the Judiciary
Howzeh Riyasat-e Qoveh Qazaiyeh /
Office of the Head of the Judiciary
Pasteur St., Vali Asr Ave.
South of Serah-e Jomhouri
Tehran
Islamic Republic of Iran
E-mail: info@dadgostary-tehran.ir
(In the subject line write:
FAO Ayatollah Shahroudi)
Salutation: Your Excellency

RUSSIA

Scholars at Risk has reported that two professors at Baltic State Technical University in St. Petersburg, Russia, **SVYATOSLAV BOBYSHEV** and **YEVGENY AFANASYEV**, were arrested on March 16, 2010, on accusations of espionage. They have since been held in pretrial detention, which was extended another 4 months in September 2010. The accusations relate to collaboration between Baltic State Technical University and Harbin Engineering University in China, in which the professors are accused of revealing state secrets. The chairman of the two professors' academic department has denied the accusations. Their arrest and detention without trial comes at a time when scholars across Russia are becoming increasingly threatened with state and parastate forms of repression.

Appeals to:

Dmitry Medvedev
President of Russia
Ilinka Str, No 23
103132, Moscow
Russia

Mr. Yuriy Chaika
General Public Prosecutor of Russian Federation
125993, Moscow
GSP-3, 15a B. Dimitrovka Str.
Russian Federation

THE FOLLOWING PREVIOUSLY FEATURED SCHOLARS REMAIN IN PRISON:

BAHRAIN

'ABDUL-JALIL AL-SINGACE, a professor of engineering at the University of Bahrain, arrested on August 13, 2010, and reportedly tortured along with other members of the Haq Movement for Civil Liberties and Democracy. He is currently held in detention awaiting trial.

Appeals to:

Shaikh Khaled bin Ali al-Khalifa
Minister of Justice and Islamic Affairs
P.O. Box 450
al- Manama
Bahrain
Fax: +973 1753 6343
Salutation: Your Excellency

His Majesty Shaikh Hamad bin Issa Al Khalifa
King of Bahrain
Office of His Majesty the King
P. O. Box 555
Rifa'a Palace
Kingdom of Bahrain
Fax:+ 973 1766 8884
Salutation: Your Majesty

BURMA (MYANMAR)

KO AUNG HTUN, a writer and former student activist arrested in Burma in the winter of 1998, sentenced to 17 years' imprisonment on charges of violating state censorship and unlawful association.

Appeals to:

Senior General Than Shwe
Chairman, State Peace and Development Council
Ministry of Defense
Naypyitaw Union of Myanmar
(for U.S. Postal Service, "Burma" should appear in parentheses after "Myanmar" on envelope only, not in the letter itself)
Salutation: Dear Senior General

Minister Counselor U Myint Lwin
Chargé d'Affaires
Ad Interim Embassy of Myanmar
2300 S Street NW
Washington DC 20008
Salutation: Dear Sir

CAMEROON

JUSTICE M. MBUH, a lecturer at the National Polytechnic Bambui in Bamenda Cameroon, arrested in September 2009 following accusations of "treason." He remains in prison awaiting trial.

Appeals to:

His Excellency Paul Biya
President of the Republic of Cameroon
Yaoundé, Cameroon

Fax: (237) 22 20 33 06
Email: cellcom@prc.cm
Salutation: Your Excellency

CHINA

GUO QUAN, a former literature professor at Nanjing Normal University, sentenced to ten years in prison and three years of deprivation of political rights in October 2009 on charges of "inciting subversion of state power."

LU XIAOBO, a Chinese writer and human rights activist, arrested in December 2008 for "inciting subversion of state power."

LÜ GENGSONG, a Chinese writer, activist, and former university teacher, arrested in the summer of 2007 on charges of "incitement to subvert state power" and "illegally possessing state secrets."

ZHENG YICHUN, professor of English at Liaoning University, arrested in the winter of 2004 and charged with "suspicion of inciting subversion of state power."

XU ZERONG, a professor affiliated with the Provincial Academy of Science and Zhongshan University, arrested in 2002 and charged with revealing state secrets for his use of historical materials in researching the Korean War.

Appeals to:

His Excellency Hu Jintao
President of the People's Republic of China
Zhong Naihai
Beijing 100032
People's Republic of China
Salutation: Your Excellency

Mr. Xiao Yang
President of the Supreme People's Court
No. 27
Dongjiaominxiang Dongcheng District
Beijing 100745
People's Republic of China
Fax: 86 10 65292345 (c/o Ministry of Communication)
Salutation: Dear President

VIETNAM

PHAM MINH HOANG, a mathematics lecturer at Ho Chi Minh City Polytechnic Institute, arrested on August 13, 2010, on charges of participating in a banned pro-democracy opposition group, the Viet Tan. He was officially charged on September 29, 2010, with "carrying out activities with intent to overthrow the socialist government" and is currently awaiting trial.

TRAN KHAI THANH THUY, a novelist and essayist, was arrested in October 2009 after she publicly defended six dissidents facing trial. In February 2010 she was sentenced to 42 months in prison.

Appeals to:

His Excellency Nguyên Minh Triêt	Nguyên Tân Dung
President of the Socialist Republic of Vietnam	Prime Minister
c/o Ministry of Foreign Affairs	1 Hoang HoaTham Street
Hanoi	Hanoi
Socialist Republic of Vietnam	Socialist Republic of Vietnam
Salutation: Your Excellency	Salutation: Your Excellency

—Written by John Clegg

HELP SUPPORT
THE JOURNAL DONATION PROJECT

Begun in 1990 with the collapse of the Soviet Union, the Journal Donation Project (JDP), a *Social Research*, initiative, is an international library assistance program that assists in the rebuilding of major research and teaching libraries in countries that have fallen victim to political and economic deprivation. Through the provision of current subscriptions drawn from over 2,000 of the most important English-language scholarly, professional and current events journals, the JDP has helped to develop significant journal archives at over 300 libraries in 30 countries. The Project has grown substantially over the years, due to the generosity of donors. Gifts from individuals, families, corporate matching programs, grant-giving foundations, and others are deeply appreciated.

Donors may wish to make a one-time donation, pledge an annual gift, give in honor of or in memory of a loved one, or designate monies for a specific project/geographic location. All donations are tax deductible.

To learn how you can help support the JDP, please contact:

Professor Arien Mack, Project Organizer and Director
New School University, Journal Donation Project
80 Fifth Avenue
New York, NY 10011
Tel: 212 229 5789
Fax: 212 229 5476
Email: jdp@newschool.edu
Website: www.newschool.edu/centers/jdp

social research
AN INTERNATIONAL QUARTERLY OF THE SOCIAL SCIENCES

INDIA'S WORLD
A *Social Research* Conference

Tuesday, May 10 - Wednesday, May 11, 2011
John Tishman Auditorium, The New School
66 West 12th Street, New York City

Join us as experts discuss key issues of contemporary Indian life, connecting the dots between government, economy, policy, and culture in India. We aim to deepen our understanding of the ways in which the country and people of India today are influenced by the world and the world by India.

Keynote Speaker AMITAV GHOSH
Tuesday. May 10, 6:00 P.M.

Tickets
Regular: $30 for full conference
Nonprofit staff and members: $20
Students, New School alumni and faculty: free

For more information and to register
Please visit **http://www.newschool.edu/cps/indias-world/program/**
or contact cps@newschool.edu or (212) 229-5776 x3

India's World is presented by the Center for Public Scholarship
in collaboration with the India China Institute

THE NEW SCHOOL FOR SOCIAL RESEARCH

Befekadu Degefe and Berhanu Nega
Guest Editors' Introduction: Accountability for Development in Africa

SUB-SAHARAN AFRICA OCCUPIES THE LOWER FOUR-FIFTHS OF THE African continent and covers an area more than twice that of the United States. Its inhabitants are differentiated from their cousins in the north physically by the great Sahara Desert and more significantly by the color of their skin.

The last 500 years have been very unkind to this part of the world. The harrowing poverty and the general backwardness of the region at the beginning of the twenty-first century owe their origin and endurance to events that were inflicted on the continent and people during these years. Colonial masters were in control during the first four and half centuries. The past 50 years were self inflicted. Such an apportionment of responsibility between exogenous and endogenous forces notwithstanding, one must hasten to point out the considerable degrees of cooperation among these two entities, since no one force could have inflicted such a heavy toll for so long without the assistance provided by one to the other.

The region's initiation into the global political economy had its genesis with the discovery of the sea route to India in the fifteenth century. This brought about incremental interaction with the then

European powers, beginning with the colonization of the coastal region, expansion into the interior, and the shipment of an estimated 10 to 15 million of the ablest of the population to plantations in the Americas (Lovejoy 2000).

This was followed by the total annexation of sub-Saharan Africa (SSA) by the powers of the day. In this regard Bismarck should be credited not only for uniting Germany but the SSA as well (Williamson 1998). As part of his "balance of power" diplomacy, he crafted the peaceful division of Africa among those who claimed parts of it. In doing so he helped bring disparate people with different customs, belief, ethnicity, and environment under one colonial power. At the end of the Second World War, Britain and France together controlled 80 percent of the region. French West Africa extended from the Atlantic to the Sudan while French Equatorial Africa extended from the mid-Atlantic to Libya. In addition to important holdings elsewhere in the region, British Africa in the eastern part extended from the Cape of Good Hope in the south to Alexandria in the north.

Unfortunately, these large territories were fragmented into smaller entities at independence. Of the 48 countries making up the region, 18 were former French colonies, 17 were British, 5 Portuguese, and 3 Belgian. The fragmentation cut across ethnic lines, dividing kith and kin between two countries as well as reducing the viability of many of these countries as an economic entity. According to the UN (United Nations 2009), of the 48 countries, 7 have a population of less than a million, 19 less than 5 million, 26 less than 10 million, 31 less than 15 million, 37 less than 20 million and 41 less than 30 million. Only three countries have a population exceeding 50 million. These are the Democratic Republic of Congo (71 million), Ethiopia (86 million), and Nigeria (150 million).

SOCIOECONOMIC CONDITIONS AT THE BEGINNING OF THE 21ST CENTURY

Not only is Africa fragmented into unviable entities, it started the twenty-first century as the poorest and the most backward of the continents, despite the rich natural endowments. Of the 49 countries designated as "least developed" by the United Nations General Assembly, 34 are from the SSA (UNCTAD 2008: xii). The population in these countries numbers no less than 500 million. This classification is based on three criteria of : 1) annual gross domestic product (GDP) below $900 per capita; 2) quality of life, based on life expectancy at birth, per capita calorie intake, primary and secondary school enrollment rates, and adult literacy; and 3) economic vulnerability, based on instability of agricultural productions and exports, inadequate diversification, and economic smallness.

According to the UNDP's *Human Development Report,* the latest Human Development Index (HDI) for SSA (including the Republic of South Africa) was 0.493, which is the lowest of all the regions (UNDP 2010, table 1: 232).

The World Bank reports SSA GDP for 2010 at $978 billion. This amounts to a per capita income of about $1,124 per annum or $3.10 per day (World Bank 2010). The minimum federal wage in the United States for that year was $7.25 per hour (U.S. Department of Labor 2010). In other words, a casual worker in the United States earns more than two times in one hour what an African earns in a day, albeit on per capita basis.

Nearly 51 percent or 440 million Africans survive on less than 1.25 international dollars a day (equivalent to U.S. $2.15), and 600 million on 2 international dollars a day (or U.S. $3.45) in 2010 (World Bank 2010; the international dollar is also known as purchasing power parity). Over the past 40 years, African food production has fallen by 10 percent since 1960 (while that of the world increased by 145 percent) as a result of which the number of the undernourished rose by 100 million to 250 million since 1990 (Juma 2010). In this regard Africa must be grateful to the rest of the world for, among other necessities, feeding it.

Not only is the SSA poor and undernourished—it also starts the third millennium as the most backward of the regions. The information communication index (ICI) prepared by the International Telecommunications Union (ITU) shows that the digital divide between the SSA and the rest of the world is not only wide but is getting wider.

Of the 44 countries with low ICI, 35 are in the SSA (ITU 2009, table 4: 22 and table 5.1: 46). The same tables show that 22 SSA countries were ranked lower in 2008 compared with their position in 2002, implying that the rest of the world has bettered itself faster than these countries.

The UNDP's report on diffusion of technology shows that there were 17 mainline and 130 cellular telephone subscribers per 1,000 persons while only 26 per 1,000 persons used the Internet in 2005 (UNDP 2008, table 13: 276).

THE STATE IN AFRICA: THE VIRTUAL AND THE REAL

The harrowing socioeconomic conditions obtaining in Africa are not an accident but the result of a rational outcome of political gamesmanship and go back to the early days of independence. Rather than creating a democratic state for the newly independent country, the colonial socioeconomic and political infrastructure was retained, justified by a need to build a nation out of the ethnically fragmented country and the mobilization of resources for national development. It was argued that civil and political liberties would lead to the ethnicization of politics leading to instability and conflict (Meridith 2005). Thus challenges to authority were minimized and outlawed.

If the first generation of leaders were honest in their intentions, this was soon abandoned by the corporals who took over through coups that flourished in the 1960s and early 1970s. These new rulers privatized the nation and used the state an instrument for the perpetuation of their rule. Since then neither political nor economic competition is allowed. Basic civil political and economic rights are anathema. In addition to increasing the capacity of the security forces and providing them with a blank check and authority, the system ensured the dependence of the people on the state. Under such rule, all incomes, in theory, accrued to the head of the system, who in turn redistributes it among "his" people.

In the zero-sum game mentality that pervades the economics and politics of the system, wealth means power, and those beyond the full control of the state become a threat. In consequence there is no private sector independent of the state and no respect for private property, the most fundamental and final expression of economic incentives (Easterly 2002).

While the authoritarian system thrived during the Cold War, it came under fire following the demise of the Soviet Union. This was to be the end of dictatorial regimes. Pressure mounted to democratize. The result was the creation of two states, one virtual and the other real. This was a smart accommodation for the half-hearted global demand for democratization while preserving the status quo ante.

The virtual is the "democratic" state. Of the 48 countries, all except the kingdoms of Lesotho and Swaziland became republics. They all adopted constitutions with distinct separation of powers and respect for people's rights and their properties. Public offices were to be held for a limited period of time and only with the consent of the people. Coup d'états, once a common African feature, were declared unacceptable and the African Union was mandated to suspend any government that came to power through ways other than the ballot box.

In addition to internalizing some of the international instruments of rights, all African countries became signatories of the various conventions relating to human and peoples' rights (UNDP 2009: 163-66, table F). They even initiated and ratified the African Charter on Human and People's Right and established the African Commission for its implementation.

This is the virtual African state, the modern and civilized face of Africa created for public relations purposes. This is the Africa that engages with the rest of the world and with which the rest of the world is willing to engage without compunction. It is to this state that donors provide assistance to and scholars research and reflect on the various aspects of their democracy and democratization. It is this state that organizes elections observed by the European Union and the United States, among others, elections that predictably fail to meet "international standards" and raise "concern." The African Union observers provide an antidote to this observation by always certifying all elections as free and fair. This done, it is back to business as usual.

Behind this veil is the real African state, which is aptly characterized as "neither African nor a state" and is the author of the many ills that the region suffers from (Englebert 1997). It is not African since it is the Africanized colonial state. It is not a state because it does not provide the most basic of public services, such as protection of the person and property.

The focal interest of such a state is to ensure the smooth flow of resources to the ruling clique and their cohorts and the survival of the regime at any cost. The entire resources of the nation are mobilized to ensure no rival or challenge emerges. And the challenges need not be actual. They could be imagined, a consequence that explains the large populations of political prisoners and emigrants in and from Africa. The educated elite and professionals who have not submitted to the will of the party pose a threat and must be dealt with. Emigration from Africa is due as much to push factors as it is to pull factors.

Politics is thus perceived and exercised as a zero-sum game. To be rich and wealthy, to have income independent of the regime, is a potential threat that needs to be resolved (McMann 2006). It is easier to rule the poor and uneducated rather than the rich and educated.

This in essence is the real African state. Some aspects and characteristics of these states are emerging through dedicated researchers, rights groups, and surveys by institutions. Freedom House reports that the greater majorities of the African people live in states that are not free (151 million) or mostly unfree (512 million). Only 140 million people (18 percent) live in countries designated as free. Freedom was defined on the basis of whether people participate freely in the political process; vote freely in legitimate elections; have representatives that are accountable to them; exercise freedoms of expression and belief; are able to freely assemble and associate; have access to an established and equitable system of rule of law; have social and economic freedoms, including equal access to economic opportunities and the right to hold private property (Freedom House 2010).

A study that parallels the Freedom House report is the Heritage Foundation's Report on Economic Freedom. The index measures the degrees of economic freedom enjoyed by residents (both nationals and foreign) based on country data that measures business, trade, fiscal, monetary, investment, financial freedoms, size of government spending, property rights, and freedom from corruption. The 2010 Index of Economic Freedom shows that 151 million people living in 17 countries lack freedom, 512 million people living in 21 countries live under conditions that are mostly unfree, and 134 million in 6 countries live in moderately free economic environment. Only two countries (Mauritius and Botswana) are designated as mostly free and both have democratic politics.

Within the Economic Freedom Categories, those measuring property rights and freedom from corruption are revealing about the causes of poverty in the SSA. While sub-Saharan Africa scores the lowest on all the different category rights and freedoms relative to the rest of the world, it posts an abysmally low grade on property rights and freedom from corruption. Out of a possible score of 100, the SSA averages 31 on property rights and 29 on rights to be protected from corruption.

These figures reveal the absence the fundamental right of ownership of property by economic agents. Without this basic right there simply is no motivation for people to work hard and produce wealth, and therein lies one of the mysteries of poverty in Africa.

Foreign Policy has generated the Failed State Index, based on 12 social, economic, and political indicators. These are mounting demographic pressures; massive movement of refugees or internally displaced persons creating; complex humanitarian emergencies; legacy of vengeance-seeking group grievance or group paranoia; chronic and sustained human flight; uneven economic development along group lines; sharp and/or severe economic decline; criminalization and/or delegitimization of the state; progressive deterioration of public services; suspension or arbitrary application of the rule of law and widespread violation of human rights; security apparatus that operates as a "state within a state"; the rise of factionalized elites; and intervention of other states or external political actors. Using scores for each of these entries, the index groups countries into four categories of Alert,

Warning, Moderate, and Sustainable. Only one SSA country (the island nation of Mauritius, population 1.3 million) ranked as moderate. The rest were either in the Alert (failed or close to collapse) designation (23 countries with 600 million people) or "Warning" category—that is, likely to fail unless measures are taken to prevent them from collapsing (24 countries and 300 million people).

RECONSTITUTING THE AFRICAN STATE

The past 50 years are the lost decades for Africa. They failed to meet the challenges of nation building, state building, and economic development. Rulers have brazenly abdicated the responsibilities of providing basic services to the people and dedicated themselves to continue with the colonial tradition of using the state to extract resources while treating the people in a most inhumane fashion. If colonialism was found unacceptable from the political and economic perspectives, the "postcolonial" African states must be rejected for the same reasons.

It is important to note that foreign governments are more concerned for the welfare of the African people than their own governments. A good number of Africans survive on international charity. This is particularly true of health services, where many of the lifesaving drugs are obtained from donors. The same is true for food. The Social Development Goals of significantly reducing poverty and its various attributes were initiated by the donor community at the Social Summit in Copenhagen in 1996 and relaunched under the new banner of the Millennium Development Goals in 2000.

It is time that Africans assume responsibility for their lives, an opportunity and obligation denied them by their own governments. To this end, there should be a reconstitution of the state, which should be based on the idea of how best it could serve the interest of the people and how quickly would the public masters become public servants.

A cruel joke has so far been played on Africa by scholars who report on flourishing free markets and high growth in the region's institutions (World Bank 2009; Sachs 2005). The World Bank defines good governance as one that enhances growth, irrespective of the regime type, and by this it usually means dictatorships.

Advocates for authoritarianism should note that in the few instances it succeeded in delivering high rates of economic growth, it was because the people enjoyed economic freedom and the private sector had the support of its government, including an encouraging investment climate and protection from external competition (Wade 1990). In China the difference between pre- and post-1979 China is due to "economic freedom" along with nationalism. People respond to "incentives," and there is no better incentive than having assurance of freedom to work and own the proceeds (Easterly 2002) as well as strong and broadly shared nationalist developmentalism as an ideology (Mkandawire 2001). That is what is needed at the minimum in a reconstituted state in Africa, and this is where most assistance is needed, including putting pressure on the regimes to reform.

It is depressing to note that the West is now competing with China to curry favor with autocrats. This is not the way to win friends or enhance global security. The war on terror is best fought not by drones and smart bombs but with the most powerful weapon at the disposal of the West: freedom of people. In this regard President George Bush articulated the correct stance when, at his inaugural speech at the beginning of his second term in 2005, he noted that "the survival of liberty in our land increasingly depends on the success of liberty in other lands. The best hope for peace in our world is the expansion of freedom all over the world" (Bush 2005). Unfortunately, he couldn't put his money where his mouth was. Reforming governance in Africa should be approached not by removing an individual from office but through holistic reconstitution of the system. The problem lies not in the ruling clique: it is systemic and systematic.

The final target should be the making of the virtual state the real state. The first step toward achieving this goal is the rule of law. This comes through the rigorous adherence to the law irrespective of one's position in society. To this end the judiciary should be granted absolute independence. However, even this requires addressing the broader issue of the democratic accountability of the state.

THE INTERNATIONAL COMMUNITY AND ACCOUNTABLE GOVERNMENTS IN AFRICA

African people are cognizant of the fact that no one except themselves can democratize each of their countries. However, a little help would certainly enhance their effort. The international community has two fundamental leverages to use to help civilize leaders and tame their barbarism. The first is the fact of African governments being more accountable to the international community than to their own people. This is because they owe their survival in office to the assistance they obtain from bilateral and multilateral sources. The international community could use this leverage to influence the behavior of African governments.

The second is due to the International Criminal Court (ICC). The indictment of a sitting head of state has sent a clear and resounding message to African dictators that they are being watched and should start behaving in a more civilized manner.

An important service provided to dictators in Africa is the provision of safe haven for the money they have stolen from the people. If laundering drug money is a crime, laundering money stolen from poor starving people or the taxpayers—who generously gave a part of their income to improve the life of the poor—should be placed in the same league. And yet governments in the rich countries are openly preventing legal proceedings targeting the repatriation of stolen wealth to the people from whom it was stolen. Providing safe haven is not only immoral but will encourage and intensify the robbery.

Scholars should deal with Africa with the honesty and intensity they bring to other areas of study. Democracy being the result of freedom is not equivalent to democracy as harbinger of freedom. The latter is oxymoronic. They should expose wrongdoings and not sanctify criminal behaviors.

Often people hear and read the exhortation that democracy takes time. The mystery to those people living under tyranny is how much time it takes to live under a regime governed by law rather than being abused by man. How long does it take to vote for a leader of one's choice? For Africans living under tyranny, they understand perfectly well when such exhortations come from their tormentors in power. It is much harder to swallow when it comes from academicians who will never choose to live under such tyranny or from the aid industry, whose very existence is premised upon improving the life of the African masses. It is time that the African people's aspirations for justice and freedom are taken as seriously as their material poverty.

ACCOUNTABILITY

The papers in this issue of the *Social Research* were solicited from scholars on the frontiers of research on Africa. We are very grateful for their contributions. Some of these papers were presented at a conference held in early December 2010 at the New School for Social Research.

The theme of accountability was selected because this is the endgame of democratic governance. If a country's government is accountable to the people, it implies the rule of law is well established and that decision makers appreciate the fact that their decisions will have serious consequences. It means that people exercise the right to select their leaders in or out of office. In other words, this subset of accountability implies a society enjoying democratic governance. The absence of accountability in a country suggests the very high degree of discretionary personal rule rather than the rule of law. And this has significant implications both for political stability and economic development in Africa.

Benchmarking the project on accountability had thus the double purpose of evaluating the conditions that currently obtain as well as suggesting the direction for reform. The papers in this issue, taken together, tell the story of what it means to live under governments that are unaccountable to their people, what needs to be done, and the role of stakeholders, domestic as well as external.

Professor Arien Mack, editor of the journal, was instrumental in bringing the publication of this issue on accountability and development in Africa at this crucial period in the debate about Africa's future. Her team's ability to organize the conference and the publication of this volume attests to the capability and professionalism of the group under the able leadership of Professor Mack.

The papers are organized under four themes: conceptual and historical; the past, present, and future of accountability; the international community and accountability; and country studies. There are three papers in each category (with the exception of the first part, which has four papers).

A summary of the papers will not do justice to their content. Nevertheless, a succinct digest is presented to help introduce each paper to readers. We ask readers to read the articles in their entirety to appreciate the problems and the learned and wise counseling proffered by the authors.

Professor Mark Haugaard's philosophic excursion explores the conditions and possibilities of instituting democracy through the analysis of power and authority as a means of resolving conflicts. Democratic power constitutes a non-zero–sum institutionalization of conflict resolution through the structuring of authority relative to certain principles, including equality, impartiality, and separation of spheres. Such democratic interactions presuppose a democratic subject who is restrained and accountable. The key to creating the latter is education.

Professor Robert Bates offers a brief but interesting tour of democracy in Africa. Defining democracy as a system of governance in which political power is employed to serve the interest of the public rather than those who govern, Bates argues that "democracy has been reborn" in Africa, and advises citizens to be vigilant as incumbents would thwart the development of democratic politics to continue in office. In this regard he traces political developments from the pre- to postcolonial period and locates the essence of accountable political systems in the private ownership of productive resources.

Agnès Callamard reviews the political, institutional, and legal environment respecting freedom of expression in Africa. She posits freedom of expression as a fundamental prerequisite for accountability and notes its positive development since the decade of the 1990s. She details the commitments of African countries to respect freedom of expression. She also expresses her emerging concern due to the fact that there have been important remissions in the curtailment of this freedom during the first decade of the twenty-first century.

Two recent developments inform and define the essence of Paul Collier's paper. First, the price of natural resources is on an increasing trend, which augers well for resource-rich countries. Second, new resources are being discovered. The issue is how best Africa could use these resources for its development. To this end he notes the unpleasant experience in the past where resources, rather than being a blessing, turned into a curse, and calls for a more accountable political system that will harness politicians and mobilize the resources for the good of the society. In addition to domestic measures, Collier points to two international initiatives (the Kimberly Process, an initiative that outlaws the marketing of diamonds, the proceeds of which were used to destabilize governments in the past, and the Extractive Industries Transparency Initiative, which aims at creating an optimal relationship between companies and governments on the one hand and governments and the people on the other) that are likely to be helpful in the crafting of a more beneficial use of resources.

George Ayittey is melancholic about Africa's current status. He contends that Africa is lost because it has forgotten its past, which would have anchored its development on a robust basis. The modern generation spurned their own culture and political heritage in favor of alien values and imposed them on the people. The result is the chaos engendered by the clash of these values with those inherited from earlier generation. Had African leaders looked into their indigenous institutions and modalities for accountability and development, Africa would have been in a stronger position. He notes the success of the Japanese, Chinese, and Indians and underlines the need for Africa to emulate them.

Van de Walle and McKie confront the issue of how African leaders are to be held accountable. While they laud the achievement of elections as an important mechanism, they nevertheless point to the survival resurgence of authoritarian regimes. They search for nonelectoral means of holding public officials accountable and suggest which of these would be the most optimal. To this end they survey recent studies offering alternative mechanisms. They conclude that variations in the ability of formal institutions to check political power are often affected by the differences in informal practices across countries.

Mueni Wa Muiu's paper argues for the restructuring of the countries of Africa and for the reconstitution of the colonial state. This restructuring would be aimed at achieving a more sustainable environment for each states. She also proposes to reduce the number of countries from the current 48 to 5, along with the reconceptualization and relocation of the politics of the region on a more responsive paradigm.

The next set of papers deal with the external determinants of accountability in Africa. Professor William Easterly castigates donors for the hypocritical relationship between themselves and recipients. Noting that development succeeds when people develop themselves, he assails the international community's relationship with authoritarian regimes that deny the people the opportunity to do so. Just as donors value their freedom, so do people in the aid dependant countries. He urges donors to condition their assistance on good behavior. He argues that accountability needs to be universalized and applied to recipients of aid as much as they do in the donor countries. In particular, donors should note the negative and debilitating impact of the assistance they provide to rogue regimes.

Clement Adibe also focuses on the different dimensions of accountability. He notes that African regimes may not be accountable to their people, but they are highly accountable to their external constituencies. In addition to the aid, Adibe notes the very close relationship between African and donor countries as repositories of money pilfered from their countries. The political, economic, and personal interests of African leaders induce them to positively respond to any and all demand from the developed countries.

Thandika Mkandawire traces the historical relationship between aid and democracy. Strong regimes (read authoritarian governments) were preferred during the Cold War. Following the collapse of the Soviet Union, aid was predicated on the development of democratic systems of governance, which gave rise to the "democrative wave." Problems of accountability emerged because donors needed to justify the transfer of taxpayers' money to other countries. This required the imposition of conditionality on the recipient countries.

In a way, this element of accountability weakened the leverage of the Western donors relative to countries that do not have to account to their constituencies (such as China), which give without expressing concern on how the aid is used. Mkandawere points out the growing concern about giving aid to "kleptocrats" or "authoritarian regimes" who use the resources to further their private wealth and/or use them to enhance their capacity to oppress their people. He also raises the issue of whether donors should require governments to be accountable to their people as a condition for the provision of assistance. He concludes that whatever good pressuring governments to be held accountable to their people may do, "pressure for accountability must ultimately come from the citizens of the recipient country."

The three country papers deal with Nigeria, Ethiopia, and Somalia. Professor Kelechi Kalu analyses the reasons and causes behind Nigeria's failure to transform itself into a well-behaved power, given its vast resources and well-educated and skilled manpower. He treats the easy explanation of corruption and the looting of national wealth by politicians as a symptom rather than cause. He instead locates the cause in the absence of or weak institutions. What is needed, he contends, are institutions that protect property, enhance peaceful coexistence of different ethnic groups, and create an enabling environment. He condemns not only the theft but even more, the fact of not investing the wealth so amassed in the development of the nation. He calls for reformulating the political environment. To this end he develops a theoretical frame that he refers to the transition-transformation schema.

Professor Berhanu Nega takes issue with advocates of authoritarian governments, who point approvingly to such governments because of their capacity to deliver high rates of economic growth and reduce poverty sooner than democratic governments. He takes Ethiopia as a case in point. It has claimed double digit GDP growth during the last seven years. It has justified its atrocious human rights record by claiming to be a developmentalist state. For Nega, development without freedom is meaningless, since freedom itself is a necessary component of development. He argues that even if one is willing to trade freedom and democracy for growth, one still challenges the veracity of the claim made by the Ethiopian government. In this task he points to inconsistencies in the data in terms of inputs and output as well as periodic adjustments made to the data to align it with the high-growth claim. He goes on to castigate donor governments and international institutions that support autocratic government, such as those in Ethiopia, and turn a blind eye to abuses of human rights.

Mwangi Kimenyi, John Mukum Mbaku, and Nelipher Moyo's paper on Somalia proposes a two-track program to bring order to this lawless country. In the immediate run they call for an international intervention, since none of the factions or a coalition will be capable of subduing the rest and bringing about a normal state or bringing the warring factions under a central government. The longer-run project should focus on a constitutional arrangement to be arrived at through consultations and negotiations, the results of which will ensure autonomy of each of the clients organized under the different warlords.

These papers are important additions to the already rich publications both on the subject of accountability and problems of African development. We hope they will generate further debate, help purify the message, and send a more nuanced and powerful message to African governments that the old ways of unaccountable governance are no longer tolerable, that the cost of authoritarian governance is too high to be allowed to continue for long. In the twenty-first century politics needs to be perceived and lived as a positive rather than a zero-sum game.

REFERENCES

Acemoglu, Daron, and James A. Robinson. *Economic Origins of Dictatorship and Democracy.* New York: Cambridge University Press, 2006.

Bush, George. W. "There Is No Justice without Freedom." 2005 <http://www.washingtonpost.com/wp-dyn/articles/A23747-2005Jan20.html>.

de Mesquita, Bruce Bueno, and George W. Downs."Development and Democracy." *Foreign Affairs* (September/October 2005).

Easterly, William. *The Elusive Quest for Growth: Economists' Adventure and Misadventure in the Tropics.* Cambridge: MIT Press, 2002.

Englebert, Pierre. "The Contemporary African State: Neither African nor State." *Third World Quarterly* 18:4 (1997).

Freedom House."Freedom in the World: The 2010 Survey." Washington, D.C., 2010.

Heritage Foundation. "Index of Economic Freedom." Washington, D.C., 2010.

International Telecommunications Union. "Measuring the Information Society: The ICT Development Index." New York: United Nations, 2009.

Juma, Calestous. *The New Harvest: Agricultural Innovation in Africa.* New York: Oxford University Press, 2010.

Lovejoy, Paul E. *Transformations in Slavery.* New York: Cambridge University Press, 2000.

McMann, Kelly M. *Economic Autonomy and Democracy.* New York: Cambridge University Press, 2006.

Meredith, Martin. *The State in Africa: A History of 50 Years.* London: Free Press, 2005.

Mkandawire, Tandika. "Thinking About Developmental States in Africa." *Cambridge Journal of Economics* 25:3 (May, 2001): 289–313.

Sachs, Jeffrey. *The End of Poverty: Economic Possibilities for our Time.* Toronto: Penguin, 2006.

United Nations. "Population Projection." New York: United Nation Population Division, 2009.

UN Conference on Trade and Development (UNCTAD). "The Least Developed Countries Report." Geneva, 2008.

UN Development Program (UNDP). *Human Development Report.* New York: United Nations, 2009.

U.S. Department of Labor. "Federal Minimum Wage." Washington, D.C., 2010.

Wade, Robert. *Governing the Market: Economic Theory and the Role of Government in East Asian Industrialization.* Princeton: Princeton University Press, 1990.

Williamson, D. G. *Bismarck and Germany 1862-1890.* London: Addison Wesley, 1998.

Wintrobe, Ronald. *The Political Economy of Dictatorship.* New York: Cambridge University Press, 1998.

World Bank. "Worldwide Governance Indicators 1996-2008." Washington, D.C.: World Bank/IBRD, 2009.

———. "World Development Indicators 2010." Washington D.C., 2010.

Young, Crawford. *The Politics of Cultural Pluralism.* Madison: University of Wisconsin Press, 1976.

Mark Haugaard
Democracy, Political Power, and Authority

IN THE COUNTRIES WHERE DEMOCRACY IS WELL ESTABLISHED, IT IS frequently so taken for granted that few citizens are aware of how unusual this political system is in historical terms. Democracy is a fragile flower that presupposes specific forms of power and perceptions of authority. Only in postcolonial societies in which the historical legacy has been relatively unconducive to democracy is its historical uniqueness appreciated.

In this paper we analyze some of the background conditions conducive to democracy. This involves distinguishing between power as domination—the predominant form of power in nondemocratic systems—and political power, which is based on structured consent. As will be explained, political power is power that is routed through authority, which constitutes a perfomative act. Authority presupposes a democratic subject who interprets the world in a highly differentiated way, is disciplined, and therefore accountable, relative to norms of equality and impartiality.

COERCION AND POLITICAL POWER
Ernest Gellner argued that one of the profoundly transformational characteristics of modernity was a process whereby "production replaced predation" (1988: 158). Gellner divided the social world according to three types of power resources: ideological, represented by the book; military, the sword; and economic, the plough. His central hypothesis was that prior to modernity, the world remained essentially economi-

cally stagnant because those who controlled the means of violence dominated the rest. Whenever those holding economic power managed to increase production, they were immediately preyed upon coercively, which created a disincentive for economic growth. However, during the eighteenth and nineteenth centuries, economic growth was simply so great that the producers of economic wealth were able to buy off, through taxation, the wielders of the sword. As I have argued elsewhere (Haugaard 2007: 75-102), this is only half the story. Key was the coming of age of a new mode of managing conflict: *democracy*. This mode of engaging in conflict presupposes the triumph of *political power*, which is a qualitatively different kind of power to the coercive power wielded by the sword. I follow Mann in arguing that there are four sources of power: ideological, economic, political, *and* military (Mann 1983: 1-33; 2008: 351). I prefer to use the term *coercive* power rather than *military* because the latter suggests state-to-state confrontation, rather than internal coercion of the subjects/citizens of the state. The distinction between political and coercive power does not have its origins in the advent of the formation of the modern state but became much stronger with its emergence, especially in those states that became democratic.

The distinction between political and coercive power involves what Max Weber called *ideal types,* which entail the construction of purified categories of analysis distilled from social life. Pure political power, devoid of violence and coercion, is a rare phenomenon. In most interactions, the two sources of power are mixed, yet some interactions are predominantly characterized by political power and, with the emergence of the modern democratic state, the conditions of possibility for political power unsupported by coercion became hugely advanced.

As ideal types, democracies exist on a scale ranging from those democracies that approximate to the ideals of democracy, where power is largely political, to, at the other end, those "democracies" where coercive predatory power is the norm. Arguably, political systems in which political power is the exception and coercive power the norm are "democracies" in name only. Because democracy has become a general term of commendation, democracy has lost its specificity (Dahl

1989: 2; Hyland 1995: 36) with the result that many of these "democracies" use the term to gain legitimacy without any semantic specificity. As such, they are predominantly coercive and predatory regimes. Speaking metaphorically, they are governed by feudal lords and would-be absolute sovereigns disguised as politicians and bureaucrats.

POLITICAL POWER

In the academic literature on power, there are two broadly contrasting perceptions of power. On the one hand, the followers of Weber, most notably Dahl (1957) and Lukes (2005; 2008), view power as domination. Power constitutes A's ability to get B to do something that B would not otherwise. A's and B's interests are assumed opposite and their relations zero-sum—A's gain is B's loss. On the other hand, a number of thinkers, most notably Arendt (1970), Parsons (1967), Barnes (1988), and Morriss (2002 and 2009), view power in terms of empowerment, or the capacity to act. In this perspective, power constitutes the core of agency as ability. For the former, the emphasis is primarily on *power over*, whereas for the latter it is *power to*. In terms of this dichotomy, Foucault (1979, 1980, 1981, 2008) has aspects of both perspectives, arguing that power is constitutive of agency; his insistence on critique of all forms of power suggests, however, that he equates power with domination.

As I have argued elsewhere (Haugaard 2010b), these two perspectives on power should not be interpreted as an either/or phenomenon and instead as a both/and. What we mean by power covers a cluster of concepts and phenomena, which include both *domination* and *agency*, and *power over* and *power to*. Speaking at a high level of generalization, it can be argued that the conflictual, or dominative, view of power most closely corresponds to politics in its predatory form, while the more democratic forms entail consensual power. In terms of the problematic of this issue of *Social Research*, it can be argued that failed democracies are predatory systems in which true *political power* is the exception, while *power as domination* is the rule. The challenge for new democracies is to replace coercive power with authoritative political power. As in Gellner's account, the predatory form of politics results in disincentive to economic development, while conversely the introduction of political power should create the conditions of possibility of replacing a predatory economy with a truly productive one.

In the literature that deals with both *power to* and *power over* there is a tendency to interpret these as two discrete forms of power, and to equate *power over* with domination (for instance, Allen 1999 and 2007 or Goehler 2009). Yet, democracy is a system for managing conflict, which entails *power over*. The key to the transition from predatory to democratic forms is the containment of conflict within consensual parameters. In a democratic system, *power over* is accepted as legitimate precisely because it does not entail predation or domination. Democratic power constitutes a blend of consensual constrained conflict. The advent of this form of power, which contains conflict within consensual norms, is the key to the transition from predatory politics to democratic politics, in the true sense of the word.

THE CAGING OF POWER

The move from coercion to democracy was a protracted process in the European context. In the early modern period (fifteenth and sixteenth centuries), a slow process of elimination of antiquated feudal forms of institutional arrangement began. They were replaced by formalized legal structures that constituted the basis for regularized exercise of power (Thornhill 2010). Central to this was the idea that the legitimacy of the law presupposes separation from the persons who exercised it. To the extent to which the feudal system was legitimate, it presupposed precisely the opposite: it constituted a rigid class—verging on caste—system in which feudal elites were considered to embody virtues, derived from essential essences, that gave them rights particular to their place in the order of things. For this reason, feudal elites considered it necessary to maintain difference in lifestyle, manners, and speech protected by sartorial laws (Elias 2000). The feudal order was reinforced by an ideological power, which privileged tradition and was reified by the great chain of being, whereby God ordered the universe, from kings and local lords to the humblest sparrow.

In the sixteenth and seventeenth centuries, attempts at state building and the emergence of standardized institutional procedures was tied to a process of centralization of power around the figure of the sovereign, who sought ideological legitimacy in the feudal order of things. Sovereigns claimed absolute power as the apex of the great chain of being. Basing absolute sovereignty on the divine right of kings was ideologically ineffective, since it constituted an attempt to reify power based upon a teleological, essentialist worldview, which was being undermined by the European enlightenment.

Structurally, this form of political authority was also inherently unstable and dysfunctional because, while standardizing, it embodied the exception at its center, in the person of the sovereign. This is paradigmatically represented by Hobbes' account of the Leviathan (1914 [1651]), where all subjects are bound by contract to the sovereign but the sovereign is exempt from contract. As observed by Locke, the subjects who contract in the Hobbesian account avoid the inconveniences of theft from foxes and pole-cats in order to subject themselves to being devoured by a lion (Locke 1924 [1690]: 163).

From a sociological perspective, in the West democracy emerged out of the massive coercive conflicts, including the Thirty Years War, and the revolutions or civil wars in the Netherlands, England, France, and the United States. In most instances, the initial outcomes of these violent confrontations were a form of modus vivendi whereby protagonists agree to a set of political structures to get them out of civil war, or the threat of civil war. They were getting out of the "state of nature" in Hobbes' sense, but in place of an absolute sovereign they adopted shared constraints. Most political systems did not emerge as fully fledged stable democracies in one go. The closest to an exception in this regard was the United States, but even there basic institutions including full extension of the franchise took nearly a century and a half, until the success of the civil rights movement in the 1960s. The overall result was the slow move from social conflict as coercively based to the adoption of shared constraints that channeled conflict into predictable structured forms. Through this caging of conflict, modern authoritative political power became the norm of politics. Slowly, the bureaucrat and professional politician replaced the absolute sovereign and their revolutionary adversaries. The secret of the success of democracy, in comparison with its competitors, was its greater capacity to replace coercive power with authoritative power. This made democracies politically stable, rule-bound, no longer predatory, and capable of repeat play. Thus they also became able to fund themselves through regular taxation, rather than raiding the resources of economic elites on an ad hoc basis and, in so doing, destroying their economies.

STRUCTURE AND GOALS

In order to make sense of the concept of the caging of conflict, which defines political power, it is necessary to break social action into two component parts: the objective or goal-oriented aspect of the action and the structures reproduced (Haugaard 1997: 119-62). All forms of social action have these two components, although in many cases only one aspect of social action, usually the goal orientation, is visible to the social actor undertaking the action. In some instances, the goal and the structured element may be identical, though they are separable analytically. In the usage of this paper (this is not a claim for "correct" usage, simply a local usage within a particular framework), *structure* refers to the aspect of an action which makes that action recognizably part of a social system. The goal-oriented part refers to the objectives of the action.

To be systemically structured an action contains meaning, which makes it interpretable as equivalent to another action at a different time and space. The most obvious instance of structured action is everyday speech. A common language is an assembled set of social structures that facilitates debate within a structured context. As language is the archetypal structured meaning-given system, it is the model that lies at the base of understanding reasoned conflict, as is argued by Habermas (1984). What constitutes reason in this case is not some kind of transcendental reason but a combination of reasonableness with regard to logical inference combined with a shared perception of meaning.

Political institutions gain their structured form from their membership of a political system as a meaning-giving system. So, to take a simple example, when one private individual, Barack Obama, announced his candidacy for the American presidency, on February 10, 2007 in Springfield Illinois, that action was a meaningful act within the structures of the American political system. Obama was structuring (Giddens 1984) or recreating the structures of the American political system by reproducing a key signifier (*candidacy*) within that system. The action of Obama had exactly the same meaning as the act of structuration performed by John McCain at a different time and place (April 25, 2007, Portsmouth, New Hampshire). The structured sameness is reproduced irrespective of the fact that their desired goals are opposed—Obama versus McCain for president. The structured content of their action was contained in the meaning of announcing their candidacy. The act of announcing a candidacy gains its meaning from a whole series of other meaningful acts, such as, party nomination, voting, inauguration, and so on.

This is not to claim that the structures are never the object of conflict within democratic politics, but when this happens the consensus that underpins the democratic system is under stress. This is precisely what happened with the decision of the U.S. Supreme Court, December 9, 2000, to end the Florida recount, which effectively awarded the presidential election to George W. Bush. Al Gore reluctantly conceded the election "for the sake of the unity of our people and the strength of our democracy," Gore's point being that a protracted conflict over what it means to be elected has the potential to destabilize the democratic process (Gore 2000). The Supreme Court decision constituted a new and contested way of winning an election, which the losing party only conceded to for the sake of the process itself.

DEMOCRACY: THE STRUCTURING OF CONFLICT

To take a long historical perspective, in comparison to other political systems, the extraordinary aspect of democracy is that it constitutes a process of conflict management in which *participants concede defeat because they are constrained by the social structures that constitute the system.* Democracy is a system for moving conflict from coercion to regularized institutional procedures. In this sense, it constitutes war by other means. For the political actors involved (presidential candidates, political parties, voters . . .) the constraints of the system operate through meaning and reason. When standing for election, politicians do their best to obtain as many votes as they can. It follows from this behavior that it is only reasonable, relative to their shared system of meaning, to concede defeat if some other politician obtains more votes. It is self-contradictory, it constitutes a *performative contradiction* relative to the local system of meaning, to pursue as many votes as possible and then claim victory with fewer votes than your rival.

To return to the conflictual view of power, if party B obtains fewer votes than party A, A gets B to do something that B would not otherwise do. Yet, it is simplistic to describe it as an outright conflict. A exercises power over B because both actors share consensus on the rules of the game. Nor is it correct to claim that such an exercise of power over B is contrary to B's interests—Lukes' definition of power (2005: 37). Part of, if not the entire reason for B conceding defeat to A is precisely that both A and B share a common interest in, and understanding of, the democratic process, which trumps their interest in winning. Structural reproduction is the common good of democracy as a set of institutional procedures for containing conflict.

An institutionalized democratic exercise of *power over* also constitutes *power to* in the sense that the willingness of B to concede defeat also entails the creation of a shared capacity for action. Even though A is exercising power over B, the willingness of either party to concede defeat, should they have fewer votes, entails that they gain a common power to act through the reproduction of the democratic system. In that sense the total power of the system has been increased—political power is positive-sum for the system as a whole. For A and B power is also positive-sum in another sense at the agency level. In a coercive conflict where A takes power from B, it is quite likely that B will remain subaltern for good. However, in a democratic contest actor B may lose this time but win next time. In that sense, B also has an interest in reproduction of the democratic rules of the game, even if they entail episodic defeat.

It is because political power is non-zero-sum that it constitutes an end in itself. The common good of democracy is not a set of goals: it is a structured process. As observed by Dahl, "our common good, then— the good and interests we share with others—rarely consists of specific practices, arrangement, institutions and processes" (Dahl 1989: 307). In this sense I would also agree with Chantal Mouffe (2002) that the objective of democracy is not consensus. Rather, it constitutes a process for converting antagonism into agonism or for converting coercion into politics. Arguably this is the kind of power which Hannah Arendt had in mind when she wrote that "power is indeed of the essence of all government, but violence is not." And further: "the power structure itself precedes and outlasts all aims, so that power, far from being the means to an end, is actually the very condition enabling a group of people to think and act in terms of the means-end category" (Arendt 1971: 51). Or more comprehensively:

> Power is what keeps the public realm, the potential space of appearance between acting and speaking men, in existence. The word itself, its Greek equivalent *dynamis*, like the Latin *potentia* with its various modern derivatives or the German *macht* . . . indicates its potential character (Arendt 1998: 200).

Democracy constitutes a set of structured procedures for containing conflict so that power does not degenerate into open violent confrontation. The actors who engage in the democratic process find themselves within a set of structured constraints the institutionalization of which entails a gain in power overall. Therefore, moving from zero-sum to positive-sum confrontation creates an incentive for moving from coercive politics to democratic politics on a pragmatic level. While democracy is frequently couched in the language of high ideals and principles, its desirability, its good, comes from the mundane world of everyday conflict.

AUTHORITY AND STRUCTURAL REPRODUCTION

Political power structures are reproduced through authority with designated spheres of legitimate power. This power, including their power over others, is not inherent in the powerful. Authoritative power issues from the subaltern who complies. There is a tendency to think of the power of the powerful as issuing from them because it is directed outward toward the subaltern and the word *powerful* suggests that power is intrinsic. Yet the source of that political power, to the extent to which it is based upon authority and legitimacy, derives from the compliance of the compliant subject.

When a person moves into a position of authority, he or she is a referent, a physical body, which acquires a new signifier. Barack Obama, who declared his candidacy, was a *private citizen* and a *senator*. These are signifiers, which attached to the physical referent of his persona. In declaring, he announced that he wished to have the signifier *president* attached to him. A position of authority constitutes a performative act (Austin 1950) or an act of structuration that is successful when it is considered felicitous by others (Alexander 2009: 66-7; Haugaard 1997: 165). A president or tax official is ontologically different from a physical object, such as Mount Everest. The latter exists whatever we believe about it, while the former are constituted by our belief (Searle 1996: 2007). Of course, the concept of a mountain is a human construct but the referent of that construct has the capacity to resist what we believe about it. In contrast, whatever we believe about social institutions self-validates. An individual may be mistaken about the powers of the president of the USA, but if a significant number of actors believe that the powers of the president are such-and-such, that is the case (Barnes 1988: 49-58). Legitimate authority is power that is commensurable with a surrounding system of thought.

Performative felicity is qualitatively different from a truth claim in that what qualifies as a statement is not subject to any kind of process of veridiction or falsification. Rather, because the referent is entirely socially constructed, it is deemed either inside or outside the conditions of possibility relative to what appears reasonable within a local interpretative horizon. As social agents we see the world by interpreting it. This applies both to social institutions and phenomena of the natural world. However, in the case of social institutions there is no foundation except for the self-validating beliefs of others. Social actors who interpret the world in a particular way consider it reasonable that the powers of authority figures include certain actions and preclude others. Relative to any transcendental foundations, this inclusion and exclusion is arbitrary, although not arbitrary relative to their local habitus. More significantly, in democracy the structures are not arbitrary with regard to the pragmatic criteria of replay and fair play. There is nothing epistemically invariable about considering this order of the world reasonable, yet it is not arbitrary. As observed by both Foucault (1989: 51) and Gellner (1988: 47) from their very different perspectives, in the medieval period priests could pronounce on science, while in the modern period they cannot. Again, it is important to emphasize, *cannot* is not literal, as in *unable* to. Of course they *can* but they would be speaking a kind of private language. They would be infelicitous or would be considered idiots in the ancient Athenian sense of the word—as people living outside society.

Any interpretative horizon sustains within it various possibilities of what is considered reasonable action. It is not that actors cannot act outside this but when they do their actions will not be validated by others. Conversely, if they act in ways considered reasonable by others, those others also find themselves constrained to respond appropriately, unless they want to be considered unreasonable, or idiots, in the Athenian sense. Epistemic constraint does not work by making actors into dupes. Rather it opens up certain conditions of possibility for felicitous action.

When a person in authority exercises power over subordinate actors in a manner consistent with that authority position, then those others find themselves constrained by the local conditions of reasonableness. If A wins an election by winning the most votes, the other contestant B who received fewer votes is constrained by an epistemic horizon he or she shares with A. Of course, B can ignore local conditions of felicity and insist that he or she has won. In that case A will consider B unreasonable and, chances are, A will not admit defeat. However, if B has coercive power resources at his or her disposal, a private army or whatever, then B can choose to ignore all this. The power-usurping B may be able to call him or herself "president," but the power of that "presidency" will be sustained through coercive rather than political power. From the perspective of political (as opposed to coercive) power, B will not be a true president.

A system of thought confers a capacity for action upon actors occupying positions of authority. These include not simply the most obvious ones of high political office: they pertain to all aspects of authority in everyday life—not only politicians and bureaucrats but, also, teachers, parents, citizens, employees, illegal aliens, and so on. As actors move through social life they move authority positions. One moment a father can tell his daughter what she eats for dinner, yet the next he may be a politician who can draft and vote on legislation that affects millions, yet he is powerless to determine what the electorate eats for dinner. These constitute the *conditions of possibility* associated with each authority position, which are defined by the possibilities of felicitous response by others. Sometimes authority positions impact upon each other: when Obama ran for the presidency he appeared on television surrounded by his family. The objective was to use the image of fatherhood to reinforce that of head of the nation, but performance nearly became infelicitous when some journalists interpreted the appearance as a father exploiting his children for high political office (Alexander 2009: 77).

The precarious performative nature of authority can best be seen where it is at the edge of what is possible. According to a recent article by Read (2010), part of the key to Nelson Mandela's success was the perception that the standoff between the African National Congress (ANC) and the apartheid regime had the potential to be changed from a zero-sum to a positive-sum conflict. However, this entailed convincing others of a change of the rules of the game, thus taking performative risks as an authority figure. While in prison Nelson Mandela became an iconic figure for the ANC, yet he was also distanced from its everyday workings and could be perceived of as out of touch. In this ambiguous position of iconic yet isolated leader, he took the risk of negotiating with the government without the preconditions that until then had been ANC policy. Performatively, he could be portrayed as a lone old man who was out of touch if he were to fail but, if he were successful, he would constitute a transformative leader who led South Africa from a zero-sum confrontation to a non-zero-sum democracy. In his own words: "my isolation furnished my organization with an excuse in case matters went awry: the old man was alone and completely cut off, and his actions were taken by him as an individual, not a representative of the ANC" (Mandela 1995: 627; Read 2010: 318).

Political power is power based on authority that stays within the parameters of the local conditions of possibility. It is power that is essentially constrained and controlled by the local system of meaning. However, these systems of meaning are not cast in stone, and Mandela effectively shifted such perceptions and, in so doing, changed the conditions of possibility. The other possibility is to impose authority irrespective of local meaning, which entails coercion and the resultant authority constitutes authority in appearance only. Of course, these are ideal types: in the real world most authority has to be backed by coercion but in a truly effective political system, the routine exercise of power takes place within the conditions of possibility set out by the generalized habitus, or collective consciousness, of the society in question.

DEMOCRACY, STRUCTURAL CONSENT, AND STABILITY

Modern power became functional through its institutionalization of legal procedures (Thornhill 2010). As political systems advance they standardize routines of power and, in so doing, become more effective than their competitors. Coercive power is power of the exception. It is the power of an uninstitutionalized environment in which order is relatively absent. What made the emergence of ordered functional power possible was the epistemic differentiation of the social world into separate spheres. Thus there emerged a political realm that was separable from the religious and economic spheres. While the normative ideals of the religious sphere aimed at consensus, the political sphere became normatively structured around constrained conflict and the economic embodied norms of competitive meritocracy.

The functionality of the conflictual political sphere is premised upon its routinization and standardization. When the political sphere emerged as a standardized realm of predictability, conflicts could be channeled through it in a manner that rendered possible conflict with regard to specific issues, yet consent with respect to the structures themselves. In an ongoing conflict actors will *not* consent to being constrained by the rules if they perceive them as skewed to their disadvantage. For instance, first-past-the-post elections (in which the majority takes all) allow for repeat play in either highly pluralist or uniform societies, because the losers have a chance of winning through repeat play. Pluralist societies deliver repeat play because diversity ensures that no given group constitutes a permanent minority. In uniform societies there are no in or out groups. However, in ethnically or religiously divided societies, minorities may find themselves perpetual losers. In that case the structures of the system are biased against them, power is zero-sum, and as a consequence, they find themselves resistant to replay.

Democracy constitutes a stable process of decision making based around the principle of equality. This stability is not based upon the universalistic appeal of equality through foundational status. It is simply that equality, and a number of other related principles, allow for repeat play. In doing so, they create the conditions of possibility for conflict becoming constrained by consent to structures. Of course, in many instances these principles are justified foundationally but these reifications are actually unnecessary for stability.

Another democratic principle is impartiality. In feudalism, power was linked to the perceived essences of the elite. Therefore, power was entirely partial, in the sense of being linked to specific personae. However, with the decline of an essentialist worldview, partiality became perceived of as illegitimate. The feudal world was sustained ideologically by a teleological foundationalism in which objects changed because of essences within them—an acorn became an oak because it had the essence of oakness within it. With the advance of modern science, teleology became discredited and was replaced by a world of atoms governed by scientific laws antithetical to the idea of essences and exceptions. The political equivalent of the atom is the citizen, who counts the same as every other citizen, governed by the same impartial laws.

In a democratic conflict it is not necessarily that subaltern actor B wants to comply, but refusal to do so becomes unreasonable. If power structures treat each as the same as every other actor, if a subaltern can perform the thought experiment of putting him or herself in the place of the powerful other and the outcomes would be the same, then it becomes unreasonable not to consent to an exercise of power. Thus there is a perceived link between political institutions, justice, and impartiality (Barry 1989: 423). The reason for this correlation between impartiality and the absence of coercion has nothing to do with justice as some kind of transcendental truth that all the actors in a democracy believe in with moral fervor—the secular equivalent of the word of God. It is simply that the norms that most closely follow the Kantian ethic of impartiality are the ones that most easily allow for repeat play. The difference between a fair game and an unfair game is that each player has an equal chance of winning.

It is important to understand that what constitutes the rules of "fair" play in their specificity is particular to context. First-past-the-post systems are perceived as both equal and impartial in societies that are either highly pluralist or homogenous. Yet, in divided societies this is not the case because repeat play will deliver continual victory for the majority group. Over time the minority will accept the outcomes of elections only because they are coerced. Yet, in divided societies the kind of consociational democratic models described by Lijphart (1977) are considered fair.

In *Political Liberalism*, Rawls observes that there is a direct correlation between justice and stability (1993: 142-3) but he does not argue for fairness based upon stability. In contrast, I would argue that fairness is desirable because it is stable, therefore noncoercive. This is not some fundamental deontological fairness, grounded in abstract philosophical theory. The key is local perceptions of reasonableness gained through replay over time, which result in stability.

In addition to equality and impartiality, stability also presupposes the separation of public and private. Actors who have political authority have to be able to distinguish the resources that belong to the state and those of private citizens. In terms of repeat play it does not make sense for an actor B to hand over authoritative power to another who then uses that power to confiscate their material resources—Locke's point, apropos of Hobbes, that it does not make sense to exchange the threat of theft by pole-cats and foxes for that of a lion.

Not only will systems that conflate political and economic power not allow for repeat play but they are also dysfunctional. Political systems that are limited in their powers of economic extraction to established taxation systems, as opposed to ad hoc raiding of resources, are economically more efficient than their competitors. Ironically, political systems that are internally coercive are less effective at mobilizing for war than regimes based on political power because they are weak in terms of economic power resources. As has been argued by Tilly (1992), a key element in the emergence of the modern bureaucratic state was the greater capacity of states with regularized taxation systems to mobilize armies. During the early modern period, war was the greatest drain on the state's economic resources. Modern industrialization presupposes the capacity to plan future profits with relative accuracy. Thus the advent of the balance sheet presupposes regularized taxation while, conversely, regularized taxation gives the state the capacity to make war effectively as it can plan its resources. Ad hoc extraction of material resources destroys the economy, while taxation makes rational planning possible. The restraint necessary to prevent the state plundering the economic resources of its subjects presupposes official authority figures capable of restraint and whose interpretative horizon includes a clear separation of public and private, of political power from economic power.

European democracies were also tempered in the fires of religious civil wars, where coercive power was everything. Again, over time, repeat play made it reasonable to move religion from the public to the private sphere in order to allow political power to develop. This did not happen as a sudden insight into civil liberties, rather it emerged as a modus vivendi response to civil war. Making religious belief private was a way of moving from coercive power to political power, from zero-sum power to non-zero-sum power. Over time this modus vivendi practice acquired normative foundations in the discourses of civil liberties.

THE DEMOCRATIC SUBJECT

Political power presupposes a certain kind of social subject who has internalized the conditions of felicity and infelicity of the age in which the subject lives. Power that disregards these background conditions of possibility does so by substituting coercive power. This raises the question: What are the key characteristics of the democratic subject who performs the authority associated with modern democracy?

The modern state emerged as part of a process of standardization of the world. Political power was made legal, codified and thus iterative. Modernity is also associated with the attempt to codify the political structures of the world as distinct from their exercise—the law became blind. Impartiality entails a subject capable of methodologically bracketing certain perceptions in favor of other ones.

The strong perception of fairness and impartiality of the democratic subject did not happen overnight. It emerged through socialization. It is not chance that the emergence of political power took place simultaneously with the emergence of modern sport. Sport was ritualized violence, in which the joys of the battlefield became constrained, literally, by the rules of the game. Central to this was the idea that the game had to be fair. Fairness did not come about overnight: games were not invented ex nilo. Rather, just as with democracy, rules emerged over time through continual testing against criteria of fairness (Elias 1986: 150-74).

Neither is it chance that the modern democratic state emerged at the same time as the state attempted to standardize education. As observed by Gellner (1983), the modern state not only assumed a monopoly of violence and taxation but control of education, which entails the mass socialization of subjects. Even where there were privately run schools, these had to conform to a state syllabus and receive state validation. Acquiring the status of a school or university became a new authority position performatively validated by the state. As observed by Foucault (1979) and those who write on governmentality (Dean 2010 and Rose 2008), modern education involved attention to detail. Lateness and lack of self-restraint or control became punishable. There emerged a new economy of the disciplined subject. Foucault and his followers criticize this, and with good reason at times, yet it is important to understand that the authority positions of complex democratic states presuppose precisely this kind of disciplined subject.

The structural aspect of social life is tied to the meaning reproduced. The same signified, or referent object, can have a different meaning, depending on the specific local interpretative horizon that is used. In social life referents include individuals with different meanings. If an actor knows someone as a relative, friend or lover that suggests an affective language game with specific criteria of reasonableness that are very different from the language game in which the other is a client, a voter, or a citizen. These modes of seeing the other entail a form of methodological bracketing of other ways of seeing that person and imply deliberately distancing oneself from one's emotional relationships. It entails specifically not thinking of the particularities of their lives—all the intimate things we may know and that tie us to that individual. Thus felicitous democratic authority presupposes *methodological bracketing*, which constitutes a self-imposed restraint whereby only certain meanings apply to specific contexts. This presupposes internalization of constraint and socialization in a differentiated perception of the world. Again, mass education instilled discipline. Not only does the endless attention to detail, time-keeping, punctuality, neatness create a disciplined subject but the division of the world into various disciplines (especially the divisions between the natural sciences, human sciences, economics, humanities, philosophy, and theology) teaches the modern subject that the world is not continuous. *Academic disciplines constitute a form of methodological bracketing* in which different descriptions of the world are made to count in different contexts.

In his well-known theory of justice, Rawls describes what he terms the "original position." In thinking about justice, actors should put themselves behind a "veil of ignorance" whereby they do not know their place in society, race, gender, wealth, concept of the good, and the general particularities of their life (Rawls 1971: 12). This has generally been criticized, most famously by Sandel (1998), because it appears to suggest that actors should put themselves in the position of an unencumbered self who lacks socialization. This description of the social actor appears unsociological in presupposing an undersocialized concept of the self. This criticism actually misses the sociological point that modern power presupposes a highly differentiated social world in which the competent agency of performative authority entails the use of interpretative horizons, or specific descriptions, that require continual methodological bracketing. The self of politics and modern bureaucracy is expected to be able to switch from, for instance, an affective language game of family to the political language game of impartiality. The other who may be a friend or lover one moment becomes a number on a file at another. This switching entails continual methodological bracketing and self-restraint. In the role of treating the other as anyone else, the democratic authority figure may have to exclude all the particular things that they may value about the other. This can be a difficult task, especially if the other is someone about whom he or she knows a lot and with whom he or she has strong affective emotional ties.

Because repeat play presupposes separation of economic, religious, and political fields, the democratic authority figure must have a strong sense of public and private not only economically but also ideologically. This ties the modern subject to a highly differentiated interpretative horizon characteristic of modernity. The premodern feudal world was relatively singular. Religious belief saturated not only the political order but also the natural order. Part of the conflicts between church and science sprang from the self-proclaimed right of scientists to the separateness of the natural world. If scientific observation suggested that the world was not the center of the universe or that species evolve, this was separate from the world of religious belief, which constituted a private ethical sphere. As a consequence of the wars of religion, repeat play entailed a further separation of the moral sphere into private ethics and public morality. The former pertains to the private sphere and the latter to political authority.

In short, authority constitutes a performative act of structuration that is considered reasonable. The criteria of reasonableness are, of course, not some historical invariable. Rather, they presuppose a specific social ontology. While individual authority figures may have the capacity to abuse power in individual instances through coercion or symbolic violence, the maintenance of the system depends on actors who, as a matter of routine, refrain from doing so. Authority must be accountable, which entails that at any point in time the person in authority can account for his or her actions in ways that make sense within the local conditions of possibility. Even when modern authority figures make previously unencountered decisions, accountability entails that any such decision must be compatible with prevailing norms of felicity. Thus modern figures of authority will apply rules to make themselves accountable. This entails leaving a paper trail. The unintended cost of accountability is, of course, the inefficiency of bureaucracy.

The modern authority figure is a highly restrained being whose political power presupposes a highly differentiated worldview. The subordinate actor over whom he or she exercises power only renders authority felicitous in the long term if that authority figure follows generalized principles of equality and impartiality, and differentiates the public and private spheres. In short, the democratic subject is rule-bound, thus accountable. This entails massive methodological bracketing of the personal, whereby democratic authority is, essentially, the product of a disciplined and interpretatively differentiated subject.

REFLECTIONS ON THE TRANSITION TO DEMOCRATIC POWER

We have analyzed democracy as ordered institutionalized power that was set against a context of the long period of transition, which constitutes the European and U.S. experience of democracy. I would like to conclude with some reflections on the implications of this analysis for contemporary shorter transitions to democracy.

Central to our analysis has been the hypothesis that democracy presupposes consent in structuration practices, which entails that political power cannot come out of the barrel of a gun—as observed by Arendt (1970: 53). Political power comes from the hearts and minds of human subjects. This has two aspects: on the one hand they must desire political power as an end in itself and, once the institutionalization has taken place, they must internalize the constraints necessary for their reproduction. The first prerequisite comes from the conviction that political power is more worthwhile than coercive power. There are two reasons actors might be convinced that democratic power is more desirable than coercion. The first is one cited by Hobbes as the reason for moving from the hypothetical state of nature: coercion makes life unpredictable, thus nasty, brutish and short (Hobbes 1914: 65). The second is that coercive power is zero-sum, while authoritative political power is positive-sum. At a systemic level, political power is positive-sum because the institutionalization of power means the creation of greater predictability with the system as a whole, which enables the development of complex coordinated activities. At an individual level, the democratic institutionalization of power means that a loss in one political contest does not constitute a perpetual loss. It is reasonable for the episodically subordinate actor to consent to defeat in the knowledge that there will be a next contest, in which that actor has the potential to win.

Convincing contesting parties to move from zero-sum coercive confrontation to positive-sum power is the key to any initial transition to democracy. As we saw, according to Read's analysis, Mandela's task was one of persuading both sides to move from zero-sum to positive-sum politics. Yet, given the extent of repression and the relative absence of the kind of political power that underpins stable democracy, Mandela's task was a formidable one. Political power presupposes consent. Consequently, part of Mandela's capacity to convince others to move from coercive confrontation to institutional power entailed a profound understanding of the habitus, or the taken for granted knowledge, of *both* opponents and his own flock. His knowledge of Boer history was impeccable (Read 2010: 333). With regard to the ANC, he saw himself as a shepherd leading from behind (Read 2010: 326-7): "a leader . . . is like a shepherd. He stays behind the flock, letting the most nimble go out ahead, whereupon the others follow, not realizing that all along they are being directed from behind" (Mandela 1995: 25-6). In acknowledging the social ontology of the other, and those he led, Mandela did not simply take their being-in-the-world as an immutable external reality. He sought to transform it. Transition to democracy entails a complex interweaving of understanding the habitus of other and attempting to transform it.

Once democratic institutions have been created, authority has to be shown to be accountable. Accountability entails that politician and official can give an account of their behavior that is consistent with what is considered reasonable relative to the meaning of their specific authority as performative acts. In order to be accountable, politicians and bureaucrats must develop a strong sense of the distinction between pursuing public and private interests because their account must make sense relative to the former, while precluding the latter.

As a whole, the society must come to understand that for democracy to be stable it must constitute a positive-sum game in which the winner does not take all. In societies in which groups have been oppressed, it can be tempting simply to reverse the identity of winners and losers. Moving beyond a zero-sum view of democracy entails that there develops an understanding that the general will is not equivalent to the sum of individual interests, as in crude majoritarianism. The general will is never a particular good, including the good of the majority. Rather it constitutes a set of principles that allows for the routinization of power.

Over time, as democracies become more established, the taken for granted knowledge that sustains democracy becomes stronger. There are few, if any, instances of a democracy that has been established for over 20 years democratically dissolving its institutions (Dahl 1989). The reason is that the structuration practices of democracy become routinized in the habitus of social actors—the institutions become part of the natural order of things. However, before that can happen it is paramount that actors interpret the rules of the game to be impartial and fair. It must make sense to them to concede defeat in electoral contests, or to accept the reasonableness of bureaucratic decisions that go against the specific interests at a given point in time, because they know that the rules apply equally to others. Actors will only accept power over them if they consider that power to be reasonable, and it is entirely unreasonable to expect anyone to accept rules of the game in which they are perpetual losers or which apply only specifically to them.

Democratic play presupposes democratic *players*, and the key to creating the latter is education. In Europe democracy took some 500 years to develop. The basic institutions began as modus vivendi arrangements to resolve conflict and only gradually became transformed into something more far-reaching and idealistic. This time frame was accompanied by a slow incremental change in habitus, which included state control of education. If such a process is to be condensed into a few years, it has to be accompanied by education that is specifically directed at creating a collective consciousness that is differentiated, restrained, and capable of distinguishing the public from the private and so on. In the first instance the change of rules may entail limited use of coercion but, overall, the objective must be to move from coercive power to true political power by creating the conditions of possibility for such power, which will entail an ontological shift in the habitus of social actors.

In some instances there may be local traditions, such as the practices of the local tribal regent observed by Mandela as a child (Mandela 1995: 25), that can be used to build a democratic habitus. Using the foundation of local habitus entails that there can be no exact blueprint for democracy. The habitus that sustains European or American democracy is different from that of most African states, therefore the details of what constitutes fairness, impartiality, and so on will not necessarily be identical. Yet the underlying principles of political power will be the same.

REFERENCES

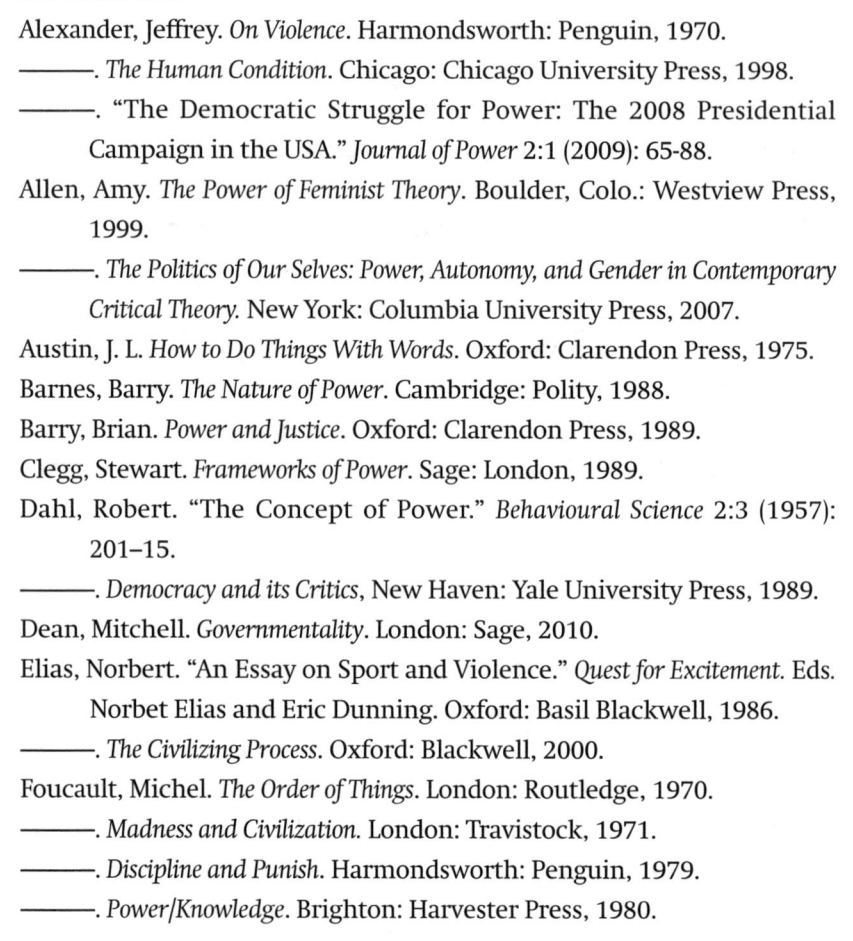

Alexander, Jeffrey. *On Violence*. Harmondsworth: Penguin, 1970.
———. *The Human Condition*. Chicago: Chicago University Press, 1998.
———. "The Democratic Struggle for Power: The 2008 Presidential Campaign in the USA." *Journal of Power* 2:1 (2009): 65-88.
Allen, Amy. *The Power of Feminist Theory*. Boulder, Colo.: Westview Press, 1999.
———. *The Politics of Our Selves: Power, Autonomy, and Gender in Contemporary Critical Theory*. New York: Columbia University Press, 2007.
Austin, J. L. *How to Do Things With Words*. Oxford: Clarendon Press, 1975.
Barnes, Barry. *The Nature of Power*. Cambridge: Polity, 1988.
Barry, Brian. *Power and Justice*. Oxford: Clarendon Press, 1989.
Clegg, Stewart. *Frameworks of Power*. Sage: London, 1989.
Dahl, Robert. "The Concept of Power." *Behavioural Science* 2:3 (1957): 201–15.
———. *Democracy and its Critics*, New Haven: Yale University Press, 1989.
Dean, Mitchell. *Governmentality*. London: Sage, 2010.
Elias, Norbert. "An Essay on Sport and Violence." *Quest for Excitement*. Eds. Norbet Elias and Eric Dunning. Oxford: Basil Blackwell, 1986.
———. *The Civilizing Process*. Oxford: Blackwell, 2000.
Foucault, Michel. *The Order of Things*. London: Routledge, 1970.
———. *Madness and Civilization*. London: Travistock, 1971.
———. *Discipline and Punish*. Harmondsworth: Penguin, 1979.
———. *Power/Knowledge*. Brighton: Harvester Press, 1980.

———. *History of Sexuality*. Vol. 1. Harmondsworth: Penguin 1981.

———. *The Archaeology of Knowledge*. London: Routledge, 1989.

———. *The Birth of Biopolitics*. Houndsmills: Palgrave Macmillan, 2008.

Gellner, Ernest. *Nations and Nationalism*. Oxford: Blackwell, 1983.

———. *Plough, Sword and Book*. Chicago: Chicago University Press, 1988.

Giddens, Anthony. *The Constitution of Society*. Cambridge: Polity, 1984.

Gohler, Gerhard. "'Power To' and 'Power Over.'" *The Sage Handbook of Power*. Eds. Stewart Clegg and Mark Haugaard. London: Sage, 2009.

Gore, Al. "Gore Concedes Presidential Election." CNN, Dec. 13, 2000 <http://articles.cnn.com/2000-12-13/politics/gore.ends.campaign>.

Habermas, Jurgen. *The Theory of Communicative Action*. Vol. 1. Cambridge: Polity, 1984.

Haugaard, Mark, *The Constitution of Power*. Manchester: Manchester University Press, 1997.

———. "Power, Modernity and Liberal Democracy." *Ernest Gellner and Contemporary Social Thought*. Eds. Sinisa Malesevic and Mark Haugaard. Cambridge: Cambridge University Press, 2007.

———. "Power and Social Critique." *Critical Horizons* 11:1 (2010a): 51-74.

———. "Power: A 'Family Resemblance' Concept." *European Journal of Cultural Studies* 13 (2010b): 1-20.

Hobbes Thomas. *The Leviathan*. Oxford: Oxford University Press, 2008.

Hyland, James. *Democratic Theory*. Manchester: Manchester University Press, 1995.

Laclau, Ernesto, and Chantal Mouffe. *Hegemony and Socialist Strategy*. London: Verso, 2001.

Lijphart, Arend. *Democracy in Plural Societies*. New Haven: Yale University Press, 1977.

Locke, John. *Two Treatises of Government*. New York: Everyman, 1993.

Lukes, Steven. *Power: A Radical View*. Houndsmills: Palgrave Macmillan, 2005.

Lukes, Steven, and Clarissa Hayward."Nobody to Shoot? Power, Structures and Agency: A Dialogue." *Journal of Power* 1:1 (2008): 5-20.

Mandela, Nelson. *Long Walk to Freedom*. London: Abacus, 1995.

Mann, Michael. *The Sources of Social Power.* Vol. 1. Cambridge: Cambridge University Press, 1983.

———. "The Sources of Social Power Revisited: A Response to Criticism." *An Anatomy of Power.* Eds. John A. Hall and Ralph Schroeder. Cambridge: Cambridge University Press, 2006.

Morriss, Peter. *Power: A Philosophical Analysis.* Manchester: Manchester University Press, 2002.

———. "Power and Liberalism."' *The Sage Handbook of Power.* Eds. Stewart Clegg and Mark Haugaard. London: Sage, 2009.

Mouffe, Chantal. *The Democratic Paradox*, London: Verso, 2000.

Parsons, T. "On the Concept of Political Power."' *Proceedings of the American Philosophical Society* 107 (1963): 232-62.

Rawls, John. *A Theory of Justice.* Oxford: Oxford University Press, 1971.

———. *Political Liberalism.* New York: Columbia University Press, 1993.

Read, James R. "Leadership and Power in Nelson Mandela's *Long Walk to Freedom.*" *Journal of Power* 3:3 (2010): 317-339.

Rose, Niklas. *Governing the Present.* Cambridge: Polity, 2008.

Sandel, Michael. *Liberalism and the Limits of Justice.* Cambridge: Cambridge University Press, 1998.

Searle, John. *The Construction of Social Reality.* London: Penguin Books, 1996.

———. "Social Ontology and Political Power." *Freedom and Neurobiology: Reflections on Free Will, Language, and Political Power.* New York: Columbia University Press, 2007.

Thornhill, Chris. "Legality, Legitimacy and the Form of Political Power: On the Construction of a False Antinomy." *Journal of Power* 3:3 (2010): 293-316.

Tilly, Charles. *Coercion, Capital, and European States.* Oxford: Blackwell, 1992.

Wittgenstein, Ludwig. *Philosophical Investigations.* Oxford: Oxford University Press, 1967.

William Easterly
Democratic Accountability in Development: The Double Standard

THE DEVELOPMENT ESTABLISHMENT TODAY TOLERATES A SHOCKING double standard on democracy for the rich versus democracy for the poor. Despite the both moral and pragmatic argument for democratic rights for all, development policy discussions give little emphasis to these rights for the poor.

To begin with the obvious Civics 101 view, accountability is a crucial mechanism in development to ensure that government does good and not ill to those affected by its actions. Under democracy, citizens can use many mechanisms—such as voting, popular protests, and spoken and written criticisms—to penalize governments that are harming individuals (even if it is only a minority of individuals). The same mechanisms reward political actors that do good by, for example, supplying public goods. When such mechanisms work, the government is accountable to its citizens. The opposite of accountability is impunity—the government can do whatever it wants to the citizens without consequences.

Once we focus on accountability, it is clear that "democracy" must include much more than majority voting. The government must be prevented from suppressing negative feedback by giving dissidents protection against arbitrary imprisonment, torture, "disappearances," or assassination. The media and other forums for public debate similarly need protection against government suppression (freedom of the press, freedom of speech, freedom of assembly). Likewise, to prevent harms against each of many different possible groups within society, rights must be guaranteed for minorities, even if a majority wants to violate those rights. Since the government also cannot be allowed to choose who are eligible to be dissidents, or who is eligible to be "media" or "public debaters," this is yet another reason to have equality before the law for *all* individuals.

Our most soaring and famous political rhetoric is devoted to these ideas:

> We hold these truths to be self-evident, that all men are created equal, that they are endowed by their Creator with certain unalienable rights, that among these are life, liberty and the pursuit of happiness. That to secure these rights, governments are instituted among men, deriving their just powers from the consent of the governed.

Of course, these ideals are never perfectly realized anywhere—as most famously dramatized by the fact that the writer of these words in 1776 was a slave-owner. But recognizing them at least as ideals has made it possible for political movements to extend individual rights by exposing such hypocrisy and appealing to these ideals, as Abraham Lincoln and Martin Luther King Jr. later did explicitly for African-Americans. In rich countries today, these principles are universally accepted, even if the realization still falls short.

The tragedy of the economic development establishment is that not even the ideal of democratic accountability to the poor seems to be widely accepted. The failure is along two separate dimensions. First, official aid agencies themselves do not explicitly accept that they should be accountable to the poor intended beneficiaries whom they sometimes affect negatively (or more often fail to affect positively) by their actions. Second, the development establishment displays indifference whether governments in poor societies (including governments they finance) are democratically accountable to their citizens.

Since, as discussed above, meaningful accountability requires individual rights, these two points, as contrasted with the ideals in rich countries, imply that the development establishment has a double standard: rights for the rich, and not for the poor.

As Berhanu Nega writes in this volume:

> the massive and rather effective campaign by the aid industry to "make poverty history" . . . [has] been successful in pressuring developed countries to provide more resources to support the development efforts of poor countries particularly in Africa without asking too much on the issue of democratic accountability (Nega 2010: 1408).

Sudanese entrepreneur Mo Ibrahim also complains about the current double standard:[1] "All Africans have a right to live in freedom and prosperity and to select their leaders through fair and democratic elections, and the time has come when Africans are no longer willing to accept lower standards of governance than those in the rest of the world" (Ibrahim 2009: 7).

This paper does not claim that it is easy to establish accountability to the poor in either sense of the two points noted earlier, and indeed the difficulty of doing so may be one of the main reasons for the persistence of the double standard. However, the failure to recognize equal rights for the poor even as an ideal arguably has caused many lost opportunities to advance accountability. The lack of accountability (in both senses of the two points) is in turn arguably one of the main causes of disappointing aid and development outcomes.

Of course, this paper recognizes that there is some recognition of democratic rights for the poor in official UN declarations and other official development discussions. The claim will be that this is very limited, because even talk about democratic rights for the poor is missing in most major public forums on development. A related claim will be that words like "accountability" in such discussions are watered down to evade the issue.

This paper first documents the above claims about the development establishment today in several different ways: analyzing aid and development documents, and looking at allocation of aid across democracies and dictatorships.

The second part of the paper looks at the history of the double standard to gain more insight into its stubborn persistence. This section finds that, although explicit racism has thankfully diminished, some important things can be found in common between the colonial era and today's development establishment. The paper concludes with some brief thoughts about why the double standard has persisted, and what hopes exist for the future.

THE DOUBLE STANDARD ON ACCOUNTABILITY IN TODAY'S DEVELOPMENT ESTABLISHMENT

We can see the double standard in the language that aid and development debates use, and in the actions of aid agencies.

Analyzing Aid and Development Documents

Of course, aid and development documents are unlikely to ever explicitly announce a double standard. Aid and development documents seem to follow a variety of rhetorical strategies that allow the double standard to persist while never explicitly endorsing it. Rhetorical strategies to evade issue of double standards include:

1. maintaining silence on the entire subject;
2. evading the democracy issue with euphemisms such as "governance," "participation," "civil society," or "stakeholders";
3. evading any criticism of autocrats with euphemisms such as "developmental state" or "strong leadership";
4. claiming a non-falsifiable "transition" away from a current regime of political oppression.

Until the 1990s, silence (Rhetorical Strategy no. 1) was the default option in aid and development discussions. The surge in interest in institutions in the 1990s, coupled with increasing activism by NGOs, made this strategy no longer viable and the other three strategies have become more popular since.

As an example take the World Bank's 2007 report, "Strengthening World Bank Group Engagement on Governance and Anticorruption" (World Bank 2007), a document of over a hundred pages that is currently one of the World Bank's most important statements on desirable institutions of government. The word "governance," which has become the universal word for the whole subject of desirable institutions, is one of those nearly content-free words that takes no stand on any issue. Merriam-Webster's dictionary defines "governance" as "government." Wikipedia defines it as the "act of governing." Anti-corruption is added to the title as a signal that it will receive most of the emphasis. Corruption is an appealing focus to sidestep issues of accountability, because the World Bank apparently sees it as a problem that is treatable with technocratic fixes (such as better corruption monitoring systems), and hence does not require more fundamental checks through citizen rights. These beliefs may lack a close correspondence with reality, but at least they seem plausible to many and there is no apparent double standard on corruption for rich and poor countries.

The paper of course cannot evade altogether the issue of government's relationship to the citizens. The evasion is mostly achieved (here and in many other similar documents) through Rhetorical Strategy no. 2: the use of what are popularly known as "development buzzwords": *country ownership, civil society, stakeholders, participation, inclusiveness, mainstreaming, empowerment, partnership.* In contrast, none of the following words appear in the main text of the governance strategy paper: *human rights, democracy, liberty, freedom,* or *equality.*

These latter words are also sometimes manipulated for political purposes and their meanings blurred, but they still have powerful resonance because of their historical association with the battle for equal rights for all. The latter words are useful in political movements for rights because they usually allow the oppressed to identify the oppressors—just who is violating rights, liberties, or freedoms.

Yet development discourse almost entirely avoids these powerful words. To give more examples, neither the 347-page World Bank 1998 "Participation Sourcebook" nor the 372-page World Bank 2006 "Empowerment in Practice" ever mentioned the historically resonant word "liberty."

The buzzwords, in contrast, fail to identify specific violations of rights and specific rights violators. If we do not have enough "empowerment," *who* is not empowered, *which* empowering actions are lacking, and *who* failed to take such actions?

Interestingly, the word "accountability" itself has become a buzzword. Accountability can have the clear meaning given in the introduction to this paper, which is precise enough for scholarly use. Unfortunately, the meaning of accountability in development policy debates is anything but precise. Stripped of context—without saying who is accountable to whom for what, when, and where, accountability reverts to being an empty word, and hence is also used even by organizations that operate with impunity. The word "participation" is so popular that the World Bank has an entire manual devoted to it, as mentioned above. The "Participation" manual then invokes another popular word when it lists "the poor and disadvantaged" as one of many "stakeholders" (others are the borrower government and "World Bank management, staff, and shareholders"). The manual does not address the issue of disagreements between stakeholders—like many of the other buzzwords, the word itself seems to imply a harmony of interests, a world of only winners and no losers. If this were not the real world, then the World Bank would have to address whether "poor stakeholders" would win a clash of interests against, say, World Bank shareholders (mainly the rich countries).

The "participation" idea is so broad that it covers both types of accountability: not only whether domestic governments are accountable to their own people, but also whether donors are accountable to the poor intended beneficiaries. In the above quote, the rich country governments, the donors, the poor country governments, and the citizens of the poor countries are all participating stakeholders. Of course, this raises more questions than it answers on both types of accountability—it leaves unclear which "stakeholders" are accountable to the others, and for which "stakes."

Other buzzwords like "country ownership" and "partnership" blur the issue of accountability of the donors to the poor people whom they affect. Who in a poor country is the "partner" that represents the country to "own" something? The answer to the first in practice is the ruler(s) in power at the moment. If the donor is indeed accountable to the ruler(s) as an elected representative(s) accountable to the citizens, then there is some indirect accountability of donors to the poor. However, the concept of country ownership does not discriminate between democrats and autocrats, so we are back to the original evasion of discussing poor people's rights.

If the donors and the recipient government are indeed "partners," that still does not answer the question of how power is allocated between the partners. The World Bank and International Monetary Fund (IMF) have gotten much grief for imposing their own conditions on recipient governments through the notorious Structural Adjustment Loans of the 1980s and 1990s. The SALs were general purpose loans to governments, on the condition that governments fulfilled detailed conditions on economic reform. The IMF and World Bank staff designed the reforms according to a standard blueprint, with little awareness of country context and no mechanism for holding the staff accountable for good or bad consequences of these reforms. Since recipient countries turned to these loans in moments of acute crisis, they often perceived little choice but to accept the conditions so as to get the loans.

In response to this criticism, they have been following for the past few years a process where the "country" develops its own "Poverty Reduction Strategy Paper" (and the loans renamed Poverty Reduction and Growth Facilities). This is then reviewed by the World Bank, IMF, and other donors to produce a "Joint Assistance Strategy."

For Ghana (an imperfectly democratic country), the Joint Assistance Strategy had the other "partners" saying to "Ghana":

Partners emphasized the need for the investment plan to be fully consistent with macro-economic stability, debt sustainability and principles for public financial management.... [T]here is need to scale up investment in infrastructure support services and the promotion of public-private partnerships, especially in transportation, energy and ICT [information and communication technologies]. There is also the need to improve the business environment: ensuring an effective regulatory environment for all key sectors, particularly ICT; reducing the administrative burden on the private sector; and promoting flexible factor markets to address rigidities in the reallocation of factors of production (land, labor, capital).

This sounds a lot like the old conditionality, except for the rather patronizing veneer of "partnership." Rhetorical Strategy no. 3 is often invoked not only to evade the issue of democracy versus dictatorship, but also because there is a genuine belief that dictators may be necessary for development (perhaps only during some initial phase of development). The view of development as a technocratic problem to be solved by experts is not very compatible with messy democratic compromises. Why let the people choose the "answers" when the experts already know the answers? Hence, there is the wistful hope for a "benevolent autocrat" who will be able to implement without constraints the technocratic solution specified by the experts.

As James C. Scott said in his classic treatise against social engineering, *Seeing Like a State*, "Political interests can only frustrate the social solutions devised by specialists with scientific tools" (Scott 1999: 94). Although wishing for a "benevolent autocrat" is acceptable language in many development discussions, it is a little too strong for others. Hence, euphemisms like "developmental state" or "strong leadership" are often used instead. These latter words do not necessarily imply dictatorship—it is more that they sidestep the issue of whether the developmental leader is or is not a dictator. So, for example, the World Bank Growth Commission in 2008 had as one of its strongest conclusions: "Growth at such a quick pace, over such a long period, requires strong political leadership" (World Bank 2008).

But what if the current autocrats are none too obviously benevolent? The donors can still invoke Rhetorical Strategy no. 4. The aid and democracy scholar Thomas Carothers noted the Transition Defense in a classic article. He quoted U.S. Agency for International Developoment (USAID) describing the Democratic Republic of the Congo in 2001 as a country in "transition to a democratic, free market society"(Carothers 2009: 169) (such "transition" is still not completely obvious in 2010).

The World Bank's response to Helen Epstein's May 13, 2010, article in the *New York Review of Books,* in which she accused the bank of supporting Ethiopian tyranny, is a classic Transition Defense. World Bank Ethiopia country director Ken Ohashi replied in a letter date June 24, 2010:

> We start ... with a belief that in every country people want ... to develop a transparent, accountable . . . governance system. Ethiopia is no exception. Our task . . . is to support that innate tendency. However, building institutions . . . takes a long time. . . . Changes are incremental, and at times they may suffer serious setbacks (Ohashi 2010).

The Transition Defense has the attraction of being nonfalsifiable. We don't know the future, so we don't know whether a negative event is a "setback" to "building institutions," or whether the "building" is a myth. We could of course observe the recent trend in "democratizing"—this has been negative in Ethiopia—but again, any negatives could be dismissed as a temporary setback.

To be fair to the donors, they do *sometimes* make overtures to democracy. The World Bank includes a measure of "voice and accountability" in its widely used "Governance Indicators" that it has produced since 1996.

Figure 1: Allocation of Foreign Aid by Classification of Recipients by Freedom House

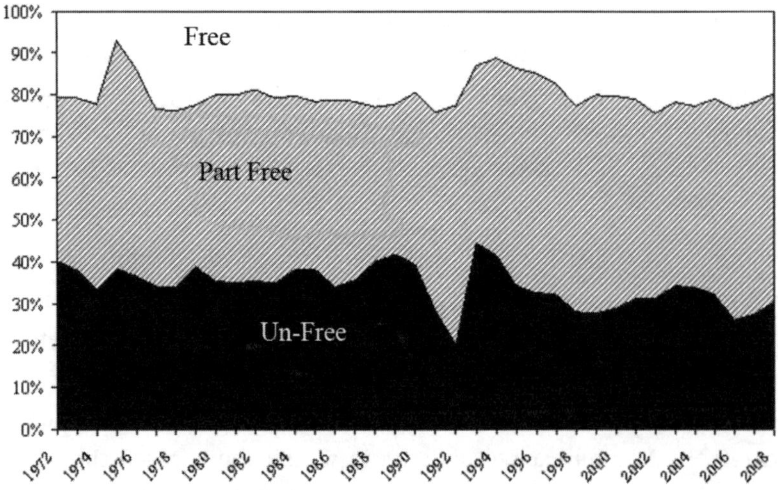

[Chart showing percentages from 1972 to 2008 with three bands labeled "Free", "Part Free", and "Un-Free"]

Source: Easterly and Williamson (2010)

However, reportedly bowing to protests by China, the bank says the indicators "are not used by the World Bank Group to allocate resources [aid]" (World Bank 2009). USAID declares its aims to be "promoting sustainable democracy" and "expanding the global community of democracies."

Donors were involved in internationally supervised elections in formerly war-torn societies like Sierra Leone, Liberia, and the Democratic Republic of the Congo. Donors also applied pressure to Kenya to conform to democratic principles after the long-time autocrat Daniel arap Moi left office, and again in 2007–2008 when there was a seriously flawed election.

However, these statements and actions are heavily qualified in practice. The World Bank announced that it will not use its own "voice and accountability" measures to influence its own aid allocation. The rhetorical and practical support for democracy is usually limited to the mechanics of majority vote elections. As noted above, majority voting is not sufficient to ensure true accountability. Moreover, elections can be manipulated by autocrats. Hence, the most important finding is the

Table 1: Top Autocratic Recipients of Aid (in billions of dollars)

Donors		Recipients	
United States	$46	China	$15
Japan	$23	Vietnam	$12
Germany	$16	Sudan	$10
World Bank (IDA)	$14	Egypt	$9
France	$14	Cameroon	$9
United Kingdom	$10	Rwanda	$5
EC	$9	Tunisia	$3

silence and evasion documented above on the democratic rights that are the basis of true accountability.

Allocation of Aid Across Types of Regimes

The aid donors also show their indifference to democracy by allocating only a small share of aid funds to democracies (see figure 1), and a surprisingly large share to unambiguous dictatorships (using the definitions of "Free," "Partly Free," and "Not Free" of Freedom House).

Admittedly, there is a genuine dilemma for donors. They want to direct aid to the poorest countries, and since democracy and poverty are inversely related across countries, there are not that many democracies to choose from among the poor nations. Yet, as figure 2 shows, some donor agencies are able to do much better at this trade-off than others. And too much emphasis on poverty relative to democracy is likely to be counterproductive if aid to an autocratic government is not going to reach the poor anyway.

The bottom line is that many autocrats receive a considerable amount of aid. Table 1 shows the top autocratic recipients of aid, as well as which donors are most responsible for financing them.

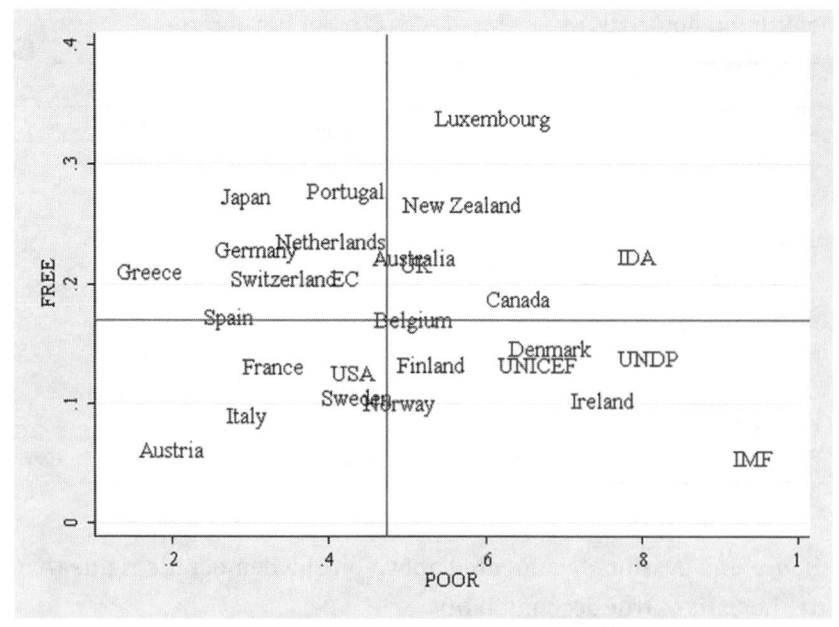

Figure 2: Donor Agencies' Shares of Democratic Recipients (vertical axis) vs. Share of Low-lincome Nations (horizontal axis)

Paul Biya, the dictator of Cameroon, has been in power 28 years. Throughout his tenure he has received a long series of loans from the International Monetary Fund that are now known as "Poverty Reduction Growth Facilities." Biya, whose government also enjoys ample oil revenues, has received $35 billion in foreign aid from all sources during his reign. Yet the average Cameroonian is poorer today than when Biya took power.

In February 2008, Biya's security forces killed 100 people during a demonstration against food price increases and against a constitutional amendment that extended Biya's rule to 2018. Many of the victims were "apparently shot in the head at point-blank range" (Amnesty International 2009). The IMF justification for the newest loan in June 2009 noted that these "social tensions" have not recurred and "the political situation is stable" (International Monetary Fund 2009).

Other long-serving aid-receiving autocrats are Chad's Idriss Deby, 1990–present ($6 billion in aid); Guinea's Lansana Conté, 1984–2008 ($11 billion); Rwanda's Paul Kagame, 1994–present ($10 billion); Uganda's Yoweri Museveni, 1986–present ($31 billion); and Cambodia's Hun Sen, 1985–present ($10 billion). The autocrats of Kazakhstan, Tajikstan, and Uzbekistan have been in power since the break-up of the Soviet Union in 1991, and each has received $3 billion.

Political Neutrality of Aid: The Impossible Dream
The aid donors also defend their financing of dictators by saying they do not want to ignore poor people who are unlucky enough to be ruled by an autocrat. They claim that project aid directed at specific areas like emergency relief, health, or education will help people directly without financing autocratic governments. Unfortunately, this argument has at least two potential weaknesses. First, aid is "fungible." Second, aid programs administered by the government may be manipulated to punish political dissidents.

Donor officials have always been aware that aid is "fungible." As the first chief economist of the World Bank said in the early 1950s, "we may think we're financing a power plant and actually we're financing a brothel" (Shantayanan et al. 1999: 1).

The fungibility problem is that if the government receives aid for something good, like electric power, health, or education, it can reduce its own spending on these areas. This then allows the expansion of spending in "bad" areas, such as on the security forces. This means aid can de facto finance the "bad" area even when it is de jure targeting the good area. So, for example, "health aid" may support government repression even when it is targeted at directly helping the poor. The claim of donors to be politically neutral is not tenable if they are de facto financing an autocrat.

Fungibility is a problem for all donors. Although the IMF claims to be providing finance to facilitate fiscal and balance of payments adjustment, it too is subject to fungibiilty—the government with the

IMF has more funds than without the IMF and so the IMF effectively finances the marginal dollar of government spending in whatever area it happens to be.

Autocrats can also manipulate aid to punish the opposition. A report by Human Rights Watch (2010) documented this kind of manipulation under Ethiopia's Meles Zenawi. Based on interviews with 200 people in 53 villages and two cities throughout the country, the report concluded that the Ethiopian government uses aid as a political weapon to discriminate against nonparty members and punish dissent. For example, farmers in three different regions reported to Human Rights Watch (HRW) that village leaders withheld government-provided seeds and fertilizer, and even microloans from nonparty members.

Investigating one donor-funded program in Ethiopia that gives food and cash in exchange for work on public projects, HRW documented the cases of farmers who completed work but were never paid and entire families barred from the list because they were thought to belong to the opposition. A former coordinator of the program confirmed: "the rule was that members of the safety net should be ruling party members. . . . [T]ruly speaking the people are hungry and the safety net is full of manipulation" (HRW 2010). An opposition leader in Awassa also told HRW that "there are children who are malnourished, who are not getting assistance in my *kebele* [village] for political reasons. They are starving to death, they are so sick. There are many" (HRW 2010).

Many individual aid officials that HRW spoke to admitted that they were aware of these abuses. One Western donor official said, "Intimidation is all over, in every area. There is politicization of housing, business, education, agriculture. Many of the people are forced or compromised to join the party because of safety net and so on, many do not have a choice—it it is imposed" (HRW 2010). Another senior Western donor official based in Addis Ababa said to HRW: "Every tool at their disposal—fertilizer, loans, safety net—is being used to crush the opposition. We know this" (HRW 2010).

The umbrella group representing 26 donors in Ethiopia (the Donors Assistance Group, or DAG), responded to the HRW report by acknowledging that safeguards to "provide checks on possible distortions... could be further strengthened." However, their overall response was to reject HRW's conclusions, noting that their own study "did not generate any evidence of systematic or widespread distortion" (DAG Statement 2010). It is difficult to know how widespread these abuses are when, on the one hand, the HRW report was based on small and not necessarily random or representative samples, and on the other hand the donors have the PR incentive to deny any political manipulation of their aid. The HRW report provides at least illustrative examples of the possibility of the kind of aid manipulation that many have feared could result from giving aid to autocratic regimes that wish to suppress opposition.

HISTORY OF THE DOUBLE STANDARD IN DEVELOPMENT

It is instructive to trace the history of the double standard in development. We will check to see whether some of the same ideas and language surfaced during the past history of racism and colonialism as in today's postracist and postcolonial present. The point is not to accuse anyone today of racism or neocolonialism, but it is to show that the break between history and today is not as great as usually claimed.

The Early Colonial Period: The Prehistory of Development

In the old days, most economists (and everyone else) considered it easy to explain differences in development between Europe and the rest of the world. In fact, the question did not even get much discussion because they considered the explanation so obvious: Europeans were superior to non-Europeans. There was some hope for the latter if Europeans coerced them to improve.

I hardly can do justice to the long history of such attitudes. One revealing example is from one of the most famous economists of all time, who was also a courageous early advocate for individual rights: John Stuart Mill. Mill's classic essay on *On Liberty* (1869) asserted forcefully "Over himself, over his own body and mind, the individual is sovereign." But Mill was unapologetic about the need for a double standard on individual rights:

> We may leave out of consideration those backward states of society in which the race itself may be considered as in its [childhood]. Despotism is a legitimate mode of government in dealing with barbarians, provided the end be their improvement.... Liberty, as a principle, has no application to any [such] state of things (Mill 1957 [1869]).

Things had not changed much by the time of the articles of the Covenant of the League of Nations after World War I, which entered into force in January 1920. Article 22 reads:

> To those colonies and territories which as a consequence of the late war have ceased to be under the sovereignty of the States which formerly governed them and which are inhabited by peoples not yet able to stand by themselves under the strenuous conditions of the modern world, there should be applied the principle that the well-being and development of such peoples form a sacred trust of civilisation and that securities for the performance of this trust should be embodied in this Covenant.
>
> The best method of giving practical effect to this principle is that the tutelage of such peoples should be entrusted to advanced nations who by reason of their resources, their experience or their geographical position can best undertake this responsibility, and who are willing to accept it, and that this tutelage should be exercised by them as Mandatories on behalf of the League.

One of the key players in founding the League of Nations was Jan Smuts, the prime minister of South Africa. He was already on record with similar language but stated more explicitly in racist terms: "The white race in South Africa" should act as "trustees for the coloured races" (Mazower 2009).

Yet even at this early date, there was some discomfort about the impunity colonial powers enjoyed relative to their subjects. The discomfort was still a long way from really accepting accountability to colonial subjects, so some of the rhetorical strategies that donors use today to evade accountability were already beginning to appear, even including use of some of the same buzzwords. For example, a relatively radical British member of Parliament argued in 1929 for giving the subjects of authoritarian colonial rule "some *participation* in the shaping of their own destinies" (Cornwall 2006; emphasis added).

The Late Colonial Period: The Invention of "Development"

The sudden emergence and acceptance of the concept of "development" during the 1940s had political roots that did not imply abandoning the double standard. One version of the story appears in a classic (and much underappreciated) book by Suke Wolton (2000), *Lord Hailey, the Colonial Office and the Politics of Race and Empire in the Second World War*. The British began stressing development in response to threats to their colonial empire during World War II. The British had to meet the ideological threat of the Japanese offering a non-European and nonracist alternative to their Asian colonies, which were also militarily vulnerable to the Japanese. The Japanese early in the war inflicted a catastrophic defeat on the British at Singapore, which also dented the empirical claim of European superiority. Japanese propaganda also tried to induce colonial subjects to rebel against their masters by pointing to British racism.

The old colonial ideology of white superiority was no longer tenable under such a threat. As a February 13, 1940, memo from Malcolm MacDonald, the secretary of state for the colonies on, noted: "continuance of the present state of affairs...provides our enemies and critics with an admirable subject for propaganda in neutral countries and elsewhere" (Constantine 1984: 220).

A long-time colonial official, Lord Hailey, in 1941 redefined the empire's mission as "promotion of native welfare." And he argued the colonies could only develop with Britain's help. Hailey said: "A new conception of our relationship...may emerge as part of the movement for the betterment of the backward peoples of the world, which stands in the forefront of every enlightened programme for . . . postwar conditions" (Wolton 1999: 51).

Racism was still so strong that ethnic slurs and epithets were only gradually becoming less acceptable. Responding to orders from MacDonald and Hailey, the BBC banned the N-word early in the war (the ban seems to imply that BBC announcers were previously using it and would have continued to use it without the new government orders).

Development rather than racism offered an alternative ideology of empire during World War II. Although we now know the end of the empire was only a few years away, this was not the expectation at the time. The Colonial Office still thought many colonies "little removed from their primitive state," so "they will probably not be fit for complete independence for centuries" (Wolton 2000: 128, 129).

To repress independence movements, Hailey made a distinction between political development and economic development, using arguments that are still popular today: "Political liberties are meaningless unless they can be built on a better foundation of social and economic progress."

Buzzwords can be found at the moment of birth of development, along with an indifference to the accountability of governments. The February 1940 British "Statement of Policy on Colonial Development and Welfare and on Colonial Research" found that the

> Government would propose to invite Colonial Governments to prepare development programmes for a period of years ahead.

From London there will be assistance and guidance, but no spirit of dictation. The new policy of development will involve no derogation from the rights and privileges of local legislatures.

The whole effort will be one of co-operation between the authorities in the Colonies and those at home. . . . Colonial Governments, who best know the needs of their own territories, should enjoy a wide latitude in the initiation and execution of policies, the primary purpose of which is to promote the prosperity and happiness of the peoples of the Colonial Empire (Padmore 1941).

The "Colonial Governments" that were supposed to prepare what sounds a lot like today's Poverty Reduction Strategy Papers, were actually made up principally of British officials unaccountable to local inhabitants, with occasional token local representation (except where there were white settlers). Not for the last time, the accountability of the government was less important than the allegedly apolitical technocratic solution to development.

The Birth of the International Organizations: The UN, World Bank, and IMF
The founding of the United Nations had a lot in common with the late colonial British effort to strategically use the concept of "development" in ways that did nothing to end the double standard. This is the story told in the recent book by Mark Mazower (2009), *No Enchanted Palace: The End of Empire and the Ideological Origins of the United Nations*.

The UN Preamble (June 26, 1945) at first seems to embody a major advance in the ideals of equal rights for all:

WE THE PEOPLES OF THE UNITED NATIONS DETERMINED
- to reaffirm faith in fundamental human rights, in the dignity and worth of the human person, in the equal rights of men and women and of nations large and small, and

- to promote social progress and better standards of life in larger freedom,

AND FOR THESE ENDS

- to employ international machinery for the promotion of the economic and social advancement of all peoples.

One realizes that all is not quite what it seems only upon learning that the author of the preamble was the same apostle of white superiority—Jan Smuts of South Africa—who had helped found the League of Nations. As Mazower tells the story, Smuts did not see the UN as a challenge to the British Empire, but an ally and defender of the empire. Smuts said in his speech to the UN founding conference in San Francisco that the United Kingdom was the "greatest colonial power" in the world, and he continued to use the old League of Nations language of "dependent peoples, still unable to look after themselves." Indeed, the UN Charter said nothing about independence for any European colonies.

It is difficult to resist the temptation to read the history backward when it actually happened forward. As already noted, few expected in 1945 the sudden collapse of colonial empires (which would have more to do with the postwar collapse of the British and French as major military powers and the proliferation of small arms to end their monopoly of force). The anticolonial and antiracist positions for which the UN later became known emerged only after a majority of their members became non-European and postcolonial, which was not the case in 1945.

The first UN report on development in 1947 shows the same combination of technocratic mindset and indifference to accountability that we already saw in the late colonial period. In the first paragraph of the introduction, we learn of "the urgent need for some mechanism to co-ordinate various departments and agencies concerned in developmental planning" (United Nations 1947: xv). What mattered most was "the administrative structure which was created . . . for the purpose of translating government planning into economic reality."

The report made no distinction between the types of governments doing this planning: colonial authorities planning for their colonies, self-governing colonies (by white settlers only, such as Southern Rhodesia), independent countries (including apartheid South Africa), and Soviet-style autocracies (Bulgaria, Poland, and Yugoslavia).

The language of the early UN document was also consistent with principles invoked in the founding of the World Bank and the International Monetary Fund that had already occurred a year earlier. The delegates to Bretton Woods were like the other examples here: apparently indifferent to accountability in the governments of those countries receiving their loans. They went even further and actually forbade the World Bank and the IMF to *ever* consider political institutions in deciding to whom to lend.

The articles for the World Bank were so insistent on this that they said it twice:

> SECTION 5. USE OF LOANS GUARANTEED, PARTICIPATED IN OR MADE BY THE BANK
> (b) The Bank shall make arrangements to ensure that the proceeds of any loan are used only for the purposes for which the loan was granted, with due attention to considerations of economy and efficiency and without regard to political or other non-economic influences or considerations.
>
> SECTION 10. POLITICAL ACTIVITY PROHIBITED
> The Bank and its officers shall not interfere in the political affairs of any member; nor shall they be influenced in their decisions by the political character of the member or members concerned. Only economic considerations shall be relevant to their decisions, and these considerations shall be weighed impartially in order to achieve the purposes stated in Article I (World Bank, IBRD Article IV n.d.).

The IMF had the same restriction in its articles in the context of changes in exchange rates from their "par values":

> SECTION 5. CHANGES IN PAR VALUES
> (f) The Fund shall concur in a proposed change which is within the terms of (c) (ii) or (c) (iii) above if it is satisfied that the change is necessary to correct a fundamental disequilibrium. In particular, provided it is so satisfied, it shall not object to a proposed change because of the domestic social or political policies of the member proposing the change (International Monetary Fund 1944).

These articles are still in force today, despite the long run trend toward ever more intrusive intervention by the fund and the bank in the sovereignty of loan recipients—from structural adjustment conditions in the 1980s to today's postconflict reconstruction and aid to failed states.

Perhaps this restriction was double-talk from the beginning. Certainly, it never made much sense on its own. First, as noted earlier in this paper, giving a loan to an incumbent ruling party is arguably political interference already. Second, the separation between economic and political policies heroically assumed that the two could be completely independent of each other—that is, they had no effect on each other. Alternatively in the above quotes, the restriction embodied the strange idea that one could seek only "efficiency" without "regard to political... influences or considerations." Like the other efforts described above, the political "prohibition" was perhaps just a way to evade the issue of accountability of donors and governments to the intended loan beneficiaries with the simplest possible device: shut up!

The Cold War: Development Takes Off

The evasion of accountability continues to show persistence across epochal changes in the global balance of power. After the end of colonialism and the beginning of the Cold War, it was still convenient to ignore autocracy as an issue in development. Whether the "Free World" had a developing country on its side was much more important than if that country was, in fact, "free." Development and foreign aid were held out as promises to neutral nations to side with the West in the Cold War, and to resist the temptation of Communist methods of achieving rapid industrialization (at the time thought to be quite successful).

This is best embodied in a best-selling book by Walt Rostow in 1960, *The Stages of Growth*, which he modestly subtitled *A Non-Communist Manifesto*. Rostow was more of a political official than an academic, a senior adviser to Presidents John F. Kennedy and Lyndon Johnson. His book promised countries could "take off" into rapid growth with foreign aid, again indifferent to whether either aid donors or domestic governments were politically accountable to the beneficiaries of the "take off."

These views reflected the intellectual climate of the 1940s and 1950s. The fascist and Communist alternatives seemed to have outperformed the democracies in the Great Depression and its aftermath. Stalinist industrialization was then seen as a great success (a mistaken perception not to be corrected for many decades). Among the democracies such as the United States and the United Kingdom, wartime coercive planning and rationing seemed to have been at the time what got them out of the Depression. The combination of all these experiences fostered the perception that development often had to sacrifice individual rights, despite the previous long-run success of the democracies in the United States and most of Western Europe.

Development economists imbibed these values without question. As one statement of the postwar consensus put it: "Economic development was not spontaneous, as in the classical capitalist pattern, but was consciously achieved through state planning" (Jolly et al. 2004: 17). Early models of development were much closer to the Soviet economic model, although not necessarily its police state features, than to European and American examples. Gunnar Myrdal (later a Nobel Laureate) said in a widely circulated lecture:

> Super-planning has to be staged by underdeveloped countries with weak administrative apparatus and a largely illiterate and apathetic citizenry.... The alternative to making the heroic attempt is acquiescence in economic stagnation which is politically impossible in the world of today.... This is why [planning] is unanimously endorsed by experts in the advanced countries (Mydral 1957).

Of course, the endorsement of planning was not quite as unanimous as Myrdal wanted. Ironically, his future co-winner of the Nobel Prize, Friedrich Hayek, had already published many of his criticisms of central planning and social engineering, although these had no influence on development economics. Another famous early dissident was P. T. Bauer. But other dissidents were completely ignored and then forgotten, such as the South African anti-apartheid activist and development economist S. Herbert Frankel.

After the Cold War: Failed States and Buzzwords
In the unipolar world that emerged after the Cold War ended, the idea of violating the sovereignty of the aid recipient countries suddenly went from taboo to contingent upon circumstances. The new aid industries of "fixing failed states," "peacekeeping," and "postconflict reconstruction" suggested that the donors could indeed get very interventionist in the political affairs of the recipient. Strangely enough, this happened while the political prohibition in the articles of the IMF and World Bank remained in effect (surely these new activities violated such a prohibition even if the original prohibition was meaningful).

One could object that the failed state contingency only applied to a small minority of extreme cases, such as Somalia or Liberia. However, the recent "consultation draft" (November 2010) of the Quadrennial Diplomacy and Development Review of the State Department had a map in which the *entire* developing world was in the "state failure" categories of "critical," "in danger," or "borderline." Such a world view can give the U.S. military justification for its intervention in Iraq and Afghanistan (or anywhere else the United States or any other great power wanted to intervene).

However, this shift toward even the most extreme political interference in aid-receiving countries did not translate into any real support for democratic rights for the poor. Relative to the past, there *was* a positive change toward discussing democracy and accountability compared to previous silence. However, as we have seen, this discussion quickly deteriorated into ineffective buzzwords and a focus only on the mechanics of elections.

Why Does the Double Standard Persist?

There are two obvious reasons why the double standard is so persistent. First, rights and accountability are about power. Accountability of X to Y means that Y has the power to make X face some consequences if X's actions affect Y. Nobody is ever accountable to powerless people, and the poorest people are likely to be the most powerless.

Rights expanded historically as mass movements campaigned for them, forcing greater democratic accountability on the ruling elite. The power of mass movements grows in response to long-run factors like the spread of education, which are obviously too complicated to analyze here. It is likely the poorest peoples today still have too little power as mass movements to end the double standard. But even here there is hope for the future as democracy continues spreading thanks to the courageous efforts of many individuals in poor societies (see figure 3). No causality is implied between the long-run trends in poverty reduction and democracy, but the hopeful trends are very real.

The second reason for persistence is that the aid status quo finds it convenient to continue a double standard. As many aid analysts have

Global poverty rate and democracy

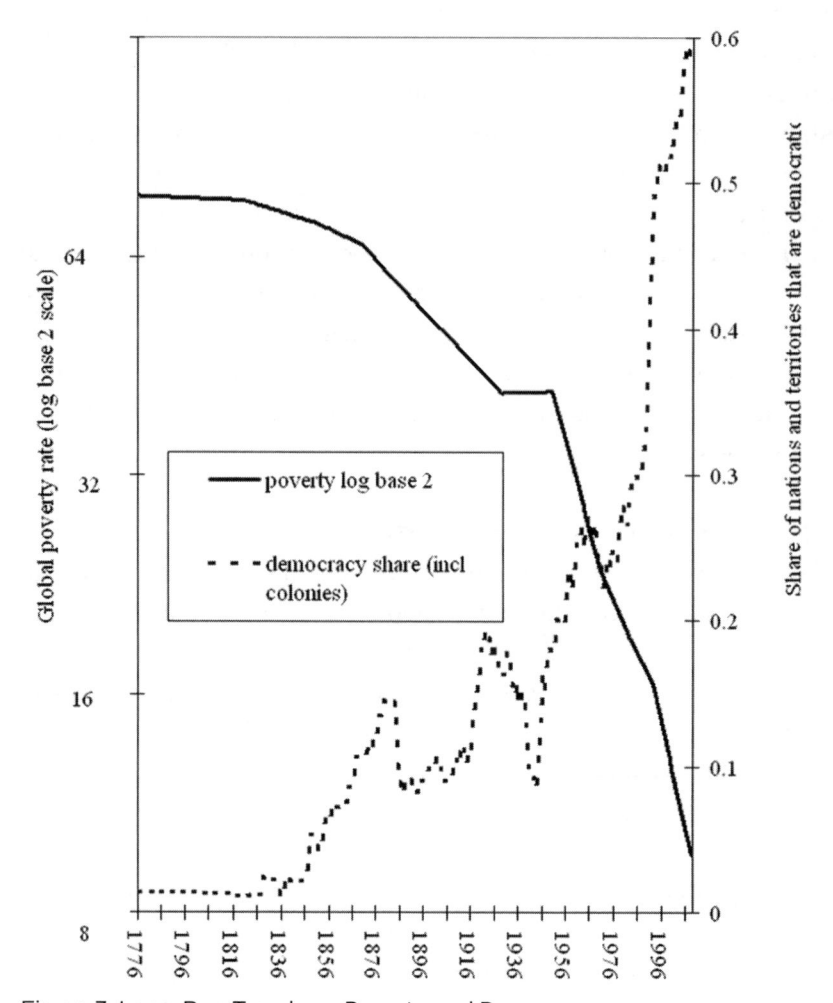

Figure 3: Long-Run Trends on Poverty and Democracy

pointed out, the aid agencies are rewarded most of all for speedily disbursing aid money. How complicated, tedious, and slow it would be to disburse aid in a way that respected the rights of the intended recipients and continually change in response to democratic feedback from those same recipients? One almost feels sorry for the autocratic unaccountable donors.

CONCLUSION

The history of democracy is that of a fight against double standards, of recognizing equal rights for black men and white men, Jews and Gentiles, Protestants and Catholics, women and men, Muslims and Hindus, the rich and the poor.

The tragedy of the development establishment is that it has never recognized the equal democratic rights necessary for the accountability of governmental bodies (both donors and domestic governments) to the peoples being "developed." These principles of individual rights and liberties have always taken a back seat to the hypocrisy of the great powers and of the development agencies, which find it more convenient to speak of development as an apolitical and technocratic problem. So continues the long history of double standards of accountability and individual rights for rich (mostly European) and poor (mostly non-European) countries.

Yet, again looking at figure 3, peoples around the world have been campaigning for greater rights and accountability on their own, with gradual but persistent success. Autocratic donors and governments have mostly failed to coercively "develop" the subjects of their efforts. Rather, development successes occurred where peoples largely developed themselves. It is to them rather than the development establishment that the greatest hope for the twenty-first century belongs.

NOTES
1. See the special issue of the journal *Development in Practice* (14:7, 2007) devoted to "buzzwords and fuzzwords."
2. However, reportedly bowing to protests by China, the World Bank says the indicators "are not used by the World Bank Group to allocate resources."

REFERENCES
Amnesty International. "Human Rights in Republic of Cameroon: 2009." Amnesty International, 2009 < http://www.amnesty.org/en/region/cameroon/report-2009>.

Carothers, Thomas. *Critical Mission: Essays on Democracy Promotion*,

Washington, D.C.: Carnegie Endowment for International Peace, 2004.

Cornwall, Andrea, "Historical Perspectives on Participation in Development." *Commonwealth and Comparative Politics* 44: 1 (March 2006): 49-65.

Constantine, Stephen. *The Making of British Colonial Development Policy, 1914-1940*. London: Frank Cass, 1984.

DAG Statement—Human Rights Watch Report: Development without Freedom – How Aid Underwrites Repression in Ethiopia, October 21, 2010 <http://danielberhane.wordpress.com/2010/10/22/ethiopias-donors-rebut-hrw-report-no-systematic-widespread-aid-misusefull-text/>.

Department of State and United States Agency for International Development. "Leading Through Civilian Power: 2010 Quadrennial Diplomacy and Development Review" <http://s3.documentcloud.org/documents/14727/state-department-diplomacy-and-development-review.pdf>.

Human Rights Watch. "Development without Freedom: How Aid Underwrites Repression in Ethiopia." Human Rights Watch, 2010 <http://www.hrw.org/en/reports/2010/10/19/development-without-freedom>.

Ibrahim, Mohamed. "Prerequisite to Prosperity: Why Africa's Future Depends on Better Governance." *Innovations: Technology, Governance, Globalization* 4 (Winter 2009): 3-8.

International Monetary Fund. Articles of Agreement of the International Monetary Fund. July 22, 1944 <http://www.imf.org/external/pubs/ft/aa/index.htm>.

———. Cameroon: Staff Report for the 2009 Article IV Consultation and Request for Disbursement Under the Rapid-Access Component of the Exogenous Shocks Facility <http://www.imf.org/external/pubs/ft/scr/2009/cr09318.pdf>.

Jolly, Richard, Louis Emmerij, Dharam Ghai, and Frédéric Lapeyre, *UN Contributions to Development Thinking and Practice*. Bloomington: Indiana University Press, 2004.

Mazower, Mark. *No Enchanted Palace: The End of Empire and the Ideological Origins of the United Nations*. Princeton: Princeton University Press, 2009.

Mill, John Stuart. *On Liberty*. Indianapolis: Library of Liberal Arts, 1957 (1869).

Mydral, Gunnar. *Economic Theory and Underdeveloped Region*. London: Gerald Duckworth and Co. Ltd, 1957.

Ohashi, Ken. Reply to Helen Epstein "Cruel Ethiopia." *New York Review of Books* (June 24, 2010) <http://www.nybooks.com/articles/archives/2010/jun/24/cruel-ethiopia/>.

Padmore, George. "Hitler Makes British Drop Color Bar." *The Crisis* (March 1941).

Rostow, Walt. *The Stages of Growth: A Non-Communist Manifest*. Cambridge: Cambridge University Press, 1960.

Scott, James C. *Seeing Like a State*. New Haven: Yale University Press, 1999.

Shantayanan, Devarajan, Andrew S. Rajkuma, and V. Swaroop. "What Does Aid to Africa Finance?" World Bank Development Research Group. Washington, D.C., 1999.

United Nations. Department of Economic Affairs. *Economic Development in Selected Countries: Plans, Programmes, and Agencies*. Lake Success, New York: 1947.

United States Agency for International Development. "From the American People" <http://www.usaid.gov/our_work/democracy_and_governance>.

Wolton, Suke. *Lord Hailey, the Colonial Office and the Politics of Race and Empire in the Second World War*. New York: Palgrave Macmillan, 2000.

World Bank. IBRD. Article IV. Washington, D.C.: World Bank <http://web.worldbank.org/WBSITE/EXTERNAL/EXTABOUTUS/0,,contentMDK:20049603~pagePK:43912~piPK:36602,00.html>.

———. "Strengthening World Bank Group Engagement on Governance and Anticorruption" (March 21, 2007) <http://siteresources.worldbank.org/EXTPUBLICSECTORANDGOVERNANCE/Resources/GACStrategyPaper.pdf>.

———. World Bank Growth Commission. Washington, D.C., 2008.

———. "Governance Matters 2009: Release of Worldwide Governance Indicators 1996-2008." Press Release No: 2009/446/DEC (June 29, 2009) <http://go.worldbank.org/Z1GB0U4590>.

Paul Collier
The Political Economy of Natural Resources

THE RISE IN WORLD PRICES OF NATURAL RESOURCES, COUPLED with the resource discoveries induced by high prices, is transforming Africa's opportunities. The economic future of Africa will be determined by whether this opportunity is seized or missed. The history of resource extraction in Africa is not encouraging. This article reviews and develops the political economy of natural resources as a guide to how Africa might avoid a repetition of that history.

The resource curse has been analyzed over several decades. Although it was initially controversial, the evidence is accumulating that it is both a reality and severe. For example, Collier and Goderis (2007) use co-integration techniques to study the time profile of the effects of resource revenues. An advantage of this approach is that whereas cross-section results, on which previous literature has largely been based, encounter familiar problems of interpretation, these results come from changes in global prices, which can reasonably be taken to be exogenous. They find that although in the short run an increase in export prices of commodities raises growth, in the long run growth is substantially reduced. Simulating the recent commodity boom for the typical African commodity exporter, they find that if global history repeats itself, after two decades output will be around 25 percent lower than it would have been without the booms.

Although the initial explanation for the resource curse, Dutch disease, was purely economic, it has gradually become evident that the key issues are political. The political economy of natural resources is about the interplay between politics and valuable natural assets. The interplay is potentially in both directions: politics can affect the exploitation of natural assets, and natural assets can affect politics. In principle, either of these could explain the resource curse, but there is a reasonable basis for thinking that both are important.

Figure 1 illustrates the simplest possible characterization. The vertical axis shows the social value of the national endowment of natural assets and the horizontal axis an ordinal measure of the quality of the political system, from poor to good. The NA locus depicts the social value of natural assets as a function of the political system: the better is the system, the more able is the society to harness the potential value of its natural assets. The PS locus depicts the political system as a function of the endowment of natural assets. The larger the endowment, the worse the political system. In general, as with any interdependent system, in equilibrium the two relationships are resolved simultaneously. As a result, the political systems best suited to harnessing natural assets are those least likely to develop once natural assets have become important in the economy.

However, it is conceptually useful first to consider each function separately. Section 1 focuses on how natural assets affect the political system. Section 2 focuses on how the political system affects natural assets. Section 3 brings the two together, discussing possible equilibria, and briefly discusses policy options.

1. HOW NATURAL ASSETS AFFECT THE POLITICAL SYSTEM

The core purpose of the state is to provide public goods. Exactly which public goods and services can reasonably be considered nonoptional varies considerably even among developed countries. However, two can reasonably be considered as meta-goods, necessary rather than optional: security and accountability. Without them development is liable to be frustrated. Without security against violence, property rights are void; and without accountability both property rights and the supply of other public goods depend upon the personal whim of the ruler. The presence of valuable natural assets can undermine both

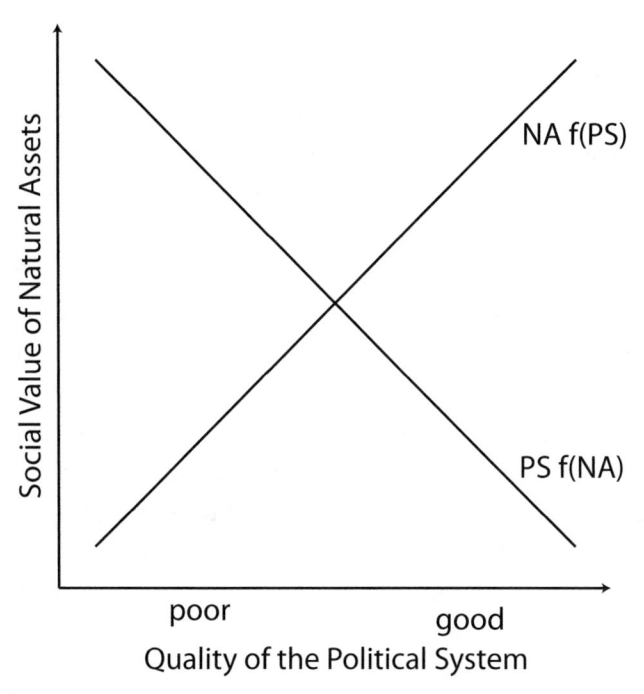

Figure 1

security and accountability. We first consider why security might be undermined and then why accountability might be undermined.

Why Natural Assets Interfere with the Security-Taxation Nexus

Tilly (1990) explains the historical emergence of effective states from an initial political structure of international military rivalry. International warfare created the need for the national public good of military spending. The resulting arms race between states created an escalating need for public money, of which the key sources were tax revenue and government debt. In order to raise debt at moderate interest rates, the state needed a secure revenue source, which reinforced the importance of tax revenue. In turn, efficient taxation required an administrative structure, fiscal capacity, which could only be built slowly. It also gave the state an interest in enabling private economic activity to flourish by providing support for legal institutions that could enforce contracts.

Finally, it was in the interests of such states to accept accountability to wealth generators. This reduced the cost of borrowing and, by curtailing risks of confiscation, promoted wealth generation. The governments that made these investments in capacity tended to win the wars and so a Darwinian process of natural selection reinforced internal pressures for the emergence of effective states.

Besley and Persson (2008) propose an economic formalization of Tilly. Their analysis has three layers: public policies, which can in principle be changed rapidly; institutions, which take longer to build and so are in the nature of investments in capacity; and the initial structure of political power, describing the interests the government represents. Different power structures and interests determine how much the government invests in institutional capacity for taxation and justice. They show that a political system that is not inclusive, and that has a high degree of regime instability, is less likely to build the capacity needed for an effective state. In turn, if these institutions are not built, subsequent policy choices on tax rates and the regulation of private economic activity are constrained.

The virtuous circle described by Tilly had ugly foundations in international warfare. Security was manifestly in the interest of the elite, but since invasion was also disastrous for the general population, it was relatively easy for people to cohere around a nationalist agenda. However, decolonization occurred following the most appalling international war in history and in the context of nuclear rivalry. Unsurprisingly, there was a sense that war was no longer an acceptable part of government behavior: it was too costly and neighborhood wars might escalate into global war. As a result of international pressure, including international mediation through the United Nations and regional groups such as the Organization of African Unity, the incidence of international war radically diminished. This did not imply that the new states were secure. On the contrary, they were highly insecure, but the threat was internal from rebellion rather than external from neighboring governments. The risk of rebellion was high because it was relatively easy. At low levels of income rebellion is cheap and common (Besley and Persson). In the absence of an effective state, economic development is frustrated. The resulting economic stagnation compounds the risk of rebellion (Miguel et al. 2004). In one respect the high risk of rebellion acts like an external threat: it induces an increase in military spending in an attempt to increase security. However, since its objective is internal repression it does not have the same properties of nation-building as an external threat. Military spending for repression is not a national public good in contrast to defense against external threat. Its conventional nonrival properties are lost: the army that defends you represses me. Indeed, the military is itself often the main threat to the regime: coups are far more common than rebellions. In response, governments deliberately reduce the effectiveness of their military by dividing it into rival units with obscure lines of authority. Perhaps as a result of the deliberate emasculation of the army as a fighting force, military spending does not appear to be effective in discouraging rebellion. The risk of coups and rebellions create a continuous sense of regime insecurity.

Thus, the typical postcolonial state did not face an external threat and so did not need to build an effective and hence expensive military. In consequence, pressure to raise tax revenue was lower and so there was less need to invest in either fiscal capacity or a legal system that would have assisted private prosperity. Regimes faced two threats of insecurity—rebellion and coups—but both of these were counterproductive. Rebellion produced a military response designed for the internal repression of dissenting groups and so did not induce nationalism, and it undermined both the economy and state capacity. The coup threat encouraged rulers to weaken their armies. The two threats combined shortened time horizons and so discouraged investment in state capacity.

How Natural Endowments Deepen the Political Problem

Many postcolonial states have valuable natural resources and these compound the problem of insecurity. The increased risk coming from natural resources has long been discussed in the case study literature

(Klare 2001), but the first statistical analyses were by Fearon and Laitin (2003) and Collier and Hoeffler (2004). These initial statistical analyses suffered from various limitations (such as a sample subject to potential bias from missing data) and potential endogeneity (because the explanatory variable was the export of natural resources as a share of GDP). If GDP were to grow slowly for other reasons this ratio might be high and so the apparent causal relationship might be spurious. Hence, the results were controversial: see for example the special issue of the *Journal of Conflict Research* (2005) devoted to the topic. One alternative approach, which claimed to resolve the exogeneity problem, was to measure natural endowments not as a share of GDP but from a global snapshot valuation of subsoil assets for 2000 made by the World Bank. On this basis a high value of subsoil assets appeared to *reduce* the risk of civil war.

However, there is now much stronger statistical evidence for the original proposition. First, the 2000 snapshot of subsoil assets is itself subject to severe endogeneity problems: as discussed below, the value of subsoil assets is dependent on the amount invested in prospecting; and so developed countries have far larger discovered endowments than the poorest countries. Second, Collier, Hoeffler, and Rohner (2008) re-estimate the Collier-Hoeffler model on a much larger sample, and use the AMELIA program to address the remaining problem of missing data (the methodology is based on multiple imputation of missing values in the data matrix). Third, Besley and Persson and Collier, Hoeffler, and Soderbom (2004) both use international commodity prices as exogenous sources of change in resource revenues for commodity-exporting countries. Their results are consistent and complementary. Besley and Persson investigate how changes in prices affect the incidence of civil war. They find that an increase in prices significantly increases the incidence. Collier, Hoeffler, and Soderbom investigate the duration of civil wars once they have started. They find that a price increase of the commodities that a country exports significantly reduces the chance that a war will be settled.

Hence, the issue now is to establish the routes by which these adverse effects occur. The channels by which primary commodities might relate to the risk of conflict have come under intense scrutiny and debate (Ross 2004a; Humphreys 2005; Rohner, 2006). Three channels seem likely. One is that primary commodity exports provide opportunities for rebel predation during conflict and so can finance the escalation and sustainability of rebellion. The most celebrated cases are the diamond-financed rebellions in Sierra Leone and Angola. Oil also provides ample opportunities for rebel finance, whether through "bunkering" (tapping of pipelines and theft of oil), kidnapping and ransoming of oil workers, or extortion rackets against oil companies (often disguised as 'community support').

A second channel is that rebellions may actually be motivated, as opposed to merely being made feasible, by the desire to capture the rents, either during or after conflict. Weinstein (2005) provides a convincing argument for this channel by endogenizing the motivation of the rebel group. He argues that in countries with valuable natural resources, many of the recruits will be motivated by loot-seeking rather than by any political cause. The rebel organization will not be able to screen out such recruits so that, even if the rebellion starts out with a political agenda, over time it is likely to become loot-seeking. The evolution of FARC—the Revolutionary Armed Forces of Colombia—from a rural protest movement to a multi-million dollar drug producer and trafficker may be an illustration. Combined with the financial feasibility effect, this implies that those rebellions that are most feasible, and so most common, are also those most likely to become motivated by loot-seeking. Natural resources can make rebellion attractive even if there is no realistic prospect of capturing the state itself. Indeed, loot-seeking may be easier during the lawless conditions that prevail during conflict than during peacetime. An intermediate position between the objective of wartime looting and the capture of the state is the secession of the resource-rich region. There is some statistical evidence that natural resources specifically increase secessionist wars (Collier and Hoeffler 2006).

These two channels need not be alternatives. A study by Lujala, Gleditsch, and Gilmore (2005) provides support for either of them. It finds that conflicts are more likely to be located in the areas of a country in which natural resources are extracted.

A third channel is that the governments of resource-rich countries tend to be less accountable to their citizens. The provocation of rebellion might be one extreme consequence of a lack of accountability, but evidently there might be many other adverse consequences. I now therefore turn to this larger issue of whether resource revenues make a government less accountable.

Why Natural Assets Generate Divergent Elite Interests

To understand the effect of resource revenues on accountability requires first a broader discussion of the conditions under which the objectives of elites are reasonably congruent with those of ordinary citizens. Broadly, these are either that both happen to share overarching goals, or that elites have no choice but to deliver what ordinary citizens want.

One dimension of importance for congruence is the size of the elite relative to the population. Adam and O'Connell (1999) develop a simple model in which the ruling elite has a choice between a national public good and redistribution toward itself. The smaller the size of the elite, the stronger is the incentive to opt for redistribution. This is one reason why democratic accountability should improve government performance: attracting support by means of public goods instead of redistribution becomes more cost effective because democracy radically expands the required support base. However, public goods may become more cost-effective than patronage with a support base considerably smaller than that implied by universal suffrage and so some governments that are de jure autocratic may approximate the priorities of a democracy.

Since the 1990s, many failing states have democratized. If elections achieve accountability to a rational electorate, then it should be expected to improve government performance. Chauvet and Collier (2009) test whether this is the case using two measures of performance, the Country Policy and Institutional Assessment (CPIA) which is a rating undertaken annually for all developing countries by the World Bank; and the International Country Risk Guide (ICRG), which is a commercial rating service. They find that on both measures elections have both cyclical and structural effects. The cyclical effect is consistent with political economy models. For example, if some good policies incur initial costs with benefits accruing later, and some bad policies have converse characteristics, then as the election approaches the government has an increasing incentive to adopt bad policies, which is what they find. The structural effect of elections is, however, normally consistent with the accountability model: the greater the frequency of elections, the better are policies and governance, except for extremely high frequencies when the adverse effect of short horizons dominates.

Electoral accountability might go wrong if voters have limited information and politicians are thereby able to embezzle the public purse with little fear of prosecution. Besley (2006) analyzes the implications of these characteristics. He shows that there is a point at which elections fail to discipline those politicians whose interests are divergent from those of voters. Beyond this point this type of politician finds power very attractive and this alters the pool of candidates facing voters. This selection effect may powerfully gear up the adverse consequence of poor incentives: in the extreme, voters may face no real choice because the entire pool of candidates consists of people who will abuse power.

However, even the context posited by Besley may be considerably closer to normality than what characterizes failing states. Commonly in these states incumbents can win elections by means of technologies that are excluded in a conventional election because they are illegitimate. Three such techniques are vote-buying, voter intimidation, and ballot fraud. In research currently under way, Collier and Hoeffler find that in conditions of poor governance, incumbents are far more likely to win elections than in conditions of good governance. A reasonable interpretation is that these illegitimate techniques are considerably more effective than the strategy of trying to be a good government. Chauvet and Collier (2009) introduce a measure of the quality of elections into their analysis of whether elections improve government performance. They find that where elections are of low quality, their normal structural effects cease to hold: elections fail to improve government performance measured both in terms of economic policy (CPIA) and economic governance (ICRG). This result is, of course, entirely consistent with economic reasoning: if governments can win elections by other means then, as implied by Besley, politics will attract crooks and democracy will become impotent.

How Natural Endowments Deepen the Political Problem

These generic problems are compounded by valuable natural assets. Potentially, governance might deteriorate in three distinct ways. First, in a democracy resource rents might reduce the efficacy of electoral accountability. Second, in an autocracy resource rents might reduce the incentive to use public goods as the means of benefiting the elite. Third, resource rents might alter the likelihood of democracy relative to autocracy. There is some support for all three of these possibilities.

Collier and Hoeffler (2009) investigate the effect of natural resource rents on the economic performance of democracy. Measuring performance by medium-term economic growth, they find that in the absence of resource rents democracies significantly outperform autocracies, whereas if rents are large relative to GDP, autocracies outperform democracies. The critical point at which the two have equivalent effects is when resource rents are around 8 percent of GDP: many resource-rich economies have a share well above this level. Hence, in some sense resource rents appear to undermine the normal functioning of democracies.

One way in which democracy might be undermined by resource rents is if governments use some of the money to maintain power by means of patronage. Not only does this waste the money, but more importantly it reduces accountability of government to the electorate. Patronage might range from jobs in public employment for supporters through to direct vote buying. There is reason to think that both are effective.

Robinson, Torvik, and Verdier (2006) build a rational choice model of democratic politics to show how public sector employment is liable to be effective as a means of patronage. Supporters know that their jobs are dependent upon their patron retaining political power. Resource rents provide the incumbent with the means to finance a large public payroll and so entrench unaccountable power. Vicente (2007) studies the effect of resource rents on political corruption in a unique natural experiment. The two West African democracies of São Tomé and Cape Verde are both islands and former Portuguese colonies with similar histories. However, São Tomé recently discovered oil. Vicente investigates whether the onset of oil revenues in São Tomé increased political corruption relative to Cape Verde. His measure of corruption was the allocation of international scholarships. He found that indeed oil significantly increased the relative political corruption of São Tomé.

Vote-buying is a more direct form of divorcing elections from accountability. Vicente (2007) and Collier and Vicente (2008) investigate vote-buying in two resource-rich democracies and show that it is both prevalent and effective. Again, resource rents expand the finance for such behavior.

Not only do resource rents make it more feasible to undermine elections, they also make it more desirable for the government to do so since they increase the financial rewards to the retention of power. However, the ability to benefit financially from resource revenues depends upon the ability of politicians to embezzle them. The barrier to such behavior is the checks and balances that financial bureaucracies conventionally incorporate as part of their constituting rules. Collier and Hoeffler (2009) develop a simple model in which resource rents facilitate the erosion of checks and balances. A crooked politician embezzles public revenues to fund vote-buying unless restrained by public scrutiny: expenditure on public goods is thus the residual left once the politician has embezzled. The key component of the model is that it endogenizes scrutiny. They assume that scrutiny is a public good that is only supplied to the extent that citizens are provoked into it by the taxation of private incomes. The crooked politician thus faces a constrained maximization problem. In the absence of natural resources, if he does not tax he has more freedom to embezzle, but there is no revenue. If he taxes heavily there is plenty of revenue but little scope to embezzle it. Hence, there is a Laffer curve in embezzled revenue, with an optimizing rate of taxation. Resource rents change this optimization problem: the politician does not want to provoke scrutiny because although higher taxes would raise more revenue, embezzlement of the resource rents themselves would be curtailed. They show that within this framework resource rents always lead to worse governance and can easily lead to a reduced supply of public goods. They then test the model, investigating whether the number of checks and balances that a society has are affected by resource rents. They find that both in the short term and with lags as long as three decades, resource rents systematically erode checks and balances.

Now consider the effect of resource rents in autocracy. Robinson et al. (2006) show that the implications of their model for democracy readily extend to autocracy. Within the model of Adam and O'Connell (1999), resource rents would increase the value of transfers and so make the interests of the elite more divergent from those of ordinary citizens. Hence, even if the elite can hold the ruler to account, performance need not improve for the ordinary citizen.

The third route by which resource rents might deteriorate the polity is if they change the likelihood of democracy relative to dictatorship. Ross (2001) shows that this is indeed the case: resource-rich countries are more likely to be autocratic. He shows that this is not due simply to the high incidence of autocracy in the Middle East: on the contrary, the autocratic nature of politics in that region is likely to be due in part to its resource abundance.

Finally, resource rents might delay fundamental change of seriously dysfunctional policies. Normally, if a government embarks upon an economic strategy that destroys the economy, change will eventually be forced upon it by the decline of revenue. However, resource rents are robust and so may weaken the impetus for decisive reform. Chauvet and Collier (2008) test this and find that resource rents significantly reduce the speed of exit from highly dysfunctional policies. A doubling of resource rents as a share of GDP approximately doubles the time taken.

A Provisional Summary

In this section I have considered whether the political system is a function of resource rents. The conclusion is that both security and accountability, which are the key attributes of an effective state that is congruent with the interests of its citizens, are likely to be adversely affected. In terms of figure 1, PS f(NA) is downward-sloping.

Manifestly, a state that provides neither security nor accountability has problems that are more fundamental than just the mismanagement of natural assets. However, resource-rich countries evidently have opportunities not open to others. Whether they harness these opportunities depends specifically upon their management of natural assets. This is the subject of section 2.

2. HOW THE POLITICAL SYSTEM AFFECTS NATURAL ASSETS

What decisions does a political system have to get right if it is to harness natural assets efficiently? Against this benchmark we can then assess why particular political systems might get some or all of these decisions wrong.

For most economic activities the role of government is peripheral; however, for the exploitation of natural assets government is center stage. Because they are natural, the ownership rights to these assets must be assigned socially: for practical purposes government has custodial rights on behalf of citizens who are collectively the owners. Government must manage the natural assets in its custody in such as way as to maximize their value to citizens. First, natural assets have to be discovered and extracted, and then the revenues must be well spent. Each of these poses substantial challenges.

Resource Extraction

To see the centrality of government in resource extraction, consider what happens in its absence. How would natural assets be exploited in a lawless society that lacks any capacity for making or enforcing property rights over natural assets so that physical control of the asset is all that matters? The outcome is characterized by three problems: maldistribution, rent-seeking, and inefficiency. Maldistribution comes about partly because the strong are advantaged over the weak. But it is compounded by chance: some territories are better endowed than others. If we imagine the population distinguished in the two dimensions of strength and luck, the natural assets are acquired disproportionately by those who are lucky and strong. Rent-seeking comes about because if ownership is conferred by physical control of territory, people will divert their effort into violence. Since violence can be offset by counterviolence, in equilibrium the value of the rents from the natural assets will be dissipated by the costs incurred by the violent. Inefficiency comes about because of the uncertainty as to whether control can be maintained in the future. If control is perceived as likely to be temporary, the private incentive is to deplete assets quickly, even if this is socially more costly than necessary.

A further consequence is that the absence of property rights interacts with the problem of information. As with inventions, unless discoveries of natural assets are protected, there is no incentive to undertaking search. It is more efficient to wait for others to find natural assets and then wrest control of them through superior violence. Hence, they remain undiscovered. Indeed, since the process of losing control of them is likely to be costly, there is even an incentive for suppressing discovery.

To summarize: in the absence of government the exploitation of natural assets is markedly socially dysfunctional. Few assets are discovered and those that are trigger violent and costly contests. Compounding these gross inefficiencies, outcomes are highly unequal, favoring those who are strong and lucky.

No area of the world has been continuously without government. However, Africa has only had government since relatively recent colonial times, and postcolonial property rights have sometimes weakened with the end of the colonial period. The most evident way in which this relative absence of government might show up is in a reduced level of discovery. Exploration is a costly and risky investment and so known reserves are determined by the economic environment rather than simply being a geological given. As of 2000, the average square kilometer of the African landmass had beneath it only around $25,000 of known subsoil assets, whereas the corresponding figure for the landmass of the Organization for Economic Cooperation and Development (OECD) countries is $125,000. Since the subsoil assets of the OECD have been heavily exploited for a far longer period than those of Africa, it is likely that the true average value of Africa's subsoil assets exceeds that of the OECD. The contrast in known assets therefore points to sensitivity of prospecting to property rights. From Africa's perspective, the good news is that there is huge remaining potential for discovery.

A variant of complete lawlessness is the "finders-keepers" rule, whereby there is a free-for-all in prospecting but enforcement of ownership once a discovery has been made. This is essentially how the American Wild West was prospected. Even this is far from ideal. The distributional disadvantage is that the rents are captured by prospectors instead of being spread more widely. The rent-seeking problem arises from the fact that the chances of striking lucky on a plot are increased if neighboring plots have had lucky strikes. Hence, the profit-maximizing strategy is to acquire many plots and leave them idle until discoveries are made, free-riding upon the prospecting efforts of others. This produces the economics of a gold rush: whole territories may be neglected for many years, and then prospected in a surge following the first discovery. Both the period of neglect and the surge are inefficient. The period of neglect arises from a standard public goods problem: knowledge is a public good and so the outcome is a stalemate in which no one incurs the costs of acquiring knowledge. Eventually, a lucky strike occurs and this sharply increases the returns to search. In response, people crowd into search activities, lowering the chance of discovery for each other and driving down the expected returns to search. Entry may be limited if the size of the plots is set by government, but if plots are very small the standard rent-seeking outcome is that the value of the rents to be acquired through search is precisely offset by the costs that people incur. The rents from natural assets are thus dissipated. The finders-keepers rule produces a long period during which private returns to search are below their social value, followed by a short period in which they exceed their social value.

Artisanal mining is in some respects analogous to the Wild West. As many prospectors crowd in to search, the size of plot is reduced, either in response to political pressure to accommodate more people, or through the sheer physical inability of individuals to retain exclusive control over a large area. This creates an externality: each additional prospector reduces the chance that other prospectors will strike lucky. Hence, the private return exceeds the social return. A second respect in which artisanal mining is inefficient is technological: artisanal mining is not able to reap the scale economies involved in mining, such as pumping out water. Since large-scale technology involves fixed capital investment, artisanal mining gives rise to a third form of inefficiency: plundering the future. With substantial fixed investment, the appropriate pace of exploitation is gradual, so that the installed capital can remain employed for a prolonged period. This implies that some areas will initially be left unprospected. In contrast, artisanal mining prospects all areas at once so that what would otherwise be future rents are dissipated in high current costs. The social inefficiency inherent in artisanal exploitation is demonstrated by the successful growth of De Beers. The company was able to buy out the claims of artisanal producers at their full value under artisanal exploitation and generate a large profit by internalizing these externalities.

Management of Revenues

The revenues from natural resources are distinctive in two key respects from other sources of government revenue: since they are derived from depleting a resource they are intrinsically temporary; and since commodity prices are highly volatile, they are unreliable. It is generally recognized that unsustainable increases in consumption are undesirable: consumption habits may form and commitments may be made, which then need to be met, so that declines in consumption are very costly. Both depletion and volatility potentially give rise to unsustainable increases in consumption.

First, consider the issue of sustainability from the perspective of depletion. Since the revenues from resources are depleting, for an increase in consumption to be sustainable at least some of the revenue must be used for asset acquisition. Potentially, there are two key issues raised by an asset strategy: How much of the revenue should be used for asset acquisition? What assets should be acquired?

To date, most policy attention has been focused on the former of these issues—how much to save? This may be because one simple answer can be derived very easily from elementary economic analysis due to the concept of Permanent Income. This is the analytic foundation for the policy rule of sovereign wealth funds (SWF). However, the issue of how much to save cannot be addressed until the prior, and more important, issue of "what assets should be acquired?" has been considered. Developing countries are capital scarce, so that assets should be accumulated by investment within the country rather than in foreign financial assets, which will, on average, be lower yielding. In effect, the SWF needs to be built up within the country. The acquisition of high-yielding domestic assets instead of low-yielding global assets has two powerful implications.

One implication is that the high yield will in aggregate imply that resource-rich developing countries can expect rapid growth. As a consequence, the value to the society of consumption in the near-term is considerably higher than consumption in the distant future when the economy has become fully developed. It is therefore appropriate for a developing country to use its resource revenues to raise consumption *closer to* the level of the distant future, rather than to use them to raise *the level of* consumption in that distant future. This strategy contrasts with the Permanent Income Hypothesis (PIH), which provides a solution for a society wishing permanently to raise its consumption: *hence the PIH is entirely focused on the interests of the distant future.*

The other implication of using revenues for domestic assets is that the high return on them now becomes dependent upon the investment process. Although the economy is capital scarce, the investment process may not be able to deliver high returns. One issue is that beyond a point the sheer volume or rate of increase of investment may encounter both managerial and physical bottlenecks that depress marginal returns. To address this issue the economy needs a strategy for absorbing investment. The strategy has two elements: smoothing investment, and raising the overall average rate at which investment can be productive.

Volatility and Irreversible Increases in Consumption
Commodity prices are highly volatile and hence so are revenues. Potentially, this affects both consumption and investment. Cuts in consumption are socially very costly and it is sometimes suggested that this justifies the accumulation of a sovereign liquidity fund (SLF) to smooth expenditures. A SLW would differ from a SWF in its intended purpose and have both a different scale and a different composition of assets, which would need to be much shorter-term. Supposing that the government knew with certainty the Net Present Value of the resource rents, it could choose the maximum path of expenditure on investment consistent with maintaining high returns, and from this compute the appropriate increase in consumption. The function of a SLF would simply be to enable expenditure to stay on this path while actual revenues fluctuated around it. In fact, given the historical path of commodity prices, a SLF would have needed to be very large in order to achieve this smoothing function and in a capital-scarce economy this comes at a high opportunity cost. A more modest and realistic alternative is to avoid fluctuations in consumption not by a SLF but by initially using most resource revenues for investment. Fluctuations in investment are much less damaging than fluctuations in consumption: the analogue to consumption is the stock of capital, not its annual increment. Hence, the need for liquidity to moderate fluctuations in investment, though

genuine, is less daunting than that needed to smooth an initially high level of consumption.

How Politics Can Interfere with Decisions

While government is central to the successful harnessing of natural assets for development, decisions concerning both extraction and the use of revenues can be distorted by political processes.

Insufficient Prospecting. A time inconsistency problem arises when governments have to attract mineral companies to invest in prospecting. The companies face a "hold-up" problem. Regardless of what governments promise mineral companies, once the companies have made their investment they have lost their bargaining power: governments have an incentive to appropriate the resource rents. The commitment problem is in one sense standard to all investment. However, it is more acute in respect of natural resource exploitation. The capital investment required for resource extraction is typically far higher than for other activities and so more is at stake. Further, the investment is typically lumpy: a country has one particular exploitable asset that requires investment of a particular scale. Once this is made opportunities for further investment may be limited. This contrasts with most other investment, where opportunities gradually increase over time so that an initial deal is implicitly enforced by the prospects of further deals. Crucially, this is a problem not for the company but for the government. Since companies can anticipate that this will happen, they hold back investments in exploration. As a result, countries with large unexploited potential reserves lose out. For example, for many years the major resource extraction company Alcoa mined bauxite in Guinea. The company knew that it would be far cheaper to process the bauxite into aluminum prior to shipping, but this would have required a huge fixed investment of around $1 billion. The company's board recognized the time-consistency problem: the government of Guinea had no means of precommitting to refrain from capturing the profits generated by this investment once it had become irreversible. Hence, Guinea lost the opportunity for what would have been its single largest investment because of a lack of commitment technology.

Too Rapid Extraction. If the society is divided and power is unstable, then whichever group is currently in power has an interest in converting as many natural assets as possible into irreversible specific capital that favors itself. For example, the ethnic group in power might locate infrastructure in its own geographic area. If the ruling group is sufficiently small, the most attractive form of asset acquisition might indeed not even be public goods but might be private wealth held in irreversible form by means of capital flight. Incumbent governments then have an incentive to incur excessive social costs of extraction, such as by agreeing to overgenerous deals to extraction companies, or to ignore social costs incurred in the region of extraction if it is inhabited by nonfavored groups. For example, ministers in the transitional government in the Democratic Republic of Congo (DRC) knew that they only had around three years in office. During this period many contracts were signed with resource extraction companies conceding very generous terms in return for signature bonuses that cashed in the value of the natural assets to the society. By 2006 royalty payments to the treasury of the DRC were generating only $86,000 per year despite several hundred million dollars of commodity exports.

Too Little Investment in National Public Goods. Natural assets are one form of national public good. The above argument not only induces the government to plunder these natural assets in order to invest in group-specific and private capital, but to underinvest in other forms of national public good. The plunder of natural assets can be accelerated by means of international borrowing against the natural assets as collateral. More generally, spending ministers will ally to oppose the national public good of saving. Profligate spending ministers and a weak minister of finance thus give rise to a common-pool problem. This leads to an upward bias in public spending claims, a tilt of the government spending profile from the future toward the present, and thus not enough saving for future generations. When the financial return on the common asset is higher than that on private assets voracious natural resource depletion can not merely waste the natural assets but reduce overall growth.

Too Little Liquidity for Smoothing Shocks. Because commodity prices are volatile, there is a strong case for accumulating liquid international assets during periods of high prices so that spending can be smoothed during the onset of downturns. However, if governments borrow against natural assets they amplify shocks instead of cushioning them: the ability to borrow fluctuates pro-cyclically with commodity prices.

The lack of cushioning is not only due to the rapacious behavior of ill-motivated governments. Since governments do not control the behavior of their successors, governments that are prudent and well motivated face a time-consistency problem. In some polities such a government might reasonably fear that a successor government is likely to be ill motivated. In this case, savings in the form of financial assets accumulated by the current government may merely transfer spending power to the future ill-motivated government. In the worst case, by saving the windfall not only does the current government fail to raise future consumption sustainably, but it transfers public spending from a period when it is of high quality to one when it is low quality. As a result, the constrained optimal decision even for the current well-motivated government may be to avoid saving the windfall in the form of liquid assets. Note that it is the future ill-motivated government that faces the time-consistency problem. Because it cannot pre-commit not to liquidate accumulated financial assets for consumption, the current government does not accumulate them and so all future governments are worse off. The future ill-motivated government would be better off if it could pre-commit only to consume along the optimal path.

What Sort of Political Systems Are Best Suited to the Management of Resource Rents?

Not all political systems are equally prone to these problems. Over and above the desirability of stable and inclusive government, which Besley and Persson (2008) show are foundation characteristics for effective government, are there particular characteristics of polities that are well suited to the management of natural assets?

Collier and Goderis (2007) find that whereas a commodity boom always increases growth in the short term, the long-term effects are contingent. Although on average in the long term the effects on the level of GDP are adverse, in some countries they are positive. They find that the decisive differentiating factor is the initial level of governance. Above a threshold all countries experiencing commodity booms have had favorable long-term effects, whereas below it all cases the long-term effects have been adverse.

Can more precision be put on the concept of governance? Mehlum et al. (2006) find that the quality of institutions is particularly important in resource rich countries. Collier and Hoeffler (2009) start to pin down what institutions in particular might be important. They decompose democracy into checks and balances, proxied by a cardinal measure of up to 17 such veto points on executive power, and a residual which can be thought of as electoral competition and is proxied by the Polity IV index, a commonly used political science scale of democracy. They find that both have powerful and opposite interactions with natural resource rents: checks and balances significantly improve performance whereas electoral competition significantly reduces it. Thus, resource-rich countries appear to need a form of democracy with particularly strong checks and balances. This is consistent with the analytic conclusion of Robinson et al. (2006) that a key characteristic of a polity that is robust to the pressures of resource rents is effective institutional safeguards against their use for political patronage.

3. SOLUTIONS IN EQUILIBRIUM

To summarize, section 1 established reasonable grounds for thinking that resource rents erode the normal functioning of the polity, making it more prone to insecurity and less likely to be accountable. Similarly, section 2 established reasonable grounds for thinking that political systems that have weak institutions are liable to mismanage natural assets.

Mutually Reinforcing Actions

Returning to the simple conceptual framework of figure 1: both relationships matter. However, rather than being determined simultaneously, equilibrium may depend upon sequence: if a country gets a sufficiently good political system well before it gets its natural endowments, the system may be robust. Thus, countries such as Norway, which had well-established democracies with plenty of checks and balances prior to the discovery of oil, may be better characterized by an exogenous political system than by interdependence. The political system may only be endogenous if it has not had time to become entrenched.

For societies characterized by interdependence, what can be done? Conceptually, two approaches appear to be jointly necessary. One is to steepen the PS locus and the other is to flatten the NA locus. Steepening the PS locus means reducing the damage inflicted by natural resources on the political system. Flattening the NA locus means improving the management of natural assets in weak political systems. The two are complementary. If the only change is to steepen the PS locus, then the initial improvement in the political system is partially undermined as the value of natural assets increases in response. If the only change is to flatten the NA locus, then the resulting increase in the value of natural assets (for example, as a result of increased discoveries) tends to undermine the political system.

Reducing the Damage Inflicted by Natural Resources on the Political System

Recently there have been two voluntary international interventions designed to reduce the damage done by natural resources to the political system.

The first was the *Kimberley Process*, which, by establishing a certification process for diamonds, made it more difficult for rebel groups to sell illicitly acquired diamonds on the world market. By making rebellion harder to finance, this tended to reduce the effect of natural resources on the risk of civil war. In 2008, President Yar' Adua of Nigeria proposed that a comparable system be established for tracking oil. Quite reasonably, he is concerned that the bunkering of oil in the Nigerian Delta is fuelling violence. A certification system for oil would make it more difficult for criminals to sell bunkered oil to refineries.

The second intervention was the *Extractive Industries Transparency Initiative*, which seeks to make scrutiny of resource revenues easier, thereby making it harder both for companies to cheat governments out of revenues that are due, and for government officials to cheat the country out of payments made by companies. As with the Kimberley Process, there is scope for extension. Transparency in revenues is a necessary first step toward transparency in expenditure but does not in itself ensure it. Further, even transparency does not ensure accountability: this depends upon an effective judicial system.

Improving the Management of Natural Assets Given the Political System

The management of natural assets can be improved within a given political system by both domestic and international actions.

Addressing the agency problem. In setting the tax and royalty rates, the government faces an internal agency problem. The government must delegate the negotiation to a small group of its members and resource extraction companies have a strong incentive to bribe these individuals. To protect itself the government needs to adopt a process that is transparent: secret negotiations are ideally suited to corruption. The agency problem is compounded by an information problem: the government has considerably less knowledge as to the true value of its natural assets than does the company. A solution to both the agency and the information problem is to auction the extraction rights, inviting bids on the royalty rate that companies would be willing to pay. The rate could be conditioned on any observable features such as the basic geology, world price, and accumulated past volume of extraction. An auction is a way of forcing companies to reveal the true value of a right to extract by placing them in competition.

Addressing commitment problems. In section 2 I discussed two distinct commitment problems, one concerned with extraction companies the other with future governments. If governments cannot make credible commitments with resource extraction companies, one solution is to establish national extraction companies. Unfortunately, this often generates a different set of problems. An alternative is to accept the right to adjudication of disputes by international courts, backed by escrow accounts.

If a government is concerned about the possible mismanagement of future governments, a solution to the time inconsistency problem is to create a commitment technology which binds all future governments *and which they would themselves support* because they benefit from it. In OECD societies this form of problem has been recognized for monetary policy where the solution has been to grant independence to central banks. In resource-rich countries the time-consistency problem concerns savings out of windfall resource revenues. This is a fiscal problem and so the equivalent of independent central banks is to develop institutional commitments on fiscal policy. Ngozi Nkonjo-Iweala, the former finance minister of Nigeria, pioneered the idea of a fiscal constitution for African natural resource revenues through the Fiscal Responsibility Act that pre-commits governments to savings.

If the finance minister is concerned that spending ministers will gang up to press for excessive recurrent expenditure, then Chinese-style resource contracts provide a commitment technology. The Chinese mode of resource extraction is a package deal in which extraction rights are exchanged directly for infrastructure rather than revenues passing through the budget. In this case there is a trade-off between transparency and the common pool problem.

Improving information for decisions. Finally, as will be apparent from the first part of section 2, the effective harnessing of natural assets for development raises complex economic issues. Societies in resource-rich countries can only get these decisions right to the extent that they understand them. Just as there has been a role for the international community to address the problem of weakened governance, so there is scope for international action to improve understanding of difficult but crucial social choices (Collier 2010). This is the intention of the *Natural Resource Charter*, an initiative of independent academics and practitioners.

REFERENCES

Adam, C., and S. O'Connell. "Aid, Taxation and Development in Sub-Saharan Africa." *Economics and Politics* 11 (November 1999): 225-254.

Besley, T. *Principled Agents?* New York: Oxford University Press, 2006.

Besley, T., and T. Persson. "The Origins of State Capacity: Property Rights, Taxation, and Politics." *American Economic Review* 99 (September 2009): 1218-1244.

———. "State Capacity, Conflict, and Development." *Econometrica* 78 (January 2010): 1–34.

———. "Wars and State Capacity." *Journal of the European Economic Association* V6 (April-May 2008): 531-540.

———. "The Incidence of Civil War: Theory and Evidence." CEPR Discussion Paper No. DP7 (2008).

Chauvet, L., and P. Collier. "What are the Preconditions for Turnaround in Failing States." *Journal of Conflict Management and Peace Science* 25 (September 2008): 332-348.

———. "Elections and Economic Policy in Developing Countries." *Economic Policy* 54 (July 2009).

Collier, Paul. *The Plundered Planet*. New York: Oxford University Press, 2010.

Collier, Paul, and B. Goderis. "Commodity Prices, Growth, and the Natural Resource Curse: Reconciling a Conundrum." Center for the Study of African Economies. Working Paper Series (August 2007).

Collier, Paul, and Anke Hoeffler. "The Political Economy of Secession." *Negotiating Self-Determination*. Eds. H. Hannum and E. F. Babbitt. Lanham, Md.: Lexington Books. 2005.

———. "Military Expenditure in Post-Conflict Societies." *Economics of Governance* 7 (January 2006): 89-107.

———. "Unintended Consequences? Does Aid Promote Arms Races?" *Oxford Bulletin of Economics and Statistics* 69 (December 2006): 1-27.

———. "Testing the Neo-Con Agenda: Democracy and Resource Rents." *European Economic Review* 53 (April 2009): 293-308.

Collier, Paul, A. Hoeffler, and D. Rohner. "Beyond Greed and Grievance: Feasibility and Civil War." *Oxford Economic Papers* 61 (August 2008): 1-27.

Collier, Paul, A. Hoeffler, and M. Soderbom. "On the Duration of Civil War." *Journal of Peace Research* 41 (May 2004): 253-273.

Collier, Paul, and P. Vicente. "Votes and Violence: Evidence from a Field Experiment in Nigeria." Center for the Study of African Economies. Working Paper Series (2008).

Fearon, James D., and D. Laitin. "Ethnicity, Insurgency, and Civil War." *American Political Science Review* 97 (2003): 75-90.

Humphreys, M. "Natural Resources, Conflict, and Conflict Resolution: Uncovering the Mechanisms." *Journal of Conflict Resolution* 49 (August 2005): 508-537.

Lujala, P., N. P. Gleditsch, and E. Gilmore. "A Diamond Curse? Civil War and a Lootable Resource." *Journal of Conflict Resolution* 49 (August 2005): 538-562.

Mehlum, H., K. Moene, and R. Torvik. "Institutions and the Resource Curse." *Economic Journal* 116 (2006): 1-20.

Miguel, E., S. Satyanath, and E. Sergenti. "Economic Shocks and Civil Conflict: An Instrumental Variables Approach." *Journal of Political Economy* 112 (August 2004): 725-753.

Robinson, James A., R. Torvik, and T. Verdier. "Political Foundations of the Resource Curse." *Journal of Development Economics* 79 (April 2006): 447-468.

Rohner, D. "Beach Holiday in Bali or East Timor? Why Conflict Can Lead to Under- and Overexploitation of Natural Resources." *Economics Letters* 92 (July 2006): 113-17.

Ross, M. "Does Oil Hinder Democracy?" *World Politics* 53 (April 2001): 325-361.

———. "Does Taxation Lead to Representation?" *British Journal of Political Science* 34 (2004a): 220-249.

———. "What Do We Know about Natural Resources and Civil War?" *Journal of Peace Research* 41 (May 2004b): 337-356.

Sachs, J., and A. M. Warner. "Natural Resource Abundance and Economic

Growth." *Leading Issues in Economic Development*. 7th ed. Eds. G. M. Meier and J. E. Rauch. New York: Oxford University Press, 2000.

Tilly, C. *Coercion, Capital and European States, A.D. 990-1992*. Hoboken, N.J.: Wiley-Blackwell, 1990.

Vicente, P. "Is Vote-Buying Effective: Evidence from a Field Experiment in West Africa." Center for the Study of African Economies. Working Paper Series (2007).

Weinstein, J. "Resources and the Information Problem in Rebel Recruitment." *Journal of Conflict Research* 49 (August 2005): 598-624.

Robert H. Bates
Democracy in Africa: A Very Short History

WHEN DISCUSSING GOVERNANCE IN AFRICA, ONE MUST BE circumspect when applying the term "democracy" (but see Sklar 1987). One reason for doing so is because the term is imprecise. As in the writings of Schumpeter (1950), "democracy" can refer to political competition and, in particular, open competition among rival political parties. Others, such as Dahl (1971), argue that to be democratic, such competition must take place within a setting infused with attendant rights and freedoms—the right to association, for example, or to free speech—and such rights must be equally shared. Still others, such as Huntington (1991) or Przeworski, Alvarez et al. (2000), would insist that even were a polity to exhibit these attributes, it could not be labeled democratic until one party had surrendered power to another upon losing a national election. While differing in the attributes they posit and the qualifications they impose, those who write of democracy join in emphasizing its essential property: that it is a form of government in which political power is employed to serve the interests of the public rather than of those who govern.

In this essay I argue that democracy, in this sense, has been reborn in Africa. The evidence, I argue, strongly suggests that its renaissance has been accompanied by changes in public policies and political practices that generate benefit for the people. But the evidence also suggests that political dangers remain: incumbent parties strive to suborn the electoral process and incumbent executives seek to prolong

---

I wish to thank Befekadu Degefe for his comments and criticisms of earlier versions of this paper.

their terms in office. As elsewhere, to retain their political liberties, Africa's citizens must "remain vigilant." Paraphrasing John Adams at the U.S. constitutional convention, Africa today may enjoy better governance, but "can [she] keep it?"

INDIGENOUS ROOTS

Without seeking to romanticize the past, we can note the democratic tendencies that infused precolonial societies in Africa. In his extraordinary series on the political history of precolonial Central Africa, for example, Jan Vansina emphasizes the radical republicanism of the lineage systems of government and the efforts they expended to elude domination by centralized states (Vansina 1966, 1978, 1990, 1999, 2005). Even within centralized kingdoms, others stress, there existed prominent fora within which citizens could challenge the royals and their bureaucrats.[1] In some, the office of the prime minister was reserved to the commoners. In others, commoner councils provided a check on the public administration. In still others, societies—some secret, others, like the *asafo*, fully public—organized a defense for commoner interests. Following a study of the precolonial political systems, one author concludes:

> The evidence suggests that, while there was inequality in the states of pre-colonial Africa, those who held positions of privilege had to assure that the benefits created by states were widely shared. For the bargaining power of the masses, relative to the elites, was strong... (Bates 1987: 42).

FOREIGN OCCUPATION

When in the nineteenth century imperial powers occupied the continent, they imposed local rulers on societies that had long resisted political authority. When they encountered societies that possessed chiefs, they either displaced these rulers and imposed rulers of their own or forged opportunistic alliances with incumbent chiefs. As many have noted, chiefs and headmen found room to maneuver in the contested space between the occupier and their people; when they did so, however, it was often in pursuit of their own agendas (Gluckman 1955). The chiefs were able to exploit their political position to acquire—and sell—land; to extract—and divert—tax revenues; and to promote the fortunes of their kin within the new political order. They were able to evade many of the restraints that previously had limited their powers, for to oppose them was to risk provoking the wrath of the colonial occupier.

Following the global conflicts of the twentieth century, the Soviet Union and United States moved to the center of the global stage. While the two great powers clashed ideologically and politically, they shared a disdain for Europe's political pretentions. And when local political forces rallied in resistance to colonial occupation, the great powers let Europe's empires collapse and new nations rise from the political rubble.

POLITICAL TRANSITION

A notable feature of the nationalist movements was the degree to which they targeted the chiefs. Few who did so opposed the institution of the chieftaincy per se; traditional political institutions still evoked respect even among the educated elite, and not only because a disproportion of its members came from chiefly families. Where the chiefs were attacked, it was because they occupied the front ranks of the colonial order and because they had employed public office to secure private advantages. In this sense, the nationalist movements drew upon and renewed the democratic impulses that lay embedded in local political institutions.

Ironically, in this period the imperial powers also began to promote the forces of democratization. Following World War II, they were no longer able to dominate the course of events outside of their European base and so sought to forge ways of shaping outcomes that they no longer could control. Whereas in the past, they could pick and impose local political leaders—that is, the chiefs—they now had to be satisfied with merely shaping the manner in which such leaders were chosen. Out of political necessity, they therefore began to introduce representative institutions. They permitted prominent locals to take office in legislative and executive councils and, after a decent interval, they permitted local citizens to choose who among them were to do so. The culmination of the process was "self-government": the assumption of full executive and legislative power by local politicians.

The administrative, coercive, and judicial arms of the colonial state exercised close oversight of this transition. These bodies treated local political organizations as subversive[2] and monitored the actions of political activists, regulated the holding of meetings, and censored the content of local publications. The imperial powers introduced democracy as a means of disengaging from an enemy they could not defeat. The introduction of democratic institutions was thus the by-product of a search for an advantageous way of negotiating the terms of a political surrender.

The colonial governments may have been forced to introduce electoral competition and representative institutions; but the apparatus they employed to shape these institutions was not one that sought to guarantee democratic rights and freedoms. Rather, it was one that sought to safeguard and protect the institutions that had secured foreign domination over the people of Africa (Young 1994).

INDEPENDENCE

It can come as no surprise, then, that the forces that took over the colonial state, while celebrating self-government and the end of imperial rule, failed to endorse open political competition and the attendant rights of political expression and public assembly. Symptomatic is the fate of opposition parties in the period immediately following political independence. Twenty-six sub-Saharan countries in Africa had gained independence by the late 1960s: the territories of the former French West and Equatorial Africa, British West and East Africa, and the Central African states of Malawi, Zambia, and Congo. "By 1960, the year in which most of . . . Africa became independent," Ruth Collier writes, "nine countries had (formed) one-party regimes" (Collier 1982: 95). By the mid-1970s, seven more governments imposed single-party rule. In the first wave of consolidation—much of which occurred prior to independence and during the period of self-government—the folding of the opposition tended to be voluntary, or at least the product of negotiation, with opposition parties "crossing the floor" and merging with the government. In the second wave, which occurred after independence, political consolidation tended to be involuntary: it was the product of rigged elections, the jailing of political opponents, and the outlawing of political parties. Then, Collier notes, came a wave of coups and the formation of military regimes. Following the coups of the early 1960s, the military had handed power back to civilians. Subsequently, however, it chose to remain in office. And by the mid-1990s, authoritarian regimes had "become a dominant feature of African political life" (1982: 96). (See figures 1 and 2 online[3] for depictions of the distribution of political regimes in post-independent Africa.)

POLICIES

In the postindependence period, governments sought to mobilize political power to promote economic development. As eloquently captured by Ndulu (2008), in part they did so because economic doctrines prescribed interventionist policies. Whether to break out of "poverty traps," to induce "backward and forward linkages," or to launch a "big push" toward economic development, economic theory advocated that governments invest in industries and intervene in markets so as to transform the structure of their economies. As Ndulu (2008) argues, political sentiment reinforced economic doctrines. By investing in firms that could produce at home what formerly had been imported from abroad, they sought to lessen their economic dependence on their former colonial masters. The power of the Soviet Union and the Chinese Communist Party's ability to expel the imperial powers provided further inspiration to those who sought to use the state to promote development.

Rather than letting market forces determine prices in the macroeconomy, many governments in Africa strove to regulate both the interest and exchange rates, keeping them artificially low: capital equipment could then be imported more cheaply. By imposing tariffs and licensing imports, governments sought to limit competition from abroad; and by licensing firms and restricting entry, they attempted to suppress competition in the domestic market as well. To promote industrial development, not only did governments thus seek to strengthen the incentives for private investment: they themselves also invested in the formation of firms or nationalized firms that had proven slow to invest.

Governments also intervened in the rural sector. By expelling private agents from agricultural markets, they gained the power to influence prices and employed that power to lower the price of farm products. In export markets, they purchased goods at low domestic prices and then sold them at prices prevailing in global markets, pocketing the difference in the form of public revenues. In food markets, they used their market power to lower the prices charged urban consumers, be they firms purchasing raw materials, such as cotton, or urban dwellers purchasing staple foods, such as maize. In their study of the political economy of Africa's development in the postindependence period, the African Economic Research Consortium (AERC) labels this mix of policies a "control regime" (Ndulu, O'Connell et al. 2008), a term I shall adopt for this essay.

As recognized by Schattschneider (1965), public policies bear testimony to the structure of power in a society; in his words, they institutionalize "patterns of bias." In postindependence Africa, the dominant political structure included the political elite, which chose public policies; a rapidly expanding public sector, charged with their implementation; and a nascent industrial sector, which was the intended beneficiary. The rural sector remained massive in size, generating over half the national income and employing three-quarters or more of the labor force, but it was excluded, economically and politically, from the new order. Those who had seized power and implemented control regimes mounted what amounted to a war of attrition against their rural populations. Note the incidence of the costs and benefits: appreciating the currency may have lowered the costs of importing capital equipment, but it also lowered the earnings of agricultural exporters and the price of food imported from abroad. Limiting imports of manufactured goods from abroad may have promoted the profitability of domestic firms; but it also enabled them to raise the prices they charged consumers, most of whom were farmers. And while intervention in agricultural markets enabled governments to tax foreign earnings and contain pressures for higher prices for consumer staples, it lowered farm revenues. Control regimes were thus systematically biased in favor of the nascent urban sector (Bates 1981; Krueger, Schiff et al. 1992; Anderson and Masters 2009). (See figure 3 online for a depiction of how, in the 1970s and 1980s, this mix of policies had been adopted by a majority of Africa's regimes.)

CRACKS IN THE EDIFICE

Control regimes could not be sustained economically. Consider, for example, the market for foreign exchange. When the local currency increases in value, the prices of foreign goods fall and the demand for imports rises. By the same token, the value of exports falls: exporters receive fewer local "cedi" for each "dollar" they earn abroad. With an increase in imports and a decline in exports, the country begins to accumulate deficits; to remain solvent, it must borrow. But when Mexico defaulted in its external obligations, private bankers stopped lending abroad and called in their loans, and Africa's states could no longer borrow in order to cover their deficits.

For Africa's citizens, the result was hardship. For lack of foreign exchange, drugs disappeared from hospitals and textbooks from schools. Trucks, tractors, and automobiles stood idle, for want of imported parts. So too factories whose machines had been purchased abroad. Because mechanical equipment could not be refurbished, the infrastructure could not be maintained. The supply of electricity became even more erratic; roads crumbled, many becoming impassable during the rains; locomotives, ferries, and steamships decayed, rendering transport more expensive and less reliable. All whose quality of life depended on the quality of this infrastructure suffered as a result of its decline. In addition, Africa's people suffered from rising prices, as governments printed money in an effort to finance their deficits.

In the midst of this decline, Africa's authoritarian polities remained in place. Indeed, the very interventions that weakened their economies added, in the short run at least, to their political power. Consider once again the market for foreign exchange: as we have argued, an appreciation of the local currency leads to an increase in the demand for imports and a decrease in the supply of exports, thus generating a shortage of foreign exchange at official prices. In black markets, however, because of the excess demand, the price of foreign exchange rises. Those manning the national bank and finance ministries thus found themselves in command of a very precious resource. By controlling appointments to these bureaucracies, the president could control its allocation, conferring benefits on friends, denying them to enemies, and thereby building a loyal band of followers—one willing to defend him, politically, even while his policies crippled the economy.

By the same measure, however, the members of Africa's political elite sacrificed their political legitimacy. Consider the vista that lay before Africa's citizens. Their economy lay in tatters, public services were in disarray, and public infrastructure in disrepair. And yet the favored few—that is, those in power—drove expensive cars, dressed in expensive apparel, and sent their family's children to expensive schools abroad. By laying hold to and manipulating prices in the economy, their rulers had, on the one hand, converted markets into political machines. But on the other, they had incited the wrath of their people, thereby preparing the ground for those who might wish to drive them from power.

Political criticism mounted not only from within but also mounted from those who held Africa's debts abroad. At first, foreign creditors sought changes in government policies. To increase their leverage, they gathered into blocs, which were organized and maintained by the international financial institutions. As coordinators of Africa's creditors, these institutions then acquired great influence. At first, they entered into dialogue with the debtor governments, pointing to alternative ways of securing their policy objectives. Increasingly, however, they spoke harshly, offering forbearance but in exchange for the governments' willingness to change their policies. Over time, the harsher tone prevailed, and Africa's governments found themselves facing growing foreign pressure to alter their economic policies.

Subsequently, the staff of the international financial institutions and, in particular, the staff of the World Bank, began to call not only for policy but also for political reform. In part they did so because of the puzzle posed by the behavior of Africa's regimes: Why would governments, they asked, choose policies that violated the economic interests of its people? They would do so, they reasoned, if their preferences were not aligned with those who owned and managed the economies productive resources. From this reasoning emerged the outlines of a strategy: by rendering a government accountable, they could harness its political ambitions. Should the citizens be able to dismiss a government that had harmed their interests, politicians would then possess an incentive to choose policies that strengthened rather than undermined the economy. In a series of publications (World Bank 1981, 1991a, 1991b, 1994), the managers of Africa's debt advocated political reform as means of attaining policy reform in Africa.

The clash between Africa's creditors and its governments appeared one-sided: the creditors were rich and powerful; Africa, poor and weak. But political as well as economic interests were in play; and the international agencies were public, not private institutions and under the control of governments. During the Cold War, Africa had become a theatre of the Cold War. Armies backed by the Soviet Union on the one side and the United States on the other clashed on the Horn and Kenya provided the United States harbor facilities and overflight rights in the region. Liberia provided the United States an outpost for tracking satellites and a refueling base for its airplanes. And Zaire (now the Democratic Republic of Congo) provided a base for forces, financed by the United States, that fought movements backed by Cuba, China, and the Soviet Union. When an arap Moi, a Sergeant Doe, or a Mobutu Sese Seko came under pressure from the International Monetary Fund or the World Bank to reform his economic policies, the State Department, the Foreign Office, or the Quai d'Orsay would step in to defend their political client. Because they held a majority on the boards of the international financial institutions, Western governments were well placed to temper the reformist zeal of their technocrats. For political reasons, the economic costs of bad policies were judged worth paying.

Those Africans who had scanned the political and economic terrain about them and been moved to demand political change thus found themselves joined by reformers abroad. But both were checked by political forces at the global level.

POLITICAL REFORM

Following the fall of the Berlin Wall in 1989, the resistance that had originated in the foreign ministries of the West collapsed. Dictators that had once proved embarrassing but useful were now simply embarrassing and were set aside as cynically as they had once been employed. The result was a rush to reform. As depicted in table 1, the process began in French speaking West Africa: in February 1990, in Benin, local reformers set up a national convention, which soon declared itself a constitutional assembly, thus arrogating to itself the power of the state; the assembly legalized opposition parties and called for open elections to fill executive positions and legislative offices. Inspired by events in Benin, reformers in other states then convened similar conventions; the practice spread through neighboring polities, then inland and southward, and penetrated into Central Africa. In concert with these domestic political forces, those in the international financial institutions renewed their push for political reform; this time their efforts met little resistance from Western governments.

Not only did the new international realities loosen the restraints under which they labored; the collapse of communism strengthened their hand. For now the international financial institutions could point to, say, the U.S. Congress and credibly argue that without political reform, governments in Africa stood little chance when competing for international aid with states just liberated from communism.

Under intense pressure from citizens at home and mounting pressures from creditors abroad, governments in Africa rapidly changed their political institutions. The pace and extent of these reforms is vividly captured in figures 1 and 2 (available online).

THE AUTHORITARIAN REACTION

When governments have been authoritarian, they have good reason to fear political competition and the possible loss of power. Authoritarian rulers commonly used public power to acquire private wealth, seiz-

Table 1

Country	Date	Duration	Election Month	F&F?	Outcome: incumbent Ousted	Retained
Benin	Feb. 90	1 week	Feb. 91	yes	?	
			Mar. 96	yes	?	
Congo	Feb. 91	3 months	Aug. 92	yes	?	
Gabon	Mar. 90	3 weeks	Dec. 93	no		?
Mali	Jul. 91	2 weeks	Apr. 92	yes	?	
Niger	Jul. 91	6 weeks	Feb. 93	yes	?	
Burkina Faso	Aug. 91	7 months	Dec. 92	yes		?
Ghana	Aug. 91	7 months	Dec. 92	yes		?
Togo	Aug. 91	1 month	Aug. 93	no		?
Zaire	Aug. 91	1 year	—	—		
CAR	Oct. 91	2 months	Aug. 92	yes	?	
Chad	Jan. 93	3 months	Jun. 96	no		?

ing land, appropriating shares in firms and financial institutions, and extorting bribes from those they rule. Were they to be deprived of the defenses available to those in office—command of the police, the jails, and the office of the public prosecutor—they would become vulnerable to reprisals. As democratic forces mobilized, then, so too did efforts to repress them. In Kenya, opposition leaders were jailed and tortured; police broke up public rallies, on occasion shooting into the crowds; and prominent critics of the regime perished in mysterious circumstances. In Togo, the military government mobilized its soldiers who, with bayonets and bullets, cleared the capital's streets of citizens rallying in support of political reform. Mobutu, Mugabe, Habyarimana: each mobilized their regimes coercive powers in an effort to suppress those demanding democracy.

As the incumbent elite became increasingly insecure, other politicians mobilized their own supporters, the better to defend their interests in the subsequent scramble for power. Some recruited thugs from the streets, who could be gathered quickly and quickly set aside; others assembled militias, which once formed remained under arms.

(See figures 4 and 5 online. Figure 4 shows the "average level of reform" and the percentage of countries reportedly harboring armed militias from 1970-1996; figure 5 shows the rise and decline of civil wars from 1960 to date.)

The period of reform was thus also a period of political violence. But there was also a subsequent decline in the frequency of conflict. Widespread violence, it would appear, was a property of the transitional dynamics of political reform rather than of the new steady state. The new democracies appear to be no more prone to such conflict than did their authoritarian predecessors; it was the transition to democracy that was violent.

In the short term, reform proved costly: it precipitated an authoritarian reaction and political violence. But in the longer term, in many states, political order returned; and along with the blessings of peace came changes in economic policy.

POLICY CHANGE

Recall the incidence of the costs and benefits of control regimes: the benefits accrued to nascent manufacturing and the rapidly expanding public sector, both based in urban centers, while the costs fell upon consumers and the producers of agricultural products, most of whom live in the countryside. Given the nature of Africa's economies, however, when politicians must campaign for votes in order to secure power, they then must compete for the votes of farmers. To win these votes, they need to champion policies that generate benefits for, rather than inflict costs upon, rural dwellers. The introduction of competitive elections thus empowered the rural majority and the patterns of political bias embodied in government policies.

Two bits of evidence pertain. The first comes from the AERC study, which argues for an "elective affinity" between authoritarian politics and the maintenance of control regimes and found that governments chosen in competitive elections were 20 percentage points less likely to adopt control regimes (Bates 2008: 196). Of more direct relevance is a World Bank study (Anderson forthcoming) of government policies toward agriculture. As an aggregate measure of these policies, the research team calculated the Relative Rate of Assistance (or RRA), which compares the degree to which government policies enable producers in the agricultural and manufacturing sectors to raise prices over and above those that would prevail in competitive markets (as benchmarked by prices in global markets). When government policies exhibit urban bias, then the measure turns negative; positive values indicate a bias toward farmers. (See figures 6 and 7 online for depictions of the greater degree of urban bias consistently exhibited by governments in Africa as compared to those in regions in the rest of the world, and the effect of the size of the rural electorate on discrimination against farming.)

The recent revival of economic growth in Africa comes from several sources: the infusion of capital from South Africa, China, and migrants living abroad, and the demand for primary products from the growing economies of Asia surely play the dominant role. Before these forces impacted upon the economies of Africa, however, the AERC researchers had noted that the adoption of a control regime, all else being equal, was associated with a nearly 2 percentage point reduction in the rate of economic growth. Given that agriculture is the largest single industry in most African economies, it is thus possible that the abandonment of control regimes plays a significant part as well.

CONCLUSION

Political competition between organized political parties provides one means to render rulers accountable, thereby aligning their interests with the interests of those they rule. Insofar as private citizens own and control the productive resources of society, the result should be that governments that are accountable will use public power with restraint: rather than using the power of the state to seize the wealth of those they rule, they will seek to protect its creation.

Further evidence of the relationship between political reform and the conduct of governments comes from the work of Humphreys and Bates (2005). Governments that face political competition in upcoming elections, they find, are more likely to honor contracts and less likely to extract bribes. (The results parallel the data contained in figure 8 [available online], which captures the World Bank's summary of the ratings of governments. For the African sample, authoritarian governments are rated as more corrupt, less respectful of the rule of law, and less effective than are nonauthoritarian regimes.)[4]

While we are still far from establishing cause and effect, the evidence is suggestive: differences in the institutions that govern Africa appear to go hand in hand with differences in the way in which governments employ their powers. Political reform appears to have elicited political restraint and a higher quality of governance.

The question is, of course, whether the reformist impulse will endure or erode. The elections in Nigeria and Kenya in 2007 underscore the potential for backsliding; so too those in Sudan and Rwanda. Also indicative are the efforts to revoke the limits on the terms of presidents, as documented in figure 9, available online.

Political liberty is always in peril. As Adams proclaimed to the citizens of Philadelphia, so he might have exhorted those in modern Africa: Remain vigilant!

NOTES
1. "You have eaten me": this wistful phrase—variously attributed to Yoruba or Lunda kings, upon assuming office—confirms the monarch's recognition that he must subordinate his private needs to the obligation of public service.
2. Indicative is that in the British colonial archives, the files on the nationalist parties bore the same label (SOC) as did those for armed insurgencies, nativist rebellions, and communist cells.
3. All figures and the appendix accompanying this article are available online at <www.socres.org/appendices/774bates.html>.
4. For the definition of an authoritarian and nonauthoritarian regime, see the appendix, available online. Applying a t-test to the difference between the means, the difference in the ratings in each of the four panels is highly significant.

REFERENCES

Anderson, K. *The Political Economy of Distortions to Agricultural Incentives.* New York: Oxford University Press, forthcoming.

Bates, R. H. *Markets and States in Tropical Africa.* Berkeley and Los Angeles: University of California Press, 1981.

———. *Essays on the Political Economy of Rural Africa.* Berkeley and Los Angeles: University of California Press, 1987.

———. "Domestic Interests and Control Regimes." *The Political Economy of Economic Growth in Africa 1960-2000.* Eds. B. J. Ndulu, S. A. O'Connell, R. H. Bates, P. Collier, and C. C. Soludo. New York: Cambridge University Press, 2008.

Beck, T., G. Clarke, et al. "New Tools and New Tests in Comparative Political Economy: The Database of Political Institutions." *World Bank Economic Review* 15:1 (2001).

Collier, R. *Regimes in Tropical Africa.* Berkeley and Los Angeles: University of California Press, 1982.

Dahl, R. *Polyarchy.* New Haven: Yale University Press, 1971.

Ferree, K., and S. Singh. *Institutional Change and Economic Performance in Africa, 1970-1995.* Annual Meetings of the American Political Science Association, Atlanta, 1999.

Gluckman, M. *Custom and Conflict in Africa.* Oxford: Blackwell, 1955.

Humphreys, M., and R. H. Bates. "Political Institutions and Economic Policies." *British Journal of Political Science* 35 (Summer 2005): 403-428.

Huntington, S. *The Third Wave.* Norman: University of Oklahoma Press, 1991.

Ndulu, B. J. "The Evolution of Global Development Paradigms and Their Influence on African Economic Growth." *The Political Economy of Economic Growth in Africa, 1960-2000.* Eds. B. J. Ndulu, S. A. O'Connell, R. H. Bates, P. Collier and C. C. Saludo. New York: Cambridge University Press, 2008.

Ndulu, B. J., S. A. O'Connell, et al., eds. *The Political Economy of Economic Growth in Africa, 1960-2000.* New York: Cambridge University Press, 2008.

Przeworski, A., M. Alvarez, et al. *Democracy and Development*. New York: Cambridge University Press, 2000.

Schattschneider, E. E. *The Semisovereign People*. New York: Holt, Rinehart and Winston, 1965.

Schumpeter, J. A. *Capitalism, Socialism and Democracy*. New York: Harpers and Row, 1950.

Sklar, R. (1987). "Developmental Democracy." *Comparative Studies in Society and History* 29 (June 2009): 686-714.

Vansina, J. *Kingdoms of the Sanannah*. Madison: University of Wisconsin Press, 1966.

———. *The Children of Woot: A History of the Kuba People*. Madison: University of Wisconsin Press, 1978.

———. *Paths in the Rain Forest: Toward a History of Political Tradition in Equatorial Africa*. Madison: University of Wisconsin Press, 1990.

———. *Beyond Chiefdoms: Pathways to Comlexity in Africa*. New York: Cambridge University Press, 1999.

———. *How Societies are Born*. Charlotte and London: University of Virginia Press, 2005.

World Bank. *Accelerated Development in Sub-Saharan Africa: An Agenda for Action*. Washington, D.C.: World Bank, 1981.

———. *Governance and Development*. Washington, D.C.: World Bank, 1991a.

———. *World Development Report*. Washignton, D.C.: World Bank, 1991b.

———. *The Political Economy of Agricultural Pricing Policies*. 5 vols. Eds. A. O. Krueger, M. Schiff, et al. Baltimore: Published for the World Bank by Johns Hopkins University Press, 1992.

———. *Adjustment in Africa: Reform, Results, and the Road Ahead*. Washington, D.C.: World Bank, 1994.

———. *Distortions to Agricultural Incentives in Africa*. Ed. Anderson, K. and W. A. Masters. Washington, D.C.: World Bank, 2009.

Young, C. *The African Colonial State in Comparative Perspective*. New Haven and London: Yale University Press, 1994.

Thandika Mkandawire
Aid, Accountability, and Democracy in Africa

AT THE CORE OF DEMOCRACY IS THE IDEA THAT GOVERNMENTS must be systematically responsive to the desires and interests of citizens as expressed through the electoral process. This is the principal mechanism of democratic accountability, since it is through this process that politicians are called to account by a sovereign electorate with powers to sanction them. The effectiveness of the process depends on the viability of democratic institutions and the citizens' engagement, political sophistication, and access to information, which in turn impact on political contestability and transparency. Ensuring accountability is difficult enough if there is only one elected sovereign in a particular space. It becomes profoundly more complex when two sovereigns act upon the same space but are accountable to different constituencies and when the power of one of the two sovereigns is likely to impinge on the accountability of the other. In this paper I consider the problem of accountability in African democracies that are heavily dependent on aid from richer democracies. Concentrating on aid as a constraint on accountability in no way suggests it is the only culprit in this respect. Many other factors impinge on accountability at the national level. Indeed, it is the interplay with and at times the connivance of local and external factors that have undermined accountability in Africa. The internal factors include the lack of transparency of national governments and the "smoke and mirrors" political practices that come along with it; the undemocratic mores of the political class (an aspect of the authoritarian legacy that does not see accountability as a moral imperative but as an undesirable aspect of democracy); the contradictory political affiliations of voters reflecting conflicting ideological, ethnic, or clientelistic loyalties that undermine the collective action required to ensure accountability; the institutional barriers to free and fair elections; the strange behavior of legislatures that have weakened themselves by ceding more powers to the executive. Each of these has been the subject of analysis in the literature on democracy in Africa.

I will argue that although many donors have invested considerable resources in support of democratization, they have also, simultaneously, proceeded to circumscribe the reach and competence of democratic institutions and their accountability to the citizenry in aid-receiving countries. Even as they swear by democracy, part of the aid establishment is still preoccupied with finding ways and means of insulating aid from the encumbrances of democratic politics in recipient countries by creating what have been aptly termed "authoritarian enclaves" (Maravall 1994). I will also suggest that the notion of accountability in developing countries, especially the aid-dependent ones, is best understood not only in the context of democratization but also in the context of the much more fraught aid/donor relationship. Aid, by its very nature, involves power relations that go beyond the adage "who pays the piper, calls the tune." Any exercise of power necessitates and creates its own institutions. Aid giving and receiving often set in motion a whole range of asymmetrical relationships that may take on lives of their own. In such a context, preoccupation with accountability is driven at least as much by ideas about the relationship between the donors and the aid recipient countries as by the inherent meaning of democracy.

Liberal democracy has been largely premised on Westphalian foundations of national sovereignty, which allowed communities to control their own destinies. In such a context democratic accountability corresponded to the territorial boundaries of the nation-state and, as David Held argues, "the theory of democracy . . . could take for granted the link between the demos, citizenship, electoral mechanism, the nature of consent and the boundaries of the nation state" (Held

1999: 90). In the post-World War II period, the reconstruction of the international order was premised on an "embedded liberalism," which, while promoting greater trade and flow of capital, left to each nation-state important tools for economic management and was indeed premised on "domestic interventionism" (Ruggie 1982). Some aspects of this regime were extended to developing countries, neocolonialism notwithstanding, and allowed each individual state a much wider range of policy choices, at least when compared to the "policy convergent" world of today. It is perhaps precisely because it accommodated both "welfare statism" and "national developmentalism" that this era is considered the "golden age" of national autonomy. More pertinent to our discussion is that a significant number of donors viewed their aid as somehow embedded within the "national development plans" drawn up by sovereign states.[1]

During the last three decades of the twentieth century, globalization severely undermined the Westphalian foundations of democracy and the embedded liberalism of the post-World War II era by restricting the policy spaces of many countries, producing "democracy deficits" in many democracies. For African countries the forces of globalization manifested themselves through the imposition of the "Washington consensus," which led to greater policy orchestration. The imposition was facilitated, first, by the collapse in terms of trade and the ensuing debt problems that forced many countries into supplicant positions when it came to donors; second, by the end of the Cold War, which ruled out the possibility of playing off one donor against another, and, finally, following the 1981 Mexican debacle, by the loss of access to private financial markets.

AID AND THE DEMOCRATIC TURN

For years, the development discourse tended to cast doubt on democracy's appropriateness to conditions in developing countries. It was argued that there was a trade-off between economic growth and political rights. The arguments were many: that democratization was a process that evolved in tandem with development, and the full features of a liberal democracy could be enjoyed only after the passage of a certain development threshold (Lipset 1959); that authoritarian rule in poor countries was not only evidence of their underdevelopment, but might also be a necessary institutional arrangement for development (development being "no easy task" and best pursued by regimes that could curtail present consumption to increase savings and investments). Indeed, among some of the leading lights of the modernization school, the quest for political order overrode concerns of accountability and representation (Huntington 1968). Or as Bhagwati argued, "the political economy of development . . . poses a cruel choice between rapid (self-sustained) expansion and democratic processes" (Bhagwati 1966). The successful performance of authoritarian developmental states gave weight to these arguments about the "authoritarian advantage" (Maravall 1994) while ignoring the many disasters of authoritarian rule. The argument for authoritarian rule was further strengthened in the era of structural adjustment as the success of Pinochet and the symbiotic relationship of that regime with the "Chicago School" suggested an elective affinity between authoritarian rule and neoliberalism (Haggard and Kaufman 1992; Montecinos 1993). One of the prominent proponents of neoliberalism had forcefully argued that "a courageous, ruthless and perhaps undemocratic government is required to ride roughshod over these newly created special interests groups" in developing countries (Lal 2000: 33). In the African case the successes of the military regimes such as that of Ghana and Uganda also fed into this argument (Bangura 1992; Haggard and Kaufman 1992).

Democracy only firmly entered the aid business in the 1990s, partly as a new commitment to human rights (especially in the post-Cold War era) and partly because of the new belief that "good governance" was essential for development. With the end of the Cold War and definitely by the end of the 1990s, the official normative discourse had squarely shifted toward democracy. Human rights and democracy became part of the foreign policy of the leading Western countries (Donnelly 1999). At the United Nations level the great divide between those states that argued for human rights and those that argued for economic rights or "the right to development" was substantially narrowed. The Vienna Declaration and Program of Action went as far as to state that these rights are "interdependent and mutually reinforcing" (cited in Donnelly 1999). In academic circles Amartya Sen (1999) articulated the view that development means the expansion of choice for individuals and societies. In addition, there was a steady flow of academic work raising doubts or laying to rest one of the stylized "trade-offs" of development (Alesina and Perotti 1994; Bardhan 1993; Burkhart and Lewis-Beck 1994; Helliwell 1994; Przeworski and Limongi 1993: 2000). Democracy was now said to be advantageous because it ensured property rights and private business (Olson 2000); it sustained critical ingredients of "good governance" (accountability and voice), which were good for development; it allowed for self-correction (Bardhan 1999); it was adverse to inflation and macroeconomic populism, which, in the Latin American case, at least, was attributed to the military and the technocracy (Bresser-Pereira 2003); it provided avenues for resolving collective action problems inherent to development and allowed for stable "developmental pacts" to emerge (Beuningen 2007; Olson 2000); it ensured political stability that was vital for economic development (Anyang' Nyongo 1988; Bardhan 1999).[2]

In light of this new understanding, significant amounts of aid were now directed toward promoting democracy through conditionalities aimed at forcing the hands of authoritarian regimes;[3] through support to ongoing processes of democratization by providing technical assistance to electoral processes (including supply of equipment, writing constitutions and monitoring election); and through contributions to the consolidation of new democracies by strengthening various institutions considered central to democratic governance.

AID, THE FISCAL BASIS OF THE STATE, AND ACCOUNTABILITY

Fiscal relations between states, donors, and citizens affect accountability relations in direct and indirect ways. Thus, a better understanding of fiscal positions of recipient states is important when seeking to promote more democratic and accountable government. During the last 20 years or so, many governments have seen their capacity to collect revenue dwindle—largely because of structural adjustment programs, which have been opposed to taxing trade (Aizenman and Jinjarak 2009),[4] and partly because globalization has made it particularly difficult to tax highly mobile capital. One consequence has been greater reliance on aid, not only for long-term investment but also for the state's short-term recurrent expenditures. During the early years of the democratization process in Africa, 60 percent or so of African countries received aid that was more than 10 percent of gross domestic product (GDP) (see table 1).

The American Revolution had, among its memorable rallying cries, the slogan "No taxation without representation." This poignantly underscored the relationship between democracy and the fiscal basis of the state. This meant that the right of the government to tax citizens could only be based on its accountability to citizens. It has been observed that "rentier economies" (Beblawi 1987)—that is, economies relying on revenues gained through the extraction of a limited number of natural resources—require little organizational and political effort in working with citizens in order to secure revenues. The situation in such cases is said to reverse the rallying cry of the American revolutionaries to read: "No representation without taxation." The political and economic implications of reliance on such rents is that there is often a disconnect between states and citizens that, in turn, tends to lead to poor governance.[5] The extraction of revenue from an enclave-like resource base gives the state an autonomy that obviates concerns about accountability to a nontaxed citizenry (Ross 1999; Wantchekon 1999; Wantchekon and Jensen 2004). Indeed, Michael Ross categorically argues that "the oil-impedes-democracy claim is both valid and statistically robust, oil does hurt democracy" (Ross 1999). In contrast, there are the "merchant states" that rely on taxation of a large number of citizens and economic activities, and thus require the organizational and political wherewithal to reach or "bargain" with large groups of citizens (Mkandawire 1995).

Table 1: Aid Dependence of African Economies (Share of Aid in GDP>10% of GDP)

Country	1970-1979	Country	1980-1989	Country	1990-1999	Country	2000-2004
Mauritania	24.5	Lesotho	40.7	Rwanda	42.7	Sao Tome and Principe	55.9
Somalia	16.5	Equatorial Guinea	39.0	Sao Tome and Principe	36.4	Eritrea	27.0
Botswana	15.4	Comoros	34.6	Guinea	19.5	Burundi	22.5
Rwanda	13.5	Cape Verde	31.8	Swaziland	18.8	Rwanda	18.4
Swaziland	12.9	Mauritania	29.1	Guinea-Bissau	16.8	Gambia	17.5
Mali	12.8	Guinea-Bissau	27.7	Equatorial Guinea	16.0	Mozambique	16.1
Lesotho	11.3	Sao Tome and Principe	25.6	Mali	15.9	Malawi	14.6
Togo	11.2	Somalia	23.9	Kenya	15.5	Swaziland	14.3
Seychelles	11.0	Gambia	23.1	Lesotho	15.4	Mauritania	14.0
Burkina Faso	10.9	Swaziland	22.5	Malawi	15.1	Guinea-Bissau	13.7
Chad	10.0	Namibia	21.5	Gambia	15.0	Uganda	12.0
		Liberia	17.7	Cape Verde	14.6	Zambia	11.3
		Mali	16.6	Djibouti	13.7	Cape Verde	11.0
		Burundi	15.6	Chad	13.4	Djibouti	10.8
		Chad	14.1	Uganda	13.3	Ghana	10.7
		Togo	13.7	Burkina Faso	13.3	Niger	10.5
		Seychelles	13.6	Tanzania	13.2	Chad	10.4
		Mozambique	12.9	Mauritius	12.6	Ethiopia	10.3
		Senegal	12.8	Sudan	12.4		
		Burkina Faso	12.2	Mozambique	12.2		
		Botswana	11.6	Central African Republic	12.1		
		Guinea	11.3	Madagascar	11.8		
		Tanzania	11.1	Nigeria	11.8		
		Rwanda	10.1	Cameroon	11.2		
				Ghana	10.6		
				Benin	10.5		
				Eritrea	10.3		
				Botswana	10.2		
				Gabon	10.2		
				Togo	10.0		

Source: World Bank.

Some writers have suggested that the rentier state model is applicable to the assessment of the aid-accountability linkages (Bräutigam 1992; Moore 2001; Therkildsen 2002). In much the same way as with mineral rents, aid, by reducing the state's dependence on its citizenry for tax revenue, can also obviate the need for citizen consent by short-circuiting the process of "bargaining" between the state and citizenry and by forcing a break in the "fiscal-social contract" (Bräutigam 1992, 2001; Moore 2004, 1998, 2001; Moss, Pettersson, and van de Walle 2008; Therkildsen 2002).[7] There are, however, fundamental differences between aid and other rents. Revenue from natural resources goes directly to the government either as taxes or royalties while aid is mediated by a wide range of factors, including conditionalities, bureaucracies, and technical assistance, each of which impinge on national sovereignty. More specifically, aid dependence not only tends to make democracy less accountable to the citizens of the country, but also makes the state accountable to foreign citizens. Beholden to taxpayers in donor countries, governments in aid-receiving countries increasingly respond more punctiliously to the demands of donors than to those of their own citizens. In the usual principal/agent approach to public services, the crucial assumption is that the client who receives the services is also a citizen who pays for the taxes, which generates a feedback loop that sustains the relationship. Such a feedback loop of accountability is broken in the aid-recipient nexus (Martens 2009; Reinikka 2009; Svenson 2008).[8]

Parliamentary democracy implies delegation and a corresponding need for accountability, along with all the principal-agency problems that it entails. However, in the context of aid, accountability takes on a more ambiguous character and tends to lean toward a more technocratic interpretation. It is also strongly circumscribed by the prior terms of engagement between aid and recipient. At the heart of the current debates on accountability is the unresolved tension between the exigencies of a technocratic view of accountability, which stresses performance and proper accounting for public resources, and the exigencies of democracy, which stresses processes and political accountability. Although the moral imperatives of solidarity and common humanity suggest that aid should be based on trust, dialogue, and partnership, the necessity for continued support for aid by voters in the donor countries calls for greater focus on financial probity and efficient allocation—which, in the receiving country, often translates into greater conditionality and the substitution of accounting for accountability.

AID AND DEMOCRACY WITHOUT ACCOUNTABILITY

In the earlier stages of the "Third Wave" of democracy, nonaccountability of the recipient governments to their own citizens was not seen as a problem; both policies and institutional reforms were premised on this nonaccountability as the default mode. The neglect or even dread of accountability as a constitutive aspect of democracy was not only confined to the aid establishment but was typical of academic work on democracy. Lindberg reports that when Schmitter and Karl "contended that accountability was the central key to most definitions of democracy, their claim was met with overwhelming indifference and occasional expressions of hostility" (Lindberg 2009). Furthermore, within academic circles, there were initially apprehensions that attention to accountability would force the new elected governments to pay too much attention to popular will and thus reverse neoliberal policies and revert to various forms of macroeconomic populism (Dornbursch and Edwards 1992).

As it turned out, these fears were assuaged, albeit partially, by the attachment of new democracies to orthodox macroeconomic policies. Evidence from Latin America showed that "new democracies outperformed their authoritarian counterparts in promoting growth, containing the growth of fiscal deficits, and limiting the growth of the debt burden" (Remmer 1990: 327). And in Africa the adhesion of the new democracies, such as Benin, Ghana, Malawi, Mali, Mozambique, South Africa, and Zambia, to orthodoxy with the zeal characteristic of acolytes was a source of great relief (Levy 2006). It could now be argued that there was an elective affinity between democracy and economic liberalism.[9] Democracy could now be championed not so much because it empowers citizens to make demands on the state but because it would facilitate the "new social contract" through which painful policies would be imposed. However, the good behavior of new democracies did not entirely allay all fears about the threat that democracy posed for the "Washington consensus." The problems faced by donors was well captured by a U.S. Agency for International Development (USAID) official:

> The emergence of political liberalization in Africa has strengthened the institutional base for long-term policy rationality, but it has weakened the capacity to adopt "good" policies in the short run. Democratic politics has created a number of difficulties for economic policymaking. In the first place, unitary states have been replaced by states in which legislative and executive power is separated. This has complicated the process of economic negotiation between assistance agencies and African governments. Agreements reached behind closed doors are now openly debated in parliaments (Wolgin 1997: 56).

Most donors still acted as if they held a view of the electorate as fundamentally irrational and beholden to all kinds of primordial values, a view that received considerable support in academic circles. For those who interpreted African politics through the lens of neopatrimonialism, the notion of representation had no meaning in Africa because, when people vote, "they are expected, or 'asked,' to do so, or perhaps because it is indispensable to be seen to be voting a certain way. On the whole, they do not vote because they support the ideas of a particular political party but because they must placate the demands of their existing or putative patron" (Chabal and Daloz 1999: 39).[10] This view was further reinforced by the oft poorly veiled contempt for local elites so prevalent in much of the political analysis of Africa. We should also recall the effect of the "irretrievably cynical view of the state" (Toye

1991) that was sustained by the public choice school and the equally cynical views of neopatrimonialism school in Africa that reduced African politics to "politics of the belly" (Bayart 1993). In one view politicians were seen as rational operators who were in politics to pursue rents that would undermine democratic decision making (Bienen and Herbst 1996; Callaghy 1990; Lindberg 2003). In the other view the elites were corrupt or too beholden to neopatrimonial or other elite interests and thus not able to act in the public interest even when they came to power through the democratic process. Where these views were held as a matter of course, elections were seen simply as the interlude of a farce or a play of immense tragedy. This understanding provided moral and intellectual support to the conclusion that the democratic process had to be circumvented by limiting the remiss of the elected elites. A number of measures were introduced to discipline these new democracies just in case they aimed to go beyond the formal processes of elections toward the substantive issues of, for example, social welfare and income distribution.

MONOLOGICAL PARTNERSHIPS

The strategies of constraining the threat of "macroeconomic populism" consisted of three pillars: the ideational, the institutional, and brutal force of finance that was exerted on economically strapped democracies. The ideational pillar involved persuading key actors that the Washington consensus was the "only game in town" and then empowering such actors. Donors often started with firm ideas about "good policies" and the instruments to be adopted. They then suggested as, the World Bank report, *Assessing Aid: What Works, What Doesn't and Why* (World Bank 1998) did, that foreign aid would be more effective if it were more systematically targeted to poor countries that pursued these "good policies." This sounds reasonable until one asks what constitutes good policies, and who makes them. Many of the constraints imposed on democratic decision-making were based on specious performance goals and spurious quantitative precision about means and ways and the insistence on "policy coherence" that produced the one-sided and stifling Washington consensus. The constraints also reflected the premium given to technocrats in the management of economic affairs, and the ascendancy of a technocratic "epistemic community" in both donors and aid-receiving countries that shares the same vision and speaks the same arcane language. This immediately raised concerns over the nature of the counterpart that would "own" the policies. One solution was something tantamount to "cloning" the recipient so that the recipient walks, talks, and looks like the donor. In a rather perverse way, to facilitate both dialogue and accountability, donors preceded to shape their counterparts in a manner that would not only make the parties mutually intelligible but that would also make the recipient pliable. Or, as Gerry Helleiner notes with respect to the World Bank,

> However much the Bank may have conceded as to the pace, sequencing and details of adjustment programmes, as the de facto intellectual leader of the aid agencies in the 1980s and 1990s, it has not significantly altered its basic recipe for development-oriented reform. But it now wants local policymakers not simply to do what it recommends but also to believe in it (Helleiner 2000).[11]

Essentially this process involved the intensification of "capacity building," which often involved indoctrination and cloning. Through various "capacity-building initiatives," whole ministries were restructured to make them compatible with both the ideological proclivities and institutional preferences of the donors. It also demanded that the remolded partners be shielded from the encumbrances of domestic politics. And so donors devoted considerable resources strengthening elements of the state and civil society that they considered proper counterparts and insisted that the institutions dominated by these groups be "autonomous" from domestic actors while receiving their sustenance and authority from access to donor financial and human resources. We are all aware of the theatrical cases where donors have drafted key government documents, which the recipients have been induced to "own" and for which they have been financially rewarded for their intellectual acumen, maturity, and commitment to reform.[12] In many cases, bureaucrats in aid-receiving countries have learned that there is no point taking initiatives or insisting on national specificities; life is made easier by relying on experts or simply downloading and slightly reworking the "best practice" documents that are nowadays readily accessible on the web. The more insidious form this takes is the preparation of such documents by carefully selected, coached, and empowered nationals hiding between the smokescreen of technocratic autonomy and the much vaunted "ownership." Parliaments have also learned it is much easier to let the technocrats in the finance ministries meet the donors demands than engage in protracted dialogues. This ritualized charade trivializes notions of deliberation and accountability by making dialogue and exchange of ideas and experiences superfluous. But more seriously, it is a mockery of the notion of transparency that is so central to accountability because it relies on a deceptive legerdemain in which documents dictated or imposed by donors are transmogrified into "nationally owned" ones.

The spartan certainty about "good policies" only led to the kind of truth that Hannah Arendt suggested had, from the view point of politics, a "despotic character" because it forecloses disputes, disagreement, and deliberation. And the more precise the donor targets and the more dogmatic the articulation of these goals was, the more likely it was that aid would constrain democratic institutions in the receiving countries. Even such an eminently sensible thesis as "policy coherence" could and did wreak havoc on accountability, especially if it produced "take-it-or-leave-it" policy options that foreclosed debate and rendered politics inflexible and collided with the deliberative nature of policymaking in democracies and contributed to the production of what I have characterized as "choiceless democracies" (Mkandawire 1999) or others have referred to as "low-intensity democracies" (Gills and Rocamora 1992) or "democratie tropacilisée," "imperfect," "illiberal," and "immature" democracy (Armony 2004)—suggesting severe limitations on the accountability and sovereignty of new democracies. This was most sharply demonstrated in the Poverty Reductions Strategy Papers (PRSPs) process, which was supposed to mirror the new "participatory" approach.[13] The quest for coherence and, even worse, the imposition of putatively coherent policies on recipient countries, would clearly undermine the prospects of developing a culture of dialogue and compromise (Mkandawire 2001). Incoherence is inherent to democratic politics, where compromise underlies decisions.

Reshaping Civil Society

One further difference between aid and other "rents" is the way they respectively structure civil society. Mineral economies have tended to create highly organized labor, which at times has acted forcefully on the political arena,[14] while aid, especially in the era of neoliberalism, has tended to favor and capture nonmembership-based segments of civil society. Aid has spawned "briefcase organizations" that are accountable to nobody but their foreign funders. One immediate consequence of the much bemoaned fragmentation of aid has been the fragmentation and hierarchization of civil society (Kaldor 2003). The hierarchization comes from the fact that "funding by official agencies and private foundations have led to the development of a market for NGOs, in which donors influence the culture and management style of NGOs, and successful NGOs transform themselves into a kind of oligopoly" (Kaldor 2003: 16). In most cases, the effectiveness of these "oligopolies" in their advocacy activities is not derived from their anchoring in domestic civil society but in the authority given to them by the donor countries and transnational civil society networks. This close relationship with donors has in some instances earned NGOs the status of a parastatal of government subcontractors in the eyes of the public (Kaldor 2003). Governments are aware that NGOs can influence donors, and many of their "consultative meetings" with NGOs are carried out not in the spirit of accountability but rather as a response to donor requirements for such meetings or to pre-empt donor's insistence on consultancy with designated portions of "civil society." One further consequence of "etatisation" of elements of civil society is homogenization of the voices of civil society around themes that donors deem pertinent at any given time (Jelin 1997; Edwards and Hulme 1996; Shivji 2004). All this militates against the Tocquevellian view that inseparably associates civic activity with the emergence and consolidation of democracy on the assumption of voluntary membership organizations. The "briefcase" NGOs that aid has spawned and sustained blunts any incentives to seek or augment their membership and thus undermines one major driver of accountability in democracies, namely civil society.

The Institutional Straightjacket
As part of their response to conditionalities, and their own internal political developments, recipient countries have made significant institutional changes. Authoritarian governments have become democratic; socialist governments have become capitalist; most governments have witnessed a dramatic shrinking of their reach and capacity. In contrast, few donors have witnessed such changes in their ideologies or institutional arrangements in relating with aid recipient countries. Indeed, in many cases changes in the aid establishment have rarely amounted to more than relabeling existing institutional arrangements. As a consequence, the current use of "governance" is still very much business as usual. One consequence of this one-sided adjustment is that the donors, accustomed to working with authoritarian regimes, now find they have problems dealing with democracies even when they are supportive of the democratic processes and the changes that have taken place.

Limiting the authority of elected government with the advent of democracy has been ensured by introducing institutional reforms that effectively eviscerate the authority of elected bodies through the "insulation" of policy technocrats and the creation of "autonomous" authorities or "authoritarian enclaves" or "reserve domains" (Linz and Stepan 1998: 48), or by circumventing oversight by national democratic institutions. There has thus been a flurry of initiatives, in the name of institution building, to create "independent" central banks, "independent" fiscal authorities, and "independent" road authorities (Boylan 1998; Boylan 2001),[15] which, while insulated from and autonomous of local representative institutions, derive their new authority from donors and are therefore beholden to them and more outward-oriented in terms of accountability. Other initiatives have involved the creation of parallel bureaucracies that constitute much of the technical assistance given and which are not accountable to elected bodies. This institutional modeling approach tends to multiply formal institutions with little regard for their effective contribution to the solidification of the democratic architecture. One effect of such parallel structures is that they undermine the notion of checks and balances so crucial to democracy, because critical parts of the executive are outside the control of the parliament and even judiciary, given the ease with which diplomatic immunity is granted.[16]

Exploiting Structural Weaknesses

Many African democracies emerged during or at the tail end of the "lost decades" that wrought so much damage to the economic fabric and capacities of the states. In many cases it is the fear of donor demands rather than citizens' wishes that have driven government policy. Such fears are often heightened by the knowledge that sanctions may have been instrumental in bringing down the ancien régime and by the desperate need to access aid money. It has been suggested in the literature that because aid always helps democratic leaders, it should give donors greater leverage over democratic recipients than over dictators: aid can buy political reforms in democracies and not in autocracies (Montinola 2010; Yuichi Kono and Montinola 2009). It is precisely because democratic regimes are more sensitive to the domestic political responses of their voters that would follow the withdrawal of aid than their authoritarian predecessor that donors have been encouraged to intensify their conditionalities. They have also exploited the now much more open mass media to make their preferences known and to voice thinly veiled threats that aid will be discontinued or reduced if their preferences are not taken into account.

MUTUAL ACCOUNTABILITY AND BUDGET SUPPORT

By the end of the 1990s the aid establishment was faced with three problems. The first was the problem of "aid fatigue," partly induced by the increased and not always favorable exposure of aid to public scrutiny and the need to strengthen domestic accountability of recipients. In many ways, the "mutual accountability" issue has arisen out of the need to rehabilitate the state. The new emphasis on good governance is no longer premised on marginalization of the state and retrenchment. It has now been recognized that the state—usually limited to the executive branch of government—is a decisive agent of national development. With the growing realization that conditionality was not working, it has become clear that national "ownership" of policies is instrumental to the efficient use of aid.

The second problem concerned the issue of efficacy, especially at the time of increased aid. Concurrent with real and promised increases in aid, there has emerged a literature suggesting that aid may, after all, not be effective in terms of promoting economic growth and combating poverty;[17] other studies suggest that it may be downright harmful (Easterly 2006; Moyo 2009). One argument was that aid conditionality has been ineffective and lack of coordination among donors has overburdened the bureaucracies of the recipient countries and led to incoherence in both the aid institutions and projects. It became clear that conditionality-driven aid had not only failed to yield the desired outcomes but also had high transaction costs for donor and recipient countries. There was therefore the need to reduce the transaction costs associated with fragmented aid delivery and complex principal/agent problems of monitoring.

The third problem came from the moral imperative of "empowering" the new democracies by ensuring their "ownership" of policies. A number of donors began to push for an aid dispensation that prized democracy and good governance. Donors began to feel that they had gone too far or, in the words of Paul Collier, then at the World Bank, "the extension of the practice of conditionality from the occasional circumstances of crisis management to the continuous process of general economic policy-making has implied a transfer of sovereignty which is not only unprecedented but is often dysfunctional" (Collier 1999: 319).

With money from outside and policy "owned" by the recipient, it was necessary to introduce the idea of "mutual accountability," which solved the "principal agent" problems that had bedeviled the conditionality aid regime and reconcile "ownership" with the need to pursue the post-Washington consensus. This new consensus among donors was enshrined in the Paris Declaration, which endorsed the view that countries must "exercise effective leadership over their development policies" (OECD 2005) partly because this is effective way to have policies implemented. This in turn was interpreted to mean that general budget support would be the right way to go since this would not only put the recipient governments in the driver's seat but would also reduce the transaction costs associated with fragmented aid delivery while strengthening domestic accountability (Renzio 2006).

The "mutual accountability" between aid agencies and national governments had to be reconciled to the democratic premises of the accountability of both partners to their respective constituencies. In a fundamental way this demands a degree of trust between the parties. Unfortunately, much of the thinking on the donor side was premised on a political economy that still viewed local elites as either rent-seekers out to capture the state or as enmeshed in neopatrimonial relations that often undermine the rational functioning of the state. The recipients resented the patronizing attitudes of the donors and the unequal nature of the framework within which "mutual accountability" was carried out.

A WIDENING POLICY SPACE?

In the 1980s and 1990s, new democracies tended to follow orthodox policies more strictly than older ones (Mkandawire 2004). Indeed, it can be argued, without being cynical, that the willingness by donors to engage in "mutual accountability" was also facilitated by the belief that donors had attained sufficient ideational hegemony in key policymaking institutions such as ministries of finance and central banks and had sufficiently ring-fenced these institutions that they could cede authority without jeopardizing the core policy regime that they still adhered to. However, as would be expected as democracy became more entrenched, deliberation and compromises and responsiveness to a more assertive electorate introduced elements of compromise in policy that were anathema to the dogmatic insistence on one "consensus." Three actors appear to account for this. The first was the growing maturity of local constituencies that with time began to make demands on their governments that were beyond the formal issues of election and that at times went against the Washington consensus.[18] The second factor has been the erosion of the spartan certainty that had hitherto made the Washington consensus sacrosanct and severely restricted dialogue on economic policy. And finally, there are the set of favorable conditions in the global economy that has somehow widened policy space for African policymakers (these include improved terms of trade and the China/India factor). As table 1 suggested, the number of countries for which aid constitutes 10 percent or more of GDP has declined. This is probably a reflection of improved performance of African economies during the last decade.

Not surprisingly, in more recent years donors have complained about loss of control of policy. A World Bank economist, noting that "the traction from policy improvement in increasing growth performance in Africa has declined over time," observes:

> The declining traction of policy influence on growth may also, in contrast to the East Asian historical experience, reflect growth trade-offs from the decision many African countries have taken to pursue a dual reform process—economic and political (democratic)—with the latter's attendant costs and policy risks: for example, from transitions across political systems and election cycles" (Ndulu 2007: 11).

CONCLUSION

Over the years the relationship between aid, democracy, and accountability has undergone significant change. In the initial years of development thinking, with its proclivity for authoritarian politics, it was taken for granted that more often than not, aid would be given to states that were not democratic. Indeed, it was assumed that "strong" (read undemocratic) states would be the ideal partner. It was only with the Third Wave of democratization that the relationship between aid and democracy was squarely placed on the agenda. While an elective affinity between democratization and economic liberalization were often proclaimed, there was serious doubt in both policy and academic circles about the capacity of new democracies to withstand political pressures that would derail the structural adjustments to which aid was tethered for much of the past three decades. Hence the muted concern over accountability by new democracies and the imposition of conditionalities that severely limited democratic institutions. With the obvious failure of conditionalities, the high transaction costs of such conditionalities and the moral absurdity of foreign "ownership" of policies in other democracies, there has been a move to address the issue of accountability and the recognition of different "principals" that donor and recipient states respectively have to respond to. Accountability in the context of aid dependence is problematic because it addresses two different constituencies: those of the donor country and those of the recipient country.

While at times donor demands have been supportive of democratic institutions, they have also tended to undermine citizens' authority over state affairs. It would be the height of irony if democracies that have pushed for democratic reforms in many countries were to undermine new democracies by making them only outwardly accountable. As things stand, the more accountable a donor is to its own voters, the more onerous and invasive will be its intervention in the receiving economy and the more likely it is to undermine the recipient democratic government's accountability to its own voters. Not surprisingly, a number of new democracies have expressed preference for the unconditional aid given by the authoritarian regime of the People's Republic of China, which has taken the construction of parliaments in Africa as serious business![19] It is perhaps better to begin by recognizing such ambiguities and tensions as given, as being in the nature of the beast as it were, and to seek to address them in order to minimize the negative and maximize the positive. If we agree that the "goodness" of governance is ultimately attributable to its democratic legitimacy, then aid must come to terms with questions of the asymmetries that undermine democracy, the politics of budget allocation, and democratic anchoring of policies in the recipient country. It would seem that in situations where a decision has been made to support regimes because they are democratic, donors should then adopt a much less hands-on policy stance.

There have always been debates within recipient countries about the readiness or capacity of national institutions to receive aid, about the moral justification of providing aid to "kleptocrats" or authoritarian regimes, about the "dependence syndrome" that aid induces, and the need for "self-reliance" as a guiding principle. As we indicated earlier, there are many serious concerns about internal limitations to accountability in the new democracies in Africa that we have not addressed in this paper. These concerns are reasonable but they do not justify attempts to circumvent the democratic process or limit the policy options available to elected bodies. Pressure for accountability must ultimately come from the citizens of the recipient country. Donors can help by making their aid flows transparent and channeling them through institutions in which elected bodies have oversight.

Accountability presupposes discretion. "Choiceless democracy," like a puppet, cannot be held accountable, although in the African case African governments were often held accountable for ventriloquized policy pronouncements.[20] To support accountability in the new democracies, there is a pressing need to rethink the institutions that underpin the current management of aid and the "policy space" that democracies have. Aid belongs to that category of economic activities in which it is prudent to proceed by trial and error. This, in turn, requires dialogue and a more deliberative partnership. It is also incumbent upon democratic aid-receiving countries that they themselves begin to look for exit strategies, at least from the more onerous and interventionist forms of aid. Increasing policy space is not entirely in donor hands. We have suggested that there are many domestic factors that may be reducing the external hold of African economies. The lessening of accountability to outsiders does not of course immediately translate into greater accountability to internal actors. Governments can improve their position by performing better in their revenue collection. Fiscal probity by democracies must not be merely a means to meet the exigencies of external debt collectors, but also a way of securing more space for democracy by reducing aid dependence.

NOTES
1. With the help, of course, of the ubiquitous experts.
2. There were, of course, dissenting voices who still insisted that democracy might not be a prior or parallel condition of development and that democracy might actually hamper development. See Leftwich (1993, 1996).
3. It was believed that while geopolitical interests had tended to undermine the threats to condition aid on demands for democracy, the demise of the Soviet Union and the triumphalism of the West now lent greater credibility to the political conditionalities making aid conditionality more potent after the Cold War (Dunning 2004).
4. The conclusion of a recent IMF study states: "The fairly robust empirical finding is that middle income countries ultimately lose about 45-65 cents of total revenue for each dollar of lost trade tax revenue. Low income countries, more starkly still, recover almost nothing: revenue losses from trade liberalization have been permanent." There is also no evidence that the introduction of value-added tax has in itself made it easier to cope with the revenue effects of trade liberalization (Baunsgaard and Keen 2005).
5. This part of the "resource curse" theme (Auty 1995; McFerson 2009; Ross 1999; Wantchekon 1999). Of course, the "resource curse" thesis about either aid or rents from minerals is not deterministic but merely suggests the high probability of "bad governance" in rentier

economies. A number of countries have remained democratic while being resource-rich. Australia, Botswana, Norway, and the United States are often cited as examples. Similarly, properly designed aid programs need not undermine democratic accountability.

6. Mick Moore goes as far as to suggest it is this aid nexus that accounts for the "bad governance in the developing countries":

> The more specific argument is that political underdevelopment stems to a large degree from what might be termed a "disconnect" between states and citizens. Compared with the states of the rich world, those of the poor world tend to be relatively independent of their citizens: to have autonomous sources of finance and other critical resources; and/or be able to use international connections and resources to rule over their citizens in a relatively unrestrained fashion. In poorer countries, public authority has been constructed in a context in which there has been less bargaining between states and (organized) citizens than has been the norm during the process of state construction in the North. In the South, state elites have more often either ignored their citizens or related to them more coercively—and have been able to do so because of the resources and support they (state elites) could garner from their relations with other states, the international state system and international markets (Moore 2001: 387).

7. The failure of donor community to treat Chad's oil revenue as if it were aid clearly suggests the differences between political economy aid and mineral rents.

8. The World Bank captures this difference in the following passage that is worth quoting at length:

> Aid differs in important ways from domestically financed services. The beneficiaries and financiers are not just

distinct—they live in different countries, with different political constituencies. This geographical and political separation—between beneficiaries in the recipient country and taxpayers in the donor country—breaks the normal performance feedback loop in service delivery. . . . For example, beneficiaries in a recipient country may be able to observe the performance of aid agencies. But they cannot reward or punish the policymakers responsible for this performance in donor countries. The broken feedback loop induces greater incentive biases in aid than in domestic programs. So aid effectiveness is determined not only by the performance of the recipient but also by the incentives embedded in the institutional environment of aid agencies. Understanding these incentives is central to any reform of aid to support service delivery better.

The divergence and distance between constituencies and clients may be important—but there is more. Even if donor constituencies adopted client feedback as a paramount criterion for aid, there would still be difficulties in exercising external influence without undermining local accountability relationships. To illustrate the inherent problem of external actors, consider enterprise finance. When financiers or venture capitalists want to influence an enterprise they are investing in, they become an equity holder and perhaps request a seat on the company's board. Clearly it would be politically infeasible for donors to request seats in the recipient's cabinet. Yet the influence that donors exercise on the recipient's public spending often resembles that of an equity financier (World Bank 2003: 203-4).

9. This point was made by former U.S. Assistant Secretary of State for African Affairs Herman Cohen, who argued that "the beginning of the movement for democratic change in Africa coincided with, and was stimulated mainly by, structural adjustment, which realigned economic power from urban elites to rural populations and the busi-

ness community" (cited in Bienen and Herbst 1996: 35).
10. These views are contradicted by an increasing number of studies of African voters, including those by *Afrobarometer*.
11. Some of the responses (cited in Helleiner 2000) by donors on their understanding of ownership are remarkably candid:

- "Ownership exists when they do what we want them to do but they do so voluntarily."
- "We want them to take ownership. Of course, they must do what we want. If not, they should get their money elsewhere."
- "We have to pressure the local government to take ownership."
- "We have to be realistic. Our taxpayers want to be sure their money is being used well. They want to know there's someone they can trust, a national of their own country, in charge."
- "I routinely instruct my staff to draft terms of reference for technical cooperation projects and then spend half an hour with a local government official on it."

12. Yvove Tsikata, a World Bank official, observes about the ownership on public expenditure review (PER) in Tanzania:

> Although the PER process is driven by mechanisms set up in Tanzania, the country's traditional aid dependence nevertheless tends to elevate the role of the donors in the process. The secretariat of the working groups is, for example, based at the World Bank offices, although the permanent secretary of the finance Ministry chairs the meetings. Comments on the reports related to the exercise are more likely to come from donors other than nationals. Moreover, although the PER is supposed to be a Tanzanian document, it still goes through the review process of the World Bank, leading to inordinate delays. This reduces the legitimacy of the Tanzanian consultative process. In the most recent cycle, the bulk of the work and consultations process

took place in Dar Es Salaam in April-May 2000 but eleven months later the final PER reports was still not available (Tsikata 2003: 43).

13. Howard Stein's account of the process is telling in this respect:

> The pertinent questions, however, given the emphasise by both the Bank and the Fund on ownership, were how the PRSPs were drafted and whether they were actually country driven, with genuine participation by stakeholders. The answer was quite disturbing. Beyond a few hurried hours on Saturday morning, there was no parliamentary participation in the writing of the PRSP. Meanwhile, the Fund and the Bank rejected two drafts presented by the Ministry of Finance before finally accepting the third. Interviews with parliamentary representatives affirmed time and again that none of the views had been reflected in the document. In fact only two sentences in the entire fifty-three-page paper were devoted to the views of Parliament: one indicating simply that they "concurred with the reported findings of the Zonal Workshop . . . and one rather banal comment about the need to consider regional differences (Stein 2008).

14. The role of Zambian labor movements in the struggle for independence and later in democratization easily comes to mind. There are, of course, cases where mineral rents have sustained "labor aristocracies" or, as in the Gulf States, Royalty Associated NGOs (RANGOs). However, in either, the attention of these privileged groups tends to be internal.

15. The independence of these institutions is not designed or intended to enhance democracy and accountability through systems of checks and balances. Rather, as Shapiro notes with respect to the centrality of independent courts in new democracies, this "may have more in common with the popularity of independent banks than with the protection of individual freedoms by functioning as devices that

signal for investors that the capacity of elected officials to interfere in redistributive policy or interfere with property rights will be limited" (Shapiro 2003: 21).

16. As Helleiner notes,

> a remarkably high percentage of bilateral development assistance to low income Africa goes directly to overseas contractors, foreign technical personnel, or to local suppliers, governmental organizations, or even local governmental officials (topping-up their inadequate salaries), without going through any local governmental budgetary system. The local governments frequently have no information on these flows or on the projects they support. Externally supported projects frequently exist as "islands" within the local economy and society, supplying certain services to a select few but otherwise unconnected in any way to indigenous development processes (Helleiner 2000).

17. Much of the evidence of this is derived from cross-country regressions analyses that yield a negative coefficient for the aid variable.
18. One such case has been the introduction by the Malawi government of subsidies for fertilizers. A more common one has been the revision of some of the tax concessions made in mining agreement that governments made under the duress of structural adjustment.
19. Commenting on the new Malawi parliament building financed by China, the Chinese ambassador, Lin Songtian, noted that "this project was a concrete action reflecting the Chinese government's commitment to supporting Malawi in its noble cause of the democratic and human right development" (Anonymous 2010).
20. Over the years donors have blamed African countries for being overzealous in the retrenchment of their civil service, of neglecting infrastructure, of not investing enough in higher education—completely oblivious of the fact these were these were consequences of policies imposed by the donors.

REFERENCES

Aizenman, J., and Y. Jinjarak. "Globalisation and Developing Countries—A Shrinking Tax Base?" *Journal of Development Studies* 45 (May 2009): 653–671.

Alesina, A., and R. Perotti. "The Political Economy of Growth: A Critical Survey of the Recent Literature." *World Bank Economic Review* 8 (September 1994): 351–371.

Anonymous. Chinese Ambassador to Malawi Taking Interview from Malawi National Radio: Forum On China-Africa Cooperation. 2010.

Anyang' Nyongo, P. "Political Instability and the Prospects for Democracy in Africa." *Africa Development* 8 (1988): 71–86.

Armony, A. C. *The Dubious Link: Civic Engagement and Democratization.* Palo Alto: Stanford University Press, 2004.

Auty, R. "Economic Development and the Resource Curse Thesis." *Economic and Political Reform.* Eds. O. Morissey and F. Stewart. New York: St. Martin's Press, 1995.

Bangura, Y. "Authoritarian Rule and Democracy in Africa: A Theoretical Discourse." *Authoritarianism, Democracy and Adjustment: The Politics of Economic Reform in Africa.* Eds. P. Gibbon, Y. Bangura, and A. Ofstad. Uppsala: The Scandinavian Institute of African Studies, 1992.

Bardhan, P. "Symposium on Democracy and Development." *Journal of Economic Perspectives* 7 (Summer 1993): 43–49.

———. "Democracy and Development: A Complex Relationship." *Democracy's Values.* Eds. I. Shapiro and C. Hacker-Cordons. Cambridge: Cambridge University Press, 1999.

Baunsgaard, T., and M. Keen. "Tax Revenue and (or?) Trade Liberalization." Working paper, International Monetary Fund, Washington, D.C, 2005.

Bayart, J. F. *The State in Africa: The Politics of the Belly.* London: Longman, 1993.

Beblawi, H. "The Rentier State in the Arab World." *The Arab State.* Ed. Giacomo Luciani. Berkeley: University of California Press, 1990.

Beuningen, Cor Van. "Democracy and Development." *Development* 50 (2007): 50–55.

Bhagwati, J. *The Economics of Underdeveloped Countries*. London: Weidenfield Nicholson, 1966.

Bhaskar, Utpal. "India, China Build Parliaments for Better Africa Ties." *Livemint.com*, January 19, 2010.

Bienen, H., and J. Herbst. "The Relationship Between Political and Economic Reform in Africa." *Comparative Politics* 29 (October 1996): 23–42.

Boylan, D. "Holding Democracy Hostage: Central Bank Autonomy in the Transition from Authoritarian Rule." Paper presented at the 56th Annual Meeting of Midwest Political Science Association, Chicago, 1998.

Boylan, D. M. *Defusing Democracy: Central Bank Autonomy and the Transition from Authoritarian Rule*. Ann Arbor: University of Michigan Press, 2001.

Bräutigam, D. *Aid Dependence and Governance*. Stockholm: Expert Group on Development Issues, Swedish Ministry of Foreign Affairs, 2000.

———. "Governance, Economy, and Foreign Aid." *Studies in Comparative International Development* 27 (2007): 3–25.

Bresser-Pereira, L. C. "National Development Strategy: The Key Economic Growth Institution." Escola de Economia de Sao Paulo/Fundacao Getulio Vargas, 2003.

Burkhart, R. E., and M. S. Lewis-Beck. "Comparative Democracy: The Economic Development Thesis." *American Political Science Review* 88 (December 1994): 903–911.

Callaghy, T. "Lost Between State and Market: The Politics of Economic Adjustment in Ghana, Zambia, and Nigeria." *Economic Crisis and Policy Choice: The Politics of Adjustment in the Third World*. Ed. J. Nelson. Princeton: Princeton University Press, 1990.

Collier, P. "Learning from Failure: The International Financial Institutions as Agencies of Restraint in Africa." *The Self-Restraining State: Power and Accountability in New Democracies*. Boulder: Lynne Rienner Publishers, 1999: 313–330.

Donnelly, J. "Human Rights, Democracy, and Development." *Human Rights Quarterly* 21 (Summer 1999): 608–632.

Dornbursch, R., and S. Edwards. "The Macroeconomics of Populism." *The Macroeconomics of Populism in Latin America*. Ed. D. A. Edwards. Chicago: University of Chicago Press, 1992.

Dunning, T. "Conditioning the Effects of Aid: Cold War Politics, Donor Credibility, and Democracy in Africa." *International Organization* 58 (April 2004): 409–423.

Easterly, W. R. *The White Man's Burden: Why the West's Efforts to Aid the Rest Have Done so Much Ill and so Little Good*. New York: Penguin, 2006.

Edwards, M., and D. Hulme. "Introduction: NGOs Performance and Accountability." *Beyond the Magic Bullet: NGO Performance and Accountability in the Post–Cold War World*. Eds. M. Edwards and D. Hulme. West Hartford: Kumarian Press, 1996.

Gills, B., and J. Rocamora. "Low Intensity Democracy." *Third World Quarterly* 13 (Summer 1992): 501–523.

Haggard, S., and R. Kaufman. "Economic Adjustment and the Prospects for Democracy." *The Politics of Economic Adjustment: Internatonal Constraints, Distributive Conflicts and the State*. Eds. S. Haggard and R. Kaufman. Princeton: Princeton University Press, 1992a.

———. "The State in the Initiation and Consolidation of Market Oriented Reform." *State and Market in Development: Synergy or Rivalry*. Eds. L. Putterman and D. Rueschemeyer. Boulder: Lynne Rienner, 1992b.

Held, D. "The Transformation of Political Community: Rethinking Democracy in the Context of Globalisation." *Democracy's Edges*. Eds. I. Shapiro and C. Hacker-Cordón. Cambridge: New York: Cambridge University Press, 1999.

Helleiner, G. "Towards Balance in Aid Relationships: External Conditionality, Local Ownership and Development." Paper presented at the Reality of Aid International Advisory committee meeting, Costa Rica, 2000.

Helliwell, J. F. "Empirical Linkages Between Democracy and Economic Growth." *British Journal of Political Science* 24 (1994): 225–248.

Huntington, S. P. *Political Order in Changing Societies*. New Haven: Yale University Press, 1968.

Jelin, E. "Emergent Citizenship or Exclusion? Social Movements and

Non-Governmental Organizations in the 1990s." *Politics, Social Change, and Economic Restructuring in Latin America.* Eds. W. C. Smith and Roberto Patricio Korzeniewicz. Miami: North-South Center, 1997.

Kaldor, M. "Civil Society and Accountability." *Journal of Human Development and Capabilities* 4 (2003): 5–27.

Lal, D. *The Poverty of "Development Economics."* Cambridge: MIT Press, 2000.

Leftwich, A. "Governance, Democracy and Development in the Third World." *Third World Quarterly* 14 (Summer 1993): 605–624.

———. *Democracy and Development.* Ed. A. Leftwich. Cambridge: Cambridge University Press, 1996.

Levy, B. "Are Africa's Economic Reforms Sustainable? Bringing Governance Back In." *Democratic Reform in Africa: Its Impact on Governance and Poverty Alleviation.* Ed. Muna Ndulo. Athens: Ohio University Press, 2006.

Lindberg, S. I. "It's Our Time to 'Chop': Do Elections in Africa Feed Neo-Patrimonialism Rather Than Counter-Act It?" *Democratization* 10 (2003): 121–140.

———. "Accountability: The Core Concept and its Subtypes." Working paper, Africa Power and Politics Programme, Overseas Development Institute, London, 2009.

Linz, J., and A. Stepan. "Toward Consolidated Democracies." *The Changing Nature of Democracy.* Eds. T. Inoguchi, E. Newman and J. Kean. Tokyo: United Nations University Press, 1998.

Lipset, S. M. "Some Social Requisites of Democracy: Economic Development and Political Legitimacy." *American Political Science Review* 53 (March 1959): 69–105.

Maravall, J. M. "The Myth of the Authoritarian Advantage." *Journal of Democracy* 5 (October 1994): 18–31.

Martens, B. "Why do Aid Agencies Exist?" *Reinventing Foreign Aid.* Ed. W. Easterly. Cambridge: MIT Press, 2009.

McFerson, H. M. "Governance and Hyper-corruption in Resource-rich African Countries." *Third World Quarterly* 30 (December 2009): 1529–1547.

Mkandawire, T. "Fiscal Structure, State Contraction and Political Responses in Africa." *Between Liberalisation and Repression: The Politics of Adjustment in Africa*. Eds. T. Mkandawire and A. Olukoshi. Dakar: CODESRIA, 1995.

———. "Crisis Management and the Making of 'Choiceless Democracies' in Africa." *The State, Conflict and Democracy in Africa*. Ed. R. Joseph. Boulder: Lynne Rienner, 1999.

———. Policy Coherence: Trends and Policy Implications for International Development Co-operation. Stockholm, 2001.

———. "Disempowering New Democracies and the Persistence of Poverty." *Globalisation, Poverty and Conflict*. Ed. M. Spoor. Dordrecht: Kluwer Academic Publishers, 2004.

Montecinos, V. "Economic Policy Elites and Democratisation." *Studies in Comparative International Development* 28 (1993): 25–53.

Montinola, G. "When Does Aid Conditionality Work?" *Studies in Comparative International Development* 45 (September 2010): 358–382.

Moore, M. "Death without Taxes: Democracy, State Capacity, and Aid Dependence in the Fourth World." *The Democratic Developmental State: Political and Institutional Design*. Eds. M. Robinson and G. White. Oxford: Oxford University Press, 1998.

———. "Political underdevelopment: What Causes 'Bad Governance.'" *Public Management Review* 3 (September 2001): 385–418.

———. "Taxation, Governance and Poverty: Where Do the Middle Income Countries Fit?" Working paper, Institute of Development Studies, Brighton, United Kingdom, 2004.

Moss, T. J., G. Pettersson, and N. van de Walle. "An Aid-Institutions Paradox? A Review Essay on Aid Dependency and State Building in Sub-Saharan Africa." *Reinventing Foreign Aid*. Ed. W. Easterly. Cambridge: MIT, 2008.

Moyo, D. *Dead Aid: Why Aid Is Not Working and How There is Another Way for Africa*: London: Allen Lane, 2009.

Ndulu, B. *Challenges of African Growth Opportunities, Constraints and Strategic Directions*. Washington, D.C.: World Bank. 2007.

OECD. "Paris Declaration on Aid Effectiveness." 2005 <http://www.oecd.org/dataoecd/12/38/38245246.pdf>.

Olson, M. *Power and Prosperity: Outgrowing Communist and Capitalist Dictatorships*. New York: Basic Books, 2000.

Przeworski, A., and F. Limongi. "Political Regimes and Economic Growth." *Journal of Economic Perspectives* 7 (Summer 1993): 51–71.

Reinikka, R. "Donors and Service Delivery." *Reinventing Foreign Aid*. Ed. W. Easterly. Cambridge: MIT Press, 2009.

Renzio, P. D. "Aid, Budgets and Accountability: A Survey Article." *Development Policy Review* 24 (2006): 627–645.

Ross, M. L. "The Political Economy of the Resource Curse." *World Politics* 51 (January 1999): 297–322.

Ruggie, J. G. "International Regimes, Transactions, and Change: Embedded Liberalism in the Postwar Economic Order." *International Organization* 36 (March 1982): 379–415.

Sen, A. K. *Development as Freedom*. Oxford: Oxford University Press, 1999.

Shapiro, I. *The Shape of Democratic Theory*. Princeton: Princeton University Press, 2003.

Shivji, I. G. "Reflections on NGOs in Tanzania: What We Are, What We Are Not, and What We Ought to Be." *Development in Practice* 14 (August 2004): 689–695.

Stein, H. *Beyond the World Bank Agenda: An Institutional Approach to Development*. Chicago: University of Chicago Press, 2008.

Svenson, J. "Absorption Capacity and Disbursement Constraints." *Reinventing Foreign Aid*. Ed. W. Easterly. Cambridge: MIT Press, 2008.

Therkildsen, O. "Keeping the State Accountable: Is Aid No Better Than Oil?" *IDS Bulletin* 33 (July 2002): 41–49.

Toye, J. "Is There a New Political Economy of Development?" *States or Markets?: Neo-liberalism and the Development Policy Debate*. Eds. C. Colclough and J. Manor. Oxford: Oxford University Press, 1991.

Tsikata, Y. "Owning Economic Reforms: A Comparative Study of Ghana and Tanzania." *Reforming Africa's Institutions: Ownership, Incentives, and Capabilities*. Ed. S. Kayizzi Mugerwa. Tokyo: United Nations University Press, 2003.

Wantchekon, L. Why do Resource Dependent Countries Have Authoritarian Governments? Working paper, Leitner Program in

International and Comparative Political Economy, New Haven, 1999.

Wantchekon, L., and N. Jensen. "Resource Wealth and Political Regimes in Africa." *Comparative Political Studies* 37 (September 2004): 816–841.

Wolgin, J. M. "The Evolution of Economic Policymaking in Africa." *The American Economic Review* 87 (May 1997): 54–57.

World Bank. *Assessing Aid—What Works, What Doesn't, and Why*. Oxford: Oxford University Press, 1998.

———. *World Development Report 2004: Making Services Work for Poor People*. Washington, D.C.: World Bank. 2003.

Yuichi Kono, D., and G. R. Montinola. "Does Foreign Aid Support Autocrats, Democrats, or Both?" *The Journal of Politics* 71 (2009): 704–718.

George B. N. Ayittey
Traditional Institutions and the State of Accountability in Africa

MYTHOLOGY ABOUT TRADITIONAL AFRICA

DURING THE COLONIAL ERA, MYTHOLOGY CLOAKED MUCH ABOUT the institutions and cultures of the African people. They were denigrated as "primitive barbarians," "noble savages" with no history or viable institutions. Colonialism was good for them because it civilized and liberated them from their terrible and despotic rulers.

The source of this mythology was the inability to distinguish between the existence of an institution and different forms of the same institution. The absence of a particular form of an institution was taken to mean a total absence of that institution. Once this distinction is made, it becomes apparent that the European colonialists introduced no new institutions into Africa—only different and more efficient forms of already existing institutions. Consider the institution of money. Money serves as a medium of exchange and store of value. In precolonial Africa, cowry shells, gold dust, salt, cattle, and other commodities served as money. The European colonialists introduced paper currency, a different and efficient form of money. It does not mean they *"invented"* the institution of money. Nor does the fact that there was no paper currency in precolonial Africa mean the natives had no conception of money.

The institution of democracy is another example. Democratic decisions can be taken by majority vote, which is the Western form. It has the advantage of being transparent, fast, and efficient. The downside, however, is that it ignores minority positions and can degenerate into "the tyranny of the majority." The alternative is to make decisions by consensus. This has the advantage of taking all minority positions into account. However, the demerit is that it can take an awfully long time to reach a consensus the larger the number of people involved. Nevertheless, the Nobel Peace Committee and the World Trade Organization (WTO) all make decisions by consensus. So too do many traditional African societies. Again, just because there were no ballot boxes in African villages does not mean African natives had no understanding of the essence of democracy.

These examples can be multiplied a hundredfold to other institutions and concepts: institutions of marriage, markets (precolonial Africa had village markets; the Europeans introduced supermarkets) and articles of governance—accountability, transparency, checks and balances, among others. They are not alien to Africa. Again, just because they are not upheld, practiced, or expressed in Western forms does not mean they were absent in traditional systems of government.

Some of this mythology needs to be cleared up for two principal reasons. First, they may lead people, especially Westerners, to believe that corrupt and despotic regimes imposed upon hundreds of millions of Africans by their modern leaders are "acceptable" to them because it is "part of their culture." Nothing can be farther than the truth. Second and even more tragic is the continual embrace or acceptance of this mythology by the culturally and functionally illiterate African elites who rule much of Africa today. Some ruling elite still cling to the mythology that democracy is "alien" to Africa because the Western form has been absent. They also think that such concepts as "accountability," "transparency," and "rule of law" are foreign to Africa. It is this cultural ignorance that led many postcolonial African leaders to spurn their own cultural heritage and copy and impose upon their people *alien* ideologies and systems. The result of this cultural folly is quite evident: the continent is littered with the putrid carcasses of failed imported systems and explains why many African countries are in crisis.

This essay focuses on accountability. The indigenous form may be different from the Western. Nonetheless, the important fact is traditional African rulers—chiefs and kings—are held accountable for their actions and were removed from office or killed (regicide) for dereliction of duty. By contrast, most modern African leaders cannot be held accountable and commit crimes with impunity.

THE TRADITIONAL SYSTEM OF GOVERNMENT

Despotism is not a new phenomenon. It is a theoretical possibility in any political system that centralizes authority or concentrates power in the hands of a single ruler. It is a construct that has engaged minds since ancient times. In the West, the writings of the classical liberals—John Locke, Alexis de Tocqueville, Thomas Paine, Voltaire, Adam Smith, James Madison, Baruch Spinoza, among others—railed against autocracy and state tyranny.[1] For example, the English philosopher John Locke, often regarded as the "father of Liberalism," established the liberal idea that government acquires consent to rule from the governed, not from supernatural authorities.

The classical liberals saw the state as a necessarily evil. As such, they sought to develop a world free from government intervention, or at least free from too much government intervention. They believed that governments were cumbersome burdens and they wanted governments to stay out of peoples' lives. The American constitution, for example, was founded on the need to limit the powers of the state in order to protect the liberties of the people. The more power the state has, the less freedom its citizens have. Classical liberals also pushed for the expansion of civil rights, free markets, and free trade.

The revolutionaries of the American Revolution (1775-1783) and the French revolution of 1789 used liberal ideas to justify the armed overthrow of tyrannical rule. The American rebellion was against the colonial power, Britain, while the French counterpart was against Louis XVI, an absolute monarch, whose predecessor, Louis XIV, famously declared: "*L'Etat, c'est moi*" (I am the State). On January 17, 1793, Louis XVI was condemned to death for "conspiracy against the public liberty and the general safety" He was guillotined (regicide), the first in a string of executions to follow, including Queen Marie Antoinette, Barnave, Bailly, Brissot, and other leading Girondins, Philippe Égalité, Madame Roland.

It would be preposterous to believe that African natives have never considered the threat of despotism in their history, never had revolutions, and that present-day despotism is "acceptable" to them. Of course, they too had their "John Lockes," "Thomas Paines," "Adam Smiths" and other "classical liberals." They had revolutions too—*kirikiri* in the Yoruba political tradition and *itwika* in the Gikuyu's. However, their works and thinking were not put in print but transmitted through the *oral tradition,* which is a poor means of communication over the ages since it relies on memory. Over time, some facts get mangled or lost forever. It generally starts like this: "Many moons ago . . ." Well, as Mandela noted:

> Then our people lived peacefully, under the democratic rule of their kings. . . . All men were free and equal and this was the foundation of government. Recognition of this general principle found expression in the constitution of the council, variously called *Imbizo*, or *Pitso* or *Kgotla*, which governs the affairs of the tribe. The council (of elders) was so completely democratic that all members of the ethnic group could participate in its deliberations. Chief and subjects, warriors and medicine men, all took part and endeavored to influence its decisions. There was much in such a society that was primitive and insecure, and certainly could never measure up to the demands of the present epoch. *But in such a society are contained the seeds of revolutionary democracy* (1984: 53; emphasis added).

That African natives have considered or encountered the threat of tyranny is evidenced by the way they structured their political systems to deal with this threat. There were two main distinct types of indigenous political organization and further differentiation within each. In the first type, ethnic groups existed as separate political entities and governed themselves independently. Of these groups, some were led by chiefs (states or chiefdoms), such as the Fanti of Ghana, the Yoruba of Nigeria, the Mossi of Burkina Faso, and the Swazi and the Zulu of South Africa. States with such a centralized authority (a chief) surrounded him with councils upon councils to prevent him from abusing his power. For example, without a council of elders, he had no power and could not pass any law.

Other ethnic groups dispensed with centralized authority altogether (stateless or acephalous, tribes without rulers) and governed themselves peacefully. Among them are the Igbo of Nigeria, the Kru of Liberia, the Tallensi of Ghana, the Konkomba of Togoland, the Fulani of Nigeria, the Somali, the Jie of Uganda, and the Mbeere of Kenya. They were the most radical—or perhaps sophisticated—in their political thinking. The French author Jean-Francois Bayart was fascinated by these societies: "The most distinctive contribution of Africa to human history has been precisely in the civilized art of living reasonably peacefully without a state" (1989: 58).

In the second type, some ethnic groups were conquered and came under the hegemony of others in kingdoms and empires. There were also two discernible political systems. The first was an imperial rule that afforded the vassal states extensive local independence or autonomy, as in the Asante and Zande empires of the nineteenth century. This type of indirect rule was the most common. The second type of imperial rule required the vassal states to assimilate an allegedly superior foreign culture. Notable examples of rule by assimilation included the Mandinka, Fulani, Hausa, or, in general, the Islamic empires in the eighteenth and nineteenth centuries in West Africa.

In virtually all the African tribes, political organization of both types began at the village level. The village was made up of various extended families or lineages, each of which had its head, chosen according to its own rules. In general, four basic units of government in African societies governed themselves:

- The chief, the central authority
- The Inner or Privy Council
- The Council of Elders, made up of lineage heads
- The Village Assembly of Commoners or Village Assembly or Village Meeting.

What follows is a brief description of governance in chiefdoms. An extensive discussion can be found in Ayittey (2006), Boama-Wiafe (1993) and others.

Chiefdoms

Chiefdoms or states had all four units of government. The chief was chosen by the Queen Mother of the royal family, the original founders of the settlement, who were reserved the right to provide a ruler for the settlement. His appointment had to be ratified by the Council of Elders. The chief, in most cases a male, was the political, social, judicial, and religious head of the tribe. As such, he had wide-ranging powers in theory but not in practice. He was assisted in governance by a small group of confidential advisers called the Inner or Privy Council. Members were drawn mainly from the inner circle of the chief's relatives, personal friends, and some influential members of the community. The Inner Council served as the first test for legislation as well as a check against despotism. The chief would privately and informally discuss with them all matters relating to the administration of the tribe. He might consult his advisers severally or jointly to form an opinion before bringing an issue to the Council of Elders. If he refused to listen to their advice, they might abandon him.

After the chief had raised an issue with his Inner Council, he would then take it to the Council of Elders for full deliberation. This was a much wider and more formal body comprising all the hereditary heads of lineages; in essence, the Council of Elders represented the commoners. Issues debated might include additional tributes, market tolls, proposed new laws, the declaration of war, and serious quarrels. The chief presided over this council and sought its opinion and advice on administration. The council might even criticize the chief over a particular issue.

Council meetings were open to the public. Routine matters were resolved by acclamation. Complex matters were debated until the council reached unanimity. Generally, the chief did not dictate; he would remain silent and listen to the council debate. If the council could not reach unanimity on a contested issue, the chief would call a village assembly to put the issue before the people for debate. The repository of the greatest political power or influence was this Village Assembly of Commoners. These village assemblies were commonplace in virtually all traditional African societies. They were variously called *asetena kese* among the Ashanti of Ghana, *ama-ala* among the Igbo of Nigeria, *shir* among the Somali, *kgotla* among the Tswana of Botswana, *dare* among the Shona of Zimbabwe, *pitso* among the Xhosa, and *ndaba* among the Zulu of South Africa.

At these village meetings, a protocol was observed. The chief would begin by explaining the purpose of the meeting. He would not announce any decision reached in council meetings; he would merely state the facts involved and order discussions to begin. His advisers would open the debate and then be followed by headmen or elders. Then anybody else wishing to speak or ask questions might do so. These deliberations would continue until a consensus was reached. If none was reached, then another meeting might be scheduled. Since consensus was difficult to reach on many issues, the traditional decision-making process is noted for the length of time, sometimes days and even weeks, to reach a verdict. But once reached, everyone, including the chief, was required to abide by it. There was no voting but the decision reached was not imposed by the chief. For lack of a better term, this system may be described as participatory democracy based on consensus.

Kingdoms

Kingdoms, ruled by a monarch, were numerous in Central Africa. They may have been comprised of chiefdoms of people of the same ethnic stock. In fact, several kingdoms were confederations of independent republics of chiefdoms of the same ethnic people—the Ashanti and Ga kingdoms, for example. Other kingdoms did have vassal states composed of people of different ethnicity.

Generally, African natives accepted the king as a necessary evil. He was necessary for the preservation of the social order but a potential danger. He could abuse his powers and be intrusive, trampling on the independence and freedom of his people. To resolve this dilemma, African ethnic groups sought, with various degrees of success, to create some personality hidden from public view but whose awe-inspiring authority could be invoked to maintain order and harmony. The African king was this personality. An understanding of his role requires a brief discourse on African philosophical belief systems.

African natives believe their universe is composed of three elements: the sky, the world, and the earth. The sky is the domain of spirits of both the living and the yet to be born as well as powerful forces: lightning, thunder, rain, drought, etc. The earth is the domain of the dead ancestors, other dead tribesmen and the activities of the living: agriculture, fishing, hunting. The world is populated by the living—the ethnic group and other tribesmen as well. It is therefore the domain of war, peace, trade and relations with other tribes. The universe or cosmos is ordered like one vast equation but organized in a strict orderly manner. Each of the three orders is represented by a god, and the three gods must be in perfect harmony with each other.

The king's primary role is to appease or propitiate the three gods and achieve harmony among them. If the sky god is "angry" there would be thunder, heavy downpours, and flooding. If the earth god is "angry," there would be poor harvests, famine, and barren women. Thus, the king had a precise function and a definite role: to maintain harmony between society and its natural environment or the universe by means of ritual action. Kings of medieval western Europe also had similar duties: to ensure the spiritual welfare of their people by acts of piety; to defend their people against outside enemies; and at home, to safeguard justice and peace. "The forms of kingship might be different:

the content in Africa and Europe was essentially the same" (Davidson, 1970: 193).

To perform his role well, the African king was secluded, his everyday life planned to the minutest detail and loaded with socially useful burdens. The Yoruba king (*Oni*), for example, could only leave his palace under the cover of darkness and he appeared in public only once a year. His life was subject to many ritual taboos and approached only with infinite respect and by designated persons of the court (Smith 1969: 111). In other societies, the king's entire personal behavior was ritually controlled. "His sex life, symbolically fused with his fertility and vigor, might be severely restricted. . . . And his movements were hemmed in by taboos, such as those against touching the soil in fields or seeing a corpse" (Kopytoff 1989: 66). In some ethnic societies, no one could see the king eat; he could not walk in cultivated fields lest the fertility of the soil might be affected. He must not be allowed to die a natural death, for that would affect the power of his sacred "medicines." Among the Suku of Congo, it has been claimed: "When the king drank, those present had to cover their faces while one of the attendants recited proverbs and sayings recapitulating historic events, praising the king for his good deeds and also hinting at those where he had shown himself to be unjust" (Gibb 1965: 460).

Most of these restrictions were designed to reduce the king to an executive nonentity, curtail the discretionary use of political power and confine him to his palace where he would be safely out of people's private lives and business. They served primarily to take the gold out of royal glitter. Thus kingship, totally ritualized, was a symbol, a puffed-up but hollow office that could also serve as a convenient scapegoat if things went wrong. As long as the king was prepared to obey these restrictions, some ethnic groups in fact did not care who the king was or where he came from. To the Goba of Namainga (Central Africa), their "kings, *qua* rootless immigrants, were useful 'slaves'" (Kopytoff 1989: 66). Along the Nile-Zaire divide, some small states requested the Alur people to furnish them with chiefs and kings. In Benin, "the Edo elders were said to have requested the *Oni* of Ife to send them a king" (Kopytoff 1989: 65).

These societies could "borrow" kings because African kings had little or no political role to play. Vansina (1987: 29), who extensively studied the kingdoms of Central Africa, found that "the king's role is small: his participation in the political decision-making process is insignificant." In fact, the king hardly made policy or spoke. He had a spokesperson, called a linguist, through whom he communicated. He hardly decided policy. His advisers and chiefs would determine policies and present them for royal sanction. His role in legislation and execution of policy was severely limited. Most traditional constitutions require the king to delegate almost all of his authority to other leaders and officials. For this reason, most kingdoms are characterized by decentralization of power and delegation of authority (for example, the Ashanti and Ga kingdoms). Custom and tradition set limits to the authority of the king, his cabinet, and advisers.

INDIGENOUS GOVERNANCE: AN ASSESSMENT

Despotism was always a political possibility but not a practical reality in most indigenous African political systems for three reasons. First, kinship was the articulating principle of government. The chief is supposed to be the "father" of the ethnic group, whose primary function is the survival of the group. It does not make sense for the chief to repress his own kinsmen or people. Repression would divide them and even if he does, lineage heads would rise up against him. Second, by sheer force of logic, despotism is incompatible with the traditional form of governance, which is geared toward consultation and reaching decisions by consensus. Despots generally consult no one and make decisions personally. Third, the nature of institutions, checks and balances, and practices are effectively antidespotic.

Checks and Balances

Indigenous African political systems had no written constitutions (neither does Britain) but a variety of checks and balances to guard against despotism and abuse of power. The Barotse (Central African Republic) were apparently terrified of giving away power. As such, every position, according to Gluckman (1965), was balanced by another: the king against his council, ranked members of the council against each other or against their deputies. The leading executive official, the state *ngambela*, also had his own *ngambela*: this deputy or "second" was a councilor holding a permanent title who was specially charged, beyond other councilors, with restraining the state *ngambela* (Davidson 1969: 199).

The Oyo empire of the Niger Delta (Nigeria) also developed an elaborate system of checks and balances. The political system centered around four powerful figures: the *Alafin*, the *Bashorun*, the *Oluwo* and the *Kankafo*. Theoretically, all power came from *Alafin,* who was considered semi-divine.

Next to the *Alafin* was the *Bashorun*, the leader of the *Oyo Mesi* or Council of Notables, made up of seven prominent lineage chiefs of the capital. Furthermore, the councilors held judicial power with the *Alafin* in the capital. But the *Alafin* had no control over the appointment of the councilors since, as chiefs, they were lineage appointed. Thus the *Bashorun*, who dominated the *Oyo Mesi*, had an ultimate check upon the *Alafin*.

The third power in the empire was the *Ogboni,* headed by the *Oluwo*. The *Ogboni* chiefs, like the *Oyo Mesi*, were lineage appointed. They also had judicial functions, but their primary function was the preservation of the Ife oracle, which could accept or reject the *Bashorun's* decision to command the *Alafin*'s suicide. But the *Alafin*'s representative sat on the Ogboni council and his opinion carried considerable weight. Thus, he could use this position to check ambitious *Bashoruns*.

The *Kakanfo* was the field marshal with his 70 war chiefs, the *Eso,* who were expected to be loyal to the *Alafin*. The army was responsible to the *Oyo Mesi,* who appointed and promoted its officers. But wouldn't the *Kakanfo* overthrow the *Oyo Mesi* and seize power? That was not possible, according to Boahen and Webster:

> Civil authority feared the potential power of the *Kakanfo* and in order to isolate him from politics he was usually of humble (slave) origin and was forbidden to enter the capital city. The political system was thus a complex and

delicate balance with checks and counterchecks against concentration of power in one man's hands (1970: 90).

Among the Tutsi of Rwanda, political power was delicately balanced between two constituent bodies to prevent abuse.

> Although the king was theoretically absolute, there were some structural checks and controls on his power. Thus royal power was somewhat limited by the pressures that the influential Nilotic lineages—often holding hereditary offices—were able to exert on the central government. The association within the royal institution itself, of two equally assertive Tutsi groups, the royal *nyiginya* and matri-dynastic patrician also kept a certain precarious balance (Gibbs 1965: 422).

The Oromo employed a different system of checks. According to Melbaa,

> the *chaffe* is the Oromo version of parliament. The *chaffe* assembly was held in the open air in a meadow under the *odaa* (sycamore) tree. The *chaffe* made and declared common laws and was the source of accumulated legal knowledge and customs. In the hierarchy of *Gadaa chaffes*, the assembly of the entire presidium of the ruling *Gadaa* class is the highest body whose decision is final. It is the assembly at which representatives of the entire population come together, at predetermined times, to evaluate, among other things, the work of those in power. If those in power have failed to accomplish what is expected of them the assembly has the power to replace them by another group elected from among the same *Gadaa* class or *Luba*. And this was one of the methods of checking and balancing political power in Oromo society (1988: 13).

CURBS AGAINST DESPOTISM
The King

A despotic African king is an oxymoron. First, African kings had little political role; most of their powers were delegated to subordinate chiefs. The traditional role of kings was spiritual: to maintain harmony or balance among the three cosmological forces—the sky, the world, and the earth. To perform this function, he was secluded in his palace in order to keep his royal fingers out of people's business. Second, he was also cocooned in web of taboos and injunctions against the office of kingship. His daily life and conduct were planned to the minutest detail. Under such circumstances, it is hard to imagine a despotic king. "Almost all [ethnic societies] have institutionalized means to keep him from abusing his power" (Bohannan 1964: 191).

The Asante king might have appeared absolute. "Yet, he had to procure the consent of the chiefs, and the chiefs the consent of the elders, in order to bring about group action" (Carlston 1968: 127). "Akan kings had no right to make peace or war, make laws, or be directly involved in important negotiations such as treaties without the consent of their elders and/or elected representatives" (Boamah-Wiafe 1993: 169). Even in the rigidly controlled Kingdom of Dahomey, Boahen and Webster found that, "Although the king's word was the law of the land yet he was not above the law. Dahomeans like to recount how king Glele was fined for breaking the law" (1970: 108). Vaughan also noted: "In many instances, the dependence upon the rule of law and a respect for law seems to have inhibited ambitious rulers. Nor should it be forgotten that regicide itself was an ultimate check upon the excesses of a king" (1986: 178).

If the king failed to perform his spiritual functions, he was disposed of. The custom stems directly from the belief in the unity of the king and kingdom—the prosperity or failure of either may be regarded as that of both, and a king can thus be held responsible for conditions in the kingdom. Should he be ill or weak, the kingdom will be in danger; or should conditions in the kingdom be bad, then there must also be something wrong with the king. Further, it followed that a change in the person of the king would change conditions in the kingdom (Vaughan 1986: 177).

If any of the three gods became "angry," it would mean the king had not ruled well. Among the Kerebe of northwest Tanzania, "two kings are said to have been deposed in this manner at the beginning of the nineteenth century: Ruhinda, who was unable to prevent an excessive amount of rain from falling, and his successor, Ibanda, who fell victim to an extended period of drought (Packard 1981: 6).

The Junkun of Nigeria believed "kings were supposed to be killed if they broke any of the royal taboos on personal behavior, fell seriously ill, or ruled in time of famine or severe drought: whenever they could no longer be regarded as fit guardians of the 'right and natural'" (Davidson 1970: 201). Among the Serer, "a *Bur* (king) who reached old age was subject to ritual murder because it was believed he could no longer guarantee that cattle and women would remain fertile" (Klein 1968: 13). Similarly, among the Shilluk of Sudan, a sick or old king was to be killed. In other societies, an old king was not killed but revitalized. He would symbolically die, be born again, regain the vigor of his youth and be fit once again to rule. This ritual was found among the Yoruba, Dagomba, Tchamba, Djukon, Igara, Songhai, Wuadai, Hausa of the Gobi, Katsena, and Daoura, the Mbum in Uganda-Rwanda, and in what was ancient Meroe (Diop 1987: 61). Although regicide has been abolished, the belief in the practice generally reflects the existence of an ideological relationship between political authority and the problem of ecological control (Packard 1981: 6).

Regicide, the ultimate form for accountability, has been abolished, so kings are simply dethroned for various reasons. There were various procedures for divestiture. While the Serer ethnic group of Senegal adopted a distinctive drumbeat to signal the end of a king's reign, the Yoruba of Nigeria demanded the king's suicide "by a symbolic gift of parrot's eggs" (Isichei 1977: 71). Several *Asantehene* (Ashanti kings) were deposed in the course of history. Among them were Kofi Kakari in 1874, and Mensa Bonsu, who was removed in 1883 for his avarice and refusal to raise an army and reconquer Gyaman (Boahen and Webster

1970: 128). In modern times, kings are still being dethroned. Such was the case of *Oba* Samuel Aderiyi Adara of the Ode-Ekiti community of Ekiti state in Nigeria:

> The traditional ruler was invited to the community meeting where he was accused of failing in his duty of moving the town forward. But attempts by the monarch to extricate himself from the allegations failed. He was lambasted for not informing the state government of the pathetic socio-economic situation in his domain and asked to vacate the throne for a more progressive minded personality in the town.
>
> While the meeting was still going on, some youths in the town invaded the venue, removed the dress of the traditional ruler, including his royal beads and crown, and chased him out of the town. Shortly after, traditional trees in strategic shrines were cut down, symbolizing the demise of the *Oba*.
>
> The spokesman for the community said it was the collective decision of both the old and young to dethrone the monarch, saying his reign was "disastrous, woeful and sorrowful" (*The Guardian* 2003: 4).

In modern times, the separation of the spiritual role kings from politics has been maintained in most European kingdoms in Norway, Netherlands, and Britain. In Asia, the Thai king also stays out of politics. However, there have been some exceptions—Middle Eastern monarchs and two African kings: King Mohammed VI of Morocco and King Mswati III of Swaziland.

The Chief

Like his counterpart, the king, a despotic chief is a rarity in traditional African political systems, despite his characterization as such in colonial literature (for example, Shaka the Zulu).

History can be written from the viewpoints of three figures: the victor, the vanquished, and a neutral observer. Naturally, African kings and chiefs who put up the fiercest resistance to colonial rule were characterized as "terrible and despotic." But to their people, they were heroes. In fact, chiefs and kings are *expected* to be hostile and act belligerently toward other ethnic groups and foreigners in order to protect their own. They would raid, depopulate, and even enslave other tribesmen. And they did so since they might become victims themselves.

However, early Europeans writers made no distinction between the tribes. To them, it was black African chiefs killing off or selling off their own black people. But it would make no sense for a chief to commit such acts against his own tribesmen. He would be weakening his own tribe for a more powerful neighbor to overrun it. Even in his own kingdom, Shaka could make no decisions of national importance without the *izikhulu*, the highest council of state. Membership of the *izikhulu* was determined primarily by birth (lineage association) as in other African chiefdoms, but political acumen was also considered as well (Guy 1979: 30).

For several reasons, a despotic chief is seldom encountered in the traditional system. First, chieftaincy is a privilege reserved for the descendants of the original founders of the village or settlement—the royal family. The Queen Mother of the royal family appoints the chief, who must descend from the original founders. Without this link to the royal ancestors, no one—even if they wield a bazooka—can declare himself a chief. Since a bad chief brings shame to the royal family, it is the duty of the Queen Mother to scold and reprimand the chief when he errs or, if necessary, recall him. In fact, the chief's fiercest critics are most likely to come from within the royal family since there are often rival claimants to the office, who watch his every move.

Second, when chosen, the chief is publicly admonished and exhorted to obey certain injunctions. Among the Ashanti, the *Okyeame* (linguist) would address the new chief as follows:

Konti, Akwamu, Bokoro, Konton, Asere, Kyidom, Benkum, Twafo, Adonten, Nifa—al the elders say that I should give

you the Stool (the throne).
Do not go after women.
Do not become a drunkard. When we give you advice, listen to it.
Do not gamble.
We do not want you to disclose the origin of your subjects.
We do not want you to abuse us.
We do not want you to be miserly; we do not want one who disregards advice; we do not want you to regard us as fools; we do not want *autocratic* ways; we do not want bullying; we do not like beating. Take the Stool. We bless the Stool and give it to you. The Elders say they give the Stool to you (Busia 1951: 12).

This admonition effectively checks despotic tendencies. After this admonition, the chief-elect thanked the elders and took a solemn oath of office:

I ask your permission to speak the forbidden oath of Thursday. I am the grandson (i.e., descendant) of the Anye Amoampon Tabraku. Today you have elected me.
If I do not govern you as well as my ancestors did,
If I do not listen to the advice of my elders,
If I make war upon them,
If I run away from battle, then I have violated the oath (Busia 1951: 12).

If he violates any of the taboos or his own oath of office, the chief would immediately be removed even though he is appointed to rule for life. Other offenses that could cause removal may include cowardice, chasing women, drunkenness, and refusal to listen to advice or acting autocratically. The potential for removal or threat of impeachment served as an effective deterrent against dictatorial tendencies.

Third, the Inner or Privy Council constituted another line of defense against despotism. Members advise the chief and might desert him if he acts autocratically. The next powerful line of defense is the Council of Elders. Without this council, the chief is powerless. The chief must consult with them at all times in decision making. They criticize the chief and might refuse to work with him if he acts despotically. Or they might ask the Queen Mother to replace him with a new chief. In some ethnic societies, such as the Ashanti, if the Queen Mother fails on three occasions to produce an acceptable chief, she herself would be removed. Olivier pointed out the following:

> Of course, even in those days, there were foolish chiefs, who thought they were brave and could do as they pleased. They did strange things without consulting anybody, such as eating their peoples' cattle, killing without just cause, waging war, and seizing young girls of the tribe. In such cases, when it became evident that the ethnic group was discontented and not likely to tolerate such oppression much longer, the fathers (or advisers) of the ethnic group would hold a great *pitso*, and in the presence of the ethnic group denounce the chief for his wrongdoings, and intimate that some other member of the royal household had been elected to act in his stead. A chief so deposed would be murdered if he remained to contest the position (1969).

Political pressure could also be brought to bear on a despotic chief. There were various commoner associations: age-grades, *asafo companies* (among the Akan), and even secret societies. In Liberia, the *poro*, which means "laws of our ancestors," was most prominent. The chief could not ban these organizations and declare his village to be a "one-party state." Freedom of association and movement were well-nigh accepted right.

If all these lines failed, the ultimate check against despotism was the foot. People might vote with their feet and abandon the chief.

The history of Africa is full of such migrations. Van der Kemp, the first missionary to the Nguni in 1800, gave the following description of the Xhosa chief Ngqika:

> He has counselors who inform him of the sentiments of his people, and his captains admonish him with great freedom and fidelity, when he abuses his authority to such a degree, that there is reason to fear that the nation will show him their displeasure. This is done if he treats the admonition with contempt, not by way of insurrection, or taking up arms against him, but most effectually, by gradual emigration. Some kraals break up, and march towards the borders of the country. They are successively followed by others, and this seldom fails to have the effect wished for (Kendall and Louw 1987: 6).

This process actually took place when Chief Ngqika passed two laws: one forbidding a man with an unfaithful wife to take the life of her seducer, and another making the chief the heir of any of his subjects who died without heirs in their direct line. "Ngqika was forced to retract both these laws when his people demonstrated their disapproval by leaving" (Kendall and Louw 1987: 6).

Traditional African societies did not "vote out" but had institutionalized ways of removing a ruler from office. In some cases, he might avoid such humiliation by accepting responsibility for his failures and abdicating voluntarily. Busia reported such a case among the Aowin people in the western province of Ghana, where a chief had never been destooled (removed) in their history. In 1946, however, all the elders except those who were closely related to the paramount chief concurred that his administration was unsatisfactory and that he should give up his stool. He agreed.

> A public meeting was held at which the Gyasehene, on behalf of the elders, gave the reasons why they had all

agreed to destool (remove) the chief. The chief in reply said he did not wish to be the cause of any disturbance in the State and he was willing to hand over the stool (throne) since all the elders were united against him. The Gyasehene walked up to the chief, took off his sandals so that his feet touched the ground, and declared him thereby destooled (Busia 1951: 37).

Also in 1989, the paramount chief of the Kaffu Bullom chiefdom in northwestern Sierra Leone, Bai Shebora Kombanda II, accepted his failures and abdicated (*African Farmer* 1990: 45). A more recent case occurred in Ghana:

> Citing the need for peace in the Akyem Abuakwa Traditional Area, the Kwabenghene and Gyaasehene, Osabarima Kwakye II, has abdicated his stool. He told the *Daily Graphic* that the standing committee of the traditional council had ordered him in May "to abdicate or else" (*West Africa* 1994: 1186).

The offenses for which chiefs were removed were many. An Asante chief could be destooled if he became blind, or impotent, or suffered from leprosy, madness, or fits, or if his body became disfigured. "Cowardice, theft, adultery, drunkenness, cruelty, extravagance and disobedience to the elders were also grounds on which the ruler could be destooled" (Amoah 1988: 175). Even in modern times, chiefs are still held accountable and corrupt chiefs are destooled in Ghana:

- Nana Karikari Appau II was destooled for the embezzlement of C50,000 ($18,182) land compensation belonging to the entire Oyoko royal family at Okumaning and the signing of a land agreement with an Italian firm, Greenwhich Chemicals Company, involving some 16,000 acres without the consent of the entire family (*Daily Graphic* 1981: 8).

- In 1984 the Adansihene, Nana Kwanti Barima II, was found "guilty of the great oath of Ashanti and destooled" (*West Africa* 1984: 1001).
- Barima Adu-Baah Kyere and his supporters, including the Gyaasehene, fled the village to unknown destination following assassination attempts on them by an irate mob, which besieged the palace, a police source said there had been a dispute between Barima Adu-Baah and section of the people of Osorase over accountability on the village's revenue (*Ghana Drum* 1994: 12).
- Nana Ekwam VIII, Chief of Gomoa Ekwamkrom, was destooled for misappropriating a sum of 780,000 *cedis* ($190,000) (*The Mirror* 1996: 1).

Historically, Africans have brooked little tolerance for corruption. Diop revealed that:

> Ghana probably experienced the reign of a corrupt dynasty between the sixth and eighth centuries. Kati tells of an extremely violent revolt of the masses against it. The members of that dynasty were systematically massacred. In order to wipe it out completely, the rebels went so far as to extract fetuses from the wombs of the royal family (1987: 65).

Good governance is not alien to Africa. As the late Lord Peter Bauer once averred: "Despotism and kleptocracy do not inhere in the nature of African cultures or in the African character; but they are now rife in what was once called British colonial Africa, notably West Africa" (1984: 104).

In the traditional system, the emphasis was on *prevention*. The king was ascribed little or no political role, "imprisoned" in his palace, and hemmed in by a myriad of taboos—all designed to prevent him from abusing his powers. Similarly, the chief is also restrained by taboos. Further, he comes from a royal family to which he cannot bring disrepute. Accordingly, he is admonished, made to swear an oath and surrounded with councils, without which he was powerless. If the king or chief broke any of the taboos, oath of office, or failed to perform his duty, he was dethroned or removed from office. The contrast with the postcolonial leadership could not be more glaring. The likes of Isaiah Afwerki (Eritrea), Idi Amin (Uganda), Samuel Doe (Liberia), Sani Abacha (Nigeria), Robert Mugabe (Zimbabwe), Mengistu Haile Mariam (Ethiopia), Meles Zenawi (Ethiopia), among others, are revolting caricatures of the traditional leadership Africa has known for centuries.

THE POSTCOLONIAL LEADERSHIP

Back in 1958 at the Pan African Congress in Mwanza, Tanzania, the delegates shrilly wailed over the fact that "*the democratic nature of the indigenous institutions of the peoples of West Africa* has been crushed by obnoxious and oppressive laws and regulations, and replaced by autocratic systems of colonial government which are inimical to the wishes of the people of West Africa." It demanded that "the principle of the Four Freedoms (*Freedom of speech, press, association and assembly*) and the Atlantic Charter *be put into practice at once. . . . Democracy must prevail throughout Africa from Senegal to Zanzibar and from Cape to Cairo*" (Langley 1979: 740; emphasis added).

After independence, however, these same pan-Africanists suddenly forgot about those lofty principles and ideals (democracy, the vote, freedom of the press, of assembly, etc.). They never built upon the "*democratic nature of the indigenous institutions of the peoples of Africa.*" Only Botswana did. Instead, the rest copied from abroad alien and lugubrious systems (one-party states) and alien ideologies (socialism, Marxism-Leninism) and imposed them on their people and continued with the *same* repressive rule that occurred under colonialism (Ayittey 1992). In fact, in some countries, they did worse. They stripped the chiefs of their traditional authority and even set out to destroy the indigenous institutions (Ayittey 2006: 342). Africa's postcolonial story is a truculent tale of cultural betrayal.

Most postcolonial African leaders wield *unchecked* power and cannot be held accountable, democratically or legally, for their actions.

Only 16 out of the 54 African countries are democratic and can vote out of office an incompetent head of state. The leadership treats their countries as their own personal property and the national treasury as their private preserve. The rule of law is a farce; bandits are in charge, their victims in jail. Since the bench is packed with their cronies and allies, they can plunder the national treasury and commit flagitious acts of repression with impunity. It is no accident that the richest people in Africa are heads of state and ministers. Former Nigerian President Olusegun Obasanjo once charged that corrupt African leaders have stolen at least $140 billion from their people in the decades since independence (London Independent 2002). More maddening, modern African leaders are above the law and commit acts of inhumanity with impunity. Consider the following:

- According to Mallam Nuhu Ribadu, the former chairman of the Economic and Financial Crimes Commission, Nigeria's military rulers stole "£220 billion ($412 billion) from the time of independence from Britain in 1960 to the return of civilian rule in 1999. We cannot be accurate down to the last figure but that is our projection" (Telegraph 2005). The stolen fortune tallies almost exactly with the £220 billion of Western aid given to Africa between 1960 and 1997. That amounted to six times the American help given to postwar Europe under the Marshall Plan. None of the bandits have been brought to justice to date.
- In May 2005, Ethiopians went to the polls that were blatantly rigged by the regime of Prime Minister Meles Zenawi. When people poured into the streets to protest, security forces opened fire, killing over 400; over 1,000 protestors were tossed into jail. None of the perpetrators of this heinous crime have been held accountable.
- In December 2007, Kenyans voted in an election that was also rigged. Street protests turned violent as politicians stoked ethnic rivalry to "win" the election. Over 1,200 were killed and over 300,000 people displaced. None of the politicians who orchestrated the violence have been held accountable.

▸ In December 2008 in Guinea, Captain Moussa Dadis Camara seized power in a military coup and pledged not to run for the presidency. When he changed his mind, thousands of Guineans packed a stadium to protest his reversal in October 2009. His security forces opened fire, killing at least 150 protesters. In addition, his troops raped a number of the female protesters in broad daylight ("In a Guinea Seized by Violence" 2009).

The litany of abuses is long and the exceptions to this state of governance distressingly few: Benin, Botswana, Ghana, Mali, Mauritius, South Africa, and Tanzania. No traditional African ruler could commit such grotesque abuses and still remain chief or king. As a Ugandan writer, Yusuf Muziransa, complained bitterly: "Many more Africans certainly have been tortured, killed, raped, maimed, and reduced to poverty in the independence era than those that suffered these abuses during all of the colonial period combined" (Muziransa 2010). In fact, if one adds up the number of Africans killed since independence through wars, the total comes to about 18 million (Ayittey 2006: 521). The wars in the Democratic Republic of Congo and Sudan alone have claimed over 9 million lives. The 18-million count is about equal to how many Africa lost through both the West African slave trade, ran by the Europeans and the East African counterpart operated by the Arabs. To many Africans, independence was in name only. One set of masters (white colonialists) was replaced by another set (black neocolonialists), with the oppression and exploitation of the African people continuing unabated.

So rampant have these acts of brutality grown that the international community has been forced to intervene and check them. In 2009, the International Criminal Court (ICC) issued an arrest warrant against Sudan's president, Omar al-Bashir, for the genocide in Darfur. The former president of Liberia, Charles Taylor, an indicted war criminal, is currently facing justice at The Hague. Further, former UN Secretary General Kofi Annan has called for an end to "the culture of impunity" that was responsible for the bloodbath that occurred after Kenya's December 2007 elections, which claimed over 1,200 lives.

Sadly, it is not the leadership alone who spurned their cultural heritage:

> African academics hailed the establishment of Confucius institutes in the continent at a seminar opened on August 12 in Yaounde, the capital of Cameroon, saying the institutions are serving as a bridge of culture and partnership between African and China. A total of 25 Confucius institutes have been opened in 18 African countries (*Xinhua* 2010).

One would have expected them to establish *Ubuntu* or *Majimbo* institutes on the continent.

CONCLUSION

"He who does not know where he came from does not know where he is going" is an old African proverb. Africa is lost because the majority of postcolonial leaders—and unfortunately some academics—do not know where they came from. They spurned their own cultural and indigenous political heritage and imposed alien ones on their people. The results were disastrous. Had they looked, they would have found the ingredients of good governance and successful development embedded in their own indigenous institutions. Said E. F. Kolajo, a writer in South Africa: "The Japanese, Chinese, and Indians still maintain their roots, and they are thriving as nations. Africa embraces foreign cultures at the expense of its own, and this is why nothing seems to work for us" (*New African* 1995: 4). In fact, according to the *Washington Times*,

> Japan's postwar success has demonstrated that modernization does not mean Westernization. Japan has modernized spectacularly, yet remains utterly different from the West. Economic success in Japan has nothing to do with individu-

alism. It is the fruit of sheer discipline—the ability to work in groups and to conform (*Washington Times* 1996: A8).

Guest offered this perspective: "Japan's example should be important for Africa, because it shows that modernization need not mean Westernization. Developing countries need to learn from developed ones, but they do not have to abandon their culture and traditions in the process" (2004: 23).

Africa faces the same challenges today in building a prosperous society. Even here, there is indigenous guidance: *Sankofa*. It literally means, "go back and get it" and is derived from the Akan proverb, "Se wo were fi na wosankofa a yenkyi" ("It is not wrong to go back for that which you have forgotten"). One of the Adinkra symbols for *Sankofa* depicts a mythical bird flying forward with its head turned backward. The egg in its mouth represents the "gems" or knowledge of the past upon which wisdom is based; it also signifies the generation to come that would benefit from that wisdom. The Akan believe that the past illuminates the present and that the search for knowledge is a lifelong process ("African Tradition, Proverbs, and Sankofa" n.d.).

NOTES

1. Classical liberals need not be confused with today's liberals, who, in many Western countries, believe in government solutions or push for the "nanny-state"; in other words, more government intrusion into the economy.

REFERENCES

"African Tradition, Proverbs, and Sankofa." Sweet Chariot: The Story of the Spirituals <http://ctl.du.edu/spirituals/Literature/sankofa.cfm>.

Ayittey, George B. N. *Africa Betrayed*. New York: St. Martin's Press, 1992.

———. *Africa Unchained*. New York: Palgrave/Macmillan, 2005.

———. *Indigenous African Institutions*. Dobbs Ferry, N.Y.: Transnational Publishers, 2006.

Bauer, Peter Lord. *Reality and Rhetoric: Studies in Economics of Development.* Cambridge: Harvard University Press, 1984.

Bayart, Jean-Francois. *L'Etat en Africa.* Paris: Fayard, 1989.

Boahen, A. A., and J. B. Webster. *History of West Africa.* New York: Praeger, 1970.

Boamah-Wiafe, Daniel. *Africa: The Land, People and Cultural Institutions.* Omaha: Wisdom Publications, 1993.

Bohannan, Paul. *Africa and Africans.* New York: The Natural History Press, 1964.

Bohannan, Paul, and George Dalton, eds. *Markets in Africa.* Evanston, Il.: Northwestern University Press, 1962.

Bohannan, Paul, and Laura Bohannan. *Tiv Economy.* London: Longmans, 1968.

Busia, Kofi Abrefa. *The Position of the Chief in the Modern Political System of Ashanti.* London: Oxford University Press, 1951.

Carlston, Kenneth S. *Social Theory and African Tribal Organization.* Urbana: University of Illinois Press. 1968.

Davidson, Basil. *African Kingdoms.* Chicago: Time/Life Books, Inc., 1969.

———.*The African Genius: An Introduction to African Cultural annd Social History.* Boston: Atlantic Monthly Press, 1970.

Diop Cheikh Anta. *Precolonial Black Africa.* Westport, Conn.: Lawrence Hill and Company, 1978.

Gibbs, Jr., James L., ed. *Peoples of Africa.* New York: Holt, Rinehart and Winston, 1965.

Gluckman, Max. *Politics, Law, and Ritual in Tribal Society.* Oxford: Basil Blackwell, 1965.

"In a Guinea Seized by Violence, Women Are Prey." *New York Times,* October 5, 2009.

Kopytoff, Igor, ed. *The African Frontier.* Bloomington: Indiana University Press, 1989.

Langley, J. Ayo, ed. *Ideologies of Liberation in Black Africa, 1856-1970.* London: Rex Collins, 1979.

Mandela, Winnie. *Part Of My Soul Went with Him.* New York: Norton, 1985.

Martin, Phyllis M., and Partrick O'Meara, eds. *Africa*. Bloomington: Indiana University Press, 1986.

Melbaa, Gadaa. *Oromia: An Introduction*. Khartoum, Sudan: Government Printer, 1988.

Olivier, N. J. J. "The Governmental Institutions of the Bantu Peoples of Southern Africa." *Recueils de la Societies Jean Bodin XII*. Bruxelles: Fondation Universitaire de Belgique, 1969.

Smith, Robert S. *Kingdoms of the Yoruba*. London: Methuen, 1988.

Vansina, Jan. *Kingdoms of the Savannah*. Madison: University of Wisconsin Press, 1975.

Vaughan, James H. "Population and Social Organization," in Martin and O'Meara , 1986.

Yusuf Muziransa."The Story of the African Unity Effort." *The Monitor* (July 25, 2010).

Agnès Callamard
Accountability, Transparency, and Freedom of Expression in Africa

IN 2008, ARTICLE 19, THE INTERNATIONAL ORGANIZATION dedicated to free expression, celebrated its twentieth anniversary by publishing research that reviewed the last 20 years' transformation in the fields of freedom of expression, the press, and access to information (ARTICLE 19 2008). The review found that the changes were dramatic, especially in the areas of legal protection for freedom of expression and technological development. This held true for Africa, also. It concluded, however, that the last 20 years had also been characterized by many unfulfilled promises and that, since 2001, year after year, "freedom of expression, the fundamental guarantor of human rights, has been *weakened and eroded in emerging and older democracies alike*" (ARTICLE 19 2008: 12-13).

Two years on and the global setback for human rights has continued (Freedom House 2010), suggesting that the trend identified in the early years of the twenty-first century is not anecdotal or incidental but entrenched and historical in nature. Not unlike a genie no longer in the bottle, the forces unleashed in the aftermath of 9/11 and in financial quarters around the world have spread out to become part and parcel of the global political and economic landscape, including in Africa.

To explore this trend and its implications, this article will first introduce the relevant normative framework and set out the relationship between freedom of expression, including transparency, and accountability. It will then offer an overview of the current state of these issues in Africa, and identify the implications for stronger accountability.

This article will present the profound and real changes that took place in Africa, specifically in the areas of press freedom and free speech, particularly in the 1990s, but will argue that there remain much unfinished business and many unfulfilled promises, including stalled legal reform, limited media pluralism, and a lack of political will to move from the rhetoric of transparency to its reality. It is in this context that a global human rights recession has struck. This article will show that the observed global human rights setback applies with equal force to Africa. The setback has not necessarily been greater in Africa than elsewhere, but neither has it been less visible or less marked. In fact, in an environment characterized by weak political institutions and a nascent, and thus fragile democratization process, it is probable that this setback will take longer to reverse.

ACCOUNTABILITY, FREE EXPRESSION, AND TRANSPARENCY IN THE HUMAN RIGHTS FRAMEWORK

Accountability is a broad term underpinned by many different understandings and applications. From a human rights standpoint, accountability is often juxtaposed with other terms, such as responsibility, duties, or obligations, which are often used in reference to the state although increasingly to nonstate actors as well. Accountability serves similar purposes as do responsibility (and liability), including protecting the rule of law, and paving the way for compensation and satisfaction of victims. But it is also essential to the protection of democratic values (Curtin and Nollkaemper 2005: 9) and key to securing control of public power: "rulers generally dislike being held accountable. Yet they often have reasons to submit to accountability mechanisms. In a democratic or pluralistic system, accountability may be essential to maintaining public confidence.... But we can expect power holders to seek to avoid accountability when they can do so without jeopardizing other goals. . . . To discuss accountability is to discuss power" (Keohane 2005: 2).

States can be made accountable through a wide range of measures: judicial mechanisms such as domestic constitutional and legal courts (including judicial review), and regional and international mechanisms (through regional courts or individual complaints procedures for UN bodies such as the Human Rights Committee); political means by way of voters and elections, and in parliamentarian democracy, also through political parties, the media, and civil society: "Political accountability is an essential characteristic of democratic government in that it refers to the organization of public power in a democratic fashion, that is, in a way that makes the government answerable to the people. It goes hand in hand with good governance, which concerns the exercise of public power in the pursuit of the public good and justice for all" (van Gerven 2005: 229).

Whichever definition of accountability is adopted, there are a number of characteristics beyond discussion. It requires duty bearers and duty holders, a reporting process, a common understanding of what needs to be reported on or against, and consequences for the actions. To be made operational, accountability thus requires providing for the following five questions: 1) Who is accountable? 2) To whom? 3) For what? 4) How (mechanisms of reporting)? and 5) For which consequences?

When applied to states or governments, this operational definition thus becomes: 1) government officials are accountable (elected officials generally); 2) to the people of the country; 3) for abiding by the laws and the constitution and delivering policies in the public interest; 4) these officials are held accountable through elections and domestic, regional, or international law, but also through scrutiny exercised by the parliament, the public, civil society, and the media; 5) the ultimate consequence of a lack of accountability (perceived or real) may be legal (e.g., trials) or political (nonreelection).

Based on this approach, it is clear that state accountability cannot be exercised without a fully functioning parliament and free and fair elections, all of which require respect for freedoms of association and expression, transparency, freedom of information, and freedom of assembly.

State accountability also requires a free and vibrant media able to investigate freely and without fear, report, question, and denounce. It further demands an independent civil society to foster voice and participation, and offer citizens a say in decisions and enhance pluralism.

The centrality of freedom of expression, including press freedom and transparency, to human rights, state accountability and democracy has been highlighted and recognized by international courts and bodies worldwide. At its very first session, in 1946, the UN General Assembly adopted Resolution 59(I), which states: "Freedom of information is a fundamental human right and . . . the touchstone of all the freedoms to which the United Nations is consecrated." This has been echoed by other courts and bodies. For example, the UN Human Rights Committee has said (HRC 1998. para. 10.3) that "the right to freedom of expression is of paramount importance in any democratic society." The European Court of Human Rights has recognized the vital role of freedom of expression as an underpinning of democracy (ECHR 1976, para. 49): "Freedom of expression constitutes one of the essential foundations of [a democratic] society, one of the basic conditions for its progress and for the development of every man."

The African Commission on Human and People's Rights has emphasized with equal force the importance of freedom of expression and the role of the media to human rights and accountability. It has highlighted "the fundamental importance of freedom of expression and information as an individual human right, as a cornerstone of democracy and as a means of ensuring respect for all human rights and freedoms."[1] It has also stressed that "respect for freedom of expression, as well as the right of access to information held by public bodies and companies, will lead to greater public transparency and accountability, as well as to good governance and the strengthening of democracy."

Freedom of Expression and Transparency: The African Perspective and Contribution

Freedom of expression, including the right to access and receive information, is a fundamental human right, central to achieving all human rights, individual freedoms, and meaningful electoral democracies. It not only increases a society's knowledge and provides a sound basis for participation within a society but it can also secure checks on state accountability and thus help to prevent the corruption that thrives on secrecy and closed political environments.

Freedom of expression is guaranteed under Article 19 of the Universal Declaration on Human Rights (UDHR), and also under more or less in similar terms by Article 19 of the International Covenant on Civil and Political Rights (ICCPR): "Everyone has the right to freedom of opinion and expression; this right includes the right to hold opinions without interference and to seek, receive and impart information and ideas through any media regardless of frontiers."

In law and public policy, freedom of expression has been interpreted and understood as including two main dimensions: the right to express one's ideas and the right to receive information and ideas. Article 19 of the ICCPR sees no barrier or separation between the right to seek and receive and the right to impart information (with the former loosely associated with freedom of information and the later with freedom of expression): they are sides of the same coin, and most important, they need each other if a society is to be true to their underlying values and in order that they be fully realized. These rights cannot be divorced, conceptually or legally.

Freedom of expression, including access to information, is protected in all three regional human rights treaties: Article 10 of the European Convention on Human Rights (ECHR), Article 13 of the American Convention on Human Rights, and Article 9 of the African Charter on Human and Peoples' Right.[2] The African Charter has been ratified by all 53 African states.

Under Article 9, the African Charter guarantees every individual the right to receive information and express and disseminate his/her opinions *within the law*. This article is sometimes deemed to include a "claw-back clause": if its use of the term "law" is interpreted to mean any domestic law regardless of its effect, state parties to the charter would be able to negate the rights conferred upon individuals by the charter.

Under international human rights standards, the right to freedom of expression may be restricted in order to protect the rights or reputation of others, and national security, public order *(ordre public)*, or public health or morals, and provided it is "necessary in a democratic society" to do so and it is done by law. This formulation is found in both the ICCPR under Article 19, and in the European Convention on Human Rights. However, the limitations set forth by Article 9 of the African Charter are imprecise and overbroad and would have placed problematic restrictions on freedom of expression, had it not been for subsequent interpretations by the African Commission.

The African Commission on Human and People's Rights (the African Commission) was established by virtue of Article 30 of the African Charter on Human and People's Rights (the African Charter) with the specific mandate to promote human and people's rights and ensure their protection in Africa. Complaints (commonly referred to as communications) can be submitted by individuals, NGOs, or state parties to the African Charter alleging that a state party has violated the rights contained therein.

Over the years, in response to these complaints, the commission has developed jurisprudence on human and people's rights in general, and the right to freedom of expression, including its legitimate restrictions. The jurisprudence function of the African Commission is particularly important given that to date the African Court for Human Rights has not been functional. It has issued only one judgment since its establishment and this was an inadmissibility decision!

One of the key interpretations by the commission has been of the so-called claw-back clauses. Early on it ruled that this provision constituted a reference to international law (not domestic), meaning that the only restrictions that can be enacted by the relevant national authorities are those consistent with state parties' international obligations.

In its very important decision, the commission noted that when in its defense a state claims that it acted in accordance with previously laid down domestic law, such laws should not override constitutional or international human rights standards; they must be consistent with the state's obligations under the charter: permitting state parties to construe charter provisions so that they could be limited or even negated by domestic laws would render the charter meaningless. According to Article 9 (2) of the charter, dissemination of opinions may be restricted by law. This does not mean that national law can set aside the right to express and disseminate one's opinions; this would make the protection of the right to express one's opinions ineffective. To allow national law to have precedence over the international law of the charter would defeat the purpose of the rights and freedoms enshrined in the charter. International human rights standards must always prevail over contradictory national law. Any limitation on the rights of the charter must be in conformity with the provisions of the charter.[3] The commission has also underlined that states could only impose necessary restrictions to rights protected by constitutional or international human rights instruments and that no situation warranted the wholesale violation of human rights.[4]

At its 32nd Ordinary Session held in Banjul, Gambia in October 2002, the African Commission adopted, by resolution, the Declaration of Principles on Freedom of Expression in Africa. The declaration is a result of the combined efforts of many stakeholders working on freedom of expression across the continent. It sets out important benchmarks and elaborates on the precise meaning and scope of the guarantees of freedom of expression laid down under Article 9 of the African Charter.

In particular, the Banjul Declaration states that "1. No one shall be subject to arbitrary interference with his or her freedom of expression. 2. Any restrictions on freedom of expression shall be provided by law, serve a legitimate interest and be necessary and in a democratic society." A similar formulation can be found in the European and American regional human rights treaties.[5]

One of the most important decisions of the African Commission was issued in 2004 when, at its 36th Ordinary Session in Dakar, Senegal, it established a Special Rapporteur of Freedom of Expression in Africa. At the 42nd Ordinary Session, held in Brazzaville, Republic of Congo, the commission renewed the mandate of the Special Rapporteur for two years and extended it to include "Access to Information."

Freedom of expression, including freedom of the press, is also enshrined in New Partnership for Africa's Development (NEPAD) Declaration on Democracy, which commits African governments to "ensure responsible freedom of expression, inclusive of freedom of the press." Media freedom and diversity are among the standards considered by NEPAD's peer review mechanism in assessing a country's commitment to human rights and good governance.

Media Regulation under International Law and African Norms

Freedom of expression also includes freedom of the press, whose legitimate regulation presents specific challenges. The media is an attractive target for control owing to its power to influence public opinion by, for example, reporting critically on government policies and exposing corruption, dishonesty, and mismanagement. The temptation is large for governments to seek to transform the media's role from that of a watchdog to a lapdog by making the work of independent or opposition journalists and publications illegal or impossible.

Article 2 of the ICCPR places an obligation on states to "adopt such legislative or other measures as may be necessary to give effect to the rights recognised by the Covenant." This means that states are required not only to refrain from interfering with rights but are also required to take positive steps to ensure that rights, including freedom of expression, are respected. In effect, governments are under a duty to ensure that citizens have access to diverse and reliable sources of information on topics of interest to them. A crucial aspect of this "positive obligation" is the need to promote pluralism within, and ensure equal access of all to, the media.[6]

In order to promote pluralism and protect the right to freedom of expression, it is imperative that the media be permitted to operate independently of government control. This ensures that the media plays its role as public watchdog and that the public has access to a wide range of opinions, especially on matters of public interest. This has important implications for media regulatory models.

The African Commission has emphasized that for the print media, self-regulation is the best system for promoting high standards in the media (African Declaration 2002: Principle IX). It has also ruled that the payment of prohibitive registration fees as precondition to the registration of newspapers was essentially a restriction on the publication of news media and a violation of freedom of expression.[7]

With regard to the broadcast media, the African Commission has stated that it may be more strictly regulated than print media in order to manage the limited available radio spectrum, but that this regulation should follow strict principles, including (Principle V):

1. States shall encourage a diverse, independent private broadcasting sector. A State monopoly over broadcasting is not compatible with the right to freedom of expression.
2. The broadcast regulatory system shall encourage private and community broadcasting in accordance with the following principles:
    - there shall be equitable allocation of frequencies between private broadcasting uses, both commercial and community;
    - an independent regulatory body shall be responsible for issuing broadcasting licences and for ensuring observance of licence conditions;
    - licensing processes shall be fair and transparent, and shall seek to promote diversity in broadcasting; and
    - community broadcasting shall be promoted given its potential to broaden access by poor and rural communities to the airwaves.

Where self-regulation has demonstrably failed, a public authority may be entrusted with some limited aspects of media regulation, provided it does not function as a quasi-judicial organ and is independent of government control ("Declaration of Principles" 2002, Principle VII):

1. Any public authority that exercises powers in the areas of broadcast or telecommunications regulation should be independent and adequately protected against interference, particularly of a political or economic nature.
2. The appointment process for members of a regulatory body should be open and transparent, involve the participation of civil society, and shall not be controlled by any particular political party.
3. Any public authority that exercises powers in the areas of broadcast or telecommunications should be formally accountable to the public through a multi-party body.

Transparency and the Right to Access Government-Held Information
Despite its importance, there is no consensus on a description of the concept of transparency and there are no legally binding international standards assessing transparency.

The international NGO Transparency International has defined transparency as "a principle that allows those affected by administrative decisions, business transactions or charitable work to know not only the basic facts and figures but also the mechanisms and processes. It is the duty of civil servants, managers, and trustees to act visibly, predictably and understandably." For its part, the Organization for Economic Cooperation and Development (OECD) has argued that transparency consists in making relevant laws and regulations publicly available, notifying concerned parties when laws change, and ensuring uniform administration and application. Yet another approach to transparency emphasizes public consultation and participation. In spite of their differences, all definitions of transparency tend to highlight openness and availability of information, whether applied to trade, finance, markets, or governments.

Particularly important to transparency is thus the ability of everyone to access information held by public authorities or those working on their behalf, and more generally information of public interest. That ability is a human right backed by a number of international and regional standards and jurisprudence, and referred to as the right to information or freedom of information.

In recognition of the importance of Freedom of Information, Principle IV of the Declaration of Principles of Freedom of Expression in Africa states that:

1. Public bodies hold information not for themselves but as custodians of the public good and everyone has a right to access this information, subject only to clearly defined rules established by law.
2. The right to information shall be guaranteed by law in accordance with the following principles:
    ▸ everyone has the right to access information held by public bodies;
    ▸ everyone has the right to access information held by private bodies which is necessary for the exercise or protection of any right;
    ▸ any refusal to disclose information shall be subject to appeal to an independent body and/or the courts;
    ▸ public bodies shall be required, even in the absence of a request, actively to publish important information of significant public interest;
    ▸ no one shall be subject to any sanction for releasing in good faith information on wrongdoing, or that which would disclose a serious threat to health, safety or the environment save where the imposition of sanctions serves a legitimate interest and is necessary in a democratic society; and
    ▸ secrecy laws shall be amended as necessary to comply with freedom of information principles.
3. Everyone has the right to access and update or otherwise correct

their personal information, whether it is held by public or by private bodies.

In April 2009, the European Court of Human Rights explicitly stipulated that Article 10 of the ECHR guarantees the "freedom to receive information" held by public authorities. The same year, the Committee of Ministers of the Council of Europe adopted the European Convention on Access to Official Documents, the first internationally binding instrument that obliges the state parties to guarantee the right to information held by public authorities to everyone, without discrimination on any ground. The European court also stressed that governments have an obligation "not to impede the flow of information" on matters of public concern.

The Inter-American Court of Human Rights recognized the right to information as implicit in the general guarantee of the right to freedom of expression in its decision of September 19, 2006 in the case of *Claude Reyes et al. v. Chile*. On August 7, 2008, the Inter-American Juridical Committee, an official body of the Organization of American States, adopted key principles governing the right to information, including recognition of access to information held by public bodies, as a fundamental human right.

In 2010, the Economic Community of West African States (ECOWAS) announced the development of a new protocol to establish regional legal standards for the Right to Information for the 15 countries in ECOWAS. Once the protocol is approved, ECOWAS will recommend that member states adopt legislation putting the standards into national law. To date, none of the countries have adopted comprehensive Right to Information laws. The new protocol will also complement the existing ECOWAS Protocol on Good Governance and Democracy, which reiterates principles of democracy and rule of law. A similar process may be under way in eastern Africa with the East Africa Community (EAC, including Kenya, Uganda, Tanzania, Rwanda, and Burundi), developing an East Africa Bill of Rights.

The growing international consensus that there is a fundamental right to access officially held information is further reflected in the number of opinions and statements made by United Nations and regional bodies.

The United Nations Special Rapporteur developed his commentary on freedom of information in his 2000 annual report to the Commission on Human Rights, noting the fundamental importance of this right not only to democracy and freedom, but also to the right to public participation and to the realization of the right to development (UN Special Rapporteur 2000).

In December 2004, the three special mandates on freedom of expression—the UN Special Rapporteur on Freedom of Opinion and Expression, the Representative on Freedom of the Media of the Organization for Security and Cooperation in Europe, and the Special Rapporteur on Freedom of Expression of the Organization of American States—issued a joint declaration that included the following statement (UN 2004):[8] "the right to access information held by public authorities is a fundamental human right which should be given effect at the national level through comprehensive legislation (for example, Freedom of Information Acts) based on the principle of maximum disclosure, establishing a presumption that all information is accessible subject only to a narrow system of exceptions."

The African Special Rapporteur has commented on freedom of information on multiple occasions, making the adoption of bills on access to information one of the key priorities for the continent. She particularly stated with reference to the role of freedom of information with regard to accountability that, "while Freedom of Information derives its origins from and is interrelated with Freedom of Expression, it occupies a special place in the human rights family, in that without the transparency and accountability of public institutions which constitute a fundamental part of its core elements, the right to express and disseminate opinions for the purpose of ensuring good governance and strengthening democracy cannot be enjoyed in its totality."[9]

PROGRESSES AND SETBACKS FOR STATE ACCOUNTABILITY IN AFRICA

The 1990s: Overall Progress Toward Greater Respect for Freedom of Expression

The first aspect to highlight is that with a few exceptions, there has been clear progress in the 1990s throughout most of Africa toward greater respect for freedom of expression, including freedom of the media.

This progress was particularly marked in the following areas:

- *Electoral politics:* The principle of competition for political power through multiparty elections has become the norm, replacing many one-party states and military dictatorships.
- *Constitutional recognition:* Constitutional protections of freedom of expression and the media are heeded and respected to a greater degree than was the case in the 1970s and 1980s (although a plethora of laws, some dating to the colonial period, are still on the statute books). Indeed, most African constitutions seek, to varying degrees, to protect freedom of expression and of the media.
- *Private ownership*: In the past the major means by which freedom of expression is exercised—the media—were often owned and controlled by non-democratic governments. In particular, broadcasting was almost always a state monopoly and private and community broadcasting were either restricted or simply not allowed. This is no longer the case. The dominance of state ownership across Africa's broadcasting sector has been loosened and privately-owned radio and television stations as well as community-owned media are emerging. Privately-owned print media have also developed and compete for readers and advertisers with state-owned and government-controlled newspapers. Countries in Africa without independent radio or television are now few and far between: Eritrea has neither independent radio nor independent TV, while Gambia, Mauritania, Guinea, and Ethiopia have no independent TV. Mali has a continental channel but it only relays

programs from other African TV outlets, while Nigeria has plenty of television outlets at the state level but the law does not allow them to have nationwide coverage.

▸ *Emerging media pluralism*: Media pluralism has led to the emergence not only of independent media outlets but also to avenues for critical voices with alternative viewpoints within society to express themselves. There has been a clear opening up of space for a diversity of voices as compared to the situation that prevailed before the 1990s, when the public sphere was restricted by the state and dominated by state-owned media (ARTICLE 19 2008).

There are examples of the media playing a key role in enhancing accountability and transparency throughout the continent. For instance, in Kenya it is the media that first reported the Goldenberg scandal (1990s) and the Anglo-Leasing scandal (2004). Similarly, it is investigative papers in Tanzania that brought to light an overpriced radar purchase by the state. In Uganda, it is the media that publicized the scandalous expense associated with the Commonwealth Heads of Governments Meeting, where state resources were pilfered (Maina 2010).

Private radio stations such as *Walfajiri* are playing an important role in helping the Senegalese people to learn about and participate in development issues and decisions. The key to *Walfajiri*'s success is its concentration on providing information in the Wolof language to the disadvantaged urban poor residing in Pikine, Guediewaye, Keur Massarr, Yemeul, and Rufisque. One particular weekly program entitled "Face the Citizenry" has enabled local communities to raise issues such as unemployment, poor housing conditions, flooding, and lack of sanitation directly with public officials, who are asked to respond by revealing what they are doing to tackle such issues. Some local research has shown that increasing media focus on delivering the people's Right to Information has resulted in more demands in the same area for social justice. The government of Senegal has also reacted by creating the National Agency for the Employment of Youths specifically to tackle the

issues raised by media programs, such as Walfajiri and "Face the Citizenry."
- *Technological transformation:* The African subcontinent has experienced an unprecedented uptake of technology, especially mobile telephony. Between 2003 and 2008, the number of cell phone subscriptions in Africa grew from 11 million to 246 million—faster than anywhere else in the world, according to the International Telecommunications Union ("ITU Telecom" 2008). And while less than 3 percent of rural areas in Africa have landline telephone connections, the ITU has estimated that over 40 percent of these areas have cell phone coverage. As mobile technology is increasingly used to access the Internet, the mobile phone revolution in Africa is closing to some degree the digital divide between Africa and the rest of the world.

The Human Rights Setback of the 2000s

Unfortunately, the democratic leap forward that characterized the end of the twentieth century—stimulated by the fall of the Berlin wall and inspired by the release of Nelson Mandela—has suffered many setbacks at the beginning of the twenty-first century. In Africa, too, many of these, although not all, were linked to 9/11 and the subsequent "war on terror" but also to the past decade's financial crisis and economic recession. According to Freedom House's press freedom index, the overall level of press freedom worldwide has dropped for each of the past eight-years, with the most significant declines evident in the Americas and sub-Saharan Africa (Freedom House 2010).

ARTICLE 19 and organizations around the world have also observed an alarming increase in attacks and killings of human rights defenders, impunity for these crimes, and regressive legislation against civil society overall. Such violations have come on top of deepening restrictions on foreign funding available for country-level human rights and democracy initiatives by civil society organizations (CSOs). The year 2010 alone has seen several examples of regressive legislative change, proposed, or enacted in countries such as Ethiopia, Uganda, and Zimbabwe. These laws are narrowing the available space for civic activity and have set poor legal precedents for the remainder of the continent.

In her latest report, made public in May 2010, the Special Rapporteur on Freedom of Expression for Africa, concluded that "we are losing some of the gains that we had made in the enjoyment of the right to freedom of expression and access to information in Africa." She attributes this regression to the adoption of restrictive media legislation that has the potential to limit the capacity of media practitioners and journalists to effectively carry out their functions; the use of restrictive laws to punish/harass journalists and media practitioners who publish articles that are critical to the government; the slow pace of the adoption of access to information laws by state parties; failure by some media practitioners to adhere to professional and ethical standards of journalism; and the lack of responses from some state parties to the African Charter on the recommendations and appeals of the Special Rapporteur ("Special Rapporteur" 2010: 11).

Among these backward steps, taken at the behest and initiative of the state or enabled by its inaction, are stalled legal and regulatory reforms for freedom of expression. Laws, some dating back to the colonial and apartheid eras, continue to undermine constitutional guarantees of freedom of expression and the media in Africa. Security legislation appears to be a particularly popular tool by which to curtail freedom of expression and media freedom. It is used to harass, arrest, and detain media workers, to close media houses, and ban publications. It also has the effect of inducing self-censorship within the media for fear of repression.

To intimidate the media, both governments and powerful figures are also using defamation laws, including criminal defamation and sedition laws. Imprisonment and hefty fines can be imposed upon journalists and media houses convicted under such legislation. Only Ghana and Lesotho have fully decriminalized defamation. According to the latest annual report on imprisonment of journalists by the Committee to Protect Journalists (CPJ), four of the world's ten countries responsible for the nearly two-thirds of all journalists in jail are in Africa: Eritrea (19), Ethiopia (4), Egypt (3), and Tunisia (2) (CPJ 2009).

In almost all African countries, independent regulation of the broadcast media is nonexistent. In some, supposedly independent regulators are undermined by interference from the executive arm of government. Many of their members are appointed for their political allegiance. Governments tend to allocate private and community radio frequencies to individuals on this same basis—aligned to their political persuasion. Often licensing of private broadcasters remains politically controlled even in the context of liberalization of broadcasting and the slow pace of change away from state monopoly of broadcasting. Often such powers are used to stifle press freedom whenever incumbents think that the media paints them in bad light. Examples include the Uganda Broadcasting Council, the Rwanda Media High Council, and the Communications Commission of Kenya (although in the case of Kenya an Independent Media Council was established in 2007, following the passage of a Media Council Law).

The Ghanaian situation is somewhat muddled. Overlapping regulatory bodies fail to deliver transparent and independent regulation, in particular with respect to media licensing. Even in South Africa, the independent regulator exists in a context of limitations from the executive. For example, legal amendments gave the South African Minister of Communications the power to appoint members of the regulatory body.

Too many private broadcasters operate without protection from direct state interference, including under threat of forced closure when their broadcasts tackle issues that are considered politically sensitive. Uganda is a case in point where, at critical moments, including during elections, privately-owned broadcasters have come under direct pressure from state organs. One of the most worrying emerging trends is political ownership of the media, bringing with it negative implications in terms of independence and impartiality.

In many African countries self-censorship—more insidious than external censorship because it results in restrictions beyond those that would be imposed by censors—is a prevalent practice or has become part of journalistic culture.

Further Regression for Freedom of Expression

Over the last few years, legal and regulatory reforms have tended to further restrict protection of freedom of expression, rather than enlarge the already minute space provided for pluralism and diversity.

The Uganda legal framework for the media is symptomatic of many of the problems characterizing media regulation in Africa. Uganda has restrictive laws that regulate media (the Press and Journalist Act) dating to 1995. ARTICLE 19 has criticized this law extensively and intervened in a case at the Supreme Court challenging the "false news" provisions of the Penal Code. The oversight bodies provided by this law, in particular the Council and Disciplinary Committee, lack the necessary independence from government. In February 2010, the government decided to amend the law. However, the new draft does not remove the problems but imposes even further restrictions, such as setting a restrictive licensing system for newspapers and providing for broad restrictions on the content of what may be published. The Ugandan government clamped down on the media during the 2009 Kampala riots, in which 21 people died and many others were injured, by closing down four radio stations and banning open-air public radio debates. One radio station remains closed, while the other three have reopened under stringent editorial conditions. The further deterioration of the situation for press freedom in Uganda was sadly demonstrated in 2010 with the murder of two journalists, Paul Kiggundu and Dickson Ssentongo (ARTICLE 19 2011).

Ethiopia remains one of the countries in Africa with a very restrictive regime for civil and political rights in general. Political freedom is highly controlled by the Ethiopian People's Revolutionary Democratic Front, while media and human rights activities are heavily restricted. The situation facing human rights defenders and journalists has continued to deteriorate since the passing in 2009 of the Proclamation on Charities and Societies and the Proclamation on Antiterrorism. The new regulatory agency established by the Charities and Societies Proclamation froze the bank accounts of the largest independent human rights group. At least six of Ethiopia's most prominent human rights activists fled the country in 2009. In July 2009, the anti-terrorism law was introduced to further restrict democratic dissent. Articles 12 and 14 of the Anti-Terrorism Proclamation give national security intelligence services unfettered powers to search and impound broadcast equipment and force journalists to reveal sources of their stories. The proclamation has been used to threaten with prosecution human rights activists and journalists for any acts deemed to be terrorism under the law's vague definition of the term. The new media code introduced in March 2010 by the National Electoral Board of Ethiopia prevents journalists from interviewing voters, candidates, and observers on the Election Day.

Many journalists have been forced to self-censor while others have fled the country. One of the most recent incidents demonstrates well the extent of the silencing. In May 2010, the Ethiopian magazine *Enku* did not appear on the newsstands as scheduled as police impounded all 10,000 copies before they could be distributed. They also arrested and charged Alemayehu Mahtemework, the magazine publisher and deputy editor and three of his staff with threatening public order for publishing a story that featured the arrest and trial of a well-known pop-singer, Tewodros Kassahun, on April 23, 2010, allegedly for a hit-and-run accident in November 2006. The editor and his staff spent five days in detention before being released. Several journalists also fled in 2009, including the editors of a prominent independent Amharic newspaper, and in February 2010 the government acknowledged that it was jamming Voice of America radio broadcasts.

The situation in Rwanda is another story of deterioration. Rwanda's laws on defamation, genocide ideology, and other restrictive media legislation have ensured an absence of media pluralism and media independence. In the months preceding the 2010 elections, journalists and political opponents have been harassed and intimidated, and two have been killed (Human Rights Watch 2010), while the Rwandan media is operating in an atmosphere of pervasive self-censorship.

Senegal is a particularly striking demonstration of the fragility of the last 20 years' progress. Its 20-point drop in Freedom House's 2010 global survey of press freedom index is the steepest decline in world for the past five years. Government support for media freedom and tolerance for critical or opposing viewpoints has declined considerably while official rhetoric against members of the press has increased. More important, the incidence of both legal and extralegal forms of harassment—including physical attacks against journalists and the closure of media outlets—has risen sharply, leading to a much more restrictive environment for the press (Freedom House 2010).

Even South Africa has witnessed significant setbacks to democracy and free expression. This is particularly highlighted by the Protection of Information Bill currently before parliament and by an African National Congress (ANC) proposal to establish a special tribunal—the Media Appeals Tribunal—that would issue unspecified sanctions for complaints against the press. The bill, meant to replace a law dating from 1982, is reminiscent of apartheid-era regulations in that it would virtually shield the government from the scrutiny of the independent press and criminalize activities essential to the vital public service of investigative journalism. Violations under the proposed law would see journalists facing heavy custodial sentences (CPJ South Africa 2010).

The liberalization of the airwaves and print media that took place in the 1990s may have achieved media pluralism (introducing many more media owners), but it did not necessarily result in media diversity (different media owners offering the widest range of content). As highlighted by ARTICLE 19 in its compilation on Broadcasting Policy and Practice in Africa (2003: 3-4), "private broadcasters entered the broadcasting arena as legitimate commercial activity and [would] operate them according to how they could make money even if it meant just playing popular music or showing popular television programmes imported from abroad with very little news or locally made programs, if any." In fact, the rapid expansion of broadcast media in Africa has highlighted numerous gaps in policy, first among them content regulation, including local content, one of the most sensitive and contentious issues in media regulation (Kariithi 2003: 163).

Broadcasting regulation is further complicated in the 2000s by the development of communication technologies, particularly the mobile phone, both in terms of their vast reach and diverse functions, including their provision of information. In Africa, as in Europe and elsewhere in the world, one of the key concerns this development is raising is the relationship between broadcasting and telecommunication regulations and thus whether these should be brought into one regulatory framework. Regardless of whether Africa opts for one or two regulators, the principle of separation between politicians, government, and regulation will remain fundamental.

Transparency: A Reform Process Hardly Initiated
Nowhere are the unfulfilled promises more clearly demonstrated than in the area of transparency. In fact, "unfinished" is a misnomer: transparency reforms have hardly begun in most of Africa.

Access to information held by public authorities enables citizens to make informed choices and allows them to scrutinize the actions of their government. It is essential to creating a relationship of trust between state bodies and the general public, allowing for transparency and public participation in decision making. Without an individual right to access information, state authorities can control the flow of information, "hiding" material that is damaging to the government and selectively releasing information the government deems appropriate for public consumption only. In such a climate, corruption thrives and human rights violations can remain unchecked.

The rapid growth on the number of such laws worldwide over the past decade highlights the increasing consensus over the importance of the right to access information. States that have recently adopted right to information legislation include Liberia, India, Israel, Jamaica, Japan, Mexico, Pakistan, Peru, South Africa, South Korea, Thailand, Trinidad and Tobago, and the United Kingdom, as well as most of East and Central Europe. These countries join a number of other countries that enacted access laws some time ago, such as Sweden, the United States, Finland, the Netherlands, Australia, and Canada, bringing the total number of states with right to information laws to close to 90. A growing number of intergovernmental bodies, such as the European Union, the UNDP, and the World Bank, have also adopted policies on the right to information.

Unfortunately, the right-to-know revolution of the last twenty years has largely bypassed Africa. Lack of political will on the part of African leaders is largely responsible for the absence of clear progress. The rhetoric of transparency has not been accompanied by the required actions.

South Africa, Zimbabwe, Angola, Uganda, and most recently Liberia are the only countries with access to information legislation. However, many present significant weaknesses and problems. The Zimbabwean legislation lacks the safeguards that would ensure maximum disclosure, and is in practice a law promoting nonaccess. In South Africa the law has rarely been put to use. In Uganda the regulations to implement the law were placed before the cabinet after a delay of four years.

In her latest report, the African Special Rapporteur on Freedom of Expression conducted a survey of the steps taken toward respecting the right to access information throughout the African continent ("Special Rapporteur" 2010). The main finding is that while the right to access to information has been entrenched in the constitutions of many countries in Africa, only a handful of these countries have enacted laws that give effect to this right. Her report also illustrates the fact that the right of access to information in these constitutions is often times lumped together with the right to freedom of expression. Consequently, this has had the potential of watering down the importance of access to information and its cause. In the majority of African countries, the right to information and access to information is restricted by other legislation and exclusions that make it a weak tool for empowering the public. In some countries the authorities have balked and failed to pass the legislation.

Transparency: Further Setback in the Late 2000s
Many countries have had bills on access to information pending adoption for many years ("Special Rapporteur" 2010: 6-10). These include Malawi, Mozambique, Zambia, the DRC, Ethiopia, Kenya, Tanzania, Burkina Faso, Ghana, Nigeria, Sierra Leone, and Algeria, all of which have had a draft bill on access to information pending adoption for at

least the last two years. In Francophone Africa, only Mali, Senegal, and Burkina Faso have initiated processes toward development of access to administrative information legislation.

Others have not even initiated the process toward such legal reforms. Ghana is an interesting example of a country that at the political level has made a decisive break with military and political rule, but seems hesitant to pass strong legislation on the right to information (ARTICLE 19 2008). The only progress made on the Ghanaian bill drafted in 2003 is that it was finally tabled in parliament in February 2010.

In South Africa, a Protection of Information Bill was introduced in 2010 by Security Minister Siyabonga Cwel, which would give officials and state agencies unchecked authority and discretion to classify any public or commercial data as secret, confidential, protected, or sensitive based on vaguely defined "national interest" considerations and without any explanation, according to ARTICLE 19 research and legal experts. National interest would, for instance, include "details of criminal investigations," a definition that risks chilling coverage of public law enforcement and judicial matters. Political appointees overseeing state intelligence agencies would have final say over which information should be classified or not. The bill places the onus on journalists to establish "public interest" (broadly defined as "all those matters that constitute the common good, well-being, or general welfare and protection of the people") to justify declassifying any information. Journalists and others found guilty of unauthorized disclosure of official or classified information could face up to 25 years in jail (CPJ 2010).

The findings of research conducted by the Media Institute for Southern Africa (MISA) between June and August 2010 across nine countries reveal nontransparent and overly secretive public institutions, making it difficult for citizens to access information in their possession and under their control. No more than 4 of 61 institutions surveyed in this research qualified as open and transparent. These findings are not particularly different from a similar study done in 2009 in which secrecy shrouded the operations, budgets, and activities of governments in southern Africa (Media Institute 2010).

The MISA report does highlight one possible positive development since 2009, although with a caveat: the increase in the use of technology by many governments across the region. From 61 institutions surveyed, 49 had functional websites. All government ministries and institutions surveyed in Botswana, Namibia, Tanzania, Swaziland, and Zambia had functional and accessible websites. However, in sub-Saharan Africa, only 3 percent of the population is online ("ITU Telecom" 2008).

Further, as indicated by MISA, while the use of information and communication technologies (ICTs) by many government institutions is commendable, most have failed to maximize them to their fullest potential. Most websites contained "obvious" rather than relevant, critical information that would help citizens make informed decisions or participate in the affairs of government. For instance, not one of the 49 websites surveyed across the region had information on their budgets and expenditure, while most of them had no information on procurement procedures or signed contracts (Media Institute 2010).

Another study testifying to the state of transparency in Africa is the yearly Transparency International corruption perception index. The latest report (TI 2009) highlights serious corruption challenges across the region, with a particular focus on the case of resource-rich countries: despite their potential for generating huge revenues that could increase social development, countries such as Angola, the Democratic Republic of Congo, Guinea, Chad, and Sudan have not been able to translate their wealth into sustainable poverty-reduction programs. Instead, high levels of corruption in the extractive industries consistently contribute to economic stagnation, inequality, and conflict. This is despite many of these countries having adopted the EITI (Extractive Industry Transparency Initiative) framework.

CONCLUSION

Over the last two or three years, two key factors have contributed to a worsening of the landscape for both freedom of expression and accountability in Africa. The first is the global human rights setback, resulting from the economic and banking crises in many countries across the globe, the "war on terror" and its security agenda, and the emergence of a multipolar world with human rights-unfriendly actors such as China exercising an increasingly crucial influence.

The second factor that has triggered a specific continent-wide setback has been the holding of a number of elections across Africa. The widespread manipulation of the competitive electoral processes over the last two years or so has both required and resulted in the curtailment of dissenting voices and independent media reporting. Both journalists and civil society were at the center and the forefront of the repression required to flaw elections results. In its latest report, the Observatory for Human Rights Defenders (2010) notes that

> Defenders were found at the forefront of crackdowns during crisis situations related to contested or flawed elections (Mauritania, Nigeria, Republic of the Congo). Those who denounced postelection violence (Kenya, Zimbabwe) or called for the holding of free elections (Sudan) were assimilated to the opposition and threatened, arrested, attacked or harassed. In other countries, defenders were subjected to campaigns of intimidation ahead of elections (Ethiopia, Rwanda). In Niger, several demonstrations against reforming the constitution to lift presidential term limits were violently repressed by the police and led to arrests of supporters, some of whom were then subjected to judicial harassment. Finally, in the DRC, defenders who had called for respect of democratic principles during an inter-institutional crisis were either threatened, arrested, or threatened with prosecution (Observatory 2010: 15).

Indeed, some of the worse abuses against the political opposition and the media, in Uganda or Ethiopia for instance, are slowly being reversed, now that those in power for several decades have managed to maintain hold of the state.

This is not to argue that there has been no progress in terms of freedom of expression and accountability. Since the 1990s, the trend as far as free expression, transparency, and accountability goes is a positive one and progress has been real. Furthermore, as highlighted in the first section of this article, African institutions (particularly the African Commission) have contributed to the global development of universal norms and standards regarding freedom of expression and accountability. But there remain too many unfinished reforms, particularly in terms of the legal and regulatory framework at the domestic level, and this has contributed to greatly weaken the potentials for stronger and effective state accountability.

The overall absence of independent, transparent, and credible regulation of the media is of specific concern: it highlights well the unwillingness of African governments and others holding some forms of political power to let go of their control over mass media. It also seriously hampers the development of the media and its watchdog function.

According to Norris (2006), the media has three key roles in contributing to democratization and good governance: as a *watchdog over the powerful*, promoting accountability, transparency and public scrutiny; as a *civic forum* for political debate, facilitating informed electoral choices and actions; and as an *agenda-setter* for policymakers, strengthening government responsiveness to, for example, social problems and exclusion. Of these three ideal functions, the first has been the most difficult to achieve in Africa (and elsewhere) because of direct repression, political manipulation and ownership, and/or self-censorship.

Yet another major obstacle to stronger state accountability is the fact that the reforms required to establish and entrench a transparency regime have barely been initiated. Six countries only have adopted access to public information laws and secrecy remains the modus operandi of governments and corporations across the continent.

The challenges ahead to ensure stronger state accountability in Africa remain mutiple and complicated, particularly as the global context is not conducive to progressive reforms and is unlikely to generate many demands or incentives for stronger accountability. More than ever, therefore, civil society activists, the media, and other actors will have to rely on their courage, determination, professionalism, and dynamism to keep watching the powerful, seeking to hold them to account, and also drive the much needed reforms process.

NOTES
1. Resolution on the Declaration of Principles on Freedom of Expression <http://www.achpr.org/english/declarations/declaration_freedom_exp_en.html>.
2. [Banjul] Charter on Human and Peoples' Rights, adopted by the Assembly of Heads of State and Government (AHSG) of the Organization of African Union (OAU) (now African Union - AU) meeting in Nairobi, Kenya on June 26, 1981.
3. See for instance and more recently ARTICLE 19 v. Eritrea <http://www.chr.up.ac.za/index.php/browse-by-institution/achpr-commission/286-eritrea-article-19-v-eritrea-2007-ahrlr-73-achpr-2007-.html>.
4. Communication 102/93 against Nigeria.
5. This formulation has been interpreted by courts and experts around the world as requiring restrictions to meet a strict three-part test: 1) a restriction must indeed pursue the legitimate aim that it claims to pursue; 2) the restriction must be imposed in a democratic framework (either by parliament or pursuant to powers granted by parliament); and 3) the restriction must be "necessary in a democratic society." The word "necessary" must be taken quite literally and means that a restriction must not be merely "useful" or "reasonable." The word "necessary" means that there must be a "pressing social need" for the restriction. The reasons given by the state to justify the restriction must be "relevant and sufficient" and the restriction must be proportionate to the aim pursued.
6. European Court of Human Rights, *Informationsverein Lentia v. Austria*, November 24, 1993, Application Nos. 13914/88, 15041/89, 15717/89, 15779/89 and 17207/90, para. 38 8. Communication 152/96, also against Nigeria.
7. European Court of Human Rights, *Informationsverein Lentia v. Austria*,

November 24, 1993, Application Nos. 13914/88, 15041/89, 15717/89, 15779/89 and 17207/90, para. 38.
8. The African Commission had not yet appointed a special rapporteur at the time. Since 2006, the African Special Rapporteur has been a member of these joint initiatives.
9. African Special Rapporteur on Freedom of Expression, Activity report, presented to the 44th Ordinary Session of the African Commission on Human and Peoples' Rights <http://www.achpr.org/english/Commissioner%27s%20Activity/44th%20OS/Special%20Rapporteurs/Freedom%20of%20expression.pdf>.

REFERENCES

ARTICLE 19. *Broadcasting Policy and Practice in Africa.* 2003<http://www.article19.org/pdfs/publications/africa-broadcasting-policy.pdf>.

———. "Speaking for Free Expression 1987-2007 and Beyond." 2008 <http://www.article19.org/speaking-out>.

———. "Joint Mission Calls on Uganda to Safeguard Free Speech Ahead of 2011 Elections." 2011 <http://www.article19.org/pdfs/press/uganda-joint-mission-calls-on-uganda-to-safeguard-free-speech-ahead-of-2011-.pdf>.

Committee to Protect Journalists (CPJ). "2009 Prison Census." 2009 <http://www.cpj.org/imprisoned/2009.php>.

———. "In South Africa, Legislation Would Restrict Press." 2010 <http://cpj.org/2010/08/in-south-africa-legislation-would-restrict-press.php>.

Curtin, Deirdre, and Andre Nollkaemper. "Conceptualizing Accountability in International and European Law." *Netherlands Yearbook of International Law* 36 (2005): 3-20.

Freedom House. "Freedom of the Press Index." Washington, D.C., 2010 <http://www.freedomhouse.org/emplate.cfm?page=16>.

Human Rights Watch (HRW). "Rwanda: Silencing Dissent Ahead of Elections." New York, 2010.

"ITU Telecom Africa Focuses on a Continent at a Crossroads." ITU, 2008 <http://www.itu.int/newsroom/press_releases/2008/10.html>.

Kariithi, N. "Issues in Local Content of Broadcast in Africa Broadcasting Policy and Practice in Africa." In ARTICLE 19. *Broadcasting Policy and Practice in Africa* <http://www.article19.org/pdfs/publications/africa-broadcasting-policy.pdf>.

Keohane, R. "Abuse of Power, Assessing Accountability in World Politics." *Harvard International Review* 27 (2005): 48-53.

Maina, H. "The Role of the Media in Promoting Good Governance in the Region." Paper presented at the 2nd EAC Conference on Good Governance, Nairobi, Kenya, August 19-20, 2010.

Media Institute for Southern Africa. "Right to Know Day 2010, September 28th" <http://www.misa.org/cgi-bin/viewnews.cgi?category=1&id=1285588675>.

Norris, P. "The Role of the Free Press in Promoting Democratization, Good Governance and Human Development." UNESCO. 2006 <http://www.humanrightsinitiative.org/programs/ai/rti/articles/undp_rti_2006/annex3_background_paper.pdf>.

The Observatory for Human Rights Defenders. "Steadfast in Protest" <http://www.fidh.org/Steadfast-in-Protest,8478>.

"Special Rapporteur on Freedom of Expression and Access to Information in Africa." Report presented to the 47th Ordinary Session of the African Commission on Human and Peoples' Rights, Banjul, The Gambia, May 12-26, 2010.

Transparency International (TI). *Corruption Perceptions Index*. Berlin, 2009.

United Nations. Joint Declaration by the UN Special Rapporteur on Freedom of Opinion and Expression, the OSCE Representative on Freedom of the Media and the OAS Special Rapporteur on Freedom of Expression. 2004 <http://www.article19.org/pdfs/igo-documents/three-mandates-dec-2004.pdf>.

———. Special Rapporteur on Freedom of Expression. "Promotion and Protection of the Right to Freedom of Opinion and Expression." UN Doc. E/CN.4/2000/63. January 18, 2000.

van Gerven, W. "Which Form of Accountable Government for the European Union." *Netherlands Yearbook of international Law* 36 (2005): 227-257.

Clement Eme Adibe
Accountability in Africa and the International Community

IN JUNE 2010, A STUNNING DEVELOPMENT OCCURRED IN RUSSIA. Jean Gregoire Sagbo, an African immigrant from Benin Republic, West Africa, was elected to the 10-member municipal council of Novozavidovo—a city that is about 65 miles north of Moscow (Narizhnaya 2010). Sagbo's election in Russia, a fledgling democracy, provides an immensely significant backdrop to this essay for many reasons. The first is that Sagbo has the distinction of being "the first black to be elected to office in Russia," which has led to his characterization by the Russian media—much to Sagbo's discomfort—as "Russia's Obama." Indeed, as Kristina Narizhnaya has observed: "In a country where racism is entrenched and often violent, Sagbo's election . . . is a milestone" (2010: 11). Second, Sagbo is not just black; he is West African, arguably the regional epicenter of much of the accountability woes in Africa. Third, the reason given by the Novozavidovo electorate for choosing Sagbo over the other contestants in this city of 10,000 inhabitants is refreshingly prescient: "they see in him something equally rare—an *honest politician*" (Narizhnaya 2010: 1; emphasis added).

I am grateful to George Kieh, Chudi Okafor, and reviewers of early drafts of this manuscript for comments and criticisms. I would also like thank the DePaul University Research Council and the College of Liberal Arts and Sciences for research grants that supported a larger project on African conflicts and governance from which this essay derives.

Finally, it is highly unlikely that Sagbo or his fellow white Russian émigré to West Africa could have won an election into a political office in Benin Republic.

To the extent that the extant discourse on accountability is inherently connected to democratic praxis, Sagbo's election in Russia provides a window into the infinite possibilities of linking accountability in Africa to the broader international community. Therefore, this essay shall examine the global context of the increasingly thorny issue of accountability in Africa. My argument is that, contrary to widespread perception that African states suffer from impunity and lack of accountability, African governments have demonstrated a remarkable degree of responsiveness or accountability in their *external* orientation toward the international community while remaining virtually unaccountable to their own citizens. Paradoxically, because of their external economic and political vulnerabilities, African states are more likely to respond to a combination of domestic reforms and external support in two issue-areas that are crucial to generating and sustaining robust demand for political accountability. These are, first, electoral support and a free press, and second, anti-corruption and wealth repatriation. In situating the following analysis within the broader theoretical and historical framework of Africa's political development, I pose the following questions: 1) What exactly is the problem of accountability in Africa? 2) To whom are African governments accountable and why? 3) Is there a role for the international community in fostering accountability in Africa?

CONCEPTUALIZING AND PROBLEMATIZING ACCOUNTABILITY IN AFRICA

The *Merriam-Webster's Collegiate Dictionary* defines accountability as "an obligation or willingness to accept responsibility or to account for one's actions." This is fitting because, as Joy Marie Moncrieffe observed, "concern with public accountability originated in England toward the end of the feudal period, with the commercial classes' insistence that the king account for how their accumulated surpluses were spent" (1998:

389). Over time, the king and his successors would also be required to account for their exercise of political power as good government increasingly became the concern of many citizens. "Accountability, therefore, was and still is defined in terms of responsibility (traditionally limited to that of the governments and public officials to the electorate) and accounting or answering for actions, particularly expenditure" (Moncrieffe 1998: 389). The emphasis on responsibility has been echoed in a rare statement on political accountability by the Southern African Catholic Bishops' Conference, a highly respected assembly of religious leaders with a long tradition of thought on the human condition in relation to all things spiritual and temporal. According to the bishops, "accountability can be broadly defined as a social relationship where an actor (an individual or an agency) feels an obligation to explain and justify his or her conduct to some significant other" (Chawatama 2009: 1). The bishops reasoned that political accountability exists when an individual or corporate body is "subject to another's oversight, direction" in the course of discharging their duties: "In principle, political accountability serves a dual purpose. On the one hand it checks the power of political leaders, preventing them from ruling in an *arbitrary* or abusive manner; and, on the other, it helps to ensure that governments operate effectively and *efficiently*" (Chawatama 2009: 2; emphasis added).

These definitions have the advantage of emphasizing the acceptance of *responsibility* by an actor, typically in the public sphere, as the crucial element of accountability. An actor, by this definition, will accept responsibility willingly or by *force* of obligation. Relying on the willful disposition of an actor to accept responsibility imposes on the public an extremely high faith in human nature that may only be possible in a perfect world of saints. Therefore, in the imperfect human societies that many of us inhabit, especially in the fledgling democracies of developing societies, accountability will depend less on personal will than on a clearly articulated and enforceable set of obligations across many strata of society. For many Africans, political accountability is a very important subject in a continent increasingly characterized by impunity, unbridled self-interest, shrinking public space, unimaginable graft, social injustice, and the resulting lethargic apathy of the masses. It would seem rather natural, therefore, that the demand for accountability today would emerge from Africa or similar social milieu. Instead, notwithstanding the earlier reference to the Southern African Bishops Conference, the accountability agenda in the international system today has been driven primarily by the international development aid agencies and international financial institutions (IFIs), comprising a vast network of Bretton Woods institutions—the World Bank, the International Monetary Fund (IMF), the International Financial Corporation (IFC)—and their regional partners, such as the African Development Bank (ADB) and the Organization for Economic Cooperation and Development (OECD). In a major review of its vast accountability programs in developing countries and the resulting academic literature, Britain's Department for International Development (DFID) provided the following conceptual model of accountability:

> Accountability refers to the nature of a relationship between two parties. A relationship may be characterised as lacking in accountability or highly accountable. In a relationship between two parties, A is accountable to B, if A is obliged to explain and justify her actions to B, and B is able to sanction A if her conduct, or explanation for it, is found to be unsatisfactory. . . . These are the two dimensions of accountability—answerability and enforceability (also called controllability or sanction) —which must exist for there to be real accountability (O'Neill, Foresti, and Hudson 2007: 3).

Not surprisingly, DFID's conception of accountability is strikingly similar to that of the World Bank—the premier global multilateral economic institution, which, like DFID, has far-ranging powers, influence, and leverage in Africa. In a seminal study entitled *Anticorruption in Transition: A Contribution to the Policy Debate*, which examined the problem of corruption in the transitional societies of east and central Europe in the last decade of the twentieth century, the World Bank opined that "political accountability refers to the *constraints* placed on the behavior of public officials by *organizations and constituencies* with the power to apply *sanctions* on them" (2000: 40; emphasis added). "As political accountability increases," the study argued, "the *costs* to public officials of taking decisions that benefit their private interests at the *expense* of the broader public interest also increase." Therefore, "accountability rests largely on the effectiveness of the *sanctions* and the *capacity* of accountability institutions to monitor the actions, decisions, and private interests of public officials" (World Bank 2000: 40; emphasis added).

The bank's definition of political accountability echoes a familiar theme in its theory of development: strong states with effective institutions and manpower are a desideratum in developing societies. It is the role of the international community—defined typically as the World Bank, its sister institutions, nongovernmental organizations, and the development agencies of Western states—to fill the gap through various capacity-building projects and appropriate policy support instruments notwithstanding the political preferences of their client-states (World Bank 1981; Stiglitz 2002). It took the bank more than a decade—from 1981 when the Berg Report was published to the publication of *Governance and Development* in 1992—to seriously consider good governance, or what it labeled an "enabling environment," as a factor in economic development (World Bank 1992; Williams and Young 1994). By that time, the heavy-handedness exhibited by a powerful clique of the World Bank and the IMF's "market fundamentalists" had wreaked significant havoc on the economies and sociopolitical fabric of African societies. An internal study by the bank admitted this much in 2007: "The international community's willful avoidance of governance issues for the previous half-century of development lending undermined aid effectiveness, at best, and, at worst, supported authoritarian regimes which impoverished their countries and repressed their citizens" (Cornett 2007: 1).

Given this theoretical tradition and the World Bank's palpable influence and policy power in Africa and other developing regions of the world, its articulation of political accountability should be taken very seriously. In my view, the bank's definition, as discussed above, has the advantage of enabling us to get at three important issues that are crucial to understanding political accountability and its applicability in various political environments. These are: first, to whom are public officials responsible (or accountable) and, second, who has the powers to sanction public officers in consonance with the principle and practice of political accountability? Third, and finally, should efficiency be the goal of political accountability?

The Object of Accountability

Public officials are primarily responsible to their *citizens* on whose behalf they act. But this notion is new, emerging from and mainly in Western Europe as a distinctive product of the Enlightenment and its accompanying political and economic revolutions. Prior to that development, governments—that organ of society that is constituted to exercise legitimate authority—were accountable to a small clique of individuals who claimed to derive their temporal powers from a higher authority—God—to whom they were accountable (Bellamy 1992; Pierson 2004). That was the case with the ecclesiastical polities of medieval Europe and much of the ancient world and their monarchical/dynastic successors before the dawn of the modern era. According to Marx:

> In early modern Europe, there was only one such form of collective sentiment that had widespread salience among the people, religion. . . . It determined "man's attitude towards the world," providing meaning and cause for all suffering or fortune, life and death, and "the dynamics of

interest." The peasant majority in particular, otherwise *disengaged or isolated from larger social forces*, looked to faith both for salvation and to explain the "organic processes and natural events" on which they were dependent . . . (2003: 36; emphasis added).

In such a society political accountability was simply deferred to God, who is the first and ultimate judge. It is hardly surprising, therefore, that governments at this stage of Europe's political development were, to varying degrees, autocratic, tyrannical, exclusionary, and also egregious violators of human rights (Marx 2003). It is to the credit of Western political theory and praxis, however, that they overcame these shortcomings through a sustained—and by no means peaceful—march toward a democratic society characterized by "a fair system of cooperation" among its varied constituents. Today, according to John Rawls, "in their political thought, and in discussion of political questions, citizens [in the West] do not view the social order as a fixed natural order, or as an institutional hierarchy justified by religious or aristocratic values" (1993: 15). By contrast, the traditional societies of modern-day Africa and the theocratic regimes that abound in the Middle East continue to lay claim to higher authority as the source of their power rather than their citizens. As Samuel Huntington (1993) suggested, this may explain much of the problem of political accountability in these societies.

But it is during the intervening period between the European Enlightenment and the present that the seed of the contemporary problem of accountability in many developing countries was sown. The forcible extension of the European state form into non-Western societies in the nineteenth century produced a mechanized and racially rationalized form of political abuse (Hochschild 1999). In Africa and elsewhere, a militarized state was implanted on heterogeneous populations that subsequently divided colonized societies into two distinct categories of people. The first category encompassed citizens, who were exclusively white, and to whom all the privileges of the Enlightenment—civil rights, economic and social entitlements, for example—were vested. As Mahmood Mamdani has argued: "The history of civil society in Africa is laced with racism . . . for civil society was first and foremost the society of the colons. . . . The rights of free association and free publicity, and eventually of political representation, were the rights of citizens under direct rule" (1996: 19). The contrast between them and the second category of people, the subjects, was sharp and palpable. The former inhabited a "state that was bounded by the rule of law and an associated regime of rights." The latter, the subjects, were exclusively natives and nonwhites, and were denied the privileges of the Enlightenment because they were "indirectly ruled by a customarily organized tribal authority." The subjects inhabited a political space that was characterized by "a regime of extra-economic coercion and administratively driven justice" (Mamdani 1996: 19). In this milieu, governments and their officers were accountable to the European citizens and the colonial "home" government only. Governments and their officials were not accountable to the *subjects* who constituted the vast majority of the population in these societies (Lugard 1965). Desperately poor, effectively marginalized, and systematically traumatized by unspeakable acts of oppression that lasted more than a century, the subject population in the colonized societies of Africa lacked the capacity to hold their governments accountable through elections or sanctions—acts that were deemed treasonable and ipso facto illegal.

It is the sad reality of Africa that when independence came 50 years ago, massive personnel changes occurred that saw the emergence of native, mostly black, public officials presiding over minimally adapted political institutions. No concerted efforts were made before and since independence to change the political culture that could support a new democratic dispensation. The notions of citizenship and equal rights remain bogged down by pre-democratic structures, practices, and thought that have produced "control regimes," with the resulting impunity that have sadly manifested in ethnic hatred, wholesale looting of public funds, idolatry of "big men," systemic mistreatment of women, hero-worshipping of expatriates, genocide, and other predatory behaviors and practices (Lewis 1996; Reno 1998; Hyden 2005; Bates 2008). Put simply, political accountability is not just a function of political institutions per se but political *culture* and ideas as well (Kalu 2004). This has been underscored in a recent policy brief by the Overseas Development Institute (ODI), which "shows that the universal application of an 'accountability blueprint' will not work. Strengthening accountability is fundamentally a political activity, requiring a robust understanding of local politics" (Wild, Foresti, and Harris 2010: 1). It requires, at the minimum, an engagement with culture.

The Powers to Punish
With regard to the second concern—who has the power to sanction public officials—the World Bank's definition of political accountability confers that power on "constituencies" and "organizations," generically conceived. That is hardly helpful, absent any underlying reasoning. For an organization that is renowned for its analytical rigor and precision, such vagueness, if not deliberate, is highly unusual. To the extent that "public" officers are nationally bounded, we can reasonably assume that the responsible constituencies to which the bank refers are national or local. The constituency could also be international, in which case the defining criterion would not be citizenship, which confers exclusive membership, but interest and power, which are, in theory, elastic universal attributes. But, what about organizations? Does the World Bank mean local, national, or international organizations? Given the extraordinary ability of the World Bank and the vast network of Western development agencies to project their power and influence around the world, it would be reasonable to assume that the bank refers to local *and* international organizations as possessing the powers of sanctions for the purpose of effecting political accountability in developing societies. It would be unimaginable, therefore, to think that, as promoters of the agenda of political accountability, the international financial institutions and

development agencies would not seek the powers to enforce political accountability. In fact, a recent critique of accountability practices by development agencies hints at their exercise of enforcement powers and the dangers they pose: "Donor interventions to build more accountable and better governed states have foundered in part because of too little emphasis on country-specific political processes and structures, a failure to recognise that seeking to impose reforms without domestic support won't work, and a lack of realism about what is achievable" (Wild, Foresti, and Harris 2010: 1).

Efficiency and Political Accountability

What emerges from the foregoing analysis is the postulation that political accountability serves two practical purposes. The first, which is political, is that political accountability gives effect to the principle of checks and balances as a bulwark against arbitrary government. The second, which is economic, is that it ensures efficiency in the operation of the *business* of government. While these may be complementary objectives, they are by no means guaranteed. In fact, they may be inherently contradictory in the real world. The record of the involvement of international financial institutions in micromanaging the struggling economies of Latin American and African states between 1980 and 2000 sadly demonstrates that when the business of government is couched in terms of efficiency, it is really about reducing costs or improving the balance sheet of government accounts so they are better able to repay their international debt even though their domestic debts go unpaid. This much was underscored by Joseph Stiglitz in his widely acclaimed critique of the "Washington Consensus": "Looking at the IMF policies . . . , its emphasis on getting foreign creditors repaid rather than helping domestic business remain open becomes more understandable. The IMF may not have become the bill collector of the G-7 [Group of 7], but it clearly worked hard (though not always successfully) to make sure that the G-7 lenders got repaid" (2002: 208).

By contrast, the political purpose of preventing arbitrary government—a political objective par excellence—may be inimical to efficiency by requiring costly obstacles and defenses that end up tying the business of government in knots. Nowhere is this more evident, for instance, than in American system's quintessentially expensive presidential system, which appears to work best in conditions of divided government. The goal here is not necessarily to make governments cheaper in this multinational federalism, but to prevent despotism and political overlordship that is more likely to occur with the concentration of powers in a unitary government. The accompanying decentralization of power in such systems raises the cost of government, thereby rendering them less efficient.

Scholars who have studied the relationship between decentralization and political accountability have found that, methodologically, "countries are penalized for having too many and too big governmental units at LG [local government] level" (Ivanyna and Shah 2010: 6). The point here is that political accountability entails a trade-off. For instance, an emphasis on efficiency may constrain the ability of a government to perform crucial administrative tasks, such as funding national, state, and local legislative bodies, or essentially symbolic yet important nation-building tasks, such as granting paid holidays to workers to celebrate religious observances or victories in international competitions, such as the World Cup or rugby. In other words, it is risky and potentially counterproductive to impose on Africans a model of political accountability that narrowly emphasizes "efficiency" in government as its ultimate goal. Doing so risks losing the profound, even if uneven, gains of the current wave of democratization in Africa and many developing countries if a poorly nuanced notion of political accountability is shoved down the throats of weak societies. In Africa, where structural adjustment programs (SAPs) and the so-called efficiency-laden "developmental state" were pushed vigorously by the Bretton Woods system in decades past, memories of the utter brutality of bureaucratic-authoritarianism without the accompanying fruit of economic growth remain fresh (O'Donnell, Schmitter, and Whitehead 1986). As Moncrieffe has insightfully recalled:

> Developmental state theory . . . minimizes the importance of accountability. For developing democracies, the theory suggests, economic growth is best achieved in contexts where the state is relatively insulated from the demands of varying interest groups; as a corollary, the ideal civil society is one that is crushed or that was weak from its inception. The emphasis, then, is on economic growth, which can be achieved at the expense of accountability (1998: 394).

ACCOUNTABILITY IN AFRICA: WHEN DID THINGS REALLY FALL APART?

The political history of Africa is rich with factual and anecdotal evidence of a long struggle with political accountability. In *When Things Fell Apart*, Bates opined that Africa's postcolonial political elites converted the otherwise accountable democratic institutions they inherited from European colonizers into a well-oiled tyrannical machine that led to the immiseration of millions of their people:

> searching for wealth and power, political elites reconfigured African political institutions, transforming them from multi- to single- or no-party systems. . . . They also narrowed the range of those entitled to political benefits. Rather than political independence serving the collective welfare, then, it instead conferred narrowly circumscribed privileges upon those who won out in the competition for political office (2008: 52).

But, as many scholars have demonstrated, the so-called democratic institutions that were bequeathed to African elites at independence had a pitiful record of political accountability, at least to

Africans (Chabal 2009). This observable gap between the theory and reality of colonial democracy in Africa may have driven Mamdani to the outrageous and unfortunate thesis that "apartheid, usually considered unique to South Africa, is actually the generic form of the colonial state in Africa" (1996: 8). In my view, though, what this debate has not captured adequately is that the well-known tyranny of Africa's political systems was often accompanied by valiant acts of resistance by ordinary citizens and the development of institutions, rituals, and norms that effectively checked arbitrary power well before the advent of colonialism.

The willful destruction of these institutions and practices by colonial administrations, and the subsequent incorporation of traditional tyrants into the new and advanced form of colonial despotism, set the stage for the current crisis of accountability in Africa. In the Yoruba kingdom of precolonial West Africa, for example, a deep-seated republican sentiment helped create a far-reaching measure—royal suicide—as a tool to check the arbitrary tendencies of powerful kings of the legendary Oyo Empire. According to Toyin Falola and Matthew Heaton, "the Oyo Mesi, a non-royal organization that served as the advisory body to the *alafin* [the monarch] . . . had the prerogative to approve of the royal lineage's choice of a new *alafin* and could enact regime change by ordering disgraced or ineffective *alafins* to commit suicide" (2008: 50). Indeed, in the two decades between 1754 and 1774, the Oyo Mesi "secured the suicides of two *alafins*," thereby ensuring the political supremacy of the Oyo Mesi (the people) over the monarchy. European colonization of Yorubaland and much of West Africa a century later dismantled this political institution and proscribed these "barbaric" acts, thereby effectively eliminating a powerful (albeit menacing) symbol and instrument of political accountability that was available to the people. Similarly, in East Africa, the traditional "practice of 'breaking a pot'—a powerful form of curse in the Mount Meru area of northern Tanzania" that served as a means of holding people accountable—is roundly derided as an abominable act of witchcraft (Kelsall 2003). The real tragedy of the destruction of these practices, as Patrick Chabal captured succinctly, was the double jeopardy that African masses now faced:

> the consequence of colonial rule was in this respect to place those Africans who were not part of the emerging political elite in a position of double subjection: "modern" and "traditional." *Modern* in that the colonial state evolved a form of governance that paid little heed to accountability. . . . *Traditional* in that the colonial system also largely removed the accountability mechanisms that had linked chiefs and subjects in pre-colonial Africa (2009: 89–90).

What Africans lost, as a consequence of the colonially engineered process of social decomposition, were two important mechanisms of accountability: vertical and horizontal accountability. The former refers to a people's ability to choose those who govern them, while the latter refers to "the separation of powers (executive, legislative, judiciary) and checks and balances to prevent the abuse" of power (Farrington 2002). Given this vacuum, military coups d'état—like the Oyo Mesi-mandated suicides of the precolonial Yoruba kingdom—emerged in postcolonial Africa as the only seemingly viable means of effecting regime change. As various forms of "control regimes" increasingly held the masses of the people hostage to their ego, their impunity became more pronounced as they ran their national economies to the ground, thereby shattering the dreams and aspirations of generations of Africans (Bates 2008). As Chabal explained it: "Having entrusted their future to their nationalist liberators, ordinary men and women came to realize that they had effectively mortgaged that future to 'modern' elites whom they could scarcely reach, let alone control" (2009: 91). W. Arthur Lewis, who, as Kwame Nkrumah's chief economic adviser, had a front-row seat in the unfolding drama, made the following observations: "The prestige is incredible. Men who claim to be democrats in fact behave like emperors. Personifying the state, they . . . build themselves palaces, bring all other traffic to a standstill when they drive . . . and generally demand to be treated like Egyptian Pharaohs" (quoted in Ogueri II 1973: 281). It quickly became apparent to ordinary Africans that "not only did the politicians fail properly to represent the ordinary men and women who had supported their nationalist campaign, they also appeared increasingly immune to the formal accountability mechanisms enshrined in the new constitutions" (Chabal 2009: 91). From Ghana to Tanzania, Africa's immediate postcolonial multiparty democracies were transformed into one-party states. Even in Kenya, with its rich history of stiff colonial resistance through the Mau Mau, Jennifer Widner observed that a once-thriving multiparty democracy—*harambee*—was reduced in no time to "nyanyo" (*follow the leader*) under the presidency of Daniel arap Moi (Widner 1993).

In response to the malaise, coups d'état became a common phenomenon throughout Africa in the 40-year period between 1960 and 2000 as military regimes came to be perceived as Messianic interventions that represented "the highest . . . stage of African nationalism and nationalist movement" (Ogueri II 1973: 282; Welch 1967). Violent coups toppled elected governments in Congo, Ghana, Nigeria, Uganda, Somalia, Libya, and Sudan, among others. As Kieh and Agbese (2004) demonstrated, when this deadly virus of coups toppled the hitherto stable regimes in Ethiopia and Liberia—the two African countries with the distinction of escaping the scourge of colonialism a century earlier—it set in motion a prolonged period of instability throughout the continent. In some countries, such as Nigeria and Uganda, the military regimes that toppled elected governments precipitated civil crises that culminated in a devastating civil war.

In all, McGowan calculated that the 48 independent states of sub-Saharan Africa experienced a total of 327 coups in "the 46-year period from January 1956 until December 2001" (2003: 339). For their destabilizing effect and violent rage, many of these coups—especially those not initiated and/or sanctioned by Western states—were roundly condemned by the international community as an atavism that offended the conscience of the "civilized" world (Decalo 1990). What was missing in these strong condemnations, however, was any prescription of a viable alternative for effective restraint on the rulers by the people—that is, an effective antidote to impunity. In this lacuna emerged insurgencies or "bush wars" as a means of increasing the personal cost of despotism in Africa. In Uganda, Yoweri Museveni's National Resistance Movement (NRM) waged a "bush war" that made Uganda ungovernable for the military regimes until he seized Kampala and formed his government in 1986. Similarly, Charles Taylor's National Patriotic Front of Liberia (NPFL) mounted a long-running military insurgency against General Samuel Doe's regime in Liberia until his forces took effective control of Monrovia in the mid-1990s. These insurgencies became the symbol of a nonprofessional, no-holds-barred armed insurrection that sent shockwaves throughout Africa's circle of ruling elites (Adibe 1997).

For all their many faults and intolerable abuses, military coups became just about the only available instrument for imposing some measure of restraint and *fear* of accountability on Africa's menacingly rogue regimes. Perhaps the best example of this is the 1979 military coup in Ghana. Here, according to Martin Meredith, "a group of junior officers led by a 32-year-old air force officer, Flight-Lieutenant Jerry Rawlings, seized power and embarked on what was described as a 'house-cleaning exercise.' Eight senior officers, including three former heads of states, were executed by firing squad" (2005: 219). Rawlings would proceed to preside over Ghana's transition to a multiparty democracy more than a decade later under enormous pressure from an increasingly agitated masses and international forces. The pressures resulted from a rapidly deteriorating economy under the stringent conditionalities of the World Bank's famed SAP, as well as the perceived excesses and hypocrisy of his otherwise sanctimonious regime. His signature economic reform policy of privatization had resulted in the sale of many publicly owned companies to private individuals in the mid-1980s. As head of the military junta, Rawlings considered himself to be above the law and was not answerable to his fellow citizens for his actions. But in 1996, when he ran as a presidential candidate in the general elections, Rawlings was forced to respond to long-running criticisms that hitherto state-owned firms had been sold to his cronies at prices that were far below their market value. That was just one of the early signs of "democratic dividend" in Ghana. According to E. Gyimah-Boadi:

> Accountability and transparency got a boost as Rawlings found himself compelled to campaign with utmost seriousness, to defend his record, and to address some of the issues raised by his opponents. For example, he conceded the truth of the widely heard criticism that, at a time of public-sector contraction and general austerity, his cabinet was bloated (1999: 412).

Impressively, Rawlings was also forced to break "his . . . silence toward the domestic press and gave an interview . . . to a privately owned radio station" (Gyimah-Boadi 1999: 412). It also emerged that while ordinary Ghanaians were forced by the regime to endure excruciating economic hardship, Rawlings's wife, Nana Konadu, had treated herself to a U.S. $46,000 jacuzzi that she reportedly installed in her bathroom—an amount that, in the view of a Ghanaian satirist, "could have built a clinic" for rural women whose cause she ostensibly championed (Mensema 2010).

To be sure, as far as financial malfeasance goes in Africa, Mrs. Rawlings's extravagance pales in comparison to Gabonese Omar Bongo's luxury estates in France or the multibillion dollar Swiss bank accounts of General Sani Abacha and other Nigerian super-kleptocrats (Shaxson 2007). Nevertheless, as Lentz observed poignantly, the jacuzzi affair goes to the heart of the paradox and monumental failure of Africa's self-styled revolutionary regimes:

> Interestingly, columnists and readers were quick to draw a parallel between Nana Konadu Rawlings's jacuzzi and the

legendary golden bed with which Krobo Edusei, a minister in the Nkrumah government of the 1960s, adorned his bedroom and which caused quite a stir at the time. . . . President Rawlings, of all people, referred to this golden bed in a recent interview with an American journalist. The luxurious bedstead, he explained, had once occupied his youthful imagination and awakened his sense of justice, ultimately leading to the "revolution" of 1979. Precisely in view of the populist rhetoric of this military coup which brought Rawlings originally to power, the . . . popular outcry about the scandalous presidential jacuzzi is quite understandable (1998: 49–50).

And so, like their European colonial predecessors that purported to bring the fruits of civilization to Africans but systematically violated their dignity instead, African military and revolutionary regimes, such as Rawlings's, which emerged ostensibly to stamp out corruption and right the ship of state ended up abusing the citizens and pushing African societies to the precipice. This phenomenon where victims of injustice, both elites and the masses, inflict even greater injustice on their neighbors and fellow citizens has been aptly captured by Mamdani in *When Victims Become Killers,* which attempts to explain the 1994 Hutu genocide against the Tutsi in Rwanda (2002).

The central paradox is that, while Africa's control regimes are nonchalant about their obligation to be accountable and responsive to their fellow citizens, they are shockingly responsive and accountable to the international community to which they are beholden. They are quick to respond to Western governments, donor agencies, and global multilateral institutions, such as the United Nations, the IMF, and the World Bank. The officials of these agencies at just about any rank have a degree of access to the highest levels of African governments that even the most senior African government officials are routinely denied. Several examples illustrate the partial nature of the political accountability problem in Africa, where governments that are unaccountable to their own citizens turn around to be very responsive to the international community. Throughout the period of the Congo crises in the 1960s and afterward, General Mobutu placed himself at the disposal of American intelligence operatives and dutifully executed their demands with spectacular distinction. He was punctual in attending the many meetings and dinners to which he was invited by the head of the CIA in Congo, and he did Washington's bidding diligently and effectively. According to Larry Devlin who, as CIA station chief in the Congo in the 1960s, got to know General Mobutu and his inner circle very well: "Mobutu provided the United States with what it wanted. He ousted Lumumba . . . and installed a government acceptable to the Western world" (2007: 263). To his own people, however, he was condescending and unaccountable: "Mobutu inherited all the trappings of a parliamentary democracy, but he ruled as a tribal chief, . . . He was not alone in employing this form of government as it was, and still is, used by other African leaders" (Devlin 2007: 263–264).

As African economies declined in the 1980s, many governments summarily ignored the advice of their own seasoned economists and experts only to eagerly accept the policy recommendations of World Bank and IMF experts even though they had questionable applicability to their situation. These governments implemented IMF policies despite the vocal opposition of the vast majority of their citizens. Stiglitz recounts a personal experience he encountered during an official World Bank mission to Morocco in 1998 to assess its privatization policy: "I discussed with villagers and government officials what had gone wrong [with poultry farming]. The answer was simple: *The government had been told by the IMF that it should not be in the business of distributing chicks, so it ceased selling them*" (2002: 55; emphasis added). Such dramatic responsiveness to Westerners, which juxtaposes the deafness of governments to domestic demands, rings true for Africans in Morocco and throughout Africa. When Nigeria's late President Umaru Yar'Adua—a refreshingly modest "servant-leader" in a country teeming with bombastic public personalities—fell seriously ill and left his country in November 2009 to seek medical treatment in Saudi Arabia, he did so without informing his fellow citizens or even his own deputy (Adeniyi 2010). When his visibly agitated fellow citizens demanded to hear from their leader after several months of incommunicado had left a power vacuum that threatened to precipitate yet another round of crises in Africa's most populous and unstable nation, President Yar'Adua hesitated. But when he reluctantly agreed to break his silence after two consecutive months of absence, he did so with a brief telephone interview he granted in January 2010 to the British Broadcasting Corporation (BBC), rather than Nigeria's state-owned media or any of its thriving private media organizations (Tangaza 2010). Sadly, it would be the only communication President Yar'Adua would have with the citizens who elected him before his untimely death in May 2010.

In my view, the crucial challenge here is to explain and remedy "the contempt in which people hold all those that occupy an intermediate position in the hierarchy" of African societies (Etounga-Manguelle 2000: 71). I shall argue in the section that follows that a crucial component of any solution to the problem of political accountability in Africa is the progressive role of the international community in the twenty-first century.

THE INTERNATIONAL COMMUNITY AND POLITICAL ACCOUNTABILITY IN AFRICA

For all its many drawbacks, the external orientation of African states provides a tremendous opportunity for the international community to be creative partners in Africa's struggle for political accountability. Africa's economic, political, diplomatic, and security vulnerabilities create policy elasticity on a scale not seen in other regions of the world. For this reason, I shall outline and examine below how and why international support in the areas of free press and elections, along with anti-corruption and wealth repatriation, will strengthen Africa's efforts to build a self-sustaining process of political accountability.

Culture, Democracy, and a Free Press: The Need for International Support
One of democracy's most enduring attributes is that, compared to other political systems, it is better able to assure change of power without recourse to violence. The new wave of democracy in Africa is the latest attempt to address an ancient dilemma: the delicate relationship between society and government. Writing during the American Revolution in 1776, Thomas Paine argued that "society in every state is a blessing, but government, even in its best state, is but a necessary evil; in its worst state an intolerable one: for when we suffer, or are exposed to the same miseries *by a government*, . . . our calamity is heightened by reflecting that we furnish the means by which we suffer" (1776/1976: 2; emphasis in the original). At the core of the accountability problem in Africa is the unresolved problem of government-society relations. Whereas European and American philosophers devoted enormous amount of time and talent to thinking about the relationship between the government and the people, there is little evidence that African philosophy has engaged this thorny issue with the seriousness and urgency that it deserves.

Throughout much of Africa, the culture of subordination of the individual to a higher authority without a reciprocal expression of the responsibility of authority to the individual abounds. In fact, according to Etounga-Manguelle: "The concept of individual responsibility does not exist in our hyper-centralized traditional structures. In Cameroon, the word 'responsible' translates as 'chief.' Telling peasants that they are all responsible for a group initiative is to tell them therefore that they are all chiefs—which inevitably leads to endless interpersonal conflicts" (2000: 71). While he may have overstated the issue, the point is that, as a general proposition, African children are taught to be beholden to their elders—parents, older siblings, relatives, and just about anybody who is older than the child. That a child has the right to challenge the parent or elders is considered an anathema in the parenting culture of many African societies (Weisner 2000: 141–155). In this cultural milieu, various forms of child abuse are rampant, yet they are rarely acknowledged by society, so authority figures go scot-free and impunity reigns, all in the name of tradition. This value is reproduced and reinforced in schools, religious organizations and, most consequentially, the government. Here, "subordinates consider their superiors to be different—having a right to privilege. Since strength prevails over law, the best way to change a social system is to overthrow those who hold power" (Etounga-Manguelle 2000: 68). Dealing with the various forms of political abuses in Africa will require a dramatic change in culture that will be more hospitable to a democratic dispensation. In its present form, the cultural foundation for political accountability in Africa is weak and, as Etounga-Manguelle has suggested, Africa may well need a "cultural adjustment program" as a precondition for political accountability and economic development (2000: 65).

The problem, however, is whether the emergence of such a culture will precede the emergence of democratic institutions or whether the institutionalization of democracy, even a weak one, will lead to the cultural change envisaged by critics. The preliminary evidence from Africa's new democracies would suggest that the latter appears to be the case. The new democratic dispensation in Africa has created an enabling environment for a serious engagement with culture. African elites have controlled the political vuvuzelas for so long that they barely hear the people they represent, let alone respond to their concerns. As the case of Ghana indicates, it was the inexorable logic of democracy that compelled Jerry Rawlings to face the local media during the 1996 presidential elections. Related to this is the structure of media ownership. State ownership of the media—a common practice throughout Africa—has given unfair advantage to the governing parties and elites, while shutting out the voices of dissent. As Gyimah-Boadi observed in the early years of Ghana's Fourth Republic, "editors of the state-owned newspapers . . . continued to use their positions to propagandize in favor of the NDC government and to spew venom at its perceived opponents" (1999: 421). Over time, this has led to tunnel vision where the president and his inner circle hear only what they want to hear and, on the rare occasion when contradictory information filters through, the bearer of the "bad news," no matter how insignificant, is summarily manhandled. In 2007 the Kenyan first lady, Lucy Kibaki, assaulted a broadcaster because "he had mistakenly introduced [the] first lady by the name of the woman widely alleged to be her love rival" (Allen 2007). Worse still, these infractions occur without any legal consequences for the perpetrators or remedy for the victims. But, as frightful as these incidents are, the very fact that they are reported demonstrates the unstoppable power of democracy to lead to the emergence of a free press and the eventual supremacy of the will of the people. In Kenya, Lucy Kibaki's inexplicable assault on the media helped precipitate a political atmosphere that led to an unprecedented powersharing arrangement between President Mwai Kibaki and the opposition party after his ruling party suffered staggering losses in the aftermath of the December 2007 elections—which many believe he lost.

The significance of these developments is that the strength and survival of democracy in Africa depend on a free press and free elections—two crucial areas where Africa's third democratic wave has shown significant weaknesses. In a recent study conducted by Afrobarometer, researchers found that 82 percent of Africans favored choosing "our leaders . . . through regular, open and honest elections" (Bratton and Logan 2006: 7). However, the study found that a third of the survey's respondents were very concerned about the "quality" of elections in Africa, and that proportion jumped to 65 percent among respondents in Malawi, Nigeria, Zambia, and Zimbabwe. By far the most disturbing finding by Afrobarometer is that "just 47 percent [of respondents] report that elections 'enable voters to remove from office leaders who do not do what the people want'," which means that "Africans have yet to be convinced that competitive [electoral] contests always guarantee the vertical accountability of leaders to the electorate" (Bratton and Logan 2006: 7).

When elections become perfunctory because rulers rig their way to power or refuse outright to vacate offices when they have been defeated, confident that the worst case scenario is that the international community will coerce opposition parties into a redundant powersharing arrangement, the vertical accountability functions of elections are lost to the society. This was precisely what happened in Kenya following the apparent defeat of President Kibaki by opposition candidate Raila Odinga in the 2007 general elections (Rice and Tran 2008). In Zimbabwe, opposition candidate Morgan Tsvangirai was on course to win the 2008 general elections when incumbent President Robert Mugabe stopped the counting of the final ballots and ordered a new election (Mbanga 2008). Not surprisingly, rather than produce policy clarity, these elections generated stagnation and widespread violence in Kenya and Zimbabwe, which then compelled the international community to intervene in ways that created a moral hazard by urging the parties to agree to a tenuous powersharing arrangement. In my view, the international community can and should do more to reverse this trend. Elections are a technical issue and, given Africa's technical deficiencies, electoral assistance should be given to states at a very early stage. This includes training of field officers, election judges and umpires, supply of voting machines and other logistical support. In addition, the fielding of a wide array of local and international teams of election observers or monitors has been shown to deter or reduce the incidence of electoral mischief (Gyimah-Boadi 1999).

By far the most important function of these international election observers is that they help legitimize the outcome of elections. This objective is, however, defeated when elections certified by international observers to be free and fair are set aside by the international community in favor of a transitional powersharing government for the singular purpose of avoiding conflict. This approach to electoral disputes plays into the hands of African big men and their sycophantic supporters. After all they are, according to Collier, "the villains" who created the political accountability problems in the first place (2007: 5). For that reason alone, they should not be allowed by the international community to defeat the "heroes." Quite to the contrary, as Collier would argue, supporting the heroes in this epic struggle for liberation in Africa is the moral and strategic duty of the international community. In this regard, the current deterrent practice of using the International Criminal Court (ICC) and specialized tribunals to try the symbols of impunity in Africa, such as Charles Taylor and the accused war criminals in Rwanda and the Democratic Republic of the Congo, should be extended to the other villains whose disregard for the will of the people constitutes the greatest threat to peace and security in Africa (Darnstädt, Zuber and Puhl 2009).

Fighting Corruption and Repatriating African Wealth

The problem of corruption has been so closely associated to Africa that it has become a kind of ethnic slur, a stigma that has in turn made it unnecessarily difficult to address by encouraging a recourse to political correctness (Sachs 2005: 312–314). Some scholars attribute the developmental deficits of Africa to corruption (Mbaku 1998; Easterly 2002). President Barack Obama made this case quite eloquently when, as U.S. senator, he addressed the issue head-on in Kenya in 2006: "It is painfully obvious that corruption stifles development—it siphons off scarce resources that could improve infrastructure, bolster education systems, and strengthen public health" (2006). As a Western politician with an African father, Obama can afford to be so direct without risking the appearance of being too harsh or patronizing or even worse.

Other scholars, such as Jeffrey Sachs, have cautioned against such association because of the paucity of hard data, arguing that "Africa shows absolutely no tendency to be more or less corrupt than other countries at the same income level. There is no evidence whatsoever that Africa is distinctly poorly governed *by the standards of very poor countries.*" (2005: 312; emphasis in the original). My interest in the problem of corruption derives from its centrality to the problem of political accountability in Africa in four significant ways. First, as President Obama (2006) noted, corruption "erodes the state from the inside out, sickening the justice system until there is no justice to be found, poisoning the police forces until their presence becomes a source of

Table 1: Comparative Data on Illicit Financial Flows and Ibrahim Performance Index

Top 20 Sources of Illicit Financial Flows, 1970-2008	Amount (U.S.$ billion)	Rank in 2009 Ibrahim Governance Index	Top 20 Performers in the 2009 Ibrahim Governance Index	Rank as Source of Illicit Financial Flows
1. Nigeria	89.5	35	1. Mauritius	n.a
2. Egypt	70.4	11	2. Cape Verde	n.a
3. Algeria	25.6	14	3. Seychelles	n.a
4. Morocco	24.9	16	4. Botswana	n.a
5. South Africa	24.8	5	5. South Africa	5
6. Cote d'Ivoire	16.1	47	6. Namibia	n.a
7. DR Congo	14.1	41	7. Ghana	20
8. Sudan	12.8	49	8. Tunisia	10
9. Angola	12.6	42	9. Lesotho	n.a
10. Tunisia	11.7	8	10. Sao Tome and Principe	n.a
11. Cameroon	11.4	33	11. Egypt	2
12. Ethiopia	10.8	37	12. Tanzania	15
13. Gabon	8.1	21	13. Madagascar	17
14. Zimbabwe	6.8	51	14. Algeria	3
15. Tanzania	6.6	12	15. Benin	n.a
16. Zambia	5.8	18	16. Morocco	4
17. Madagascar	5.3	13	17. Senegal	n.a
18. Kenya	5.1	22	18. Zambia	16
19. Mozambique	4.9	26	19. Gambia	n.a
20. Ghana	4.5	7	20. Mali	n.a

Sources: Kar and Cartwright-Smith (2010); Mo Ibrahim Foundation (2010).

insecurity rather than comfort." Second, corruption is tantamount to an egregious violation of trust, thereby weakening social capital, the very essence of the social contract upon which modernity rests. Third, corruption is a dangerous expression of impunity by those who have access to public funds and power against the masses who do not. Fourth, and most significantly, corruption is the principal mechanism of capital flight from Africa as the surest haven for illicit money is typically outside of the society from where it is stolen.

A recent study by the Washington-based group Global Financial Integrity found that, between 1970–2008 "African countries . . . experienced massive outflows of illicit capital mainly to Western financial institutions" to the extent that "the continent as a whole has turned into a net creditor to the world" (Kar and Cartwright-Smith 2010: 10). By illicit capital they mean "money that is illegally earned, transferred, or utilized," money that "breaks laws in its origin, movement, or use" (Kar and Cartwright-Smith 2010: 7). Illicit capital flight occurs through two principal mechanisms: external accounts, which several African countries maintain with Western banks rather than their own cash-strapped banks; and "mispricing of trade transactions" (Kar and Cartwright-Smith 2010: 3). According to Kar and Cartwright-Smith: "Trade misinvoicing has long been recognized as a major conduit for illicit flows. By overpricing imports and underpricing exports on customs documents, residents can illegally transfer money abroad" (2010: 10). The total amount of money lost to Africa through these two sources between 1970 and 2008 is huge: $854 billion—"enough to . . . wipe out the region's total external debt outstanding of around US$250 billion" (Kar and Cartwright-Smith 2010: 10).

An interpretation of the data in table 1 reveals some pertinent facts. Among African countries, the top sources of illicit capital flight are Nigeria, Egypt, Algeria, Morocco, Côte d'Ivoire, Democratic Republic of Congo, Sudan, and Angola. Interestingly enough, these countries are also among the most unstable states in Africa and rank among the worst in the Ibrahim Index of African governance (see table 1). Although South Africa and Ghana, which both rank high in the Ibrahim Index, also rank among the top 20 sources of illicit capital flows from Africa, the highest ranked African states in the Ibrahim Index—Mauritius, Cape Verde, Seychelles, and Botswana—do not appear at all on the list of sources of illicit capital flows. At the very least, their omission implies that to curb the problem of illicit capital outflows is to increase the chances of producing more Botswanas in Africa. That prospect alone is reason enough to tackle the problem of corruption and repatriate African wealth to the states where they are most needed.

Because the culprits are both Africans and external actors, the solution to the problem of illicit capital flows will require the participation of Africans and the international community. Domestically, building effective state institutions and legal regimes to fight corruption have been the focus of many African democratic regimes, such as Nigeria and Kenya. But as the uneven progress in these countries has demonstrated, African efforts alone will not suffice. To date, international efforts to fight corruption have been laudable, but they have been insufficient. Stronger enforcement of existing corruption laws by European and U.S. governments has implicated major transnational conglomerates, such as Siemens and Halliburton. A tighter international regulatory regime under the United Nations system may be needed to move anti-corruption enforcement measures from a voluntary national practice. Better still, to move away from the symbolism of anti-corruption in Africa, a robust international regime is needed to address the principal source of the financial drain, and that is the maintenance of external accounts by African governments in the form of "foreign reserves." It is stunning that this practice, which began during the colonial era as a commentary on the lack of capability in Africa, has continued into the twenty-first century. The recent boom in commodity prices has swelled the balance of payments accounts of many African states, especially the mineral-rich states. These multibillion-dollar accounts are held in American and European banks where they are put to the service of these economies while African banks and governments seek Western financing at high interest rates to capitalize their financial institutions or fund budget deficits.

THE EMERGING POLITICAL ACCOUNTABILITY REGIME IN AFRICA

Two promising developments in the twenty-first century provide a solid foundation on which to anchor the preceding proposal for international support for Africa. The first is the New Partnership for Africa's

Development (NEPAD), which emerged in 2001. NEPAD is the product of the convergence of two forces in the twilight of the twentieth-century: the emergence of a permissive international environment and the palpable optimism felt across Africa with the arrival of a bumper crop of democratically elected leaders soon after the amazing transformation of South Africa from apartheid to multiracial democracy. The NEPAD document was exceptionally candid about its diagnosis of the African dilemma and, for purposes of political accountability, it demonstrated an uncharacteristic ability of African leaders to capture the pulse of the people. "Across the continent," the authors wrote, "Africans declare that we will no longer allow ourselves to be conditioned by circumstance. We will determine our own destiny and call on the rest of the world to complement our efforts" (African Union 2001: 2). To underscore the political tailwind driving the agenda in the new century, the authors of NEPAD noted that: "There are already signs of progress and hope. Democratic regimes committed to the protection of human rights, people-centred development, and market-oriented economies are on the increase. *African peoples have begun to demonstrate their refusal to accept poor economic and political leadership* (African Union 2001: 2; emphasis added).

People power, exemplified by the convening of several sovereign national conferences in many African countries in the late 1990s, is beginning to shape the continental agenda unlike anything in the past. Nowhere is this push for accountability more obvious than in NEPAD's African Peer Review Mechanism (APRM). This groundbreaking accountability measure requires that African governments voluntarily submit themselves to periodic assessments by their peers to determine the extent to which they have fulfilled their NEPAD obligations. Using a complex matrix that measures compliance in four areas—Democracy and Political Governance, Economic Governance and Management, Corporate Governance, and Socio-Economic Development—a technical committee constituted by the secretariat collects and reviews countries' data to determine their level of compliance. The result is shared with the host government, the local media and civil society organiza-

Figure 1: External Financing (Loans and Grants) as a Percentage of National Budget (2010)

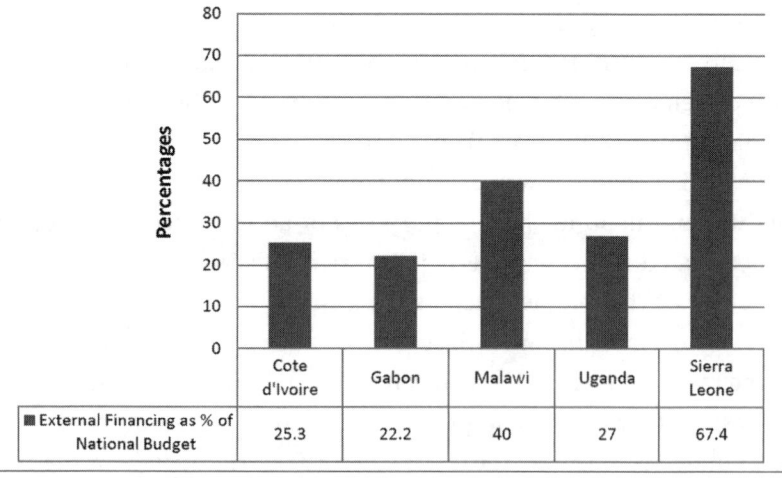

	Cote d'Ivoire	Gabon	Malawi	Uganda	Sierra Leone
External Financing as % of National Budget	25.3	22.2	40	27	67.4

Data generated from: Government of Sierra Leone (2009); Republic of Uganda (2009); Reuters (2009); Africa Online (2009); Republic of Malawi (2010).

tions, and subsequently distributed to the African Union secretariat and member states, the United Nations, and donor agencies.

The APRM is quickly developing into a norm in Africa, where it has become a bragging right of sorts that touts a regime's transparency and democratic credentials. By mid-2010, 29 countries had acceded to APRM and a dozen of them have been peer-reviewed. They are Algeria, Benin, Burkina Faso, Ghana, Kenya, Lesotho, Mali, Mozambique, Nigeria, Rwanda, South Africa, and Uganda. The potential uses of the APRM by the international community to promote accountability in Africa are limitless. For example, as a complement to international ratings agencies, such as Moody's and Standard and Poor's (S&P), the APRM could be used to channel the flow of donor aid to states or private capital through the bond market (as Dambisa Moyo has advocated), thereby ensuring that regimes that demonstrate greater accountability are rewarded and those that failed the accountability test are punished by the market (Moyo 2009). This will be especially effective given that several African governments rely on external grants and loans to finance their budget deficits. As figure 1 shows, even Gabon,

Table 2: 2009 Ibrahim Index of African Governance

Key Indicators	Constitutive Elements
1. Safety and Rule of Law	a) Personal Safety—Violent crime, social unrest, human trafficking, domestic political persecution b) Rule of Law—Independent judiciary, property rights, UN sanctions, orderly transfer of power c) Accountability and Corruption—Transparency, accountability of public officials, corruption in government and public officials, prosecution of abuse of office d) National Security—Domestic armed conflict, government involvement in armed conflict, flow of refugees and internally displaced persons, international tension
2. Participation and Human Rights	a) Participation—political participation, strength of democracy, free and fair elections, electoral self-determination b) Rights—human rights, political rights, collective rights, civil liberties, ratification and reporting of core international human rights conventions c) Gender—gender equality, ratio of girls to boys in primary and secondary education. women's participation in the labor force, women in parliament
3. Sustainable Economic Opportunity	a) Economic management—quality of public administration, budget management, strength of the banking sector, public debt management, strength of reserves b) Private sector—competitive environment, investment climate, access to credit, extent of bureaucratic red tape, trading costs across borders c) Infrastructure—reliable electricity supply, mobile phone subscribers, computer and internet usage d) Environmental and rural sector—environmental sustainability, access to land and water for agriculture, dialogue between government and rural organizations
4. Human Development	a) Poverty and Health—HIV-AIDS, TB, infant mortality, immunization, welfare regime, degree of social exclusion b) Education—access and quality of education, teacher-student ratio, primary school completion rate, secondary and tertiary enrollment rates

Source: Adapted from Mo Ibrahim Foundation (2009).

a small-sized major oil-exporting country, is financing its 2010 budget to the tune of 22 percent from external sources. The level of dependence on external financing rises significantly for nonoil producers in the sample during the same period—from 25 percent in Côte d'Ivoire to 67 percent in Sierra Leone. Such a level of dependence should make for an effective application of financial leverage to promote an important economic and political value: accountability.

The Mo Ibrahim Foundation Formula for Political Accountability

The second positive development on which to anchor international measures in support of political accountability in Africa is the extraordinary work of the Mo Ibrahim Foundation. Founded in 2007 by Mo Ibrahim, the Sudanese-born multibillionaire, the foundation "is committed to supporting great African leadership that will improve the economic and social prospects of the people of Africa" (Mo Ibrahim Foundation 2009). The foundation's two programmatic initiatives that are geared to this end are the Ibrahim Index of African Governance and the Ibrahim Prize for African Leadership. The Ibrahim Index is a set of governance and accountability indicators originally created for the foundation by Robert Rotberg and his colleagues at the Harvard University Kennedy School of Government's Program on Intrastate Conflict and Conflict Resolution. As an indicator of the quality of governance in Africa, the goal of the Ibrahim Index is to inform and empower "citizens to hold their governments and public institutions to account" and, to that end, "stimulate debate in a constructive way and establish a framework for good governance in Africa" (Mo Ibrahim Foundation 2009).

As a broad measure of government and accountability, the 2009 Ibrahim Index focuses on four broad indicators (see table 2):

1) Safety and Rule of Law. This category examines the performance of African states with regard to personal safety issues such as violence and state persecution; the supremacy of the rule of law, exemplified by the existence of an independent judiciary and property rights, among others; visible measures against corruption; and national security.

2) Participation and Human Rights. This category has three components. The first, participation, measures the extent to which

a country has free and fair elections and the adequacy and independence of institutions charged with conducting elections. The second component, rights, measures the basket of human, civil, and political rights available to citizens and the extent to which they are respected by governments. The third component, gender, measures the degree of gender equality, the ratio of girls to boys in primary and secondary schools and the level of women's participation in the formal economy and their representation in parliament.

3) Sustainable Economic Opportunity. This indicator measures the strength and quality of economic management, the private sector, infrastructure and environmental management.

4) Human Development. The two components of human development that are measured here are educational access and quality, and poverty and health care.

Taken together, the foundation believes that these four criteria provide a broader picture of governance in Africa. On that basis, the Mo Ibrahim Foundation publishes an annual list of the Ibrahim Index Scores and Rankings of all the 53 African countries. Mauritius, Cape Verde, Seychelles, Botswana, South Africa, Namibia, Ghana, Tunisia, Lesotho, and Sao Tome and Principe have dominated the top 10 spots on the Ibrahim Governance Index since the ranking began in 2006. Among the worst performers have been Somalia, Chad, Zimbabwe, Democratic Republic of Congo, and Sudan. Aside from bragging rights, being at the top of this list reinforces positive perceptions of the political and economic climate in Mauritius, Cape Verde, Botswana, and Ghana, which translates into greater inflow of tourism dollars and foreign direct investment than might otherwise have occurred. For example, the impressive economic growth of Botswana, which has consistently been among the top five performers on the Ibrahim Index, has been cited by prominent scholars as evidence of a positive relationship between good governance and economic performance (Sen 1999: 149–150). By contrast, being at the bottom of the Ibrahim Index does not help an African state. The presence of some of the worst violators of human rights in Africa—Zimbabwe, Somalia, Sudan, Democratic Republic of Congo—at the bottom of the ranking has reinforced negative perceptions of these countries in Africa and the outside world as unstable and downright risky.

The second component of the Mo Ibrahim formula for accountability and good governance in Africa is the Mo Ibrahim Prize for Achievement in African Leadership. Modeled after the Nobel Peace Prize, the Ibrahim prize "is awarded to a democratically elected former African Executive Head of State or Government who has served their term in office within the limits set by the country's constitution and has left office in the last three years" (Mo Ibrahim Foundation 2009). Like the Nobel Committee, the Ibrahim laureate is chosen from a list of nominees by a distinguished committee which, at present, comprises former UN Secretary-General Kofi Annan (chair), Marti Ahtisaari, Mary Robinson, Graça Machel, Salim Ahmed Salim, and Aisha Diallo. To encourage African leaders to seek the highest office by electoral means, shun corruption, govern effectively, and selflessly and ensure peaceful power transition by vacating office promptly at the end of their constitutionally-determined term limits, the Ibrahim laureate receives a $5 million cash prize over ten years and $250,000 annually for life, making it the largest such award in the world. To date, there have been only two prize winners: President Joachim Chissano of Mozambique (2007) and President Festus Mogae of Botswana (2008). As evidence of the strictness of their criteria, the prize committee failed to find any former African president to award the coveted prize in 2009 and 2010.

The combination of the APRM, the Ibrahim Index, and the Ibrahim Prize provides a powerful instrument to gauge and engage the substantive work done by Africans to develop a self-sustaining system of political accountability. The local ownership of this process could be reinforced by the international community through the processes and measures discussed in this essay.

In conclusion, anecdotal and direct references to the desirability of an empire, even if a benevolent one, as a solution to Africa's ailments do very little to advance the agenda of political accountability in the minds of many Africans whose struggles against domestic and external sources of tyranny are hardly a matter of distant memory. In this regard, the astonishing proposal advanced by Niall Ferguson in *Colossus* is but an unfortunate reminder of the burden that Africans still carry in the twenty-first century:

> I believe the world needs an effective liberal empire and that the United States is the best candidate for the job. Economic globalization is working. . . . But there are parts of the world where legal and political institutions are in a condition of such collapse or corruption that their inhabitants are effectively cut off from any hope of prosperity" (2007: 301).

Such vocal yearning for an era that lives in infamy in the minds of many Africans demonstrates an unusual level of insensitivity to the problem of accountability in contemporary Africa where despots, such as Mugabe, cling to such references for their political survival. As I have argued in this essay, accountability is not about economic prosperity alone, important though that might be. Instead, it is fundamentally about the right and freedom of a people to shape their own destiny. For that reason, the quest for political accountability in contemporary Africa is the last phase of a continent's "long walk to freedom" (Mandela 1994).

REFERENCES

Adeniyi, Segun. "The Yar'Adua I Knew." *Vanguard* (June 6, 2010) <http://www.vanguardngr.com>.

Adibe, Clement E. "The Liberian Conflict and the ECOWAS-UN Partnership." *Third World Quarterly* 18:3 (1997): 471–488.

African Union. *The New Partnership for Africa's Development (NEPAD)*. Addis Ababa: African Union Secretariat, October 2001.

AllAfrica Online. "Côte d'Ivoire: The 2010 Budget Amounted to 2.481 Trillion CFA." (November 28, 2009) <http://www.allafricaonline.com>.

Allen, Karen. "Kenya's First Lady Slaps Official." BBC (December 13, 2007) <http://news.bbc.co.uk/2/hi/7143097.stm>.

Bates, Robert. *When Things Fell Apart: State Failure in Late-Century Africa.* Cambridge: Cambridge University Press, 2008.

Bellamy, Richard. *Liberalism and Modern Society: A Historical Argument.* University Park: Pennsylvania State University Press, 1992.

Bratton, Michael, and Carolyn Logan. *Voters But Not Yet Citizens: The Weak Demand for Political Accountability in Africa's Unclaimed Democracies. Afrobarometer* Working Paper 63 (September 2006).

Chabal, Patrick. *Africa: The Politics of Suffering and Smiling.* London: Zed Books, 2009.

Chawatama, Regis. *"Political Accountability."* Cape Town: Southern African Catholic Bishops' Conference Parliamentary Liaison Office. Briefing Paper #211 (July 2009).

Collier, Paul. *The Bottom Billion.* Oxford: Oxford University Press, 2007.

Cornett, Linda. "Good Governance and Anti-Corruption in Theory and Practice." Washington, D.C: World Bank, April 11, 2007.

Darnstädt, Thomas, Helen Zuber, and Jan Puhl. "The International Criminal Court's Dream of Global Justice." *Spiegel* (January 14, 2009).

Decalo, Samuel. *Coups and Army Rule in Africa.* New Haven: Yale University Press, 1976.

Devlin, Larry. *Chief of Station, Congo.* New York: Public Affairs, 2007.

Easterly, William. *The Elusive Quest for Growth: Economists' Adventures and Misadventures in the Tropics.* Cambridge: MIT Press, 2002.

Etounga-Manguelle, Daniel. "Does Africa Need a Cultural Adjustment Program?" *Culture Matters: How Values Shape Progress.* Eds. Lawrence Harrison and Samuel P. Huntington. New York: Basic Books, 2000.

Falola, Toyin, and Matthew Heaton. *A History of Nigeria.* Cambridge: Cambridge University Press, 2008.

Farrington, John. *Decentralisation and Political Accountability.* London: Overseas Development Institute, March 2002.

Ferguson, Niall. *Colossus: The Rise and Fall of the American Empire.* New York: Penguin Press, 2005.

"Gabon Targets 6.5 Percent Growth in 2010." *Reuters* (December 14, 2009). www.reuters.com.

Government of Sierra Leone. "*Government Budget and Statement of Economic and Financial Policies For the Financial Year, 2010.*" Freetown: Ministry of Finance and Development, December 4, 2009.

Gyimah-Boadi, E. "Ghana: The Challenges of Consolidating Democracy." *State, Conflict, and Democracy in Africa*. Ed. Richard Joseph. Boulder: Lynne Rienner Publishers, 1999.

Hochschild, Adam. *King Leopold's Ghost*. New York: Houghton Mifflin, 1999.

Huntington, Samuel P. "The Clash of Civilizations?" *Foreign Affairs* 72:3 (Summer 1993): 22–49.

Hyden, Goran. *African Politics in Comparative*. Cambridge: Cambridge University Press, 2005.

Ivanyna, Maksym, and Anwar Shah. *Decentralization (Localization) and Corruption: New Cross-Country Evidence*. Washington, D.C.: World Bank Institute, Policy Research Working Paper 5299 (May 2010).

Kalu, Kelechi, ed. *Agenda Setting and Public Policy in Africa*. London: Ashgate Publishing, 2004.

Kar, Dev, and Devon Cartwright-Smith. *Illicit Financial Flows From Africa: Hidden Resource for Development*. Washington, D.C.: Global Financial Integrity, March 2010.

Kelsall, Tim. "Rituals of Verification: Indigenous and Imported Accountability in Northern Tanzania." *Africa* 73:2 (2003): 174–201.

Kieh, George, and Pita Agbese, eds. *The Military and Politics in Africa: From Engagement to Democratic and Constitutional Control*. Aldershot: Ashgate Publishing, 2004.

Lentz, Carola. "The Chief, the Mine Captain and the Politician: Legitimating Power in Northern Ghana. *Africa* 68:1 (1998): 46–67.

Lewis, Peter. "From Prebendalism to Predation: The Political Economy of Decline in Nigeria." *Journal of Modern African Studies* 34:1 (1996): 79–103.

Lugard, Lord. *The Dual Mandate in British Tropical Africa*. Hamden, Conn.: Archon Books, 1965.

Mamdani, Mahmood. *Citizen and Subject: Contemporary Africa and the Legacy of Late Colonialism*. Princeton: Princeton University Press, 1996.

———. *When Victims Become Killers: Colonialism, Nativism, and the Genocide in Rwanda*. Princeton, NJ: Princeton University Press, 2002.

Mandela, Nelson. *Long Walk to Freedom*. Boston: Little, Brown and Company, 1994.

Marx, Anthony. *Faith in Nation: Exclusionary Origins of Nationalism*. New York: Oxford University Press, 2003.

Mbaku, John, ed. *Corruption and the Crisis of Institutional Reforms in Africa*. Lewiston, N.Y.: Edwin Mellen Press, 1998.

Mbanga, Wilf. "Zimbabwe's Unfolding Drama." *Open Democracy* (April 7, 2008) <http://www.opendemocracy.net>.

McGowan, Patrick. "African Military Coups d'état, 1956–2001: Frequency, Trends and Distribution." *Journal of Modern African Studies* 41:3 (September 2003): 339–370.

Mensema, Akadu Ntiriwa. "Konadu Rawlings Who Born Hypocrisy." *Modern Ghana* (March 5, 2010) <http:// www.modernghana.com>.

Meredith, Martin. *The Fate of Africa: A History of Fifty Years of Independence*. New York: Public Affairs, 2005.

Mo Ibrahim Foundation. "2009 Ibrahim Index of African Governance." (October 1, 2009) <http://www.moibrahimfoundation.org/en/section/the-ibrahim-index>.

Moncrieffe, Joy Marie. "Reconceptualizing Political Accountability." *International Political Science Review* 19:4 (October 1998): 387–406.

Moyo, Dambisa. *Dead Aid*. New York: Farrar, Straus and Giroux, 2009.

Narizhnaya, Kristina. "A Russian Milestone: 1st Black Elected to Office." *Yahoo News* (July 25, 2010) <http://news.yahoo.com>.

Obama, Barack. "An Honest Government, a Hopeful Future." August 28, 2006 <http://obama.senate.gov/speech/060828-an_honest_gover/print.php>.

O'Donnell, Guillermo, Philippe Schmitter, and Laurence Whitehead, eds. *Transitions from Authoritarian Rule: Latin America*. Baltimore: Johns Hopkins University Press, 1986.

Ogueri II, Eze. "Theories and Motives of Military Coups D'état in Independent African States." *Africa Spectrum* 8:3 (1973): 280–302.

O'Neil, Tammie, Marta Foresti, and Alan Hudson. *Evaluation of Citizens' Voice and Accountability: Review of the Literature and Donor Approaches*. London: DFID, 2007.

Paine, Thomas. *Common Sense*. Cutchogue, N.Y.: Buccaneer Books, 1976.

Pierson, Christopher. *The Modern State*. New York: Routledge, 2004.

Rawls, John. *Political Liberalism*. New York: Columbia University Press, 1993.

Reno, William. *Warlord Politics and African States*. Boulder: Lynne Rienner Publishers, 1998.

Republic of Malawi. *2010/11 Budget Statement*. Lilongwe: Ministry of Finance, May 28, 2010.

Republic of Uganda. *Budget Speech: Financial Year 2010/11*. Kampala: Ministry of Finance, Planning and Economic Development, June 11, 2009.

Rice, Xan, and Mark Tran. "Fiery Speaker with the Populist Touch." *The Guardian* (London) (January 2, 2008) <http://www.guardian.co.uk>.

Sachs, Jeffrey. *The End of Poverty: Economic Possibilities For Our Time*. New York: Penguin Publishers, 2005.

Sen, Amartya. *Development as Freedom*. New York: Anchor Books, 1999.

Shaxson, Nicholas. *Poisoned Wells: The Dirty Politics of African Oil*. New York: Palgrave Macmillan, 2007.

Stiglitz, Joseph. *Globalization and its Discontents*. New York: Norton, 2002.

Tangaza, Jamilah. "BBC Hausa Interview with President Yar'Adua." BBC (January 12, 2010) <http://www.bbc.co.uk/blogs/theeditors/2010/01/bbc_interview_with_president_y.html>.

Weisner, Thomas. "Culture, Childhood and Progress in Sub-Saharan Africa." *Culture Matters: How Values Shape Progress*. Eds. Lawrence Harrison and Samuel P. Huntington. New York: Basic Books, 2000.

Welch, Claude. "Soldier and State in Africa." *Journal of Modern African Studies* 5:3 (November 1967): 305–322.

Widner, Jennifer. *The Rise of a Party-State in Kenya: From 'Harambee'! To 'Nyayo'!*. Berkeley: University of California Press, 1993.

Wild, Leni, Marta Foresti, and Dan Harris. *Why Accountability Matters*. London: Overseas Development Institute, May 2010.
Williams, D., and T. Young. "Governance, the World Bank and Liberal Theory." *Political Studies* 42:1 (1994): 84–100.
World Bank. "Accelerated Development in Sub-Saharan Africa." Washington, D.C.: World Bank, 1981.
———. "Governance and Development." Washington, D.C.: World Bank, 1992.
———. "Anticorruption in Transition: A Contribution to the Policy Debate." Washington, D.C.: World Bank, 2000.

Kristin McKie and Nicolas van de Walle
Toward an Accountable Budget Process in Sub-Saharan Africa: Problems and Prospects

WHY HAS SUB-SAHARAN AFRICA'S DEVELOPMENT LAGGED BEHIND virtually every other region of the world over the last five decades? Scholars agree that a unique combination of domestic factors (such as weak state institutions, difficulties of accessing markets, and clientelistic political systems) and international factors (including the nature of foreign aid and the fluctuating demand for Africa's natural resources) have likely combined to create an environment in Africa that has hindered socioeconomic development. However, one obstacle to development that both scholars and development practitioners have begun to focus on recently is the lack of accountability in the national budget process. Even though a number of mechanisms of accountability have been built into public expenditure management and auditing procedures in many sub-Saharan African states, a host of legal, capacity, and political constraints often hinder these mechanisms from being able to effectively monitor and sanction executive misuse and diversion of public funds. Accordingly, this essay seeks to synthesize some of the recent research on a select group of these mechanisms of accountability, namely parliamentary budget committees, supreme audit institutions, citizen budget monitoring, and advocacy groups and elections, paying particular attention to the factors that impede the ability of these mechanisms to consistently demand accountability from the executive regarding budget management, and by extension, development priorities in sub-Saharan Africa.

The article will open with a brief look at Africa's level of development compared to other regions of the world in order to illustrate the continent's relatively poor performance. Next, we will explore the theoretical linkages between development, the budget process, and accountability that form the basis for our analysis. After disaggregating the concept of accountability into horizontal and vertical strands, the remainder of the article will survey some recent case-study research that highlights the challenges facing four specific mechanisms of accountability within the budget process: parliamentary budget committees, supreme audit institutions, citizen budget monitoring and advocacy groups, and lobbying/elections. In their own way, all of these mechanisms seek to hold the executive responsible for ensuring that the national budget is designed and implemented in a manner that best promotes national development goals. We will conclude with a discussion of some innovative strategies various actors have developed to increase the level of accountability in the budget process.

THE BUDGET PROCESS, ACCOUNTABILITY, AND DEVELOPMENT: THEORIZING THE LINKAGES

No single metric can fully capture the variation in the progress of development across regions of the world, but comparative data on the level of the population that lives below the poverty line provides telling evidence that average citizens continue to face consistently higher levels of economic deprivation in sub-Saharan Africa than in every other region of the globe. According to data collected for the United Nations 2010 Millennium Development Goals Report, in 2005 approximately 51 percent of sub-Saharan Africans lived on less than $1.25 per day, compared to 39 percent in South Asia, 19 percent in Southeast Asia, 8 percent in Latin America and 6 percent in the Middle East region (United Nations 2010: 6). While fortunately this proportion is down from the 58 percent of sub-Saharan citizens who subsisted at this level in 1990, it is still well above the proportion of the population living at or below the poverty level in every other regions of the developing world.

While sub-Saharan Africa's relatively low level of economic development is clearly caused by a complex mix of domestic, international, structural, and contingent factors, one aspect that has received increasing attention over the course of the last two decades has been governance factors, as scholars and policymakers have come to agree that a major cause of Africa's economic crisis has been institutional and political in nature (Bates 2008; Ndulu et al. 2008; van de Walle 2001). Simply put, the nature of political institutions, and the manner in which they have been managed, have served to constrain and complicate the process of economic development. In the brief space allowed us here, we focus on a small but critical component of this issue: the lack of a transparent and efficient national budget process in many African states.

The budget process can be broken down into three main phases, each of which is linked to a country's development trajectory in distinct ways. First, in the *budget formulation phase*, a country's spending priorities are set. Spending priorities impact development because sustained development can only occur if governments invest in the type of programs, projects, and initiatives that lay the groundwork for socioeconomic growth by advancing human capital and spurring economic activity. Second, in the *budget execution phase*, a country's spending priorities are actualized through the transfer of funds to the receiving ministries and subnational units to fund budget initiatives. The manner in which budget execution is undertaken impacts development in a country in terms of the effect it has on the quality of physical infrastructure that is built, the availability of crucial social services, and the efficiency of government entities to facilitate economic advancement. Finally, the third phase of the budget process is the *monitoring and evaluation phase*. In this phase, various types of audits are performed to ascertain to what degree the budget process, as implemented, has resulted in "(a) the proper and effective use of public funds; (b) the development of sound financial management; (c) the proper execution of administrative activities; and (d) the communication of information to public authorities and the general public through the publication of objective reports" (DFID 2005: 1). Such monitoring and reporting is central to development because it tracks how allocated funds are actually spent and highlights areas of mismanagement and corrupt practices that hinder the full implementation of development projects. Only through careful evaluation (and subsequent reforms of the system where needed) can both governments and citizens ensure that the national budget process stimulates effective and sustainable development in the country.

Realizing the important links between the budget process and socioeconomic development, many donors have recently begun to funnel more developmental aid money to recipient countries in the form of "direct budget support" (DBS), rather than funding specific development projects in an ad hoc manner. DBS connotes foreign aid that is infused directly into the general government coffers to be disbursed through the country's regular budget allocation process. DBS is thought to encourage "greater local ownership of the development process by reinforcing accountability relationships within governments and drawing on and developing the capacity of governments to define and manage programs" (Franz 2004: 2). Such local ownership and capacity building surrounding the budget process is hypothesized to allow recipient countries to better and more sustainably address development targets such as poverty reduction. However, while DBS aid does put greater responsibility for meeting development goals into the hands of developing countries, the internal accountability within the budget process that Franz mentions does not arise automatically with the advent of direct budget support. Various studies assessing the impact of direct budget support programs in Mozambique (Hodges and Tibana 2004), Malawi (Rakner et al. 2004), and Tanzania (Kelsall 2002) among others find that the potential effectiveness of DBS is often hindered by the clientelistic nature of the political systems in many aid-dependent African counties, which highly discourages the development of a culture of accountability within governments.

If the budget process and direct budget support are to become an effective vehicle for development, mechanisms of accountability within the public expenditure management system must be reinforced. In recognition of this fact, "strengthening domestic accountability mechanisms through parliaments, audit institutions and civil society has also become a more prominent objective of both donor and recipient countries" (de Renzio 2006: 628). Yet, the question remains how best to foster meaningful and operational mechanisms of accountability within the budget process in countries where the political economy and historical practices lead most government officials to see the state as a source of patronage rents rather than a medium of development. The first step in addressing this question requires gaining an understanding of the nature of the challenges facing the various mechanisms of accountability that de Renzio highlights—namely parliamentary budget committees, supreme audit institutions, civil society organizations, and elections. Understanding the factors that constrain these mechanisms from effectively influencing and regulating the budget process will allow us to hypothesize ways to strengthen them so that the entire budget process in sub-Saharan African states can become more efficient, transparent, and developmentally focused.

Toward this end, the goal of the remainder of this paper is to review and synthesize recent case-study research on the difficulties faced by parliamentary budget committees, supreme audit institutions, citizen monitoring and advocacy groups, and democratic elections in holding the executive branch to account regarding public expenditure management. Before undertaking this analysis, we will pause briefly to explore the concept of "accountability" within the political context in order to ground our discussion of the various mechanisms of accountability that will be reviewed.

Defining Political Accountability

Political accountability is a relational concept that describes how one entity is answerable to another in a specified manner that can be enforced. Schedler describes the relationship as such: "A is accountable to B when A is obliged to *inform* B about A's actions and decisions, to *justify* them, and to suffer *punishment* in the case of misconduct" (Schedler 1999: 17, emphasis added). Within the budget process are two different forms of accountability: horizontal accountability and vertical accountability. Horizontal accountability refers to a relationship in which one government entity holds another government entity to account (O'Donnell 1998). Generally described as a system of checks and balances, examples of mechanisms of horizontal accountability that are regular features of modern budget processes include the powers of parliamentary budget committees and supreme audit institutions to approve, oversee, and audit the executive's management of public finances. Conversely, mechanisms of vertical accountability include procedures through which citizens can hold their elected leaders to account. Mechanisms of vertical accountability related to the budget process include civil society organizations such as budget-monitoring groups and elections, both of which provide citizens avenues to advocate for their policy preferences, monitor leaders' actions, and ultimately remove them from power if they are perceived to have failed to manage development expenditure well. While constitutions and other legal provisions in most African countries provide for the existence of each of these four mechanisms of accountability and specifies their role in the budget process, each face a number of legal, capacity and political challenges that weaken their ability to effectively hold the executive to account during the various stages of the budget process. Exploring the dynamics of some of these challenges comprises the remainder of this article.

CHALLENGES CONFRONTING MECHANISMS OF HORIZONTAL ACCOUNTABILITY IN THE BUDGET PROCESS

The formal system of "checks and balances" between government entities involved in the budget process that is enshrined in most African constitutions is designed to promote transparency and accountability in public expenditure management. While case-study evidence suggests that mechanisms of horizontal accountability such as parliamentary budget committees and supreme audit institutions are beginning to play a more prominent role in the budget process across the continent, they still face many constraints that make it difficult for them to hold the executive accountable for misappropriation of public funds.

Parliamentary Budget Committees

Most sub-Saharan constitutions ascribe their national parliaments a number of legislative oversights functions within the public expenditure management process. Among these, parliaments are tasked with authorizing and scrutinizing public expenditure, including amending and approving the budget each year as part of the formulation phase, and investigating any mismanagement in budget allocation as reported by the auditor general in the evaluation and monitoring phase. For example, in Uganda, Article 155 (1) of the constitution specifies that the proposed budget be laid before parliament annually and Article 163 (5) gives parliament the power to take appropriate action to investigate alleged misuse of public funds (Constitution of Uganda 1995). These oversight functions of parliament are often facilitated by parliamentary budget committees, a specially designated group of members of parliament (MPs) who take the lead in analyzing the proposed budget and monitoring the implementation of public expenditure initiatives by gathering testimony from key experts and evaluating reports from the auditor general and other independent executive agencies tasked with reporting on expenditure malfeasance.

However, even though these formal rules delineating the power of the legislature over public accounts should, in theory, give parliaments the oversight necessary to hold the executive accountable for executing an effective developmental budget, many different types of constraints greatly reduce parliaments' ability to check the discretion of the executive in the various phases of the budget process.

Legal Constraints on Parliamentary Oversight

As mentioned above, most African constitutions contain articles that ascribe to parliament legal oversight authority over the budget process and public expenditure in theory. Yet, in practice, vague, unenforced, or contradictory laws often hamper MPs' ability to meaningfully hold the Ministry of Finance and the larger executive branch accountable in their development spending. One illustration of this is that, in many sub-Saharan states, parliament's accountability function during budget formulation is constrained because it lacks the power to amend the budget proposal before voting on its passage. For example, Article 108 in the Ghanaian constitution stipulates that the parliament can only decrease or request that the Ministry of Finance reallocate funds but cannot increase public spending at its discretion or mandate a reallocation (Stapenhurst and Alandu 2009: 3). In many instances, this lack of true budgetary amendment powers means that the legislature simply rubber stamps the budget as presented by the Ministry of Finance without challenging any of the executive's prerogatives.

In addition to a lack of amendment powers, another factor that hinders parliament's ability to hold the executive accountable during the budget process is the existence in some countries of laws that contradict the power of the legislature as the sole authority to approve public expenditure. For example, in Benin, Article 68 gives the executive the power to pass the national budget by decree in the event of a "national crisis." Between 1994 and 2002, the Soglo and Kerekou governments invoked Article 68 no less than three times (Adamolekun and Laleye 2009: 131), thereby removing the power of the purse from the parliament and putting sole authority over the budget into the hands of the executive. The vague definition of a "national crisis" allows the government to circumvent a parliamentary approval of the budget virtually at will. Clearly, such laws severely impede the legislature's ability to check the power of the executive during the budget process, especially since they are likely to be invoked precisely when it appears that a legislature might challenge the executive's proposed expenditure priorities.

Finally, the monitoring and evaluation phase of the budget process allows the legislature to hold the executive to account through hearings and investigations into expenditure mismanagement initiated through a parliamentary public accounts committee (PAC) and based on reporting by an auditor general. However, although PACs are legally allowed to summon and collect testimony from ministry heads and subpoena documents in order to investigate allegations of wasteful, corrupt, or illegal spending practices, the most that a PAC can do in practice is recommend disciplinary action or censure against offending officials. Yet, these recommendations are nonbinding since most African legislatures do not enjoy prosecutorial powers (Dorotinsky and Floyd 2004: 204). Thus, it is up to the attorney general (AG) or other governmental offices to take up these recommendations and enact punishments for offenders, but this rarely happens. For example, Stapenhurst and Alandu (2009: 19) find that Ghanaian MPs report that PAC investigation findings transmitted to the AG for prosecution are often not brought to trial. Interviewees surmised this was because the AG is constitutionally also a minister of state and selected by the president, and thereby likely to refrain from prosecuting fellow members of the executive branch.

In these myriad ways discussed above, the ability of parliament to hold the executive accountable for diverting development funds away from their intended targets and other violations of pro-poor expenditure management is partially hampered by vague, unenforceable, and contradictory legal structures regarding the balance of power between the legislature and the executive across sub-Saharan Africa. But even if all of these legal constraints were removed, other challenges, such as capacity constraints and political interests, would still greatly limit African parliaments' ability to effectively hold their executives to account during the budget process.

Capacity Constraints on Parliamentary Oversight
National budgets and auditor general reports analyzing public expenditures are very technical documents that are not easily deciphered by individuals who do not possess an accounting or financial background. This means that many members of sub-Saharan African parliaments, including members of public accounts committees, are ill-equipped to understand and scrutinize these types of documents, making it difficult

for PACs to monitor the extent to which proposed budgets are in line with developmental goals and the extent to which public funds that are disbursed actually mirror planned expenditures.

In more established democracies, PACs are often assisted by legislative budget offices, which employ economists, accountants, and public policy professionals who aid MPs and parliamentary committees in analyzing budget documents. For example, in the United States, the Congressional Budget Office, which has existed since the 1970s, is staffed by approximately 250 professionally trained employees who support the work of the House and Senate budget committees. In contrast, many African parliaments, including the national assemblies of Malawi and Zambia, do not have parliamentary budget offices (PBOs) attached to them or dedicated researchers who can be called upon to assist in budget analysis (Wehner 2004: 16). Even in those sub-Saharan countries where PBOs have been established in recent years (Uganda in 2001, Kenya in 2008), the lack of adequate or timely budget information from the executive and a high rate of turnover of the skilled professional staffing the PBOs (as they are hired away by donor or private groups for higher salaries) impede the ability of PBOs and therefore PACs in providing a meaningful oversight of the budget across the continent.

Besides a lack of adequate support staff, the capacity of parliamentary budget committees in many sub-Saharan African states is also encumbered by funding shortfalls and physical space constraints. In terms of funding issues, many parliaments in sub-Saharan Africa do not set their own yearly budgets and must rely on the Ministry of Finance to both allocate and disburse operating funds to parliament each fiscal year. This often means that ad hoc parliamentary activities, such as public accounts committee investigations, require parliament to request supplementary funds from the executive in order to carry out such mandates. This often results in a conflict of interest, since the executive is reluctant to provide funds to parliament to investigate one of the ministries under the executive arm of government. As a result, funds for PAC committee activities are often delayed, are too meager to cover committee expenses, or are never disbursed at all. For example, in Benin, Adamolekun and Laleye report that "in one or two cases when a legislative inquiry was established, the inadequacy of funds ensured its premature termination—the executive did not provide the extra funds needed to complete the inquiry" (2009: 136).

Linked to the insufficiency of parliamentary funding is a lack of physical space in which parliamentary committees can conduct their business. Barkan reports that in Ghana, as well as in many other African countries, too few rooms exist within the National Assembly building where parliamentary committees can meet (2008: 130-131). PACs and other committees either have to convene in public spaces, where debates are not free from partisan pressures, or not meet at all, which Rakner et al. find is the norm with the PAC in Malawi (2004: 18).

These capacity constraints prevent legislature from enforcing executive accountability regarding budgetary integrity and sound policy planning. Yet, even if reforms were undertaken to increase parliamentary funding, establish PBOs across the continent, and create permanent meeting spaces for committees, the political constraints within the budget process would still impede parliamentary oversight functions in many sub-Saharan African states.

Political Constraints on Parliamentary Oversight

Many unique aspects of African political competition create incentives that compel members of parliament to forgo many of their oversight powers over the executive during the budget process. More than anything, MPs want to win reelection to their seats in parliament, which means that all of their actions and decisions are taken with this goal in mind. Across sub-Saharan Africa, where political parties are largely nonideological/nonprogrammatic in their policy platforms, and where an inherited history of neopatrimonialism creates dominant party systems in many countries, MPs feel pressure to retain favor with the ruling party leadership and to be viewed as looking after their own constituencies first and foremost (de Renzio 2006: 638; Kasfir and Twebaze 2009: 75). Both of these structured incentives affect the willingness of MPs to exercise parliament's accountability role within the budget process. First, remaining in the good graces of the ruling party generally means not standing in opposition to critiquing the executive's budget proposal and the way in which the executive executed the allocation of budget funds. In an interview, one senior member of the PAC in Ghana stated that "the PAC can only be successful in tackling petty corruption—and that, if the Committee tried to investigate cases of grand corruption, party discipline would be invoked to ensure that the majority party MPs on the Committee would squash inquiries" (Stapenhurst and Alandu 2009: 19). Thus, MPs are de-incentivized from suggesting changes to the proposed budget or pursuing investigations against high-level government ministers following allegations of fraud and misuse of public accounts due to political pressures.

Second, the pressure MPs feel to serve their constituencies above all else means that individual members reap the biggest rewards for eschewing a focus on development at the national level in favor of a narrow focus on promoting the delivery of benefits to their own district or municipality. The notion that these constraints affected how members of parliament approached their role in the budget process was confirmed by MPs in Malawi during a study conducted by Rakner et al.:

> MPs interviewed informed us that by blocking or delaying a budget, they risked being perceived as "anti-development," a perception that was not easily accepted by their constituents, fellow parliamentarians, or the executive. Our study found MPs tending to want to quickly pass the budget as they are under pressure to see money go to their constituencies. In addition, we found that political loyalties to the party are preventing some MPs from articulating national issues (2004: 22).

Clearly, MP incentives would have to change for them to more fully play their constitutional role as overseers of the budgetary process. Barkan maintains that such transformation is possible in legislatures where a "coalition for change" emerges that consists of an informal group of legislators, who for a mix of reasons are committed to improving the institutional performance of the legislature. Only when such a coalition emerges can parliament transform itself from a rubber stamp for the executive's budget agenda into a meaningful mechanism of accountability in the budget process.

Supreme Audit Institutions
Supreme audit institutions (SAIs) are government bodies that conduct external reviews of the receipt, disbursement, and application of public funds and report their findings to the legislature, executive, and the public. Most sub-Saharan African states inherited their SAI model from either the British (Westminster) or French tradition during the colonial era and have retained them into the present. Each model comprises a different regulatory framework for the structure and operation of the supreme audit institution, which are generally known as the Office of the Auditor General in Anglophone countries and the Court of Audit (Cour des Comptes) in Francophone states. In the Westminster system, the auditor general reports directly to the parliament, the AG's office is staffed by accountants and auditors, and its main duty is to prepare audit reports on the financial operations of the government for the public accounts committee of parliament to review. In contrast, the Court of Audit in Francophone countries is officially part of the judiciary (and thus in theory independent from both the executive and the legislature), staffed largely by lawyers, and reports on government compliance with laws and regulations rather than strictly fiscal operations (Dorotinsky and Floyd, 2004: 200; Wang and Rakner, 2005: 6). While the differences between the two audit models create some variation in the effectiveness of SAIs in their accountability function across sub-Saharan Africa (see Lienert 2003 for a complete analysis), similar

legal, capacity, and political constraints are present across all countries in the region; these hinder the SAIs' ability to hold the executive to account in the budget process.

Legal Constraints on SAI Oversight

To be effective, supreme audit institutions require the ability to review all government expenditures that have been disbursed during the yearly budget cycle. Research shows that SAIs in countries such as Botswana, Kenya, Namibia, Tanzania, and Zambia (Kerapeletswe and Shilimela 2008) do have comprehensive audit authority, meaning they have de jure access to all government accounts. However, the mandate of SAIs in other countries such as Cameroon, Nigeria, Equatorial Guinea (International Budget Partnership 2010) and, until recently, Uganda (Wang and Rakner 2005: 11) are restricted because the public finance laws in force in these polities do not give SAIs full discretion in the scope of their audits. For example, in Uganda, most expenditures that fall under the Office of the President and Ministry of Defense are categorized as "classified." Until the passage of the Public Finance and Accountability Act in 2003, the Ugandan auditor general was restricted from reviewing and reporting on any of these classified accounts, which critics allege provided a sizeable base for patronage and often lead to the misappropriation of public funds (Kasfir and Twebaze 2009: 85). The passage of the act in 2003 partially addressed this shortcoming in the auditor general's mandate by allowing for an audit of classified expenditure, but only after auditors received special authorization based on the meeting of specific conditions. In addition, the 2003 law specified that any reports stemming from this special audit were not to be made available to the parliamentary accounts committee or the public, but only presented to a special committee of MPs (Wang and Rakner 2005: 11). These continued restrictions raised questions about the extent to which the executive would really be held accountable for these classified accounts and also sparked debate on who exactly should decide what expenditures should be labeled as "classified." The new National Audit Act of 2008 appears to largely remove these restrictions, but it remains to be seen how much information regarding classified accounts will actually be made available to the auditor general in a timely manner and in a form that is complete and usable (2005: 19-20). In countries where significant portions of government expenditures are not subject to auditor general oversight, SAIs cannot function as effective mechanisms of accountability because they cannot track the extent to which public funds are diverted from developmental priorities to fund patronage and other illicit expenditures.

Capacity Constraints on SAI Oversight

Even if SAIs are afforded comprehensive audit authority over all government accounts, the capacity shortcomings many African SAIs face make it difficult for auditors to fulfill their obligations and effectively hold the executive to account during the monitoring and evaluation stage of the budget process. First, many sub-Saharan African countries lack both the required number and quality of professional staff to produce useful annual audit reports in a timely manner. For example, in 2004 the Malawi auditor general's office only had five professionally qualified accountants on its staff of 300 (Wang and Rakner 2005: 13) while in 2006 the 127 auditors on staff at the Botswana SAI struggled to do the work that analysts argue should be done by 200 (Lekorwe 2008: 5). Such personnel problems have only been compounded in recent years given the fact that staff numbers are rarely increased when SAIs mandates are expanded to include performance (alternatively called value-for-money) audits in addition to more traditional regularity (fiscal) audits, which are increasing over the past decade in response to donor recommendations (di Renzio 2006: 639). The increased training for SAI staff undertaken in a number of countries in recent years has often proven to be a mixed blessing since because the more experienced and qualified personnel tend to migrate to better paying positions with private and donor organizations (Wang and Rakner 2005: 13).

African SAIs also face informational capacity issues that impinge on their ability to complete thorough and timely audits of government expenditures. In theory, SAIs rely on the internal audit bodies within government ministries to provide them with complete data on the accounts of their divisions and report this information in a clear and organized way in order to undertake the national audit. However, many African countries do not have internal audit mechanisms within ministries, meaning that the SAIs in these countries have to source account information from ministry ledgers themselves before they can even begin their audit. For example, the African Development Bank reports that Guinea, Lesotho, Madagascar, Namibia, and Sierra Leone all had internal audit capacities in less than 20 percent of its line ministries in 2008 (CABRI and ADB 2009). Even in those countries that do have internal audit capabilities within ministries, the same staffing, training, and technical issues that face SAIs also plague these internal audit divisions, and the release of accounting information to the SAI by these internal bodies are often severely incomplete and delayed (Kerapeletswe and Shilimela 2008: 37-40). For example, Wang and Rakner found that the 2002-2003 Ugandan SAI audit report put disclaimers on 82 percent of the total expenditure for the year. As they explain, a "disclaimer means that the problems with the accounts were so severe that the auditor general could not make the necessary assessment of them" (Wang and Rakner 2005: 36). As a result of the informational deficiencies from below, the ability of the SAI to finish and submit comprehensive fiscal year audit reports is also compromised, and some African SAIs run months or even years behind in issuing reports. In fact, out of 26 countries surveyed in 2008, 9 published SAI audits more than 12 months after the end of the fiscal year (CABRI and ADB 2009: 5).

Political Constraints on SAI Oversight
Autonomy is key to SAI ability to hold the executive to account on public expenditure (Stapenhurst and Titsworth 2001). An SAI that is not autonomous from central government influence and control in

matters of appointment, tenure and funding will not be effective mechanisms of accountability because their staff will not be free to act as a true external reviewer. Perhaps the most important factor related to SAI autonomy is the law regulating the removal of the auditor general. Fortunately, constitutions and statues in Botswana, Kenya, Namibia, Tanzania, Zambia, and many other sub-Saharan African countries contain safeguards against arbitrary dismissal of the auditor general, which stipulate that the sitting auditor general can only be removed from office by a vote in parliament and generally only for specified reasons such as gross misconduct (Kerapeletswe and Shilimdela 2008: 37). However, the 2010 Open Budget Survey reveals that a number of sub-Saharan states, including Burkina Faso, Cameroon, Mozambique, Equatorial Guinea, and Uganda do not have such safeguards. As such, SAI heads can be removed from office at the sole discretion of the president (International Budget Partnership 2010). Clearly, this creates a situation in which an auditor general may feel political pressure to under-report financial mismanagement that would paint the party or individuals close to the president in a poor light.

CHALLENGES CONFRONTING MECHANISMS OF VERTICAL ACCOUNTABILITY IN THE BUDGET PROCESS

The mechanisms of horizontal accountability within the budget process reviewed in the previous sections are complemented by a second set of vertical accountability mechanisms that allow citizens to hold political leaders to account for enacting a budget that directs national resources toward key developmental priorities. As part of the democratic social contract, "citizens have both the right and responsibility to demand accountability and to ensure that government acts in the best interests of the people" (Malena and McNeil 2010: 5). Democratic governments have thus created both de jure (voting) and de facto (monitoring and lobbying) means for citizens to exercise their oversight functions. However, just like African legislatures and SAIs, mechanisms of vertical accountability, such as civil society budget-monitoring groups and elections, are also constrained by various legal, capacity, and political constraints.

Civil Society Budget Monitoring and Advocacy Groups

The "good governance" agenda that dominated Western donor thought during the 1990s promoted the enhancement of accountability, transparency, and participation within democratic systems and opened up space for greater public involvement in the budget process in many developing countries (Robinson 2007: 7). Initiatives like participatory budgeting following the Porto Allegre, Brazil model and the widespread use of Poverty Reduction Strategy papers by the International Monetary Fund (IMF) and World Bank have facilitated the emergence of nongovernmental citizen budget groups that seek to improve citizen engagement in budget formation and analysis and enhance the poverty focus of public expenditure (2007: 8). For example, across sub-Saharan Africa, diverse groups such as the Uganda Debt Network, the Public Service Accountability Monitor in South Africa, and Muslims for Human Rights in Kenya have all become active in budget monitoring and advocacy over the past decade and a half. Although these and other civil society budget groups have successfully increased citizens' awareness and engagement with the budget process in their respective countries, they have all been hindered in their ability to promote greater accountability in public expenditure management for a number of reasons.

Legal Constraints on Civil Society Budget Group Oversight

Despite the fact that the majority of African constitutions contain language that extends to citizens basic civil rights, such as the freedom of expression and assembly, civil society groups may face legal restrictions that limit their ability and incentives to engage in activities that would hold the government to account. For example, the recently implemented Uganda NGO Registration (Amendment) Act of 2006 and the corresponding NGO Registration Regulations of 2009 impose several restrictive conditions on the establishment and operation of all nongovernmental organizations in the country. Included in these rules is the requirement that all NGOs must register with the NGO Registration Board and, upon registration, the board may insert into the registration certificate conditions "particularly relating to: a) the operation of the organization; b) where the organization may carry out its activities; c) staffing of the organization" (Uganda NGO Registration (Amendment) Act 2006, Article 2). Not only do such conditionalities on operations, jurisdiction, and personnel jeopardize the autonomy of NGOs, but violations of other vague restrictions can lead to the abrupt deregulation of an NGO. For instance, Regulation 13 of the 2009 document mandates that organizations notify local authorities seven days in advance if they plan to "make direct contact with people in their area of Uganda" and also declares that "organizations shall not engage in any act which is prejudicial to the interests of Uganda and the dignity of the people of Uganda" (NGO Registration Regulations 2009: 13). Both these and other vague laws regarding NGO operations have limited the actions of the Uganda Debt Network and related civil society groups that engage in budget advocacy because they fear being shut down if they engage in behavior judged to be too political (Muhumuza 2010: 8).

Citizen budget-monitoring groups are also hindered in their ability to check executive discretion in the budget process due to a lack of Freedom of Information (FOI) laws in many African countries. The group Muslims for Human Rights (MUHURI) in Kenya, which attempts to conduct social audits of Constituency Development Fund expenditures by local members of parliament, reports having trouble obtaining the necessary information to conduct full budget reviews because Kenya lacks a FOI law (International Budget Partnership 2008: 3). The enactment of Freedom of Information laws would greatly facilitate citizen budget-monitoring groups because, as it currently stands, a number of African countries do not publish budget documents for public consumption even though they are produced for government use. For example, Nigeria does not publish midyear reviews, end-of-year reports, or audit reports (International Budget Partnership 2010), yet these documents are produced and could theoretically be made available through an FOI request.

Capacity Constraints on Civil Society Budget Group Oversight
Citizen budget-monitoring groups such as the Uganda Debt Network and the Public Service Accountability Monitor (PSAM) in South Africa have enjoyed some success in their countries due to their ability to develop links with both government and other nongovernmental collaborators, use the media strategically to reach their audience, disseminate information in a way that is accessible to average citizens, and design specific activities at different stages of the budget process to keep citizens engaged throughout the cycle (de Renzio, Azeem, and Ramkumar 2006: 4). However, despite these skills, citizen budget groups are nonetheless hindered in delivering even more robust monitoring and advocacy work by a number of internal capacity constraints. First, funding is often an issue among citizen budget monitoring groups. While the Malawi Economic Justice Network (MEJN) has struggled to track public expenditures, produce budget reports and policy papers, and conduct awareness workshops on a limited budget (2010: 104), the Uganda Debt Network has experienced the opposite funding problem—managing the burdens of being reliant on donor funding from many different sources, which includes the inability to engage in long-term planning and the need to use staff resources to liaise with donors rather than engage in monitoring and advocacy work (de Renzio, Azeem and Ramkumar 2006: 19-20). Other internal capacity constraints, such as a high rate of qualified staff turnover, lack of computer equipment, office space, vehicles and other resources necessary to carry out their mandate, along with a lack of technical knowledge, are additional constraints that many citizen budget monitoring groups must contend with on a daily basis.

Apart from internal capacity constraints, one of the main hindrances to effective monitoring of the executive's public expenditures by citizen budget groups is the poor quality of information they must work with. Even if governments are mandated by law to publish various budget documents during the course of the fiscal year, this does not ensure that the information contained in the reports will be comprehensive or useful in terms of accountability purposes. For example, while the 2010 Open Budget Survey Report assigns Uganda grades of A (extensive) or B (significant) for the comprehensiveness of information provided in documents related to budget formulation—such as the executive's budget proposal and the enacted budget report—Ugandan President Yoweri Museveni's government scores grades of C (some) and D (minimal) for budget documents related to monitoring and evaluation, such as the midyear budget report and the final audit report. Even worse, the same survey finds that Tanzania and Sudan provide hardly any useful budget information for public consumption, assigning both countries mostly C, D, or E (scant/no information) grades over the eight budget documents assessed as part of the 2010 survey (Uwazi-Twaweza 2010: 6). Clearly, the capacity of citizen budget groups to effectively monitor the executive's expenditure management is greatly constrained when the relevant budgetary information available to them is so minimal and of such poor quality.

Political Constraints on Civil Society Budget Group Oversight

Finally, civil society budget-monitoring and advocacy groups may be somewhat limited by the civic environment in which they operate. For such groups to be effective, citizens must possess the political will and efficacy to *want* to play an oversight role in the budget process. Most contemporary literature on vertical accountability seems to assume that democratization, which most sub-Saharan states experienced in the 1990s, "will automatically unleash public desires and expectations for answerability" (Bratton and Logan 2006: 4) from their elected governments. However, public opinion data from across sub-Saharan Africa paints a different picture of the degree to which citizens view themselves as having a role to play in holding elected representatives accountable between elections. The percentage of African citizens who think voters are responsible for holding, elected representatives accountable is strikingly low in many sub-Saharan states, including Namibia (6 percent), Mozambique (8 percent), South Africa (11 percent), Nigeria (18 percent) Mali (24 percent), and Ghana (28 percent) while the mean for all sub-Saharan countries surveyed as a low 34 percent (2006: 9). With such low proportions of citizens who view themselves as being part of the accountability dynamic in their respective countries, citizen budget monitoring and advocacy groups are partially constrained by the lack of a constituency who view them as facilitating a needed check on executive power during budget formation, execution and reporting.

Elections

As discussed above, free and fair elections provide the main mechanism of vertical accountability in a democracy, since citizens can vote out of office leaders who underperform. With regard to specific budget issues, the presence of elections make it less likely that governments will be able to get away with pursuing budgetary practices that are at odds with what they have promised the citizenry, or with the preferences of a majority of the citizenry. However, democratic theorists have long understood the imperfect nature of vertical accountability. Many characteristics of African political competition hinder the ability of citizens to effectively hold their leaders to account through elections.

Capacity Constraints on Electoral Accountability

For elections to effectively hold leaders to account, it is imperative that voters can ascertain *who* exactly should be denied re-election based on poor performance. As Powell has noted, a condition of accountability is the "clarity of responsibility"—in other words, the ability of citizens to know which politicians are actually responsible for policy outcomes (2000: 47-67). Even in mature democracies, this clarity is not always forthcoming. It may be clouded by divided government (for example, in presidential political systems) since the politicians in the legislature can blame the president for policy outcomes, while the latter in turn blames the former. Similarly, when power is shared by a coalition of parties, as is currently the case in both Kenya and Zimbabwe, the attribution of responsibility may also be complicated, particularly when members of the coalition seek to evade responsibility. Paradoxically, the clarity of responsibility also is negatively correlated with the level of democracy in a country, given that authoritarian rule in Africa has long been associated with hyper-presidentialism, in which it should be clear that all policy outcomes result from the actions of the executive (van de Walle 2003). Responsibility is, instead, harder to attribute in some of the more democratic countries, with more powerful legislatures and party coalitions sharing power.

Political Constraints on Electoral Accountability
Besides the difficulty voters have attributing blame to specific leaders for developmental delays, several other issues are likely to undermine mechanisms of vertical accountability in the new African democracies. A first and primary reason for limited vertical accountability has been the relatively few cases of real political alternation in power. Many of the old, pre-democracy leaders remain in power, despite the emergence of regular multiparty elections. Some old authoritarian dinosaurs survive, such as Paul Biya in Cameroon, Idris Déby in Chad, or Denis Sassou-Nguesso in Congo-Brazzaville, as they have learned how to countenance some real political competition, without however losing power. In other countries, like Togo or Gabon, a dynastic logic prevents real political change. In yet other countries, the change in individual leaders should not obscure the fundamental continuity of the regime, as the same single party remains in power (Tanzania, for instance), or democratization has not prevented the very same old political elite networks from remaining in power (Kenya, Zambia). For many of these countries, the poor quality of multiparty elections undermines accountability. Simply put, the field is tilted against citizens voting out incumbents, no matter how bad their economic policies. Even, when the field is more or less level, the continuity in the political elite probably serves

to perpetuate old political traditions and patterns, including perpetuating the old neopatrimonial logics that undermine the consolidation of veritable institutions of accountability.

A second impediment to electoral accountability is the weakness of opposition parties, resulting in a lack of political party electoral competition. Parties serve to aggregate citizen preferences and give them voice and coherence. In particular, opposition parties can draw attention to abuses in the budgetary process by incumbents, and help convince voters to enforce electoral accountability. African opposition parties, however, remain weak and poorly institutionalized, even in the more democratic states. Opposition parties lack the resources to contest presidential power effectively, and presidential resources can and have been used effectively to undermine them. Too many parties remain mired in clientelistic linkages to voters and do not effectively seek to mobilize voters on issues of importance to them (Bleck and van de Walle 2011).

So far, this section has focused on indigenous constrains on electoral accountability. In much of contemporary Africa, however, the international context serves to undermine these mechanisms of vertical accountability as well. In particular, a number of observers argue that the dependence of governments in the region on foreign aid serves to diminish leaders' accountability to their constituents (Moss et al. 2008). High levels of aid lessen the need of governments to seek resources from citizens, which weakens the social contract between citizens and state as governments no longer need to gain popular support for their policies. Evidence suggests that governments that do not rely on domestic taxation for their revenues are more likely to be nondemocratic and perform less well in economic terms (Morrison 2009).

Moreover, high levels of aid dependence shifts accountability from the domestic to the international sphere. Aid-dependent governments worry more about keeping donors happy and commensurately less about keeping their citizens content. Even when it is designed to promote sound developmental budgetary practices, donor conditionality and the international agency micro-management that typically comes with it undermines domestic processes in favor of international ones. For instance, in many countries, the national budget process becomes subordinate to the Poverty Reduction Strategy Papers (PRSP) process, which governments need to implement to receive donor support. Ideally, of course, the PRSP is designed to promote local ownership, and integrate itself with domestic systems of accountability, but recent studies emphasize how different the reality is from the ideal (OECD 2008).

PROGRESS AND PROSPECTS

Although we have largely concentrated on the weaknesses and limitations of the main mechanisms of accountability within the budget process across sub-Saharan Africa, recent developments in many countries demonstrate that greater budget accountability is beginning to take root across the continent. For example, an increasing number of states are establishing parliamentary budget offices in order to assist public account committees and the parliament at large in analyzing budget reports and accounts. A parliamentary budget office was recently established in Kenya; work has commenced on a building to house a PBO in Nigeria and there has been talk of also creating such offices in Zambia and Ghana (Johnson and Stapenhurst 2007: 376). Similarly, supreme audit institutions from different countries are beginning to share best practices with each through the establishment of the African Organization of Supreme Audit Institutions (AFROSAI). As part of this new collaboration, in March 2010 an 18-member delegation from the Uganda Auditor General's Office visited their sister office in Ghana to gain knowledge of performance audits (Government of Ghana website).

Mechanisms of vertical accountability are also making strides in strengthening their oversight monitoring and advocacy capabilities. For instance, the Institute for Democracy in South Africa (IDASA) has learned that citizen budget-monitoring groups can have a great impact on policy by focusing on specific sectors within the larger national budget. IDASA's Children's Budget Unit and their alliance partners were able to convince the government of South Africa to increase the level of funding it allocated to the Child Support Grant initiative, an unconditional cash transfer to support families below a certain set income level, and also successfully lobbied to have the age of eligible children increased to 14 (Robinson 2007: 19). By targeting a narrow sector of the South African budget, and also by combining the resources of many civil society organizations in an alliance, the experience of IDASA and their partners show how citizen budget groups can greatly impact public expenditure priorities in their countries. Finally, as free and fair elections become routine in a growing number of countries, political parties and citizens are likely to gain experience and confidence so that elections become more efficient instruments of accountability. Overall, understanding the main legal, capacity, and political challenges facing the various mechanisms of accountability in the budget process in sub-Saharan Africa can help these actors to strengthen their ability to promote a transparent and accountable budget process that results in greater socioeconomic development across the continent.

REFERENCES

Adamolekun, L., and M. Laleye. "Benin: Legislative Development in Africa's First Democratizer." *Legislative Power in Emerging African Democracies*. Ed. Joel Barkan. London: Lynne Rienner Publishers, 2009.

Azeem, V., P. de Renzio, and V. Ramkumar. *Budget Monitoring as an Advocacy Tool: Uganda Debt Network Case Study*. Washington, D.C.: International Budget Project, 2006

Barkan, Joel. "Legislatures on the Rise?" *Journal of Democracy* 19 (2008): 124-137.

Bates, Robert. *When Things Fell Apart: State Failure in Late-Century Africa*. New York: Cambridge University Press, 2008.

Bleck, Jaimie, and Nicolas van de Walle. "Parties and Issues in Francophone West Africa: Towards a Theory of Non-mobilization." *Democratization* 17 (2011).

Bratton, Michael, and Carol Logan. "Voters but Not Yet Citizens: The Weak Demand for Vertical Accountability in Africa's Unclaimed Democracies." *Afrobarometer* Working Paper no. 63 (2006).

Collaborative Africa Budget Reform Initiative (CABRI) and African Development Bank (ADB). *Budget Practices and Procedures in Africa 2008*. Pretoria: CABRI. 2009 <http://www.cabri-sbo.org/cabri percent20afdb percent20eng percent20front percent20web.pdf>.

de Renzio, Paolo. "Aid, Budgets and Accountability: A Survey Article." *Development Policy Review* 24:6 (November 2006): 627-645.

DFID. *Characteristics of Different External Audit Systems*. DFID Briefing, Policy Division. London: UK Department for International Development, 2005.

Dorotinsky, W., and R. Floyd. "Public Expenditure Accountability in Africa: Progress, Lessons and Challenges." *Building State Capacity in Africa: New Approaches, Emerging Lessons*. Eds. B. Levy and S. Kpundeh. Washington, D.C.: World Bank, 2004.

Frantz, Brian. "General Budget Support in Tanzania: A Snapshot of its Effectiveness." Washington, D.C.: USAID. 2004 <http://pdf.dec.org/pdf_docs/PNADA029.pdf>.

Government of Ghana, "Ugandan Audit Delegation Tours Ghana, 02 March 2010" <http://www.ghana.gov.gh/index.php?option=com_content&view=article&id=1548:ugandan-audit-delegation-tours-ghana&catid=28:general-news&Itemid=162>.

Government of Uganda. "Uganda NGO Registration (Amendment) Act 2006." Kampala: 2006.

Hodges, A., and R. J. Tibana. *The Political Economy of the Budget in Mozambique*. Oxford: Oxford Policy Management, 2004.

International Budget Partnership. "Social Audits in Kenya: Budget Transparency and Accountability." 2008 <http://www.internationalbudget.org/files/ImpactMUHURI1.pdf>.

———. *Open Budgets Transform Lives: The Open Budget Survey 2010*. Washington, D.C.: International Budget Partnership, 2010 <www.internationalbudget.org/files/2010_Full_Report-English.pdf>.

Johnson, J, and R. Stapenhurst. "The Growth of Parliamentary Budget

Offices." *Performance Accountability and Combating Corruption.* Ed. Anwar Shah. Washington, D.C.: World Bank, 2007.

Kasfir, Nelson, and Stephen Twebaze. "The Rise and Ebb of Uganda's Parliament: Striving for Autonomy in a No-Party State." *Legislative Power in Emerging African Democracies.* Ed. Joel Barkan. London: Lynne Rienner Publishers, 2009.

Kelsall, Tim. "Shop Windows and Smoke-Filled Rooms: Governance and the Re-politicisation of Tanzania." *Journal of Modern African Studies* 40:4 (2002): 597-619.

Kerapeletswe, C., and R. Shilimela. *Budget Processes and Transparency in Southern and Eastern African Countries.* Working Paper No. 8. Windhoek: Southern and Eastern Africa Policy Research Network (SEAPREN), 2008.

Lekorwe, M. H. "Supreme Audit Institution." *Transparency, Accountability and Corruption in Botswana.* Ed. Z. Maundeni. Cape Town: Made Plain Communication, 2008.

Lienert, Ian. "A Comparison between Two Public Expenditure Management Systems in Africa." *OECD Journal on Budgeting* 3 (2003): 35-66.

McNeil, Mary, and Carmen Malena. *Demanding Good Governance: Lessons from Social Accountability Initiatives in Africa.* Washington, D.C.: World Bank, 2010.

Morrison, Kevin. "Oil, Nontax Revenue, and the Redistributional Foundations of Regime Stability." *International Organization* 63 (2009): 107-138.

Moss, Todd, Gunilla Pettersson, and Nicolas van de Walle. "An Aid-Institutions Paradox? A Review Essay on Aid Dependency and State Building in Sub-Saharan Africa." *Reinventing Foreign Aid.* Ed. William Easterly. Cambridge: MIT Press, 2008.

Moyo, D. *Dead Aid: Why Aid is Not Working and How There is a Better Way for Africa.* New York: Farrar, Straus and Giroux, 2009.

Muhumuza, William. "State-Civil Society Partnership in Poverty Reduction in Uganda." *Eastern Africa Social Science Research Review* 26:1 (2010): 1-21.

Ndulu, B., S. O'Connell, J. Azam, R. Bates, A. Fosu, J. Gunning and D. Njinkeu. *The Political Economy of Economic Growth in Africa, 1960-2000.* New York: Cambridge University Press, 2008.

O'Donnell, Guillermo. "Horizontal Accountability in New Democracies." *Journal of Democracy* 9:3 (1998): 112-126.

OECD. "Making Aid More Effective by 2010: 2008 Survey on Monitoring the Paris Declaration" (2008).

Powell, G. Bingham. *Elections as Instruments of Democracy.* New Haven: Yale University Press. 2000.

Rakner, L., L. Mukubvu, N. Ngwira, and K. Smiddy. "The Budget as Theatre: The Formal and Informal Institutional Makings of the Budget Process in Malawi." Washington, D.C.: World Bank, 2004.

Robinson, Mark. *Budget Analysis and Policy Advocacy: The Role of Non-Governmental Public Action.* Brighton, UK: Institute of Development Studies, University of Sussex, 2006.

Schedler, Andreas. "Conceptualizing Accountability." *The Self-Restraining State: Power and Accountability in New Democracies.* Eds. Andreas Schedler, Larry Diamond, and Marc F. Plattner. London: Lynne Rienner Publishers, 1999.

Stapenhurst, R., and J. Titsworth. "Features and Functions of Supreme Audit Institutions." PREM Note 59. Washington, D.C.: World Bank, 2001.

Stapenhurst, Rick, and Michael Alandu. "The Accountability Function of the Parliament of Ghana." Paper presented at the Consequences of Political Inclusion in Africa Workshop, American University, Washington, D.C. April 24-25, 2009.

United Nations. *The Millennium Development Goals Report.* New York: United Nations, 2005.

Uwazi-Twaweza. "Can People Follow Their Money: Budget Transparency in East Africa" Policy Brief EA.01/2010E. International Budget Partnership, 2010 <http://www.internationalbudget.org/pdf/Can_people_follow_their_money.pdf>.

van de Walle, Nicolas. "Presidentialism and Clientelism in Africa's

Emerging Party Systems." *Journal of Modern African Studies* 41:2 (2003): 297-321.

Wang, V., and L. Rakner. *The Accountability Functions of Supreme Audit Institutions in Malawi, Uganda, and Tanzania*. Bergen: Christian Michelsen Institute, 2005.

Wehner, Joachim. *Back from the Sidelines: Redefining the Contribution of Legislatures to the Budget Cycle*. WBI Working Papers. Washington, D.C.: World Bank Institute, 2004.

Mueni wa Muiu
Colonial and Postcolonial State and Development in Africa

"OUR AFRICA": THE COLONIAL STATE AND THE BIRTH OF IMPUNITY IN AFRICA

> [W]e have been engaged in drawing lines upon maps where no white man's foot ever trod; we have been giving away mountains and rivers and lakes to each other, only hindered by the small impediment that we never knew exactly where the mountains and rivers and lakes were.
> —Lord Salisbury, British Prime Minister (quoted in Ndulo 2003: 330)

THE CULTURE OF IMPUNITY BEGAN WITH THE ONSET OF THE SLAVE trade and in the midst of the chaos self-appointed leaders became the norm. This culture persisted with the imposition of colonialism. From its inception, the colonial state acted with impunity in all aspects of life. As various studies have demonstrated (see UNESCO *General History of Africa* 7; Ajayi 1974, 1976, 1988, 1989; Ake 1981, 1996, 2000; Young 1982, 1994), colonialism was based on violence. No colonial power consulted Africans as to whether or not they wanted to be colonized. Brutal force was required first to control the population and second,

---

I wish to thank Guy Martin for his comments on the manuscript.

to impose the will of the colonial powers. Some revisionists argue that colonies were a burden. In the case of Algeria, the French President Charles de Gaulle noted that it was costing France without any substantial benefits (de Gaulle 1982: 74). The first goal of the various colonial powers (England, France, Germany, Italy, Portugal, and Spain) was to take over the economic control of the colonies by controlling not only the raw materials but the markets as well. At the heart of this control was African labor, which was essential for any success of the colonial venture.

In addition to economic needs, some countries, like France in Algeria and Senegal, wanted to restore their "honor" after having been defeated by the Prussians. Since the colonized people wanted to retain their way of life, violence became the norm. If workers were needed, the colonial soldier appeared with a *bunduki* (gun), as he did when cash crops were to be planted. Europeans were associated with fear and death:

> We have conquered in the past when we were forced to find new land for our growing people, but the white man conquers when he does not even need the land, he is already fat and well fed. He conquers for power. The administrators defeat our bodies, and the men of God defeat our hearts, we are left as nothing. At least when we conquered other people we took them and made them as ourselves (Turnbull 1962: 230).

As a result, a culture of "them" vs. "us" developed. "Them" in this case referred to all colonial institutions—which were alien as well as tools of exploitation and oppression. "Us" comprised the majority of the people who were exploited by these institutions. Furthermore, these institutions (be they the army, parliament, police, or schools) all required Africans to operate within an alien culture that denied their very existence (Kenyatta 1961: 269). Schoolchildren were punished and mocked for speaking in their indigenous languages (Magubane 1996: 31). Their parents were also denied employment and services for failing to adopt Christianity. At a Natal mission conference in 1920, D. D. T. Jabavu, a prominent Cape politician, clearly demonstrated the contradictions between missionary preaching and its treatment of "heathen" Africans: "[railway] waiting rooms are made to accommodate the rawest blanketed heathens; and the more decent native has either to use them and annex vermin or to do without shelter in biting wintry weather" (Muiu 2008: 36). Relations between the colonial state and its subjects were marked by extreme tension and suspicion that required the constant use of military force. The brutal and inhuman nature of the colonial state further divorced the people from all its institutions (Agbese and Kieh 2007: 8). Colonialism was based on exploitation, which took the form of collecting taxes, mobilizing people for labor, or forcing them to plant cash crops (Rodney 1985: 338). As George Martelli shows, in the case of the Congo Free State (CFS), the charter companies were authorized to use force to collect taxes (Martelli 1962: 163). The delivery of rubber in the CFS is captured by Roger Casement, a Belgian diplomat in the Congo charged with investigating the atrocities committed against the Congolese people: "Those who brought short weight or their wives, were detained [in the 'house of hostages'] until the difference was made up, or until they had worked it off" (Martelli 1962: 169).

Such a state had to be authoritarian for it to be efficient. It was a top-down model where the colonial officer gave the orders. Except in areas where indirect rule was practiced (such as present-day Ghana and Nigeria), the colonial state was also a centralized one. Indirect rule did not necessarily mean that the Nigerians were governing themselves; it was just an efficient way of governing large areas where the chief still answered to the colonial officer in charge. Indirect rule distorted indigenous institutions. To soften the brutality of the colonial state were various missionary organizations that appeased the majority of the people by promising a better afterlife. The rest of the African population was treated as victims of indigenous leaders who had to be protected from their leaders through the "dignity" of colonial labor and taxes. For maximum economic efficiency, it was very important that the colonies serve as plantations for the colonial powers. Whatever the colonial power needed—from cocoa, coffee, peanuts, minerals to rubber—the colony was forced to produce without any regard to human rights. E. D. Morel has demonstrated the inhumane methods used by the Belgians in the Congo to force the Congolese to produce rubber (Morel 1969: 120). The needs of the colony were not important. Trade relations benefitted the colonial power:

> Colonial powers imposed unfavorable terms of trade and strongly skewed economic activities towards extractive industries and exportation of primary goods. These conditions stimulated little demand to improve skills and educational levels of the work force, a situation that continued into post independence states (Ndulo 2003: 320).

It was not unusual for a British citizen who had never left England to speak of "our" Africa (Muiu 2008: 22-28; Magubane 1996). That sense of ownership over everything African gave colonial powers the impunity that came to be the hallmark of the colonial state. The colonial state did not decide which country it would trade with nor what crops were suitable for growing (Kaniki 1985: 382-419). All these decisions were made by the colonial powers. Forests were cleared without any consideration to environmental or religious importance (Turnbull 1962: 182). Cash crops were introduced without detailed studies on the impact of such crops on the environment and the water supply. The case of the pineapple in Kenya is a good example. The colonial government introduced pineapples as a cash crop in Thika in central Kenya, but until then, the residents of Thika and the surrounding areas could easily feed themselves as well as the nation. Large tracts of land were cleared, cutting precious trees to plant pineapples for Kenya Canners, which has been taken over by Del Monte.

That the colonial state did not have the interests and needs of Africans is demonstrated by the artificial nature of its borders. Not only did the borders ignore ancient trading patterns within the continent that could have shown how ethnic groups related to each other, they were also insensitive to relations between ethnic groups. Various ethnic groups were divided between different countries as is the case of the Somali who are in Djibouti, Ethiopia, Kenya, and Somalia. The Masai were also divided between Kenya and Tanzania. The Hausa were divided between Niger, Nigeria, and Cameroon. Viewed in historical perspective, colonial rule was short (about 60 years) in most African countries. But it was very brutal and disruptive of the indigenous institutions. According to Ndulo: "The foremost act of disruption was the unification of ethnic communities, under the umbrella of sovereign states, created pursuant to the Berlin Conference of 1884; these communities were granted with overriding political control within their whole area of jurisdiction" (Ndulo 2003: 331).

Rival ethnic groups were lumped together in the name of the colonial state, which privileged urban over rural areas (Ndulo 2003: 332). Indigenous religious institutions were demonized (Turnbull 1962: 204). The artificial nature of the colonial state continues to be a major obstacle to unity and nationalism that moves beyond ethnic identity (Fieldhouse 1986: 56-57) As Ndulo has shown, colonial rule was "philosophically and organizationally elitist, centralist, and absolute" (Ndulo 2003: 331). The colonial state implemented policy, endowed with unlimited power (331).

The school became the most efficient means of brainwashing the African child by turning students against their parents who were believed to be "savages" for rejecting Christianity (Emmanuelson 1927: 53; Kenyatta 1961: 270). This method of brainwashing was highly perfected in South Africa, where converts to Christianity were forced to move away from their homes. These converts settled on land that was owned by missionaries, where they could be controlled and monitored throughout the year. Contact with the "heathen" was forbidden.

The disruption of indigenous institutions continued throughout the colonial period into the post-colonial state (Potholm 1979: 35; Ndulo 2003: 331). In indigenous political systems, age-set organizations, the culture of compromise, and well-respected customs that had been passed on from generation to generation had been the hallmark of governance (Muiu and Martin 2009: 23-47). The chief governed with the advice and consent of advisers, and all decisions were based on debate and consensus (Levtzion 1980). But this eminently democratic aspect of indigenous governance was ignored by colonial powers. Ndulo reminds us that

> since the advent of colonialism, however, African societies have experienced fundamental and protracted economic and social changes. The era of colonialism initiated—and the era of independence consummated—a dynamic process of disruption in [ethnic] organization and . . . life. After those changes, unlike in pre-colonial times, the financial, political, and military security of African societies no longer depended on traditional organization and custom but rather on new political and economic institutions (Ndulo 2003: 330).

Colonial institutions neither reflected those in the colonial powers nor the African ones. Most important, a system of values that informed indigenous institutions and spiritual needs of Africans was destroyed. To the European powers, Africa was a blank slate:

> the traditional political systems of Africa were most frequently founded on the concept of the family, and their destruction adds to the destruction of the whole indigenous system of values. The old government is relatively easily replaced by the new, but something just as important, if not more so, is irretrievably lost in the process. It

cannot be regained under the new system any more than the system of values that underlie our concept of government can or should be adopted (Turnbull 1962:175).

The case of parliament is a good example of a bastard institution. In Britain, parliament is an important tool for governance, where elected officials decide on important issues without intimidation. The colonial legislature, however, did not represent the people. It was a tool for colonial leaders to manipulate to achieve their objectives. Mojeed Olujnmi Alabi reminds us that "in Africa, the legislature was never designed, neither has it been allowed to play, the kind of role that similar institutions have and still play in other political systems" (Alabi 2009: 233).

Colonial rule also manipulated indigenous institutions for its own use. Thus, in South Africa, the British used Zulu regiments for labor recruitment. In some cases, such as the Embu, the Kikuyu, and the Akamba in Kenya, ethnic differences were created where none existed before. In South Africa, the differences between the Zulu and the Xhosa became as distinct as those between Africans and Europeans. Since the colonial state was an extractive system, all infrastructure was externally oriented. Coastal towns and urban areas were privileged over rural areas. As a result, colonial state cleavages developed: between urban and rural (where the former was economically privileged). Three types of knowledge also emerged. First was indigenous knowledge, which was ignored in the colonial state. Second, Islam also resulted in its own elite, which was increasingly demonized. Third was the Christian elite, which was favored by the colonial state. All these types of knowledge were at odds with each other. That divide accelerated with independence and the introduction in the late 1970s and early 1980s of the structural adjustment programs (SAPs) by the international financial institutions (the International Monetary Fund [IMF] and the World Bank) (Alubo 2007: 206-223).

THE POSTCOLONIAL STATE: ACCOUNTABLE TO WHOM?

The colonial legacy, in addition to enduring long after independence, has had a major influence in the style of governance prevalent in Africa. Colonial rule bequeathed to independent African states undemocratic governments and bureaucracies that emphasized hierarchy, compliance, and discipline without addressing other equally important concerns such as public accountability, responsiveness, and participation (Ndulo 2003: 332).

Uhuru (independence) for African countries is a three-stage process: the first entails the physical removal of colonial powers from African countries, the second is the ongoing struggle against neocolonialism, and the final stage entails economic independence and unity for all Africans. The postcolonial state was "post" in name only. It retained all colonial institutions. Except for those who benefited directly from the new state, the postcolonial state inherited the mistrust, fear, and hate that the majority of the people felt toward the colonial state as a foreign entity that was imposed on them. The divorce between the rulers and their subjects that began with the onset of slavery persisted during the postcolonial period. Citizens were further marginalized from the institutions of power. The state became the major source of wealth and, therefore, the most sought-after office. The needs and interests of the majority of the population were ignored, further alienating them from the state. In some rural areas the villagers could not tell the difference between the new African leaders and the colonial ones. To such people *Uhuru* was a continuing nightmare that only made their lives worse by denying them access to basic necessities such as food, health, shelter, and security (Devenney 1998: 165-81; Swanns 1999: 1, 4).

In most cases, *Uhuru* accelerated the disintegration of indigenous institutions as it expanded the terrain of operations for transnational organizations, bilateral financial institutions, and Western powers. Large tracts of fertile land from which the local people were excluded were controlled by major mining companies, as was the case in Zaire (now the Democratic Republic of Congo). In Kenya, Brooke Bond controlled the best land on which tea was grown for export. Coffee and flowers were also grown without any consideration of the health dangers to the workers or the environmental damage. In Cameroon, large tracts of rain forest were cleared to export timber to foreign markets.

Starting in 1968, the World Bank became involved in population control programs. Countries requesting loans from the bank were forced to introduce population control policies: "Thus its [World Bank] spending on population control programs increased dramatically, from $27 million in 1969-70, to $500 million in 1990; $ 1.3 billion in 1993; and $ 2.5 billion in 1995. On July 17, 2008, the United States Congress approved $600 million to be used for family planning in developing countries" (Muiu & Martin 2009: 81).

Given the excessively high death rate resulting from conflict, disease, malnutrition, and starvation, and given the size of the continent, it is underpopulation that is the main obstacle to development rather than overpopulation. Since Africa's resources have been monopolized by Western powers for their exclusive use, allowing Africa's population to grow would provide Africans with the natural and human resources necessary for their own development.

Transnational organizations were not limited to cash crops—pharmaceutical companies also became involved. Animal-based research was considered to be too slow in producing the desired results. So Africans became guinea pigs for drug trials. The AIDS epidemic made impoverished Africans more vulnerable to these companies, as a variety of types of medical trials were carried out on them in many countries, ranging from Botswana and Kenya to Nigeria and South Africa. Once the medicine tested (especially for tuberculosis) began working, the trials would cease and the medicine would be made available for sale in Western markets (Muiu 2002: 81; Hartman 1991: 28-39).

In the 1980s and 1990s, the World Bank and the IMF increased their activities in African countries through SAPs that aimed at disengaging the state from the economy by privatizing state institutions. The colonial state was progressively stripped of its economic power as various foreign firms bought state companies for a pittance. Christian Aid estimates that as a result of liberalization, sub-Saharan Africa has lost "$272 billion over the past 20 years. Had they not been forced to liberalize as the price of aid, loans, and debt relief, sub-Saharan African countries would have had enough extra income to wipe out their debts and have sufficient left over to pay for every child to be vaccinated and to go to school" (AfricaFocus Bulletin 2005). Even in South Africa, which transitioned to majority rule in 1994, was forced to pay the debt accumulated by the apartheid regime when the first postapartheid government of President Nelson Mandela came to office (Muiu 2008). Most of the funds borrowed by the apartheid regime were used for the purchase of weapons that wrecked havoc not only in South Africa but also in the neighboring frontline states by killing thousands upon thousands of Africans. An exponentially rising and chronic debt continues to be the chain that binds African countries to their Western overseers, allowing the latter to constantly meddle in their internal affairs (Muiu and Martin 2009: 84-102).

The policies of the international financial institutions (IFIs) also made the exploitation of farmers more intense. Without state marketing boards, farmers were at the mercy of "middlemen" who set the prices as they saw fit. In the case of string beans grown in eastern Kenya for export to the United Kingdom, farmers were forced to spend more on labor only to get a quarter of the proceeds back from the middleman. Furthermore, farmers were not in control of their produce. It all depended on what was needed in foreign countries. The amount of chemicals needed to grow labor-intensive crops was such that in some cases the land was contaminated and had to be kept fallow for years before it could be used again. Meanwhile, the basic food needs of the population were not met as flowers, coffee, tea, and sisal replaced such staples as beans and maize. As a result, countries like Kenya, Nigeria, and Zimbabwe, which could feed themselves from the 1960 to the 1980s, were by the 1990s, forced to import food. World Bank and IMF officials became the key policymakers in most African countries (Mkandawire and Soludo 2000: 176). As a result, some observers have described the IMF and World Bank "as a dictatorship of nameless, faceless, and unaccountable technocrats, obsessed with private market-driven growth that sees the masses of impoverished people as incidental to the wealth creation project" (Bond 2004: 88). These "experts" are never blamed for any economic failures. Jeffrey Sachs further notes that since independence, African countries have relied on their former colonizers for economic development with very little positive results for the former (Sachs 1996: 20).

The fact that colonial powers granted independence did not mean that access to the resources of the colonies would cease. For Charles de Gaulle, in the case of Algeria, "the key question is to know whether Algeria will become Algeria against France or in association with her" (de Gaulle 1981: 50, 95). The negotiations for a free Algeria revealed the economic importance of Algeria to France:

> Simply put our interests reside in the free exploitation of the oil and gas that we have discovered ... close cultural and technical cooperation ... and privileged access for French firms to the oil of the Sahara for research and exploitation purposes, ... [and] maintaining our army in Algeria wherever we choose (de Gaulle 1981: 130, 132).

During the negotiations for independence in Tanganyika (Tanzania), the Tanzanians were informed that they could have their independence as long as they did not interfere with the resources; these belonged to the British. Independence was granted based on the terms and conditions set by the colonial powers. The leaders who replaced the colonial powers soon discovered that if they wanted to stay in power and remain alive they had to play the part scripted by their overseers. Such a role entailed allowing colonial powers continued access to their countries' labor and raw materials. Furthermore, as Chinweizu has demonstrated, most of these countries' constitutions were drafted without the input of their people. Transnational companies that had operated in the colonies during colonialism continued their operations, and in some cases expanded them. For example, Del Monte cleared even more land, further destroying the environment. The last nail in Africa's economic freedom was hammered in 1994 when South Africa moved from minority to majority rule:

> The transition was business saying: "We'll keep everything and you [the ANC] will rule in name.... You can have political power, you can have the façade of governing, but the real governance will take place somewhere else." ... It was a process of infantilization that is common to so-called transitional countries—new governments are, in effect, given the keys to the house but not the combination to the safe (Yasmin Sooka, quoted in Klein 2007: 203-4).

COSMETIC CHANGES

It is good for the wind to blow so we can see the backside of the hen.
(Ibo proverb)

The continued existence of the colonial state was predicated upon seven conditions. First, change (if any) must be gradual and for the exclusive benefit of the West (including the former colonial powers and the United States). According to this ahistorical perspective, which ignores the existence of various ancient kingdoms in Africa, democracy is presented as an alien ideology. Thus, Peter Lewis notes that "historically, most African regimes have had little accountability to their people, as rulers have maintained political control largely through authoritarian institutions and patron-client networks" (Lewis 2008: 95). Since the presidency is also the main avenue for wealth accumulation and patronage, elections have increasingly become violent. Incumbent governments continue to rely on election-rigging and manipulation so they can remain in office (Ake 1985; Joseph 1987; Ikpe 2009). A disturbing pattern has emerged that assumes that democracy can be maintained in a context of extreme poverty. Since there is no transformation of governance institutions in which the state is the key actor, elections have become a revolving door for the elite. Adebayo Olukoshi reminds us that "for democracy to endure, the embrace of the formal rules and processes of liberal political pluralism would have to be anchored in mechanisms for enforcing popular sovereignty in the political system" (1998:11). The present emphasis on cosmetic changes derives from the type of democracy that is introduced into these weak states. According to Richard Joseph:

> Assessments of democracy's prospects in Africa should attend more closely to democracy as more than just a set of rules for managing power struggles among elites. In the context of the great material deprivation of the masses of the people, democracy is an avenue by which their legitimate aspirations for a better future can be expressed and claims for redress made (Joseph 2008: 96).

What emerges from these attempts at democratic transition is a pattern that does not take into account the interests, priorities, and needs of the majority of the population. Instead, it is an elite affair in which the interests of all the powers involved, be they the elite, bilateral agencies, foreign firms, and foreign countries, are protected in accordance with their economic, military, and strategic needs. In essence the type of democracy promoted in African countries allows the various actors involved to conduct business as usual rather than to address the basic needs of the majority of the population. The arrogance of Western countries and their agencies is demonstrated by the kind of democracy that these actors encourage in African countries. No attempt is made to incorporate indigenous forms of democracy into modern ones. Instead, African countries are forced to adopt only a nominal and formal type of democracy. As Turnbull rightly observes, "we feel that our form of democracy is the only reasonable government, and we introduce it because it is the only form that makes sense to us and that we know how to handle" (Turnbull 1962: 175). Writing in 2005, James Bovard adds:

> There seems to be a tacit presumption in Washington that if an anti-U.S. candidate wins a foreign election, the election was flawed. The spread of pro-U.S. regimes is apparently the same as the triumph of the will of the people, since the people are or should be pro-U.S. This is a new form of U.S. manifest destiny—aiming not to militarily conquer foreign lands, but merely install pro-U.S. governments over foreign peoples (Bovard 2005: 73–74).

In a state meant to marginalize the people, this kind of democracy is ideal, as maximum violence is used to silence and eliminate those who work toward self-sufficiency and control over their natural resources and the economic sector (Alubo 2007: 221 224).

Second, any change in the economy must be gradual. Demands for better pay or working conditions cannot be tolerated since the objective of transnational companies is to make the maxim profit in the shortest time possible. Since the colonial state is in essence a puppet one, it is also a dependent one. It is not allowed to "grow" beyond its existing borders. Under no circumstances do Western powers allow any degree of economic independence on the part of African states. Furthermore, this process must not include changing trading partners. Kenya is a good example of how fragile the colonial state is. The Ibo proverb that it is good for the wind to blow so we can see the backside of the hen is appropriate in this case. Kenya, once the breadbasket of East Africa and the bastion of British settler colonialism, learned firsthand what it means to say "no" to the master.

It all started when the Kenyan government decided to switch from using Land Rovers for all its police and administrative personnel (which, after independence had been purchased from Britain at great cost) to using Toyotas for a quarter of the price. This was followed by agreements between the Kenyan and Chinese governments for the latter to develop Kenya's road infrastructure as well as to modernize military equipment and carry out offshore exploration for oil. The Kenya government refused to back down, even under intense pressure from both the European Union and the United States. In December 2007, ethnic clashes broke out in Kenya, thereby freezing any economic growth. At the time of writing, work had stopped on some of the roads that the Chinese were working on, and road-building equipment stands idle. In colonial Kenya, British colonial officers "[played] off Kikuyu against Masai, and one set of Kikuyu against another" (Trench 1993: 7). This policy of "divide and rule" continues as modern media (from text messages to the radio) is put to maximum use to spread hate messages either against the Luo or the Kikuyu to an ignorant population. Some politicians have also played the ethnic card to keep the people so preoccupied, unsuspecting, and busy fighting each other that they do not ask why they are hungry. It is interesting to note in this regard that diplomats from the United States and the United Kingdom were so involved in the 2007 elections (both local and national) that it was not unusual for candidates to be wined and dined in the various embassies. As in previous occasions, those elections had nothing to do with the welfare of the people (Kenya Human Rights Commission 1998; Muiu forthcoming).

Third, since only cosmetic changes are allowed within the colonial state, leaders who fail to follow the "rules" are either replaced through elections, paid to leave office or—in the worst cases—assassinated. Once elections fail to remove a leader who has ignored the rules, a government of national unity is constituted as has happened in Kenya and Zimbabwe. Constitutions are rewritten to give more powers to the losing candidate who becomes prime minister in the government of national unity. Such rulers are more accountable to their overseers than to their own people. In Mali, President Amadou Toumani Touré (known as ATT, the first president of Mali from 1991–1992) revealed at a conference in Montreal, Canada how he was paid $5 million by the Canadian Government so he would step down in 1992 after serving for one year (Touré 2001). This was done to present him as a good example of a leader who did not stay in power and observed the rules of democracy.

It worked! ATT was elected president in 2001 as a reward for stepping down in 1992, after the incumbent president, Alpha Oumar Konaré Toumani, had served his two terms in office (Touré 2001). Those who "rig" elections are penalized through the withdrawal of loans and visits to the various capitals of major powers.

Fourth, NGOs that sometimes work against the host governments' goals and often as spies for foreign ones (especially in countries in conflict) must be allowed to continue their programs and activities in these countries, even if these are detrimental to the people (which is the case for those involved in population control) (Martin 2005). Leaders who want to maintain good relations with their overseers must allow these enemies of freedom to continue their operations unless they want to face the same fate as Thomas Sankara of Burkina Faso, whose first act on gaining power in 1983 was to curtail the activities of all foreign NGOs. Four years later, Sankara was assassinated. In some African countries, such as, Kenya, Mali and Nigeria, NGOs have become agencies for recycling the political elite. Once these elites leave office, they create NGOs and use their government contacts to get funds—as former president Alpha Oumar Konare has done in Mali (Muiu and Martin 2009).

Fifth, a colonial type of education that trained Africans to hate all things African must continue in all these countries. The average textbook in most African schools does not teach African history from Kush to the present nor does it teach that Africa is a diverse continent that includes Africans of all racial and ethnic backgrounds. These textbooks focus on individual countries with their small dependent economies without any regard to the other countries on the continent. People are not encouraged to move from one African country to another because there are more travel restrictions placed on fellow Africans than other groups. South Africa is a case in point. There, xenophobia against other Africans such as Congolese, Kenyans, Nigerians, and Zimbabweans is so intense that these dare not appear on the streets (Muiu 2008).

Sixth, African countries must allow foreign military bases on their soil. Such bases are well equipped to silence opposition to a favored leader and to identify the sources of mineral wealth and of potential trouble spots (that is, the opponents of neocolonialism). In the name of fighting the war on terror, the United States uses its military bases in Kenya to strike against Somali terrorists. That well over 250,000 Somalis are now refugees in Kenya is of no concern of the United States. Yet this excess population puts a severe strain on the country's infrastructure and on the economic opportunities available to the people.

Seven, Africans must be treated as "victims" who do not know what is best for them. They must believe that "change" is occurring. Now and again a woman wins political office, while peace continues to be elusive. Small and incremental political changes (such as the election of President Ellen Johnson Sireleaf in Liberia) silence radical groups who believe that one day these countries will also catch up with their Western counterparts. It is important that the leaders be willing to allow these countries to carry out their operations peacefully. How these leaders control their populations is their business, provided they do not use unacceptable methods such as taking land from settlers, as Robert Mugabe did in Zimbabwe. Once African leaders become an embarrassment, "opposition" parties are created while charges of human rights violations escalate. Following Claude Ake

(1996), no one dares to ask whether one group of people can develop another, no matter how well meaning it is. Furthermore, no one seems a bit surprised that of all the regions of the world, the richest continent is forced to develop outside its culture and values (Muiu and Martin 2009).

A ROAD MAP FOR AFRICA'S DEVELOPMENT

Where, then, does the future of Africa lie? Pita O. Agbese and George Klay Kieh note that "there is a general consensus that the postcolonial state in Africa has failed to cater to the needs and aspirations of Africans" (2007: xi). The colonial state is the main obstacle to the economic, political, and social development of the African countries and peoples. In its present form this state exists only for the benefit of Western powers and exclusively serves their economic, labor, market, and security needs. The first step toward development will be to make the African state accountable to the majority of the people. A state that is based on accountability and transparency will have more economic interactions with other African states. According to Julius Nyerere:

> Africa . . . is isolated. Therefore, to develop, it will have to depend upon its own resources basically, internal resources, nationally, and Africa will have to depend upon Africa. The leadership of the future will have to devise, try to carry out policies of maximum national self-reliance and maximum collective self-reliance. They have no other choice. *Hamna!* ["There is none" in Ki-Swahili] (quoted in Saul 2005: 159).

An accountable state will also take control of its natural resources and economy. Without controlling the natural resources within their borders, Africans will always be poor and dependent. Such a struggle will be long and difficult. Colin Leys writes:

> For all countries of the world, recapturing control over their own destinies requires the re-establishment of social

Federation of African States (FAS)

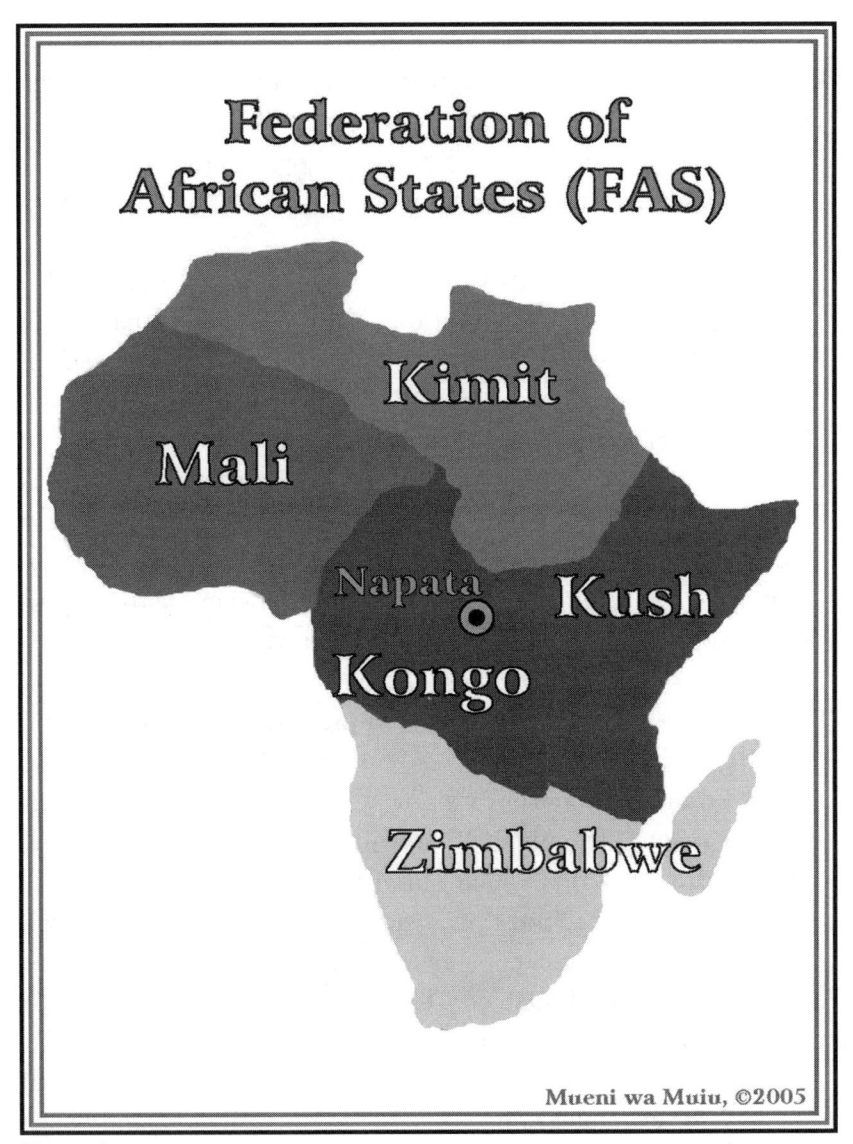

Mali · Kimit · Napata · Kush · Kongo · Zimbabwe

Mueni wa Muiu, ©2005

Figure 1

control over capital and the re-subordination of markets to social purposes [and] for the weaker regions of the world, such as sub-Saharan Africa, this is literally a matter of life and death (quoted in Saul 2005: 105).

Control over the economy means that Africans do not owe any debt to the IFIs. Since loans were provided by the IFIs to the African countries and elites without the knowledge and consent of the majority of the people, no country or agency has the right to force Africans to suffer indefinitely because of reimbursing the debt (Muiu and Martin 2009: 204).

The second step calls for the reconstruction of the colonial state based on the history, traditions, culture, and spiritual values (respect for the ancestors and for human life and compromise) of Africans. The reconstitution of the African state will be based on a Federation of African States (see figure 1). *Kimit* will consist of Algeria, Libya, Morocco, Egypt, Tunisia, and Western Sahara plus the Arab population of Mauritania, Northern Sudan, and Northern Chad. Similarly, Benin, Burkina Faso, Cape Verde, Cote d'Ivoire, Gambia, Ghana, Guinea, Guinea-Bissau, Liberia, Mali, Niger, Nigeria, Senegal, Sierra Leone, and Togo, plus the African population of Mauritania, will make up the new state of *Mali*. The Congo (DRC), Congo Republic, Cameroon, Southern Chad, Central African Republic, Equatorial Guinea, Gabon, São Tomé and Principe, Uganda, Rwanda, and Burundi will be within the new state of *Kongo*. Southern Sudan, Ethiopia, Eritrea, Djibouti, Somalia, Somaliland, Kenya, Tanzania, Zanzibar, Seychelles, and Comoros will make up *Kush*. *Zimbabwe* includes Angola, Botswana, Namibia, Malawi, Mozambique, Madagascar, Mauritius, Lesotho, Swaziland, South Africa, Zambia, and Zimbabwe. The new federal capital city will be called Napata. It will not belong to any of the five states.

Each region will have a key state based on population and resources (for example, Kongo, Egypt, Ethiopia, Nigeria, and South Africa). The FAS will be protected by a federal army made up of diverse members from the five states. All external economic relations will be conducted by the federal government. In the FAS, governance will be based on the positive aspects of indigenous institutions: consensus, shared governance, conflict resolution based on equal protection of all parties involved. Political power will be shaped like a pyramid: the village/town council will have the most power. The presidency will have the least power. Various councils will advise the leaders, but the people will have the right to remove a leader from power. All Africans will be free to travel throughout the continent. Justice will be based on conflict resolution and problem-solving rather than on retribution and punishment. Instead of serving jail time, criminals will be forced out of the community as they perform community service. There will be no death penalty throughout the FAS (Muiu and Martin 2009: 207).

Third, as one travels from Cape Town to Cairo, one is puzzled by the level of moral decay. Modern forms of justice have failed to fill the emptiness that resulted from the destruction of the African judicial system. Such systems aimed at solving problems rather than punishment. Social norms and the fear of the community forced most Africans to obey the law based on customs. According to Turnbull:

> morality is conceived of as being far above the mere obedience to the letter of a written, police-enforced law. But more important still is that in the past the [ethnic group] finds the incentive to work for the future, and to maintain its present integrity. If the past is destroyed, through taught disbelief, or through exposure to scorn and ridicule, or because of the twisted, unperceptive "evidence" of science, the result can only be total collapse (Turnbull 1962: 250).

If Africans are to limit the moral decay that pervades most aspects of modern life, the justice system must be totally transformed. Such changes must be made in consultation with the majority of the people, who must be at the center of development. Transformation of the educational system must also reflect the interests, priorities and needs of the people by linking indigenous knowledge with modern technology.

As George Ayittey cogently observes,

> foreign cultural practices and systems were foisted on the African cultural body politic. Disaster was inevitable as these foreign systems did not fit into Africa's socio-cultural milieu. The turmoil, chaos, and destruction that have ravaged postcolonial Africa can be seen as the rejection of these transplanted foreign organs. The continent is littered with the carcasses of failed foreign systems, imposed on the African traditional body. . . . Africa's salvation does not lie in blindly copying foreign systems but in returning to its own roots and heritage and building upon them (Ayittey 2005: 129, 366).

Africans are fully capable of deciding what works best for them. They can select what they want from Western culture but as the foregoing discussion has demonstrated, Western countries, agencies, and the African elite have continued to operate as if Africa belongs to them and as if they alone know what is best for Africa and its people.

Fourth, once the borders are reconstituted, African economies will have a much larger territory within which to operate. Rather than closing their borders to fellow Africans, within the Federation of African States, African experts will be free to operate in any region of the continent. Instead of these countries acting as puppets of Western ones, they will trade with each other. Such trade will entail the improvement of infrastructure throughout the continent. People and goods will be allowed to flow freely.

Fifth, the FAS democracy will be based on the needs of the people rather than on abstract individual rights that privilege private property over human rights. Four characteristics will inform such a democracy. First, the majority of the people will have decision-making power. Second, the goal of democracy will be to satisfy concrete economic, political and social needs. Third, in addition to individual rights, collective rights will be protected. Finally, it will be an inclusive democracy that does not leave out any particular group based on class, gender ethnicity, or race (Ake 1996, 2000). If a leader fails to meet the four conditions listed above or becomes an agent of foreign interests, the people shall have the right to remove her/him from office. What matters will be not be how long one is in power but *what* a leader does for all the people, not just one sector of the population. The paramount concern of a good leader will be to protect Africa and the interests, priorities, and needs of all Africans by any means necessary. Once the people know that they alone can transform the conditions they are facing and that they belong to more than just one state, then they will choose leaders from among themselves who share the same values.

Sixth, since Africans will operate within a state that they have created, they will not steal from it. The state will no longer be perceived as a leader's personal entity but as belonging to all citizens. Impunity will cease to be the norm as corruption whether by the elite, transnational companies, or foreign countries is curtailed. As Janine R. Wedel notes "corruption at its most basic [is] a violation of public trust" (Wedel 2009: 205).

In conclusion, the greatest quality that Africans have consistently demonstrated over the years is their resiliency and their ability to adapt to change in the most difficult circumstances. They are capable of deciding the best road map for their own economic, political and social development. Even the most isolated ethnic groups are not static. These groups change according to the conditions facing them as well as a function of the relations of power with other groups. Similarly, African culture is not static; it has changed over time based on various influences. It is this strength and adaptability to changing circumstances that will allow Africans to triumph. To do so they will have to create a national consciousness and unity which "the colonial powers, at all events, seem to have failed spectacularly enough [to create]" (Turnbull 1962: 250). "The serious problems facing Africa should prompt a fundamental reexamination and redirection, rather than a feeling of hopelessness and a mindset of blaming everything on the colonial past" (Ndulo 2003: 329). Only then will Africa be free from conflict, corruption, dependence, disease, fear and hunger.

REFERENCES

Africa Demos 3:4 (March 1995).

AfricaFocus Bulletin. "Africa: The Costs of Free Trade" (July 5, 2005) <http://www.africafocus.org>.

Agbese, Pita Ogaba, and Klay George Kieh. Preface to *Reconstituting the State in Africa*. Eds. Pita Agbese Ogaba and George Klay Kieh Jr. New York: Palgrave Macmillan, 2007.

———. "Democratizing States and State Reconstitution in Africa." Introduction to *Reconstituting the State in Africa*. Eds. Pita Agbese Ogaba and George Klay Kieh Jr. New York: Palgrave Macmillan, 2007.

Ajayi, J. F. A. "The Aftermath of the Collapse of Old Oyo." *History of West Africa*. Eds. J. F. Ade Ajayi and Michael Crowder. London: Longman, 1974.

Ake, Claude. *A Political Economy of Africa*. Harlow, U.K.: Longman, 1981.

———. *Democracy and Development in Africa*. Washington, D.C.: The Brookings Institution, 1996.

———. *The Feasibility of Democracy in Africa*. Dakar, Senegal: CODESRIA Books, 2000.

Alabi, Mojeed Olujinmi A. "The Legislatures in Africa: Trajectory of Weakness." *African Journal of Political Science and International Relations* 5:3 (May 2009): 233–241.

Alubo, Sylvester. "The Imperative of Reconstructing the State in Nigeria: The Politics of Power, Welfare, and Imperialism in the New Millennium." *Reconstituting the State in Africa*. Eds. Pita Agbese Ogaba and George Klay Kieh Jr. New York: Palgrave Macmillan, 2007.

Ayittey, George B. N. *Africa Unchained: The Blueprint for Africa's Future*. New York: Palgrave Macmillan, 2006.

Bond, Patrick. *Talk Left, Walk Right: South Africa's Frustrated Global Reforms*. Scottsville, South Africa: University of KwaZulu –Natal Press, 2004.

Bovard, James. *Attention Deficit Democracy.* New York: Palgrave Macmillan, 2005.

Carter, Gwendolen M., and Thomas Karis, eds. *From Protest to Challenge: A Documentary History of African Politics in South Africa, 1882–1964.* Four vols. Stanford: Hoover Institution Press, 1977.

Chinweizu. *The West and the Rest of Us: White Predators, Black Slaves and the African Elite.* New York: Vintage Books, 1975.

De Gaulle, Charles. *Mémoires d' Espoir: Le Renouveau, 1958–1962.* Genève: Editions Crémille & Famot, 1981.

Devenney, Mark. "South African Literature, Beyond Apartheid." *South Africa in Transition: New Theoretical Perspectives.* Eds. David R. Howarth and Aletta J. Norval. New York: Macmillan Press, 1998.

Emmanuelson, O. E. "A History of Native Education in Natal between 1835–1927." Masters Thesis, Natal University College, 1927.

Fieldhouse, D. K. *Black Africa, 1945–1980: Economic Decolonization and Arrested Development.* London: Unwin Hyman, 1986.

Hartman, Betsy. "Population Control as Foreign Policy." *Covert Action Information Bulletin* 39 (Winter 1991–92): 28–39.

Ikpe, U.B. "The Impact of Manipulated Re-elections on Accountability and Legitimacy of Democratic Regimes in Africa: Observations from Nigeria, Zambia and Kenya." *African Journal of Political Science and International Relations* 3:7 (July 2009): 300–310.

Joseph, Richard. *Democracy and Prebendal Politics in Nigeria.* Cambridge: Cambridge University Press, 1987.

———."Progress and Retreat in Africa: Challenges of a 'Frontier' Region." *Journal of Democracy* 19:2 (April 2008): 94–108.

Kaniki, M. H. Y. "The Colonial Economy: The Former British Zones." *General History of Africa.* VII: *Africa Under Colonial Domination 1880–1935.* Ed. A. Adu Boahen. Paris: UNESCO, 1985.

Kenyatta, Jomo. *Facing Mount Kenya.* London: Secker and Warburg, 1961.

"Killing the Vote: State-Sponsored Violence and Flawed Elections in Kenya." Nairobi: Kenya Human Rights Commission Report, 1998.

Klein, Naomi. *Shock Doctrine: The Rise of Disaster Capitalism.* New York: Metropolitan Books, 2007.

Levtzion, Nehemia. *Ancient Ghana and Mali*. New York: Africana Publishing Co., 1980.

Lewis, Peter. "Growth without Prosperity in Africa." *Journal of Democracy* 19:4 (October 2008): 95–109.

Magubane, Bernard M. *The Making of a Racist State: British Imperialism and the Union of South Africa 1875–1910*. Trenton, N.J.: Africa World Press, 1996.

Martelli, George. *Leopold to Lumumba: A History of the Belgian Congo, 1877–1960*. London: Chapman and Hall, 1962.

Martin, Guy. "The West, Natural Resources and Population Control Policies in Africa in Historical Perspective." *Journal of Third World Studies* 22:1 (Spring 2005): 69–107.

Mazrui, Ali. "Who Killed Democracy in Africa?" Paper presented at the conference on Democracy, Sustainable Development & Poverty: Are they Compatible? Development Policy Management Forum, Addis Ababa, Ethiopia, December 4–6, 2001.

Mkandawire, Thandika P., and Charles C. Soludo, eds. *Our Continent, Our Future: African Perspectives on Structural Adjustment*. Dakar, Senegal: CODESRIA, 1999.

Morel, Edmond. D. *The Black Man's Burden*. New York: Monthly Review Press, 1969.

Muiu, Mueni wa. *The Pitfalls of Liberal Democracy and Late Nationalism in South Africa*. New York: Palgrave Macmillan, 2008.

Muiu, Mueni wa, and Guy Martin. *A New Paradigm of the African State: Fundi wa Afrika*. New York: Palgrave Macmillan, 2009.

Mutua, Makau wa. "Why Redraw the Map of Africa: A Moral and Legal Inquiry. *Michigan Journal of International Law* 16 (Summer 1995): 1113–76.

———. "Globalization and Hegemony: Which Way Africa?" *The Journal of African Policy Studies* 8:11 (2002): 68–88.

———. *Economic or Political Genocide? Case Studies from Kenya and Zimbabwe*. (forthcoming).

Mwakikagile, Godfrey. *The Modern African State: Quest for Transformation*. Huntington, N.Y.: Nova Science Publishers, 2001.

Ndulo, Muna. "The Democratization Process and Structural Adjustment in Africa." *Indiana Journal of Global Legal Studies* 10:3 (2003): 315–368.

Nyerere, Julius K. "Reflections." *Reflections on Leadership in Africa: Forty Years After Independence: Essays in Honour of Mwalimu Julius K. Nyerere on the Occasion of His 75th Birthday*. Ed. Haroub Othman. Dar es Salaam, Tanzania: Institute of Development Studies/University of Dar es Salaam, 2000.

Olukoshi, Adebayo O., ed. *The Politics of Opposition in Contemporary Africa*. Uppsala: Nordiska Afrikaininstitutet, 1998.

Potholm, Christian P. *Theory and Practice of African Politics*. New York: Prentice Hall, 1979.

Rodney, Walter. "The Colonial Economy." *General History of Africa. VII: Africa Under Colonial Domination 1880–1935*. Ed. A. Adu Boahen. Paris: UNESCO, 1985: 332–381.

Sachs, J. D. *Sources of Slow Growth in African Economies*. Cambridge: Harvard Institute for International Development, 1996.

Saul, John S. *The Next Liberation Struggle: Capitalism, Socialism and Democracy in Southern Africa*. New York: Monthly Review Press, 2005.

Shivji, I. *Fight my Beloved Continent: New Democracy in Africa*. Harare, Zimbabwe: SAPES, 1988.

———. "The Pitfalls of the Democracy Debate," *CODESRIA Bulletin* 2:3 (1989).

Simmons, H. "Repackaging Population Control." *Covert Action Quarterly* 51 (1994): 33–44.

Swanns, Rachel L. "After Apartheid: White Anxiety." *New York Times*, November 14, 1999.

Touré, Amadou Toumani. "Chaire Téléglobe-Raoul Dandurand en études Stratégiques et diplomatiques."Keynote address, Colloquium on "L' Avenir des Opérations de Paix en Afrique Université du Québec à Montréal Canada, Montreal, May 26, 2001.

Trench, Charles C. *Men Who Ruled Kenya: The Kenya Administration, 1892–1963*. London: Radcliffe Press, 1993.

Turnbull, Colin, M. *The Lonely African*. New York: Simon and Schuster, 1962.

UNESCO. *General History of Africa* Eight vols. Paris: UNESCO 1989–1999.
Verschave, Francois-Xavier. *L'envers de la dette: Criminalité politique et économique au Congo-Brazzaville et en Angola.* Marseille: Agone, 2001.
Wanyande, Peter. "Structural Adjustment and Governance." *African Perspectives on Governance.* Eds. Goran Hyden, Dele Olowu, and Hastings W. O. Okoth Ogendo. Trenton, N.J.: Africa World Press, 2000.
Wedel, Janine R. *Shadow Elite: How the World's New Power Brokers Undermine Democracy, Government, and the Free Market.* New York: Basic Books, 2009.
Young, Crawford. *The African Colonial State in Comparative Perspective.* New Haven: Yale University Press, 1994.

Mwangi S. Kimenyi, John Mukum Mbaku, and Nelipher Moyo
Reconstituting Africa's Failed States: The Case of Somalia

FOR A LONG TIME, DEVELOPMENT EXPERTS HAVE EMPHASIZED THE central role that a well-crafted set of economic policies plays in the development process.

For example, a stable macroeconomic environment is considered crucial in providing the types of incentives that would enhance the ability of entrepreneurs to engage in wealth-creating activities—that is, there must be stability in order for the economy to secure the high levels of savings and investment that are key determinants of economic growth. Thus, economists have emphasized the importance of prudent monetary policy necessary to create conditions of price and interest rate stability. Likewise, models of economic growth have emphasized the critical role played by human capital, innovation, and knowledge in the growth process. These models show that although physical capital is an important component of the growth process, it is the accumulation of human capital that seems to be even more important in explaining growth trajectories. There is no doubt that all these elements are crucial to economic growth and development. However, it has become increasingly evident that at the core of the development process are sound institutions of both economic and political governance. Sound institutions determine the choices that individuals and firms make concerning investments in both human and physical capital, savings, and also long-term investments. The character of institutions also determines the choices that governments make in regard to the provision of public goods and services, maintenance of law and order, protection of property rights, and the performance of other duties. In addition, institutions establish rules that regulate sociopolitical interaction and determine the incentives that participants in both political and economic markets face. Institutions impact the development process through their influence on whether citizens live in peace or engage in destructive conflict (institutions can provide the structures for the peaceful resolution of conflict); whether scarce resources are invested in productive ways or are siphoned-off through corruption and devoted to nonproductive pursuits; whether individuals engage in productive and value-creating activities; or whether they shift their energies to destructive, rent-seeking activities; and whether, in fact, nations focus on policies that enhance the ability of future generations to undertake sustainable development; or whether public policies protect the human environment or destroy it. In short, we cannot effectively examine economic and human development in any country without placing the discussion in the context of the country's institutional arrangements.

The fact that institutions are a critical determinant of economic, social, and political development is apparent when one takes a close look at the development record of virtually all the countries in Africa. By and large, African countries have had extremely poor postindependence economic growth records. Even countries that are richly endowed with natural resources, such as oil and other minerals, have had very poor economic growth records despite the fact that, over the years, these countries have earned massive revenues from the export of their natural resources. These revenues, most of which have accrued to the government, could have been used to provide the social overhead capital needed to enhance rapid economic growth and development. Instead, the revenues were squandered by corrupt and opportunistic civil servants and politicians on nonproductive activities. The failure to effectively and efficiently use these abundant natural resource endowments and the earnings derived from them to achieve high rates of economic growth has been due to the absence of institutions that 1) adequately constrain state custodians (e.g., civil servants and politicians) and prevent them from engaging in corruption and other forms of opportunism (e.g., rent seeking); 2) enhance the management of ethnic diversity and minimize political violence, including destructive ethnic mobilization; 3) guarantee the security of property rights and hence, encourage and enhance indigenous entrepreneurship and wealth creation; and 4) provide market participants with incentives that enhance mutually beneficial exchange. Instead, most African countries have been pervaded by institutions that have failed to adequately constrain the state, enhancing the ability of civil servants and politicians to engage in corruption, financial malfeasance, and other forms of opportunism (Mbaku et al. 2001: 83-90).

Perhaps more important is the fact that these weak and poorly designed institutions have discouraged and in many instances stunted indigenous entrepreneurship and prevented the creation of the wealth that these countries could have used to deal with their multifarious public obligations. Hence, poor economic performance in the African countries is not due to the lack of critical resources such as human capital, savings for investment, and other resources, but the absence of the institutions that enhance the ability of entrepreneurs to engage in productive and wealth-creating activities and, which at the same time, adequately constrain state custodians and prevent them from engaging in opportunistic behaviors. As argued by Mancur Olson (1996: 22), many developing countries, including those in Africa, have not been able to capture or realize "many of the largest gains from specialization and trade" because they lack "the institutions that enforce contracts impartially, and so they lose most of the gains from those transactions (like in the capital market) that require impartial third-party enforcement." In this paper, we consider the failure of African countries to build growth-sustaining institutions as the primary explanation for their inability to achieve sustainable economic growth and development during the post-independence period.

There are several indicators of the quality of a country's institutions. Some of the more widely accepted indicators include those that evaluate the quality of institutions on a number of dimensions, such as government effectiveness, voice, corruption and accountability, political stability, and the quality of government regulatory activities. Other pertinent measures of the quality of institutions include economic freedom and political and civil liberties. By and large, sub-Saharan African countries, as measured by these global indicators of the quality of national institutions, appear either to have failed to provide themselves with effective and appropriate institutional arrangements or have institutions that are either weak and poorly designed or are not locally focused, and hence have no relevance to the political and economic realities in these countries. In fact, some African countries are now considered "failed states" due to the fact that within these countries there does not exist any single state authority capable of or willing to perform the legitimate functions of government or because there is no recognized authority, which like a legitimate government, has been granted the right by the people to monopolize the use of violence to, for example, maintain law and order. In such failed states, the institutions of governance collapse, subsequently producing an institutional environment that is not conducive for economic growth and development. State failure is usually associated with lawlessness, a collapse in the provision of essential public goods and services—if any public goods and services are provided at all, their allocation is undertaken arbitrarily and capriciously—a failure to protect the person and property of citizens, and a severe deterioration in the institutional structures that guarantee the security of property rights, resulting in the unwillingness of entrepreneurs to engage in productive activities, including, especially, the creation of wealth.

In this paper, we focus on Somalia, one of the clearest examples of state failure in Africa today. First, we will provide a brief overview of state failure in Africa and illustrate the discussion with examples from

Somalia's experiences during the last two decades. Second, we present proposals for the reconstruction and reconstitution of the Somali state. In addition, we examine a number of approaches that we consider critical to the rebuilding of the state. Given the current state of disorder in Somalia, we suggest that it is unlikely that the various factions will come together and strike a negotiated agreement leading to durable peace. As such, we suggest that the first step should be external intervention, and even possibly occupation, until all hostilities can be brought under control and a state of order is established. Third, we propose a number of complementary strategies, such as the provision of social services and the elimination of the various illegal sources of revenue that appear to finance the competing parties that are responsible for exacerbating the conflict. Finally, we propose institutional reforms, which we believe will establish an enabling environment for peaceful coexistence of all of Somalia's various population groups; the emergence of a robust civil society, which will serve as a check on the exercise of government agency; the continued development of the country's embryonic entrepreneurial class, which is essential for sustainable economic growth and development; and minimizing corruption, rent seeking, and other growth-inhibiting behaviors.

CHARACTERIZING STATE FAILURE

Of the countries listed on *Foreign Policy*'s 2010 Index of State Failure, the top five are African countries. Ranked by the level of state collapse/failure, they are Somalia, Chad, Sudan, Zimbabwe, and the Democratic Republic of Congo (DRC). Furthermore, in the list of the top ten failed states, only three countries—Afghanistan, Iraq, and Pakistan—are not in Africa. This evidence seems to show that Africa is over-represented in a list of the world's fragile and failed states. Poverty, health pandemics (e.g., HIV/AIDS, tuberculosis, and malaria), extremely high levels of material deprivation, human rights violations, especially the exploitation of women and young girls, and violence directed at minorities are problems that have become endemic and hence need urgent attention. However, in failed states, one cannot effectively deal with these problems until these states have been reconstructed and equipped with institutions that enhance peaceful coexistence and encourage engagement in productive activities. In other words, there cannot be economic growth and development in Africa's failed states until the necessary reforms have been undertaken and each country provided with institutional arrangements that reflect the values of the relevant stakeholders.

There are certain basic functions that the state must perform to be recognized as a sovereign territorial unit. These functions include providing territorial control or security, rule of law, basic social services, economic goods, and political services. While there is no common definition of state failure, states generally fail when they are unable to perform these basic functions for long periods of time over a substantial portion of their territory (Clement 2005: 4). There is a hierarchy of the goods and services that the state is required to provide to its population, the most important of which is security. Consequently, state failure is almost always characterized by the inability of the state to protect its citizens from internal or external aggression (Rotberg 2005: 3). Weber argues that the state must have a monopoly on "legitimate physical violence" (1964: 154). When the state does not have a monopoly on violence, as is the case in Somalia and the DRC, it is on the path toward failure. Similarly, if the state is not legitimately based on the agreed upon governing laws, this too can result in state failure.

It is important to recognize that state failure is a dynamic process. Failed states take on many different forms. However, they can be recognized by their symptoms, which include, but are not limited to, a combination of civil strife, corruption, economic collapse, poor infrastructure, pervasive poverty, little or no rule of law, lack of territorial control, and political instability, which in Africa usually includes destructive ethnic mobilization.

States can also be considered to have failed when they exhibit predatory behavior on the majority of their citizens—that is, the state becomes the source of violence directed at a section of its population.

Indeed, when states fail to ensure the well-being of their citizens, they may be classified as failed states (Collier 2009: 219-220). In Africa today, Zimbabwe is considered an example of this form of state failure.

Drivers and the Consequences of State Failure

The drivers of state failure are often dynamic and differ from one state to another. These drivers include a combination of external/international factors, structural and economic factors, political and institutional factors, and social factors. Indeed, state failure is a multifaceted issue. Vallings and Moreno-Torres (2005: 11-13) argue that weak institutions are the primary driver of state failure. Institutions allow the state to maintain the rule of law and manage the often conflicting interests of the collective effectively. When these institutions are weak, the state is vulnerable to failure. The constant changes in state institutions and inconsistent rules within fragile states ultimately lead to their failure when combined with other factors. Ineffective and unaccountable institutions leave room for abuse of power by the executive, elites and nonstate actors alike.

In the African context, the legacy of colonization has proved to be a driver of state failure. This has been found to be true in other regions of the world as well. The way in which the state was formed—whether the state is the product of gradual evolution or the artificial product of the decolonization process—matters critically for the strength of the state (ERD 2009: 50). The colonization process brought together people of different languages, ethnicities, traditional government structures, and religious beliefs to form a political, economic, and administrative unit that could easily and effectively be controlled by the colonialists. European colonialism created "states" in Africa that, often, could only be held together through the employment of significant levels of force. Today some African governments are simply unable to assert full control over the territory of the artificial states, which they inherited from the colonialists. A good example is the DRC, whose government has been unable to extend its control to all parts of the vast country since independence from Belgian in 1960.

Some researchers assert that it is the process of political or military transition that contributes to state failure. Many African states failed after the transition from colonies to independent states. The second wave of state failures in Africa occurred in the 1980s and 1990s when countries were transitioning from single party or dictatorships in some cases to democracies. Goldstone et al. (2004: 438-439) argue that countries whose political systems are in the process of transition are at a much higher risk of state failure. Another external factor that is associated with state failure is regional instability. States do not operate in isolation; instability among neighbors can destabilize the state (Vallings and Moreno-Torres 2005: 20). This is especially true in the case of Liberia and Sierra Leone—the conflict in Liberia contributed to violence and instability in Sierra Leone in the 1990s. Hence, the neighborhood in which the state finds itself is an important indicator of fragility.

The "resource curse" has gained prominence as a determinant of state failure in Africa. The abundance of mineral resources, especially oil, has been found to increase the probability of state failure. Competition for resources often fuels violent conflict further weakening the state. Violent conflict is both a symptom and a driver of state failure. States become more fragile as a result of violent conflict; congruently, violent conflict is more likely to occur in fragile states. The enduring nature of conflict is one of the most common characteristics of failed/failing states. Heterogeneity in the ethnic, religious, and class composition of the state has been found to contribute to state fragility (Rotberg 2003: 5). Social cohesion among groups in a state is necessary for creating effective political institutions. The state's ability to provide political goods is diminished by tension between groups.

Economic factors such as extreme poverty, low income, and overall economic decline have also been cited as indicators of state failure. Not all poor states are fragile states. However, every failed or failing state in the world today is a low income country. The inability of the state to deliver economic well-being for the majority of its citizens over a prolonged period of time increases the likelihood of failure. Other researchers have pointed to poor governance, environmental stress, militarization, demographic stress, and predatory elites as additional drivers of state failure. In truth, not one of the drivers examined in this section can single-handedly lead to state failure but rather it is a toxic combination, which differs from state to state, that precipitates state failure.

The impact of state failure on citizens can be quite diverse. Rotberg (2004: 8) points out that while state failure can create very lucrative economic opportunities for national elites, it can impose significant economic and social costs on the rest of the people. In fact, state failure often forces a severe deterioration of the living standards of many citizens, especially, as is the case in Africa's failed states, those of historically marginalized and deprived groups (e.g., women, children, ethnic minorities, rural inhabitants, and those who have been forced by economic circumstances, to live on the urban periphery).

Due to neglect, economic infrastructures in failed states are often in very poor conditions. Roads, electricity, water, sewage disposal and treatment plants, educational and health facilities, including hospitals, and other basic services collapse or are insufficient to meet the needs of the population. The deterioration of health care and education services is perhaps the most devastating and long-lasting consequence of state failure. Death from treatable/preventable diseases increases, literacy rates fall, and often life expectancy decreases.

The state's inability to perform basic functions often results in poor economic performance, rising unemployment, and decreasing real household income. Corruption is rampant in failed states, further constraining entrepreneurship and wealth creation. Government control, if any, does not extend beyond the capital city and select urban areas, resulting in increased migration to urban areas and worsening conditions in rural areas. Rapid urbanization presents an additional challenge for the state, as it is unable to provide enough social services to meet the needs of the newcomers. Consequently, urban areas in failed states are characterized by high crime rates and rising unemployment and underemployment (Osaghae 2006: 9).

In virtually all failed states, public goods and services that were previously provided by the state become increasingly privatized as nonstate actors (citizens, NGOs, international donors) step in to fill the void left by the government. However, as nonstate actors continue to perform functions that previously were exclusively within the purview of the state, the latter is further weakened as the space within which the state operates continues to decrease. In the case of Africa, people living in failed states usually retreat from state protection and seek solace or protection in the so-called ethnic association, an NGO that invariably assumes the functions (e.g., provision of public goods and services, including security) that were previously performed by the state.

One important casualty of the failed state is deterioration of the educational system—the state's failure to provide basic public goods and services also extends to education. The subsequent collapse of the educational system, especially at the primary and secondary level, makes it virtually impossible for the country to secure the human capital needed for staffing positions in both the public and private sectors. Perhaps more important is the fact that the few individuals in the country who have acquired significant levels of human capital (that is, professionals such as doctors, engineers, university professors, accountants, and other skilled professionals) flee the country in search of opportunities for self-actualization in more stable economies abroad. Brain drain, as this phenomenon is called, has become endemic to virtually all of Africa's failed states, including Somalia.

SOMALIA: THE PATH TO STATE FAILURE

Somalia is the quintessential failed state. By any definition, the Somali state is recognized as having failed in 1991. This is somewhat puzzling, since Somalia is one of the most homogenous countries in Africa in terms of ethnicity (85 percent Somali), religion (99 percent Sunni Muslim), and language (85 percent Somali). The primary divisions in

Somalia are along clan and subclan lines. The main clan families in Somalia are Darod, Dir, Issaq, Hawiye, and Digil-Mirifle. Within these major clans are numerous subclans. It is along these clan and subclan identities that subnational tension or violence occurs in Somalia (Clarke and Godsende 2003: 132).

The nation-state that is Somalia was created in 1960 when British Somaliland and Italian Somalia gained independence and merged. After independence, the country had a brief period of democratic governance. A national constitution was adopted by referendum in 1961 and a National Assembly created to represent the various clans/subclans. In March 1969 the National Assembly elected Abdirashid Ali Shermarke as the president of the country. By October of the same year, President Shermarke was assassinated by one of his bodyguards and Major General Mohamed Siad Barre took control of the apparatus of government in a military coup d'état.

After the coup, General Barre placed all executive and legislative power in the Supreme Revolutionary Council, which was chaired by him. General Barre then abolished the constitution and adopted a system of "scientific socialism," which effectively aligned the country with the Soviet Union (Powell et al. 2006: 3).

During the colonial period, Somalis were separated into five political jurisdictions. Somali populations could be found in *British Somaliland*, *Italian Somalia*, *French Somaliland* (now called Djibouti), *northwestern Kenya*, and *Ethiopian Ogaden*. As a result, from its inception as an independent polity in 1960, Somalia was prone to territorial disputes with its neighbors. Just four years after independence, Somali forces were embroiled in a border dispute with Ethiopia over the Ogaden region. In 1977, General Barre invaded the Ogaden region but a counterattack by Ethiopian military forces forced the Somali to withdraw by 1978 (Clarke and Godsende 2003: 135-139).

Using "scientific socialism," Barre nationalized access to land, water, banks, and other productive assets. Much of the nationalized assets were redistributed to General Barre's own clan and supporters.

Somalia's economy began to decline progressively as a result of Barre's distorting policies. Barre's regime was at first supported by the Soviet Union, which provided the country with development and military aid in the 1970s. However, the relationship between Somalia and the Soviet Union soured when General Barre invaded the Ogaden region. Taking advantage of the Cold War, General Barre shifted his allegiance to the West, which became Somalia's new benefactor and provided the country with economic aid throughout the 1980s. As the Soviet Union began to deteriorate and socialism no longer appeared to be as much of a threat to the security of the West, Barre's and Somalia's importance to the West decreased and aid trickled in at a much lower and slower rate. This, coupled with the poor economic policies implemented by General Barre, hurt the Somali economy so significantly that, by early 1990, the country was on the verge of collapse.

Throughout the course of his reign, General Barre grew increasingly more repressive toward other clans, especially the Isaaq clan in the north. By the late 1980s, numerous groups had risen to oppose Barre's rule, including the Somali National Movement (whose membership was made up primarily by the Isaaq clan), the United Somali Congress (primarily an instrument of the Hawiye clan), the Somali Patriotic Movement (staffed mostly by Ogadenis), and the Somali Salvation Democratic Movement, which had been created by members of the Majerten clan (World Bank 2005: 10).

In 1991, Barre was overthrown by rival clans and the central government subsequently collapsed. Numerous factions tried to take control of the government but failed and what ensued was a civil war. Since then, the international community has attempted numerous interventions, including one led by the United States in 1993. In addition, Ethiopia, Egypt, Yemen, Kenya, and Italy have all tried to bring the various factions together and form some central authority capable of exercising control over the entire territory. None of these efforts has succeeded.

Barre's opportunistic and extremely violent regime helped to fuel mistrust among clans in Somalia. Eventually, many clan groups came to the conclusion that they could not trust a central government but had to depend only on their own clan/subclan for security, as well as economic and social development. Consequently, numerous clan-based warlords emerged to fight for control of the apparatus of government. Civil war soon ensued, but none of the warlords was able to take full control of the country. The civil war in 1991 and 1992 destroyed the country's economic capacity, killed approximately 250,000 people, brought about a devastating famine, and created a serious refugee problem (World Bank 2005: 11).

In an attempt to reconstitute the central government, the Transitional Federal Government (TFG) was created in 2000 at the Arta Peace Conference with the help of the international community. Although numerous attempts have been made by the United Nations and other multilateral organizations to strengthen the TFG, its rule does not extend beyond Mogadishu. In fact, as 2010 came to an end, the TFG was increasingly able to exercise control over only a few neighborhoods of Mogadishu. Despite the military support that it was receiving from African Union forces, the TFG continues to face severe opposition from numerous insurgent groups.

Fractionalized State

In the absence of a functioning state, numerous factions have laid claim to portions of the territory. Each faction has established its own "government" in the form of an organizational structure and each possesses substantial capacity to impart violence. These factions include the semi-autonomous governments of Somaliland and Puntland; the TFG; Islamist militant groups such as Al-Shabab, Hizbul-Islam, Ahlu Sunna Wal-Jamaa; Islamic courts that control parts of the south-central Somalia; and recently, pirates whose sole interest is monetary gain (Kimenyi 2010: 2).

Located in the northwest and northeast region of the country, Somaliland and Puntland declared their independence from Somalia in 1991 and 1998, respectively. Though they are not internationally recognized, these semi-autonomous states have been able to provide relative peace and stability within their borders. Both states adopted a clan-based system of government and have achieved some success in maintaining law and order.

Despite these improvements, both Somaliland and Puntland face significant economic challenges. Much like the rest of Somalia, poverty and unemployment is widespread. Remittances/informal money transfers from the diaspora and livestock exports are the primary source of income in Somalia. The country's informal money transfer system or *hawala* is one of the largest money transfer systems in Africa, used to finance numerous activities from daily household expenses to the illegal operations of pirates.

The lack of economic opportunity has led some factions, primarily in Puntland, to specialize in piracy. This low-cost, high-return industry has become one of the most profitable industries in Somalia. While it is difficult to get an exact figure, it is estimated that pirate activities in Somalia brought in over $50 million in 2008, making it the most lucrative industry in Somalia (Worth and McDonald 2008: 1).

In the south-central region of the country, the Federal Transitional Government, Al-Shabab, Hizbul-Islam, and Ahlu Sunna Wal-Jamaa continue to fight for control over territories.

Al-Shabab and Hizbul-Islam were created in the wake of the defeat of the Union of Islamic Courts (UIC) by Ethiopian and TFG troops in 2006. These Islamist militant groups continue to fight the TFG and each other for territorial control. Al-Shabab is rumored to have ties with Al Qaeda, adding a global security element to state failure in Somalia.

Ahlu Sunna wal Jamaa, a group of moderate Sufi clerics, was initially created to counter the rise of radical Islamists through nonviolent methods. However, with the rise of Al-Shabab and Hizbul-Islam, Ahlu Sunna was forced to pick up arms. In March 2009, Ahlu Sunna joined forces with the TFG to fight Al-Shabab and Hizbul-Islam, but by September 2010 the alliance had fallen apart. Ahlu Sunna argued that while it was making gains in its fight against Al-Shabab, the TFG was steadily losing territory and failing to protect the people (Ibrahim and Gettleman 2010: 1).

The large supply of weapons in Somalia continues to fuel fighting between the various factions. Small arms are so prolific in Somalia that they are a form of currency in most parts of the country. Countless UN resolutions have failed to stop the flow of weapons through Somalia's porous borders. Instead, Mogadishu has become a key arms hub in East Africa with weapons flowing freely to and from Kenya, Ethiopia, Sudan, and the DRC (Kimenyi 2010: 2).

The various ethnic and religious factions in Somalia have established local fiefdoms within which they levy taxes and administer their rule. Due to these gains, factions in Somalia have little to no interest to work toward reconciliation.

RECONSTITUTING THE SOMALI STATE

The foregoing discussion has sketched the process that culminated in the collapse of the Somali State. By all counts, and as shown by both the Index of Failed States and the Rankings of Fragile States, today Somalia is a dysfunctional state, not capable of adequately performing most of the tasks expected of states. Probably no other sovereign state in modern history has remained in a collapsed state for as long a time as has Somalia. The collapse of the state has produced extensive human suffering—loss of lives, displacement of people, and in many areas, the total collapse of legitimate economic activities. Today, a large proportion of the Somali people have been displaced from their homes and now live as refugees in neighboring countries. The collapse of the state has therefore made it extremely difficult to focus on economic development.

Under the current state of affairs in Somalia, it is not possible to talk of state rebuilding or reconstruction—the violent mobilization currently being undertaken by groups determined to capture the apparatus of state must be brought to an end. In other words, in order for the process of state rebuilding to begin, peace must first be established in Somalia. Thus, the first line of business in the reconstruction of the Somali state must be to focus on halting ongoing atrocities and bring order to the country. One must create in the country an environment that guarantees the security of the people of Somalia—these are the people whose input is critical for the construction of the types of institutions that will enhance long-term economic growth and development. Ideally, if one of the clan-based factions were to dominate, then other factions would be compelled into a negotiated peace settlement. However, as things stand today, it is unlikely that any of the warring factions has the capacity to dominate others militarily. Furthermore, and even more important, no faction has broad support from the people and thus none of the factions can claim national legitimacy. It is precisely because of the lack of a politically or militarily dominant faction that each of the various factions has been unwilling to compromise and instead have all been adamantly uncooperative about subjecting themselves to any central authority. The balance of power among the warring factions has created some state of stable conflict equilibrium that is unlikely to change to peace without significant external involvement. To rebuild the Somali state, then, we propose a number of strategies. These strategies must be appropriately sequenced, starting with those that focus on dealing with ongoing hostilities.

External Intervention and Occupation

The first strategy in rebuilding Somalia must focus on securing immediate peace and establishing the necessary conditions for safeguarding the person and property of citizens. For this strategy to work, given the constraints imposed by the intransigent nature of the warring factions, there must necessarily be an infringement of the sovereignty of Somalia. To establish peace and halt the human rights abuses, there is need for substantial military intervention by external forces. We propose that this task should be led by the African Union, with the support, cooperation, and technical and material assistance of the United Nations. The military intervention necessary to establish some order must entail substantial ground forces. Today, many nations, including the United States, have largely abandoned their involvement in Somalia. The UN-supported African forces are few in number and largely ineffective. These troops have not been able to keep peace even in the limited parts of Mogadishu supposedly controlled by the Transitional Federal Government. What is now required is a large external force that is well equipped to deal with any type of internal aggression. It is certainly likely that many students of African political economy will criticize such intervention as a form of modern colonialism. However, it is important to recognize that without external intervention to establish peace and allow Somali citizens to engage in the type of state reconstruction that will help them regain control of their country, the violence will continue and many people will continue to suffer and die needlessly. For more than 20 years, there has not been a legitimate state authority in Somalia. Instead, power has been usurped by various warlords whose violent activities have created conditions in the country that have made life intolerable for the majority of people, created a serious refugee problem, and completely destroyed the economy's productive capacity. Perhaps more important, external intervention is now a matter of urgency to avoid any further human rights abuses, a problem that has been made worse by the fact that the various factions involved in this conflict do not respect international humanitarian law or the rules of war.

What we are proposing here is the establishment of an external "governmental entity" that will bring an end to the bloodshed, establish democratic structures through which the people of Somalia, regardless of clan affiliation, can engage in productive discussions to design and adopt the political principles that will form the foundation for the construction of their governance institutions. In addition to bringing about peace and security and establishing the necessary structures for subsequent Somali-led negotiations, the external authority will, in the short run and until a new Somali government is established, provide necessary public goods and services in order to arrest any further deterioration in the living standards of the people and pave the way for a return to economic prosperity.

The proposal for external control of Somalia is not radical at all, nor is it an attempt to subject the people of Somalia to some form of modern-day colonialism. The type of intervention we are seeking to establish in Somalia has been tried successfully in Bosnia, Kosovo, Liberia, and Sierra Leone, states that during sometime in the past two or so decades have either failed or have been on the brink of failure. In these countries, peace and cession of human rights abuses was only achieved after intervention by some external authority. We must also note situations in which failure by the international community to intervene resulted in regrettable outcomes—the genocide in Rwanda, which resulted in the wanton massacre of 800,000 people, could have been averted had an external authority, such as the United Nations, intervened. We feel strongly that if an external authority does not intervene and do so soon, the killing in Somalia will continue, probably for at least another 20 years. Eventually Somalia will begin to look like another Rwanda. Somalia, has, of course, disintegrated to the point where its sovereignty appears to exist only on paper since there presently does not exist any such nation called Somalia. It would be a terrible mistake not to "infringe" on this sovereignty in order to save lives and restore the dignity of the Somali people. Sovereignty, after all, should not be unlimited and should never be invoked by any country as an excuse to subject its citizens to acts of oppression, murder, rape, and starvation.

Curtail the Flow and Trade of Small Arms
Beyond containing aggression by the various factions, it is necessary to halt the flow of small arms and, as much as possible, disarm the population. As we have noted, state failure is characterized by substantial diffusion of the monopoly on violence to different factions in the society. The flow of arms to Somalia has greatly contributed to the diffusion of the monopoly on violence. Since the central govern-

ment collapsed in 1991, Somalia has evolved into one of the most vibrant markets for the trading of small arms—its porous borders provide illegal arms traffickers with the means to easily export guns to other countries (Schroeder and Lamb 2006: 71-72). Not only does this situation pose many problems for security in Somalia, but it also threatens security in other countries, especially those countries that are Somalia's neighbors. It is not possible to sustain peace unless clear strategies to deal with the flow of arms are put in place and enforced. In the longer run, it will be necessary to put in place strategies and incentives that would expedite the disarming of Somalia's many clan-based militias. Unless such actions are taken, stability might not be assured and may complicate the governance of the country in the future.

Suffocate Lines of Illicit Revenue

As has been already discussed, the collapse of the Somali state has also created opportunities for different factions to engage in illicit or extra-legal revenue-generating activities. We have suggested that these activities have in turn acted to fuel the conflict and to lower the incentives for the factions to be part of a unified state. With state failure, the various factions have been able to monopolize some revenue sources and thus it is not in the interest of the factions to have a functional state (Kimenyi 2010: 4). The rise of piracy is a good example of the consequences and causes of state failure. One cannot possibly hope to rebuild the state unless the international community cooperates in preventing piracy, which has become common practice in the Indian Ocean and a significant source of revenue for many of Somalia's clans. Likewise, many of Somalia's clans are involved in the illegal drug trade, also a lucrative source of revenue that fuels the conflict. To rebuild the Somali state, it is critically important that the international community devote significant resources and effort towards the destruction of the lines of illicit revenue that fuel Somalia's conflict and lower the incentives for factions to collaborate in state reconstruction.

Job Creation, Especially for the Youth

Engaging in conflict and other illicit activities is, to some degree, based on a cost-benefit analysis that takes into consideration the opportunity cost of the activity in question. It is unlikely that peacebuilding efforts would be sustainable unless accompanied by the creation of alternative employment opportunities, especially for the restless and frustrated youth who roam the urban areas seeking opportunities to earn a living (Renner 1999: 38-39). This is especially crucial for young males who, in African societies, are expected to engage in productive activities so that they can support a family. As part of rebuilding the state, it is necessary that there be well-coordinated efforts to create jobs or provide an environment which enhances entrepreneurship. Given the dire state of the economy and the high unemployment rate that currently exists in the country, especially among young people, job creation strategies may have to initially focus on public works, such as infrastructure construction.

Delivery of Social Services

After restoring order, the next important strategy in rebuilding the state is for the international community to emphasize investments in the delivery of social services, especially, water, education, health (which must include sanitation, especially in the urban areas), and also food security (Vauz and Visman 2005: 18-20). As can be expected, the collapse of the state is associated with limited capacity in the delivery of public goods and services, and in many areas the government is totally absent and hence, there are no public goods and services. In Somalia, local provision by different warlords has, no doubt, been important in some areas but over all, service delivery in Somalia has largely collapsed. The lack of access, especially by the poor, to welfare-enhancing and lifesaving public goods and services has obvious implications for the long-run development of the people. Of even more immediate concern is that limited investment in human capital will continue to make engaging in conflict an attractive alternative to gainful employment. Unless the security goals are also accompanied with improved delivery of public goods and services, the effort may not be sustainable and could face major opposition not only from the warlords but also from the people.

Organizing for service delivery in a collapsed state is itself challenging and one must seek innovative approaches. A particularly important aspect is that donor resources aimed at delivering services are likely to be misused as a result of corruption and the weak systems of accountability. Such circumstances may, therefore, require working through third party nongovernmental organizations in the initial stages of building the state. The setting-up of independent service authorities in such states has been suggested as a way to deal with the lack of a robust civil society that could facilitate the effective and efficient delivery of services where the state has failed. Obviously, the appropriate service delivery modalities will depend on the capacity of nonstate actors to organize for service delivery and how well they are accepted by the people.

Again, recent examples of successful initiatives show that service delivery is a critical aspect of state building in hitherto collapsed states. Citizens will place less value in engaging in conflict if they see peace dividends, such as their children going to school, improved water supply, and significantly improved access to health care. On the other hand, failure to include a strategy for service delivery is likely to render unsustainable any attempt to reconstruct the state.

Constitutionalism and Institutions of Governance
So far, we have focused on immediate short-run strategies to rescue a failed state. We believe that these strategies are necessary to establish the environment within which citizens can then engage in negotiations to build more permanent and sustainable governance institutions. Thus, once the initial stabilization phase is accomplished, it is necessary to focus on strengthening the institutions of governance that ensure peaceful coexistence of the people and provide the appropriate incentives for individuals to engage in value-creating transactions. It is the

building of institutions of governance that are founded on principles of constitutionalism that will guarantee that gains in building the Somali state are consolidated and the country does not revert to a failed state. Thus, after establishing order that guarantees security, it is necessary to build political institutions that are founded on constitutionalism.

In proposing strategies for building institutions for governance, it is important to take into account the source of state failure that has characterized Somalia. It is clear that the various factions in Somalia have expressed a demand for a fair degree of autonomy (that is, the factions behave much like semi-autonomous units that do not want to be under strict control of a central authority). Recognizing and respecting the expressed preferences for autonomy is critical in the process of building self-sustaining institutions. But such units of collective choice must be sufficiently constrained from imposing their preferences on other units. It is also the case that most of the factions are relatively small and occupy tiny geographical areas such that it might not be necessarily optimal to organize the state as a federal state with autonomous subregional governments. Furthermore, not all factions are organized in specific territorial space. Taking all these factors into consideration, we propose an intermediate model of governance that falls between a highly centralized governance model and a highly decentralized one. This model is the *functional overlapping competing jurisdiction* developed by S. B. Frey (2005: 546-549).

Self-Determination and Autonomous Subregional Governments

To some extent, the factious character of the Somali state is a result of the self-determination tendencies of the country's various factions. These groups have expressed a desire to establish self-governments that exhibit a fair degree of autonomy. One strategy to accommodate the factional preferences is to establish a decentralized federal system of governance (Mbaku 1997: 199-207). The federal structure of governance is based on the idea that jurisdictions in a federal system tax and provide goods and services to their citizens such that benefits and costs are internalized. This model also assumes that competition between jurisdictions exist and is manifested through voting with one's feet such that individuals choose to locate in jurisdictions whose tax-benefit structures align closely with their preferences. In the federal arrangement, efficiency is further enhanced by the exit and voice options available to the voters. The federal arrangement makes it possible for the various factions to establish regional governments with a fair degree of autonomy while all factions remain part of the larger Somali state (Bryden 1999: 135-136).

However, in some cases, such as Somaliland and Puntaland, there are already functional governments that have sought recognition as independent states. While it might be a bit premature to propose that Somalia be split up into several independent states, it must be acknowledged that autonomous regional governments can be a stabilizing force. As such, we propose that a key aspect of a new constitutional order must be to accommodate fairly autonomous regional units of collective choice. It is also possible that in some cases, peace and stability may require the establishment of separate independent states.

Functional Overlapping Competing Jurisdictions

The standard federalist model may not be well suited for Somalia. Given the expressed desire of autonomy by the different factions, it is unlikely that a federal system would adequately accommodate the interests of the various factions. Also, the autonomous states solution may not be viable as some of the factions are fairly small. Thus, it is important to seek a balance between autonomy and viability. In particular, factions may not be well suited to the delivering of services—they may be too small to deliver services efficiently. Rather than thinking of units of governance that are defined by some *physical boundaries*, a viable alternative approach is the establishment of *functional overlapping competing jurisdictions*. Under such arrangements, while regional units are defined by their physical boundaries, delivery of services is provided jointly by various jurisdictions. Furthermore, service jurisdictions vary depending on the type of service provided. The Functional Overlapping Competing Jurisdictions (FOCJ) model is promising where there are strong demands for autonomy and viability is of concern (Frey 2005: 546-549). We believe that this innovative approach for organizing society would be ideally suited for Somalia.

The Functional Overlapping Competing Jurisdictions, as articulated by Bruno Frey, is a modification of the standard federal model. The most important features of the institutional arrangement is that, in addition to the geographically defined local governments, new governments defined by the tasks performed are established—that is, the new governments are defined by the specific functions that they perform such as primary education, water, health, and so on. Thus, the model involves the establishment of a network of competing administrative units based on functions. The units defined by function extend over different geographical units—encompassing regions controlled by different factions or clans. Like the federal arrangement, individuals and communities have a choice on which administrative unit they want to belong to and have avenues to express preferences. Under the FOCJ model of governance, individuals can belong to more than one functional jurisdiction—for example, for the purpose of securing educational services, an individual may choose to affiliate with one FOCJ and in order to have access to clean water, choose to belong to a completely different FOCJ.

We suggest that the FOCJ model has the potential to solve some of the crucial institutional problems that have been at the center of the collapse of the state. In particular, the approach can allow even small factions to establish their own local governments while uniting with others in the provision of particular services. Thus the approach would remove the fear of domination of smaller factions by larger and more militarily-dominant factions.

Nonterritorial Federalism
We have noted that a number of the factions do not really occupy distinct territorial space. Thus, establishing traditional federalist insti-

tutions that are based on territorial jurisdictions would not accommodate some of these factions. As a result, in addition to establishing territorial federalism, it may be necessary to consider the inclusion of elements of nonterritorial federalism (Kimenyi 1998: 58-61).

CONCLUSION

There is no indication that the various warring factions in Somalia today are likely to engage freely in negotiations that can lead to durable peace. Simply, the various factions do not see the possibility of mutual gains through compromise. Furthermore, none of the factions is sufficiently strong militarily to compel others to negotiate peace. Also, the fact that factions are in control of various sources of revenue makes it possible for them to continue to finance the conflict. As such, the state of war is likely to continue and Somalia will remain a failed state with the consequential deepening of the suffering of the people. Thus, we have suggested that the situation in Somalia demands urgent internationally coordinated efforts. Given the state of lawlessness that exists in most of the country today, we have also suggested that restoring order and clearing the way for state reconstruction to begin may require occupation by external forces. While external forces will be infringing on national sovereignty, it is important to note that such intervention is clearly a more efficient and effective way to deal with the country's present quagmire than to hope that the various warrying factions will, in the long run, engage in negotiations to achieve peaceful coexistence. To complement the military option necessary to ensure security of the people and property, we have proposed strategies such as halting the flow of small arms, creating jobs, especially for the youth, and also the provision of basic services.

In the longer term, the people of Somalia must engage in building institutions that create conditions for peaceful coexistence and that make it possible for individuals to engage in productive activities. While we have observed that an appropriate constitution must take into account the fact that the various factions have expressed strong desire for autonomy, it is important to note that such a constitution must be locally focused so that it reflects the values of the relevant stakeholders, while at the same time incorporating certain universal core values of an effective and development-oriented constitution: participatory, accountable, and transparent governance; peaceful coexistence and stability; respect for human rights; sustainable development; and social justice. We have, therefore, suggested options that make it possible for factions to express their preferences as communities while at the same time cooperating with each other on issues of mutual interest. We have also noted that, some of the communities have already established self-governing entities and it is important that we accept the possibility that some of these regions may end up as completely autonomous states.

REFERENCES

Bryden, Matt. "New Hope for Somalia? The Building Block Approach." *Review of African Political Economy* 26 (March 1999): 134–140.

Collier, Paul. "The Political Economy of State Failure." *Oxford Review of Economic Policy* 25 (2009): 219–240.

Clarke, W., and R. Gosende. "Somalia: Can a Collapsed State Reconstitute Itself?" *State Failure and State Weakness in a Time of Terror.* Ed. Robert I. Rotberg. Washington, D.C.: Brookings Institution Press, 2003.

Clement, Caty. "The Nuts and Bolts of State Failure: Common Causes and Different Patterns?" Paper delivered at the annual meeting of the International Studies Association, Hilton Hawaiian Village, Honolulu, Hawaii, March 5, 2005.

Di John, Jonathan. "Conceptualising the Causes and Consequences of Failed States: A Critical Review of the Literature." Crisis States Research Centre. Working Paper 25 (January 2008).

European Report on Development (ERD). *Overcoming Fragility in Africa.* Robert Schuman Centre for Advanced Studies, European University Institute: San Domenico di Fiesole, 2009.

Frey, Bruno S. "Functional, Overlapping, Competing Jurisdictions: Redrawing the Geographic Borders of Administration." *European Journal of Law Reform* 5:3/4 (2005): 543–555.

Goldstone, J., R. Gurr, M. Marshall, and J. Ulfeder. "It's All About State

Structure: New Findings on Revolutionary Origins from Global Data." *Homo Oeconomicus* 21 (2004):429–455.

Ibrahim, M., and J. Gettleman. "Helicopter Attacks Militant Meeting in Somalia." *New York Times,* September 26, 2010.

Kimenyi, Mwangi S. "Harmonizing Ethnic Claims in Africa: A Proposal for Ethnic-Based Federalism." *The Cato Journal* 18 (Spring/Summer 1998):43–63.

———. "Fractionalized, Armed and Lethal: Why Somalia Matters," (2010) <http://www.brookings.edu/articles/2010/0203_somalia_kimenyi.aspx>.

Mbaku, John M. *Institutions and Reform in Africa: The Public Choice Perspective.* Westport, Conn.: Praeger Publishing, 1997.

Mbaku, J. M., P. O. Agbese, and M. Kimenyi. *Ethnicity and Governance in the Third World.* Aldershot: Ashgate Publishing, 2001.

Olson, Mancur. "Big Bills Left on the Sidewalk: Why Some Nations are Rich, and Others are Poor." *Journal of Economic Perspectives* 10 (Spring 1996): 3–24.

Osaghae, Eghosa E. "Engaging State Fragility in Africa from Below." Unpublished paper, Igbinedion University, Okada, Nigeria, 2006.

Powell, B., R. Ford, and A. Nowrasteh. "Somalia after State Collapse: Chaos or Improvement?" Independent Institute. Working Paper 64 (2006). Renner, Michael. "Ending Violent Conflict." Worldwatch Paper 146, April 1999.

Rotberg, Robert I. "Failed States, Collapsed States, Weak States. Causes and Indicators." *State Failure and State Weakness in a Time of Terror.* Washington, D.C.: Brookings Institution Press, 2003.

———. "The Failure and Collapse of Nation-States: Breakdown, Prevention, and Repair." *When States Fail: Causes and Consequences.* Princeton: Princeton University Press, 2004.

Schroeder, M., and G. Lamb. "The Illicit Arms Trade in Africa: A Global Enterprise." *African Analyst* 1 (2006): 69–78.

Vallings, C., and M. Moreno-Torres. "Drivers of Fragility: What Makes States Fragile?" Department for International Development, PRDE Working Paper 7 (2005).

Vauz, T., and E. Visman. "Service Delivery in Countries Emerging From Conflict." Department for International Development report prepared by Centre for International Co-operation and Security (CICS), University of Bradford, 2005.

Weber, Max. *The Theory of Social and Economic Organization*. Trans. A. M. Henderson and Talcott Parsons. New York: The Free Press, 1947.

World Bank. "Conflict in Somalia: Drivers and Dynamics." World Bank Paper IBRD 33483 (2005).

Worth, R., and M. McDonald. "Pirates Said to Take Supertanker Back to Somalia." *New York Times,* November 18, 2008.

Kelechi A. Kalu
Nigeria: Learning from the Past to Meet the Challenges of the 21st Century

AROUND 1472, PORTUGUESE SAILORS ARRIVED ON THE SHORES OF what is today the Nigerian city of Lagos. They came primarily for the purpose of participating in the slave trade. Eventually, internal battles for the control of the slave trade resulted in treaties between Britain and King Kosoko, ceding the territory of Lagos to the British in 1861. After the Berlin Conference (1884–1885), the colony of Nigeria was created as part of the so-called scramble for Africa by the European powers. Internationally, the effects of these events on governance and development in Nigeria should not be debilitating because British colonialism ceased to be a factor in Nigeria's political economy at independence in 1960. Nevertheless, the psychological impact of these external influences on Nigeria and its peoples remain. It is hoped, however, that through a well-planned and implemented educational program, these negative influences should be eliminated within a generation.

Although based on a different history, considerations for positive outcomes in Nigeria can be made by comparing Nigeria's post-indepen-

---

I thank the editors and John Mukum Mbaku for comments on an earlier draft that significantly improved the structure and quality of the essay. I also thank Devyn Paros for research assistance and Darby O'Donnell for help with the diagram. An earlier version of the paper was presented at the Center for International Studies/National Resource Center for African Studies at Ohio University.

dence political economy with that of South Korea, Malaysia, India, and other formerly colonized territories whose nationalism and economic development are rooted in their people's sense of patriotism and national identity. In 1960, Nigerians, through independence, acquired the task of nation building—focused planning, management of human and natural resources, and internal rearrangements of institutions and power. The nationalist leaders' approaches to 1) the establishment of governance institutions, 2) the building of nationalism, 3) maintenance of the rule of law, and 4) enhancement of the emergence of robust civil society institutions as frameworks for national development affected Nigeria's advancement. This paper examines how Nigerians have, since independence, articulated and implemented their national interest through the establishment and maintenance of a robust and viable state as a vector for national development.

Britain introduced a system of governance termed "indirect rule" to Nigeria as a way to enhance control of the colony's various ethnonationalities, as well as minimize the costs of exploiting the resources of the colony for the benefit of the metropolitan economy. Indirect rule, as a way to effectively organize various social classes and ethnonationalities, had been developed by British authorities through their experiences both at home and in India where indirect governance had emerged as an effective and efficient tool for exploitation and social organization of different classes and ethnonationalities. British colonialists applied that hierarchical leadership structure primarily to northern Nigeria, where there already existed institutional structures for the effective application of this approach to governance. Perhaps more important was the fact that northern Nigerians were already quite familiar with the feudal aristocratic leadership framework that had been imposed on them through religious conquest and that had subsequently established institutional structures that were amenable to the introduction of Britain's system of indirect rule. Thus, British colonial authorities merely brought to the Nigerian colony what British subjects and citizens had been forced to accept through wars of conquest—a hierarchical and feudal aristocratic governance structure that ordered the lives of the masses on the basis of class and royalty. Religious conquest and the establishment of a feudalistic governance structure in northern Nigeria provided the institutional environment within which the British handily implemented their system of indirect rule.

Starting with the nature of governance, this paper seeks to explain why Nigeria's development policies have failed, and the extent to which from the country's past governance and development failures can inform the design of policies for achieving sustainable development in the twenty-first century. Developed in the United Kingdom and honed in India, indirect rule was one of the most important constraints to the development of democratic governance in Nigeria, since it reinforced in the minds of Northern oligarchs a sense that they were "born to rule" or that they had been divinely ordained to rule the new Nigerians. In the postindependence period, many northern oligarchs and a variety of both military and civilian sycophants in the southern part of the country actually convinced themselves that they were divinely ordained to provide the new country with leadership, without which politicized religious, ethnic, and regional identities would be let loose on the masses. Simply put, Nigeria reflects the paradigm of those who created it.

Nevertheless, the colonizers are not the main source of Nigeria's underdevelopment—as evidenced by the fact that former colonial offices are, today, occupied by a stubborn and self-serving group of Nigerian elites whose understanding of leadership is governance with neither responsibility nor accountability to the governed. Without serious discussion on the particularities of the different ethnonationalities that inhabit the country, as well as on the establishment of an institutional environment within which all these diverse groups can coexist peacefully, Nigeria will remain a colonial British imposition: a failed central governance structure with a workable state.

THE CAUSES OF POOR AND INEFFECTIVE GOVERNANCE IN NIGERIA TODAY

Politics in Nigeria today is often characterized by an obsession with primitive accumulation. Instead of administering the laws and serving the public, state custodians (that is, civil servants and politicians) often abandon their mandates and seek only to maximize their self-interest and, in the process, have marginalized their fellow citizens. Since independence, a handful of elites (this includes military and civilian leaders) have managed to capture and use the apparatus of state for their personal capital accumulation purposes. Thus, during the last 50 years, Nigeria's political economy has been characterized by a high level of corruption and other forms of political opportunistic processes (for example, rent seeking) designed to enrich the ruling elites and their benefactors, but which have significantly impoverished most Nigerians. Notably, those who are most affected are the historically deprived and marginalized citizens (women, ethnic minorities, rural inhabitants, and those who have been forced by various circumstances to eke out an existence on the periphery of the country's various urban areas).

Further, most of Nigeria's elites rarely invest their ill-gotten gains in the domestic economy. Unlike their counterparts in Asia and Europe, who spend corruptly acquired loots within their own countries and regions and thus contribute to domestic economic growth, Nigeria's corrupt political elites invest their corruption-related wealth abroad, mostly in Europe and the United States. Although corruption is an insidious and growth-inhibiting institution that has been responsible for a significant part of Nigeria's continued underdevelopment, if the corrupt elites had invested their stolen wealth in the domestic economy, some of the negative impact of corruption could have been mitigated. Such investments could have created jobs for various population sectors and generated revenues to further fight poverty.

Today's Nigeria's ruling elites are not that different from the colonialists who brought various ethnonationalities together to form a political and economic entity that they could control and effectively exploit for the benefit of the metropolitan economy. Indigenous elites in today's Nigeria are engaged in a similar enterprise—they have used brute force to impose and maintain political, economic, social, and physical boundaries within Nigeria—not for the purpose of advancing economic and political development, but to enhance their ability to exploit public resources for their own benefit. These constraints to citizens' free movement and ideas distort economic incentives and significantly stunt the type of trade and exchange that is critical for economic growth and development. For example, undisciplined security forces often mount checkpoints on the few passable roads that exist in the country and demand and collect bribes from motorists as a condition for passage. In the Niger Delta (especially in Bayelsa, Rivers, and Delta states)—a region of Nigeria that is notorious for the lack of roads and other usable infrastructures—most people consider themselves trapped and unable to exit to other parts of the country to engage in productive activities and improve their quality of life. Consequently, many citizens see themselves as trapped behind an artificially constructed wall of poverty and deprivation designed and maintained by the elites in Abuja—aided by their foreign benefactors, the transnational oil companies that exploit the delta's resources for their own benefit and that of the country's corrupt and decadent political class. Materially deprived Nigerians who make up the bulk of the country's population feel powerless. They do not believe they can change the rules that regulate Nigeria's politics either through the ballot box or any other means. In the meantime, the ruling elites who have effectively privatized the state continue to employ its structures as instruments of plunder to enrich themselves at the expense of citizens.

In October 2010, Nigeria celebrated 50 years of independence. Unfortunately, the last 50 years have been characterized by high levels of corruption and political violence, including destructive ethnic mobilization and a level of poverty and social decay unbecoming of a country with such enormous endowments of natural resources.

So, why is there so much political opportunism in Nigeria? Why has postindependence Nigeria been so pervaded with poor and opportunistic governance? Why, for example, has Transparency International consistently rated Nigeria as one of the most corrupt countries in the world? Why is Nigeria, a country rich in natural resources, also one of the poorest countries in Africa?

Poverty and underdevelopment in Africa, including Nigeria, have been blamed on a number of factors: pervasive military intervention in national politics; natural disasters, including droughts (in the north) and floods (in the south); explosive rates of population growth; political instability, including violent ethnic mobilization; dependence on the Western industrial countries for trade, food and development aid, and loans; political and bureaucratic corruption, including public financial malfeasance; and agro-ecological degradation. In addition, some observers have blamed Nigeria's continued poverty on policy mistakes committed by well-meaning, poorly educated, incompetent, and unscrupulous civil servants and politicians.

The foregoing, however, are not the causes of poverty and underdevelopment in Nigeria. Corruption, for example, is not the cause of Nigeria's continued economic regression but a symptom or manifestation of its poorly developed and ill-defined institutions. Poor economic performance in Nigeria during the last half-century and the failure of the country's leaders to effectively utilize the enormous revenues received from the export of petroleum to invest in sustainable economic growth and development are not necessarily due to policy mistakes committed by ill-prepared and incompetent civil servants and politicians. While postindependence Nigerian leaders have made their share of policy mistakes, available evidence points to political opportunism (corruption and rent seeking) as the primary source of many of the country's policy failures. That is, most of what has appeared as policy errors have actually been deliberate and purposeful policies promoted by the country's opportunistic elites who are seeking ways to enrich themselves at the expense of fellow Nigerians (see Joseph 1987; Bates 1981; Diamond 1988). Although many of those economic programs generated significant benefits for the ruling elites and their benefactors, they imposed significant costs on the rest of Nigerians. Policies such as the structural adjustment programs (SAPs) nearly bankrupted the Nigerian economy, stunted indigenous entrepreneurship, and significantly increased levels of poverty, especially among historically marginalized and deprived groups. Nevertheless, these programs enriched a few politically dominant groups financially and enabled their monopoly of the supply of legislation (see Ihonvbere 1994).

Although, like many other African countries, Nigeria has suffered from a lack of committed leaders who desire to serve the national interest, quality leadership is not a sufficient condition for the effective management of national resources. The foundation for sustainable economic growth and development is a set of locally focused and development-oriented institutions. Such institutions must: 1) guarantee the protection of the individual's property; 2) enhance peaceful coexistence and provide a mechanism for the effective management of ethnic diversity; 3) adequately constrain state custodians so that they cannot engage in any form of opportunism; and 4) promote indigenous entrepreneurship and wealth creation. Thus, as Nigeria enters the next 50 years of its life as a sovereign nation, it must provide a democratic constitution with laws and institutions that are capable of adequately constraining the state (thus weeding out opportunistic custodians); enhancing entrepreneurship; and providing an enabling environment for the peaceful coexistence of the country's various ethnonationalities. In the following section, we will examine the role of institutions in Nigeria's search for development.

INSTITUTIONS AND DEVELOPMENT IN NIGERIA: SEEKING A SUSTAINABLE SOLUTION

To prepare itself for more effective governance and sustainable development in the twenty-first century, there is an urgent need for Nigeria to reconstruct and reconstitute the state in order to provide institutions and judicial structures that minimize political opportunism by state custodians; enhance peaceful coexistence of the country's diverse ethnonationalities; provide the platform for all of the country's citizens to engage in productive activities; promote the emergence of a robust civil society that can serve as a check on the exercise of government agency; and promote entrepreneurship and wealth creation.

According to Mancur Olson, the most critical and important constraint to economic development in today's developing countries is that the national economy cannot achieve its potential output through uncoordinated efforts of its citizens (1996: 22). An economy, no matter where it is located, cannot produce on its production possibilities frontier if it is not able to fully and efficiently exploit all the gains from specialization and trade. Poor countries such as Nigeria capture gains from self-enforcing exchanges. The main reason is that these countries do not have "the institutions that enforce those transactions (like in the capital market) that require impartial third-party enforcement" (Olson 1996: 22). Like most other African countries, Nigeria does not have fully functioning institutions that guarantee long-term security of property rights. Consequently, the country has not been able to attract the type of domestic or foreign investments that can transform the economy into capital-intensive manufacturing. Poor institutions enable state custodians to design and implement perverse economic policies, which produce benefits for them but discourage free exchange and wealth creation, severely stunting the development of a robust domestic entrepreneurial class. For example, without first taking into account how sustainable wealth is created in an economy and without establishing an institutional framework that protects private property rights and holds individuals accountable for their economic behavior, the 1972 Nigerian Indigenization Decree resulted in opportunistic behavior by civil servants and their foreign collaborators, forcing the program's failure.

In countries like Nigeria that lack institutions that guarantee long-term security of property rights, domestic or external investors tend to maximize short-term benefits from their activities in the market. Consequently, they undertake allocative processes that are destructive to the overall economic environment. For example, where pervasive corruption has rendered the investment climate extremely uncertain and property rights unsecure, owners of wealth may avoid investing to improve the sustainability of their resources and instead opt for excessive exploitation in order to extract as much benefit as possible before ownership of those resources is taken away from them, most likely through corrupt means. In Nigeria, this type of approach to investment can be seen clearly in the oil fields of the Niger Delta region, where short-term approaches to oil exploitation have destroyed most of the human environment.

Sustainable management of a country's resources, as well as the maximization of the gains from specialization and trade, requires national institutions that guarantee the long-term security of property rights. As Olson argues, the "intricate social co-operation that emerges when there is a sophisticated array of markets requires far better institutions and economic policies than most countries have. The effective correction of market failures is even more difficult" (1996: 22). Thus, without the right institutions, in both private and public sectors, opportunism will distort a country's public policy and equitable efforts to allocate resources. Eventually, entrepreneurship, economic growth and development will be stunted (Mbaku 2004: 269–271).

D. C. North states that institutions "are the rule of the game in a society or, more formally, are the humanly devised constraints that shape human interaction" (North 1990: 3). And, since institutions determine the incentives that traders in both political (that is, civil servants and politicians) and economic (entrepreneurs/business owners and consumers) markets face; they have a significant impact on the behaviors of citizens, whether their activities are in the private or public sector. In today's Nigeria, two issues are critical—how to adequately constrain civil servants and politicians and minimize their opportunism; and, how to enhance the ability of citizens to engage in productive activities to create the wealth that the country needs. Unfortunately, Nigeria's existing institutions trace their origins to colonially imposed arrangements, which were used to provide perverse incentives for traders. Those incentives discourage productive activities and encourage state custodians to engage in various forms of opportunism. This embeds corruption and rent seeking in Nigeria with the concomitant absence of a robust entrepreneurial class in the economy.

According to D. C. North, "that institutions affect the performance of economies is hardly controversial. That the differential performance of economies over time is fundamentally influenced by the way institutions evolve is also not controversial" (1990: 3). Regarding what role Nigeria's enormous resource endowment play in its development, Olson provides some insights. He says that improvements in the quality of life in a country are not determined by the extent of the country's endowments in natural resources or access to human and physical capital. A country can create the latter in the process of development. For Olson, the quality of a country's institutions is determined by its sustainable economic growth and development (1996). Where local laws and institutions guarantee free exchange, adequately protect property rights, force civil servants and politicians to be accountable to their constituencies, and enhance peaceful coexistence, wealth creation is likely to be maximized. Without such wealth, a country must continue to depend on external benefactors for resources to meet basic social obligations and hence, cannot plan for development. As the last 50 years in Nigeria have shown, civil servants and politicians can stunt entrepreneurship and economic growth through plunder and other opportunistic activities that threaten trade, both locally and internationally. Thus, the most effective way to fight poverty in Nigeria is to create and sustain institutions with laws that support markets and enhance the ability of traders to engage freely in exchange (see, e.g., Mbaku 2004: 270–271).

THE CHALLENGE OF INSTITUTION BUILDING IN NIGERIA

As in other parts of Africa, British colonialism brought to Nigeria laws and institutions that were never intended to enhance the ability of the indigenous peoples to maximize their values or govern themselves fully and effectively. Instead, the colonial institutional arrangements, like those in other European colonies in Africa, were designed to enhance European exploitation of Nigerian's human and material resources for the benefit of the metropolitan economies. The colony of Nigeria was very important to Britain. As argued by Lord Frederick Luggard (1926), the architect of British colonial policy in Nigeria, the colony represented, to Britain, an important source of raw materials for metropolitan economic growth, as well as a market for excess output from the United Kingdom. Hence, colonial laws and institutions were designed to serve the purpose of the colonial mission. As argued by Robert Fatton, Jr., these institutional arrangements were not democratic, "nor were they participatory, accountable to the people, or transparent" (1990: 455). In fact, British colonial officers in Nigeria made no effort to incorporate traditional systems of conflict resolution into colonial laws. Instead, they tried, often successfully, to rid the colonized society of any vestiges of traditional systems of governance and introduce Eurocentric systems that enhanced control and exploitation of the country.

Through decolonization, the British, working together with the rising Nigerian elites, were supposed to reconstruct and transform the critical domains and produce governance systems that were locally focused. Informed by the contextual values of all relevant groups, such systems would reflect the realities in the colony and be capable of enhancing full and effective governance in the newly independent country. Of course, such locally focused institutions could only be created if the decolonization process was participatory and dominated and controlled by relevant stakeholders. Unfortunately, and like that in virtually all the African colonies, Nigeria's decolonization process was reluctant and opportunistic and did not involve the full and effective participation of African peoples. In fact, the process was dominated and controlled by a few urban-based elites and their British benefactors and failed to provide Nigerians with the opportunity to determine the nature of the institutions that would become the foundation for governance in postindependence society. Further, the compacting of the colonial constitution, the foundation for the state and the government, was actually undertaken in the United Kingdom, away from the people. In addition, the discussions were in English, a language that was understood by only a very small group of Nigerians. It is no wonder that the outcomes were laws and institutions that fail to reflect the values of relevant groups in Nigeria that also were little understood by the people. Perhaps more important is the fact that the decolonization process did not offer Nigerians the opportunity to examine such issues as the National Question, citizenship, and property rights over natural resources, and what the form of government they were inheriting from the United Kingdom would mean for them. As a result, the postindependence constitution did not entrench structures for the peaceful resolution of conflicts arising from many of these problems. Immediately after independence, Nigeria was greeted with convulsive conflicts that started in the western region, then orgies of killings in the north and the consequent civil war. In terms of property rights, citizenship, indigeneity, marginalization, and other national issues, productive resolution of those initial conflicts remain at the core of Nigeria's development problems. The Niger Delta imbroglio, perhaps Nigeria's most intractable postindependence problem, is an issue that could have been examined thoroughly during a bottom-up, people-driven, participatory and inclusive (that is, democratic) constitution-making process with a structure entrenched in the final constitution to deal effectively with any conflicts arising from the allocation of resources tapped from the delta.

Since the document brought from Lancaster House to Nigeria was shared with part of the population, it can be argued that the people were given the opportunity to contribute to its improvement. However, as argued by LeVine, "constitutional debates were only rarely conducted outside the assizes of the drafting groups, and in most cases the finished product, while often the subject of intense public discussion, remained intact" (1997: 204). Thus, a well-crafted constitution compacted through a democratic constitution-making process would have been significantly different from the colonially induced model because it would have been based on ideas and values shaped by locally focused realities. Unlike the colonial institutional arrangements, the main objective of such a constitution would be the maximization of the welfare of Nigerians and sustainable allocation of the country's resources. Public policy under such a constitution would be geared toward serving the needs of all Nigerians rather than those of a few urban-based elites and their foreign benefactors. Since the postindependence constitution did not reflect the values of the peoples whose lives it governed, many Nigerians considered the institutions inherited from the British as illegitimate and alien impositions. The final outcome of the Lancaster House-based exercise was a constitution that reflected the values and ideals of the new country's urban-based elites—most of whom had been educated in the United Kingdom and the United States and had accepted Western culture and values—and not those of the country's relevant communities. Thus, the top-down, elite-driven, nonparticipatory constitution-making approach adopted by Nigeria's emerging elites disenfranchised the bulk of the population, depriving them of the opportunity to make their own laws.

Some scholars have suggested that many of Africa's postindependence constitutions were outcomes of political exigency (see LeVine, 1964). As the argument goes, Africans, including Nigerians, were eager to gain their independence and be rid of colonial tyranny. Thus, they were willing to forego democratic state reconstruction, gain independence, and then return to the issue of constitution-making in postindependence society. After indigenous elites had captured the evacuated structures of colonial hegemony, the country would then revisit the issue of constitution making and engage, this time, in a bottom-up participatory process in which all relevant stakeholders would be provided the facilities to participate fully and effectively in constitution making. For Nigeria, and indeed most African countries, that was never to happen. Historically, those who enjoy incumbency either in authoritarian or democratic regimes often do not wish to give up their advantages. For Nigeria, military intervention in 1966 ended any hopes to revisit constitution making to create a more effective set of institutions. In 1999, before the military finally returned to the barracks, however, it forced its own version of a constitution on Nigerians, again making it difficult for citizens to engage in any form of democratic constitution-making. Today the country remains saddled with institutions that inadequately constrains state custodians but constrains wealth creation. Currently, the most urgent task for Nigerians is engagement in democratic constitution-making to design and adopt laws and institutions that are locally focused. Such institutions should reflect the values of the country's relevant communities; provide the structural mechanisms for effective maintenance of the state—which includes the constructive management of ethnic diversity—and enhancement of wealth creation.

GETTING THE INSTITUTIONAL AND POLITICAL ECONOMIC DEVELOPMENT ISSUES RIGHT

While state maintenance depends on the type of institutional structures established to carry out the functions of governance, a key assumption for reconstruction in Nigeria must be the notion that state formation results from specific historical outcomes controlled by social and political forces (Caporaso and Levine 1996: 182–183). Although state structure and norms result from activities of certain individuals, power networks, or alliances, the state's legitimacy is anchored in its capacity to refract ideas and preferences of specific groups—preferably those of the country's relevant stakeholders—into a general purpose outcome that engenders most citizens' ownership claims as participants in the creation or maintenance of the state. In other words, the nature of the state and its institutions of governance and power are essential to formulating policies that lead to nationalism and popular legitimacy of the leaders and their decisions.

Even though a state emanates from the activities of distinct political and social forces, it is not necessarily autonomous because societal norms require specific outcomes in a given historical epoch. A successful state also consistently acts as a vector of development and source of ideological positions of its constituent members for long-term stability and survival. Although the Nigerian state was externally imposed, its stability and relevance depends on its uses of transparent and transformative collective resources to serve the public interest. Power contestations over oil resources in the Niger Delta demonstrate how citizens' marginalization and poverty undermine the corporate existence of the state, especially in this instance where custodians of the state have privatized the Nigerian state and its apparatuses of power and use them to maximize their private interests. Further, the extent to which Nigeria's political institutions serve the needs and interests of its citizens will mediate and maintain state legitimacy and the obedience/loyalty of citizens and determine how the law uses various institutions of governance to ensure social justice and equity in the allocation of resources.

State stability and legitimacy are enhanced when the state ensures citizens' equitable access to and use of public goods and services such as health care, clean drinking water, education and opportunities for human capital development, good road networks and other infrastructures critical to social and economic interaction, and electricity and other public utilities. It is also critical that the state be able to create and maintain an institutional environment that protects property and intellectual rights in order to encourage and enhance entrepreneurship and the creation of wealth and economic growth through innovative thinking and creativity. A successful and effective state uses public policy to transform societal relationships in ways that encourage and enhance peaceful coexistence. It also provides the wherewithal for citizens to engage in productive activities to create the wealth that they need to meet their obligations and significantly improves the ability of the private sector to serve as a solid foundation for national growth and development. Thus, while colonial policies fostered the exploitation of raw materials from Nigeria to feed industrial production in the United Kingdom and thus failed to create opportunities for the development of an integrated economy in Nigeria, the postindependence state must become a vector for the establishment, within Nigeria, of a modern, well-integrated, and fully functioning economy that offers employment opportunities to all Nigerians who desire work. Such a state will be capable of fully and effectively utilizing the country's huge natural resource endowments to create the wealth needed to deal with mass poverty and significantly improve the welfare of all citizens.

Postindependence Nigeria does not have a mandate to continue to perpetuate the illiberal and dysfunctional type of governance systems inherited from the British colonizers. Although at independence Nigerians did not reconstruct and reconstitute the colonial state to provide themselves with locally focused, liberal, and more effective governance structures, postindependence Nigeria must transform critical domains through democratic constitution making to provide itself with a development-oriented constitution. That new framework should adequately reflect the values of the country's diverse groups and focus on enhancing entrepreneurship, adequately constraining state custodians, and promoting peaceful coexistence and the efficient management of ethnic diversity.

Even though the last 50 years have been characterized by brutal military rule, high levels of corruption, and financial malfeasance—as well as significant increases in poverty and material deprivation—the country and its citizens have the opportunity and ability to turn things around. By engaging citizens in genuine institutional reforms, which can provide them with a democratic system of governance constructed around effective legal institutional framework, the state will ensure justice and fairness in social interactions. However, accomplishing that requires a focus on how to provide citizens with a good knowledge of democratic norms and a clear understanding of the nature of politics within the contexts of state and government.

In *Politics and Society in Contemporary Africa*, Naomi Chazan and her colleagues argue that the concept of the state is characterized by three components. The first component is comprised of the decision-making structures of the state (legislative, executive, political parties, and parliaments), which are responsible for making the decisions that advance the collective interests of the people. The second component of a state is the decision-enforcing institutions such as bureaucracies, parastatal organizations, and security forces. The third is the decision-mediating institutions, characterized by courts, tribunals, investigatory commissions, and the state through its structures, the organization of its people and resources, and how its public policy agendas are set to establish policy priorities, is an institution of power with definite interests (Chazan 1999: 38–39). Since the constitution establishes the rules and principles that govern the relationship between the state and its constituencies, the state and the constitution are creations of the citizenry designed to enhance the ability of the latter to peacefully coexist, resolve their conflicts peacefully, and allocate their resources in an efficient and equitable manner. Thus, ethnic or religious conflict, for example, can be resolved peacefully without resorting to violent ethnic or religious mobilization by and within the decision-mediating institutions of the state, as established by the constitution. Such legitimate outcomes are based on the extent to which the *government* (that is, the specific occupants of public offices) is willing to render fair and binding decisions on national and specific issues based on the rule of law and without bias against or in favor of any individual or group based on ascriptive traits such as ethnicity, place of birth, or religious affiliation.

Rather than the state, the government, whose agents are drawn from the society, is responsible for nation building. An organization of power, the state is not a neutral concept and emanates from specific political and social forces making it the responsibility of government to manipulate the organization of citizens and resources to advance the national interest. For Nigeria, the responsibility of the political, traditional and intellectual elites was to become the power brokers at independence. However, according to J. F. Ade Ajayi (1982), Nigeria's new elites failed because they, especially the intellectuals, knew more about what they did not want—colonial rule—than what was supposed to replace it after independence. He asserts that the new elites' understanding of development was mostly abstract and that they were not trusted by the colonized Nigerian elites, whose offices owed loyalty to Britain. With time, the country's emerging technocrats were forced out of office and replaced by opportunistic military officers and professional politicians whose main interest was primitive accumulation. Those politicians, who together with the military, have ruled Nigeria during the last 50 years, have never been able to provide the people with their vision of the state and government, nor have they succeeded in conceptualizing and presenting to the people their understanding of Nigerian citizenship. These postindependence rulers/politicians concept of nationalism remains a mystery. What is clear, however, is that whether military or civilian, they have shown interest only in primitive accumulation and have therefore not made any efforts to produce both a state and government in Nigeria capable of serving the national interest. As a consequence, the Nigeria state is "yet to evolve stable political structures that are imbued with a sense of national commitment and notions of social justice, around which the loyalties of the masses could be mobilized" (Ajayi 1982: 6).

With the nation-building project assigned to the state instead of government, the occupants of early postindependence government spaces blamed their lack of vision and crass opportunism on the state. By neglecting the decision-making, enforcing, and mediating roles of the state under the control of the government and society, Nigeria's postindependence leaders ignored the development of a collective national consciousness.

Lacking the foregoing clarifications, a number of scholars have tended to analyze Nigeria's sociopolitical issues from a Marxist production-relation point of view. Such analytical obfuscation in the Gramscian tradition sees no demarcation between the *state* and the *social classes* that sustain it. This confuses the difference between both the Nigerian state and the specific ethnic or class origins of the head of state and ignores the spuriousness of the idea that elevates the three most populous ethnic groups to dominant national status. As part of the nation-building effort, intellectual disaggregation of the notion of

Nigerian nationalities will allow clarity on the origins and identities of various leaders and their commitment to the national question. For example, although executive leaders like Generals Gowon, Babangida, and Abacha are actually members of minority ethnic groups, they often refer to themselves as Hausa (a majority ethnic group) because of the benefits associated with that membership nationally. In Nigeria, the individual so identified assures himself a constituency that anchors his political ambitions and acquires some level of legitimacy for his leadership position in the country's political system. The ethnoregional group accepts the usurper and adopts him as a "native son" in order to share in the "booty" that the new leader is expected to appropriate from the national treasury through corruption and other forms of political opportunism. Thus, by referring to himself as Hausa, General Abacha, who had seized the apparatus of government through a military coup, was assuring himself of an important constituency that was bound to support his illegitimate rule and help him gain legitimacy. In exchange, he would make a concerted effort to distort resource allocation in favor of his benefactors—the agglomeration of over 80 ethnic nationalities in northern Nigeria collectively referred to as Hausa. This consolidation of ethno-identities for political expedience is a process that has characterized Nigerian political economy since independence in 1960 and is used to manipulate the ethnic sensitivities of the masses about the origins and accountability of the country's executive leadership.

The failure to differentiate between state and government and the inability to separate the state from the social class and ethnic origin of the head of government saps national energy because they underscore differences rather than nation building: a project that emphasizes commonality of consciousness as a framework for developing a unity of purpose. Building a sound collective consciousness for a national development program will strengthen the Nigerian state, government, and the various ethnic nationalities. A strong national development program must contain the mechanisms needed to increase everyone's access to clean water, indoor plumbing, good road networks, electricity, sound education, skills-based employment, and life-enhancing health-care services, which are necessary for the survival and stability of the Nigerian state. Provision of these basic necessities does not require democracy; they require a governance platform that empowers citizens to be active participants in their own economic and political well-being—a productive framework of law and order.

The neglected nation-building project at political independence that engaged citizens to become Nigerian—irrespective of ethnic origin—still holds the key to both stability and economic growth in the country. As William E. Hudson argues, "the foundation of the state rests on the initial consent of all citizens, irrespective of differences in wealth or social status. . . . [And] the initial social contract means that government itself has a democratic obligation to understand that its powers derive from the initial consent of citizens, and to enforce laws and protect political rights equally" (Hudson 2004: 7). The agitations for resource control in the Niger Delta, the series of kidnappings across the eastern part of the country, and the various religion-based instabilities and conflicts reflect the frustrations and perceived inability and incapacity government.

However, lacking focused development policies that encourage economic growth, the only thriving industry in Nigeria is the practice of the elites hijacking democratic processes, the state, and its oil largess through fraudulent elections. Unfortunately, and given the deadly game of politics in Nigeria, unemployed youths from economically devastated regions have learned to imitate the political elites at the local level as evidenced by widespread kidnapping of children, foreign oil workers, and vulnerable relatives of Nigerian legislators and economic elites for ransom. Given that the youths from the Niger Delta and eastern parts of the country are mostly implicated in the economic terrorism of the kidnapping industry, and that the government has been unable to control the increased kidnapping or provide a platform for viable economic activities across the country, some question the survivability of the Nigerian state. And if not constitutionally rectified, these issues will threaten the corpus of the Nigerian state.

INSTITUTIONS AND TRANSFORMATIONAL DEVELOPMENT IN NIGERIA

John Boye Ejobowah argues that the problem in Nigeria is not institutions; there are many institutions to enhance democratic and governance process and the "country has the necessary institutional mechanisms for committing actors to cooperate and to respect autonomies. The problem is the country's inability to mount credible elections" (Ejobowah 2009: 520). Ejobowah's argument ignores the fact that the absence of credible institutions with the capacity to hold everyone accountable makes for poor and hijacked elections. Although credible elections sometimes produce winners and losers who accept the outcomes, they do not guarantee accountability in the governance process because credible elections do not produce corruption-free politics. Even as Nigerians bemoan public officials corruption and leaders lack of accountability in their roles as stewards of public trust, ordinary citizens often behave like those in the Nigeria of Chief Nanga in Chinua Achebe's novel *A Man of the People.* In the novel an educated Odili runs for public office with the zeal and energy of a newly minted progressive against Chief Nanga—the man of the people—whose main qualification for public service is his acquiescence to and participation in official corruption. Although Chief Nanga, the predecessor to money bags-as-politicians in contemporary Nigeria eventually won the election, it is necessary to note that the constituency's support for Odili was not based on their expectation that his candidacy would bring about transparent governance, equity, fairness, and the engendering of the rule of law. Instead, as one of the characters states after a rally,

> I always say that what is important nowadays is no longer age or title, but knowledge. . . . There is one word which entered my ear more than anything else not only entered, but (the word) built a house there. I don't know whether you others heard it in the same way as I did. That word was that our own son should go and bring our share. That word

entered my ear. The village of Ananta has already eaten, now they must make way for us to reach the plate. . . . If the very herb we go to seek in the forest now grows at our very back yard, are we not saved the journey . . . ? He knows where to go and what to do when he gets there; he should tell them that we are waiting here like a babe cutting its first tooth; anyone who wants to look at our new tooth should know that his bag should be heavy (Achebe 1967: 126–127).

Since postindependence political, intellectual, traditional, and colonized elites neglected to build institutions and structures to promote nationalism, the consequence is a situation where politicians in civilian and military uniforms in silent and, sometimes, mortal acquiescence, continue to enter pacts that exonerate all official corruption committed by "our man." Indeed, poor national policies that fail to provide employment, access to health care, clean water, education, and public safety are all connected to weak institutional structures and low levels of nationalism that result in hopelessness, social and political anomie, and abject poverty. In the Niger Delta and other vulnerable regions, unemployed youths who experience these ills are sometimes manipulated by political oppositions to cause havoc, assassinating the future for citizens and the nation. Therefore, strengthening the Nigerian state requires strong governance institutions built around nationalism rather than ethnicity. It also requires transparent and effective enforcement of law and order and a national platform where citizenship is the dominant and accepted identity to transform the state from conditions of persistent transition to economic and political transformation.

The following Transition Transformation Model (TTM) shows conditions of persistent transition move largely on a horizontal path (A→D),[1] and are unidirectional from one phase to another. The Nigerian situation illustrates how minimally the lives of most citizens have been affected by transitions from colonial status to independence, and from

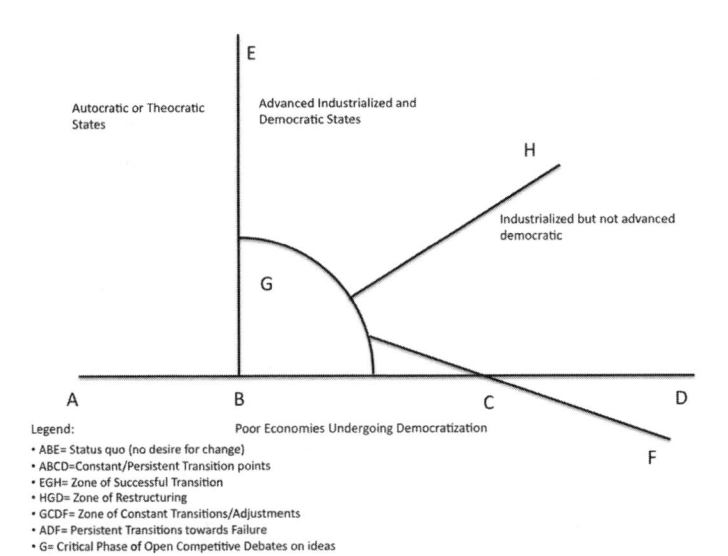

Legend:
- ABE= Status quo (no desire for change)
- ABCD=Constant/Persistent Transition points
- EGH= Zone of Successful Transition
- HGD= Zone of Restructuring
- GCDF= Zone of Constant Transitions/Adjustments
- ADF= Persistent Transitions towards Failure
- G= Critical Phase of Open Competitive Debates on ideas

Figure 1: Transition Transformation Model

authoritarian military dictatorships to electoral competitions. Each phase retains the same old cast of political and economic characters and policies; often, changing from military to civilian outfits without changes in substantive ideas on economic and political processes or personalities. For example, in the 2010–2011 election season, former military strongman Ibrahim Babangida and his supporters argue that if Olusegun Obasanjo could go from military dictatorship to civilian presidency, why not Babangida? For these cabals and their sycophants, the argument is not about the best leadership for the country but the best privileged. Certain markers also carry with them the badge of honor for public leadership; for example, Obasanjo was jailed and Babangida still carries a bullet from the civil war. Consequently, the transitional path for Nigeria is characterized by the absence of viable nation- or policy-building efforts for developing infrastructural frameworks for economic and political stability.

Mainly competing among themselves for the right to rule as a strategy to loot the treasury, Nigeria's elites continue to ignore the fact that strategic approaches to decision making enhance national stability, industrialize and diversify the economy, and ensure the safety of all citizens, including theirs. Changing that approach will reduce collaboration with the postindependence indigenous *extractive elites*, thus stemming the use of external collaborators as conduits for resource evacuation from Nigeria.

For example, 30 years after its inception, the Ajaokuta Steel Project remains unfinished. Indeed, after sinking billions into the project, the government attempted to sell it to an Indian company in 2009. However, following public outcry, the government invited the same Russian company that failed to complete the project to ascertain the extent of damage the Indian company, if hired, would cause the plant. That uncompleted project continues to garner funding from the federal budget. This means that, consistently, no clear connections are made between ideas and their implementation and few practical strategies for institutional innovations receive thorough and critical assessment on alternative approaches—a practice that is unlikely to continue in an environment of institutional accountability.

As Thomas Kuhn (1970) argues, institutions that do not think innovatively by taking alternative viewpoints seriously often become complacent, gradually eroding their relevance. Reflecting satisfaction with existing sets of ideas, such complacency ignores the relevance of alternative viewpoints to larger national visions of progress. This absence of active patriotism explains the refusal to use educational strategies to co-opt government and the masses to organize credible elections. Nigeria's current leaders are fully aware of the tendency of citizens to choose political lassitude and see no reason to respond to demands for accountability unless pressured by rival regional or national elites. In the international financial arena, Nigeria's governing elites tend to respond more to external than internal pressure. In the process, they promote currency devaluation because the devalued naira does not affect their access to foreign financial institutions, shopping sprees, or the size of their bank accounts at home and abroad. The persistence of such responses to external conditions in the transitional state is not conducive to building and sustaining ideas about politics, citizenship, liberal democracy, ideologically based party systems with viable alternatives, entrepreneurship, economic growth and, therefore, leadership transformation. This means that political and economic development must be based on serious reflection and dialog between Nigerians. Such explorations of the best way forward to the institutionalization of governing structures will enhance and protect public and personal safety and property rights (including the state) against all would-be spoilers.

In the model shown in figure 1, the G-component indicates a transition point where debates would occur, establishing the foundation for the consent of the governing and the governed. Although its focus was on the different ethnonationalities' conception of the national question, President Obasanjo's 2005 political reform agenda failed woefully as a platform to engage Nigerians through their representatives in a national dialog because it was contrived. Many of the calls exhibit religious, regional, ethnic, and resource-based agitations for recognition and inclusive public policies in Nigeria. Subsequent calls for a Sovereign National Conference reflect the absence of a persistent national dialog about the basic structure and framework for the Nigerian state. Indeed, Obasanjo's civilian tenure (1999–2007) was a missed opportunity for Nigerians to reassess opportunities for such a constitutional convention, which could have been established after its first two years, giving citizens' representatives the opportunity to engage proposals on how groups could work together to advance the country within a framework of rule of law. Clearly, it was a mistake not to seize the Obasanjo regime's efforts to move the country forward by instituting a national constitutional convention.[2] The Jonathan Goodluck regime should learn from that mistake and ensure its legacy within Nigerian history by convening a constitutional convention outside the familiar disturbances of electoral politics to ensure that, irrespective of who wins the 2011 elections, Nigerians will have a constitutional dialogue that leads to popular ratification of enforceable national law. That convention should be separate from the National Assembly and devoid of government control. Such an approach will lead Nigeria into the zone of successful transformations (EGH) rather than into a collapse of formally constituted authorities (ADF), characterized by illegitimate regime rule, destruction, and a hopeless future. Avoiding the ADF zone will reduce growing and familiar disregard for human lives, natural resource plundering, and general feelings of hopelessness by the international community and domestic elites about reconstituting formal authority in Nigeria.

ECONOMIC ISSUES AND DEVELOPMENT IN NIGERIA

Economic development issues involving crude petroleum at the national level in Nigeria often assume mortal combat proportions. However, the economic development agenda can be resolved through effective political decision-making by committed leaders. According to Rotimi T. Suberu, the demands and grievances of Nigeria's oil-producing communities are the: 1) disposition of mineral land rents, 2) application of the derivation principle to the allocation of federally collected mineral revenues, 3) appropriate institutional and fiscal responses to the ecological problems of oil-producing communities, 4) responsibility of oil-prospecting companies to oil-producing communities, and 5) appropriate arrangements for securing the integrity and autonomy of the oil producing communities within the federal arrangement of powers (Suberu 1996: 27–39; Kalu 2005). The reasonableness of the above demands aside, it is important to note that although the constitution of Nigeria charges states with protecting the environment and maintaining ecological health in their respective territories, it is the federal government that controls and disposes the proceeds from the land. Further, under the exclusive legislative list (section 39), the federal government also retains all rights to "mines and minerals, including oil fields, oil mining, geological surveys and natural gas" (Federal Republic of Nigeria 1999: 131).

As is currently evident in the Niger Delta, the federal government's involvement in the control of lands and resources without a clear land-tenure law for states is a source of contention. Traditionally, land rights are vested in the local communities. However, the 1978 Land Use Decree vested land ownership in any state of the federation in the state governor as trustee. Thus, traditionally and legally, the federal government has no direct claims to states' lands (Suberu 1996: 27–28). And, with the government not clearly defining its obligations in property rights, prevailing federal government structure with a plausible legal framework of land tenure reform, crude petroleum remains a contentious issue and a source of instability because benefits from the land and its resources are unavailable to the people.

A snapshot of Nigeria's socioeconomic indicators for the following periods: 1962 (immediately after independence), 1974 (immediately after the civil war), and 2008 (after two continuous terms of the first civilian government without a military coup) reveals the extent of the land tenure basis of Nigeria's problems (see world databank, World Development Report 2010 and UN Statistics Division). Although Nigeria's GDP rose from approximately $5 billion in 1962, and $25 billion in 1974 to $207 billion in 2008, the GDP per capita for the respective years are $104, $399 and $1,370. Also, Nigeria's export of goods and services increased as did foreign direct investment. One measure of citizens' well-being is life expectancy, which was 38 years in 1962, 42 in 1974, and 48 in 2008. Also, fertility rate has approximately remained the same at 6.6 per woman, indicating that women lack adequate formal education and the provision of adequate health care. They have remained homemakers, subsistence farmers, and baby manufacturing factories. The under-five mortality and the infant mortality rates did not change significantly and is likely worse for the conflict-ridden Niger Delta region, which produces high export earnings from crude petroleum. While overall schooling has increased at all levels, the quality of education has declined remarkably as a result of frequent strikes by teachers and students and irregular payment of teachers' salaries. This means that the rents the federal government collects from the oil companies for land use is not strategically reinvested to ensure the well-being of the traditional landowners and other citizens. The government's inattention to the environmental devastation in the region—including the focus on crude petroleum to the exclusion of other economic activities such as the refining of crude petroleum in oil-producing regions as well as agricultural and other activities—is problematic. Indeed, although Nigerian universities graduate students with degrees in petroleum and other aspects of engineering, the country exports crude petroleum but imports refined petroleum products that if produced in the country would create employment for many citizens.

Making Nigeria's public policies on the basis of strategic options and choices rooted in realistic efforts at resource mobilization will create opportunities for honest private sector employment. Also, rather than collecting money at policed checkpoints in certain regions, effective institutional structures for income tax mobilization for infrastructural development will gradually divest the government from all economic activities and engender its function as a regulatory agent in the national economy. Societal restructuring based on strong economic and political institutions that ensure fairness and transparency in economic interactions will encourage diaspora Nigerians to invest in value-added activities and reduce the number of remittances with its forced economic dependence and consequent culture of consumerism without adequate employment.

CONCLUDING REMARKS

The transition-transformation schema above illustrates that transformation is both vertical and horizontal, leading to either improved economic and political change in the lives of citizens or a deterioration. Thus, while transitions move a society or state from one point to another on the continuum, they create political space and initiate change. But overall change depends on whether or not the winning bloc, class, or political party has good leadership with coalition forces committed to transformative change through internal restructuring and value-added investments.

The phase of open competitive debates on ideas (area G), is critical for states and individuals seeking transformative change through internal restructuring (Kalu 2005). Essentially, that is what most Nigerians, but especially the ethnic, religious, and resource-based agitations desire. Alternative ideological frameworks emerge during this phase of open competitive political debates on transformative ideas. Political parties or decisional coalitions also contest for power using ideas clarified by political vision, a strategic framework, and coalitions of various classes. Indeed, after the first republic, most of the political parties that have contested elections in Nigeria have lacked transparent platforms with clear ideologies and programs of action. This critical phase of open competitive debates on ideas determines whether the outcome is one of persistent transition or transformation.

To the extent that young, skilled, educated, and patriotic Nigerians sit on the sidelines, transformation will remain difficult. Open competitive political spaces have either been circumscribed by the nature of the transition (characterized by coups and contrived self-successions as evidenced by Obasanjo's regime in 2005) that failed to consolidate constitutional liberalism. What is needed is a revolution of expectations about the role of public servants by citizens willing to hold leaders accountable for their actions. Given persistent leadership failures since independence, honest civil society organizations, intellectuals, market women, students and diaspora Nigerians should pressure current leaders to call a constitutional convention. Ultimately, success must be based on the tested assumption that while institutions are important, it is committed individuals who build enduring institutional structures of liberal constitutionalism by holding each other accountable for the success or failure of public policy. Blaming faceless government while refusing to pay taxes or be accountable for our individual and collective performances and behaviors on public matters will not change poor policies or improve national well-being.

Grounding Nigeria's goal for a democratic and constitutionally based system of governance requires that all citizens strive to create space for peace, a sociopolitical environment characterized by the rule of law, social justice, equity, respect for legitimate authority, and individual and collective security. It is necessary to set "up . . . acceptable and legitimate processes of dialogues, consultations and discussions on the future of . . . [Nigeria], the rights and obligations of citizenship and the role and relative power of democratic institutions" (Aina 2001) without preconditions. From such an assembly will emerge constitutional norms and political institutions that Nigerians will be proud to adopt as instruments for legitimate authority and governance. It may well be that the outcome of such national dialogue could lead to a break up of the country. But I am hopeful that Nigerians are strong and the country is neither on the brink of collapse nor will it collapse because citizens have engaged in a discussion about how to live together in a productive nation. Rather, the absence of a popularly ratified and accepted constitution that enables the state's capacity to serve its functions as a mediating institution in citizens' pursuit of individual and collective goals will foment perceived and real inequalities among the various ethnonationalities in Nigeria.

Indeed, the proposed constitutional convention would likely provoke ethnic consolidation, where various ethnic nationalities band together to protect relevant cultural practices and interests. However, that is a good thing because there is nothing inherently conflictual about ethnicity; it is *politicized ethnicity* that produces conflict. With that in mind, the proposed national dialogue within the framework of a constitutional convention will enhance ethnic competitiveness, but privilege citizenship as a dominant identity. That identity will be achieved through education and private enterprise as the predominant employer of labor and transparent implementation of public policies in the interest of the citizens. Thus, while resolving issues of political discourse at the constitutional conventions, competing groups will be able to articulate and understand the structure of power as well as how individuals acquire and maintain power. Understanding the structure and processes of power in the contemporary political arena is likely to result in losers in a given political contest accepting their losses and preparing for future competitions. Insufficient availability of resources and marginalization of ethnic minorities must not be contending explanations for the governance challenges that continue to sap the energies of Nigerian citizens. Indeed, through political dialogue, perhaps it will become clear for Nigerians that it is the wealth of the majority that builds the wealth of the nation, not that of the minority elites (Jordan, 1985: 380). The process by which the constitution is constructed, the extent to which citizens participate in its creation and/or ratification, leadership integrity, and the overall investment of public and private resources in value-added projects will ensure citizens respect for legitimate authority, reliance on effective institutions of government and civil society as platforms for transformative development in Nigerian life.

NOTES
1. Geometrically, lines are connected dots. Thus, the lines of transition should be read as transitions from one point to another; for example, from military dictatorship to electoral politics.
2. The basic frame of reference for President Obasanjo's National Political Reform Conference (NPRC) in 2004—which enabled him and the governors to select conference delegates based on political party affiliation, personal appointments by the president and the governors, and the time schedule for the conference—ensured the failure of the process to achieve its stated aim of political and constitutional reform. These subverted the intent of a national constitutional convention and the idea that the peoples' elected delegates represent their interests. The NPRC failed to achieve its aims, intensifying the agitations as most of the intended delegates and the focus of the conference did not reflect serious efforts at the process of enthroning liberal constitutional democracy in Nigeria.

REFERENCES

Achebe, Chinua. *A Man of the People*. New York: Anchor Books, 1967.

Ajayi, J. F. Ade. "Expectations of Independence." *Daedalus* 3:2 (Spring 1982): 1–9.

Aina, Tade Akin. "Reclaiming the Foundations of Democratic Development in Africa." Ms., 2001.

Bates, Robert H. *Markets and States in Tropical Africa: The Political Basis of Agricultural Policies*. Berkeley: University of California Press, 1981.

Caporaso, James A. and David P. Levine. *Theories of Political Economy*. New York: Cambridge University Press, 1992.

Chazan, Naomi, Peter Lewis, Robert Mortimer, Donald Rothchild, and Stephen John Stedman. *Politics and Society in Contemporary Africa* 3rd ed. Boulder, Colo.: Lynne Rienner Publishers, 1999.

Diamond, Larry. *Class, Ethnicity and Democracy in Nigeria: The Failure of the First Republic*. New York: Syracuse University Press, 1988.

Duvall, Raymond, and John R. Freeman. "The State and Dependent Capitalism." *International Studies Quarterly* 25 (March 1981): 99–118.

Ejobowah, John Boye. "Rewriting Nigerian Federal Constitution: A Prescriptive Argument for a Self-Sustaining Arrangement." *Canadian Journal of African Studies* 43 (2009): 507–535.

Fatton, Jr., Robert. "Liberal Democracy in Africa." *Political Science Quarterly* 105 (1990): 455–473.

Hudson, William E. *American Democracy in Peril*. Washington, D.C.: CQ Press, 2004.

Ihonvbere, Julius O. *Nigeria: The Politics of Adjustment and Democracy*. New Brunswick: Transaction Publishers, 1994.

Ihonvbere, Julius O., and John Mukum Mbaku."Introduction: Establishing Generalities and Specificities in Africa's Struggle for Democracy and Development." *Political Liberalization and Democratization in Africa: Lessons from Country Experiences*. Eds. Julius O. Ihonvbere and John Mukum Mbaku. Westport, Conn.: Praeger, 2003.

Jordan, June. *On Call: Political Essays*. Boston: South End Press, 1985.

Joseph, Richard A. *Democracy and Prebendal Politics in Nigeria: The Rise and Fall of the Second Republic*. Cambridge: Cambridge University Press, 1987.

Kalu, Kelechi A. "Constitutionalism in Nigeria: A Conceptual Analysis of Ethnicity and Politics." *The Nigerian Juridical Review* 8 (2000–2001): 53–84.

———. "Echoes of Instability: Implications for State, Society and Democratic Consolidation in Nigeria." *The Constitution: A Journal of Constitutional Development* 5 (March 2005): 1–36.

———. "Introduction: The Role of Ideas, Theory and Models of Public Policy Processes in Africa." *Agenda Setting and Public Policy in Africa*. Ed. Kelechi A Kalu. Aldershot, UK and Burlington, Vt.: Ashgate Publishing, 2004: 1–19.

Kuhn, Thomas. *The Structure of Scientific Revolutions*. 2nd. ed. New York: New American Library, 1970.

LeVine, V. T. *The Cameroons: From Mandate to Independence*. Berkeley: University of California Press, 1964.

———. "The Fall and Rise of Constitutionalism in West Africa." *The Journal of Modern African Studies* 35:2 (1997): 181–206.

Lugard, Frederick. *The Dual Mandate in Tropical Africa*. London: Blackwood, 1922.

Mbaku, John Mukum. *Institutions and Development in Africa*. Trenton, N.J.: Africa World Press, 2004.

———. *Corruption in Africa: Causes, Consequences, and Cleanups*. Lanham, Md.: Lexington Books, 2007.

Nigeria, Federal Republic. *1999 Constitution of the Federal Republic of Nigeria*. Lagos: Federal Government Press, 1999.

North, D. C. *Institutions, Institutional Change and Economic Performance*. Cambridge: Cambridge University Press, 1990.

Olson, Mancur. "Big Bills Left on the Sidewalk: Why Some Nations are Rich, and Others are Poor." *Journal of Economic Perspective* 10:2 (1996): 3–24.

Prah, Kwesi Kwaa. "Culture, the Missing Link in Development Planning Africa." Paper presented at the roundtable discussion on

Mainstreaming Human Security and Conflict Issues in Long-term Development Planning in Africa: A New Development Paradigm? Accra, Ghana, July 9–10, 2001.

Suberu, Rotimi T. *Ethnic Minority Conflicts and Governance in Nigeria*. Ibadan: Spectrum Books Limited, 1996.

World Bank. *World Development Report 2010: Development and Climate Change*. Washington, D.C.: World Bank, 2010.

Berhanu Nega
No Shortcut to Stability: Democratic Accountability and Sustainable Development in Ethiopia

AFTER A COUPLE OF DECADES OF INFATUATION WITH MARKET fundamentalism, economists and development practitioners have learned a practical lesson from the lackluster performance of African economies: market based reforms by themselves are not sufficient to generate long-term prosperity (Stiglitz 2003; Abouharb and Cingranelli 2007). In addition to well-functioning markets or even for markets to function well, it is recognized that the larger sociopolitical and institutional environment, or what Hall and Jones (Hall and Jones 1998) call the social infrastructure, has to be properly in place. The efficacy of markets is significantly affected by the institutional environment in which economic agents operate. Accordingly, what is sought by development economists dealing with Africa is not only the comparative advantage in goods and services that would enable African economies to benefit from an open international trade environment, but also to identify what Schneider (2008: 116) calls their "comparative institutional advantage" in order to isolate the key institutions that facilitate or inhibit long-term development in a specific country or geographic region. It is now widely acknowledged that the dire economic situation in many of the poorest African countries has a lot to do with the social and institutional structures that prevail in these societies. These structures exposed African countries to unaccountable governance systems that mire these societies in incessant conflicts, appalling corruption, and myopic and opportunistic leaders who failed to exploit the region's enormous resources effectively and for the benefit of the larger society. In short, the economic and societal problems of the continent were largely a result of the horrendous governance that Africans have to endure and the societal conflict that this engendered for a very long period (Ayittey 1999; Calderisi 2006; Moss 2007).

By any measure, Ethiopia is one of the poorest countries in the world. According to the most recent Human Development Index, Ethiopia ranks 171 out of the 182 countries covered by the report (HDR 2009).[1] According to the more comprehensive Multidimensional Poverty Index, Ethiopia ranks 103rd out of 104 countries with 90 percent of the population considered MPI poor.[2] Along with the grinding poverty, Ethiopia is also known for authoritarian governments throughout its long history. While the specific nature of the regime and its ideological inclinations differ (an absolute monarchy until 1974, a communist totalitarian dictatorship from 1974-1991, and an ethnic-based authoritarian regime since 1991), the tradition of authoritarian rule continues to this day. Another common element in all the regimes that have ruled Ethiopia has been their passionate claim to have interest in the economic and social development of the country. Modernizing the Ethiopian economy and catching up with the rest of the world has always been the constant nationalist battle cry in the otherwise ideologically disparate positions of the different regimes in Ethiopia.[3] Both the 1974 revolution against Emperor Haile Selassie and the overthrow of Mengistu Haile Mariam's totalitarian dictatorship have been, at least partly, conducted with the promise of a better economic future and a more humane governance than in the past.

Although the promise of modernization and economic prosperity has partly fueled the pressure for change, no significant improvement in the life of the average person has occurred under the successive regimes.

Not only has prosperity eluded Ethiopian society, but the increasing poverty combined with ethnic fragmentation and the inability of the state to address these problems in a more transparent and accountable manner has made the problem even more complicated and the country's stability increasingly questionable. Ethiopia is now the seventeenth most fragile state in the world according to the most recent Failed States Index compiled by the Fund for Peace and Foreign Policy magazine.[4]

The link between the country's poverty, its political instability, and the prevalence of unaccountable authoritarian governance over a long period of time is hard to miss for anyone who looks at the country's history closely. However, this link had not been a subject of serious public political discourse within the country until the first meaningful democratic election in the country's history in 2005. In the period leading up to the 2005 election, there was a clear understanding among the country's political elites (including the ruling party), the donor community, and the Ethiopian public in general that the country's long-term prosperity and its survival as a nation requires that the political system address the tensions in the society by establishing a democratic system.[5] With the tragic failure of the democratic experiment in 2005, however, the official discourse from the ruling party has shifted back to the discourse of "developmentalism" and modernization shorn of democratic accountability. The claim here is that rapid economic growth to be delivered by a "developmentalist"[6] state; this is what the country needs to achieve stability and prosperity rather than a liberal democratic order. According to supporters of the current government, the regime in power since 1991—led by the Ethiopian People's Revolutionary Democratic Front (EPRDF)—is exactly suited for this kind of development and is delivering rapid economic growth and social progress that has essentially stabilized the country. Although the donor community still talks about the importance of democratic accountability for the country's long-term stability, the current policy of donors seems to implicitly agree with the delinking of economic prosperity and political stability from democracy and accountability in Ethiopia. This can be seen from the rapidly increasing foreign aid that is flowing into the country and the common argument presented by donors justifying their increased financial support for the government.

However, as this paper will show, there is a solid theoretical as well as empirical ground to justify the link between political stability, democratic accountability, and economic prosperity in general and in the Ethiopian context in particular.

DEMOCRATIC ACCOUNTABILITY, POLITICAL STABILITY, AND ECONOMIC DEVELOPMENT

Democratic accountability implies the process through which those who govern are accountable to the public in whose name they govern. It identifies the obligations of political leaders to answer for their decisions and actions to the general public. This obligation is a central feature of any well-functioning democratic society. Democratic accountability ensures that people in power rule within the limits provided to them by the laws and norms of society—that they will not abuse their authority. It also ensures that governments operate in a fair and efficient manner in providing the public goods that society has reason to expect from government.

In an environment where democratic accountability prevails, government policy is expected to reflect the broad interests of society. Government functionaries remain reasonably clean from corruption and the state is not captured by narrow interest groups. With government enforcing the rules of the game fairly and equally, citizens will be motivated to make economic decisions that promote their interest.

For accountable governance to endure, there needs to be mechanisms and structures in place that ensures continuity. These mechanisms include a system of checks and balances within the government structure and clearly established rules that are equally applicable to everyone in the society, including those in power. What is also needed is active citizenship. In other words, accountability "is intimately linked to citizen participation, leadership responsiveness, and the rule of law, three other pillars that both define and reinforce the practice of democracy" (Bratton and Logan 2006).

Along with an accountable government is the need for an independent media. Without an independent media that serves as the eyes and ears of the public, even when governments are elected freely, there is no mechanism to keep government functionaries honest and accountable between elections. For meaningful accountability to exist, there must be a mechanism through which the government restrains itself through some kind of functioning separation of powers within the political system. This system of what O'Donnell (1994) called horizontal accountability requires that the government at all levels respect the constitution and abide by the laws of the country.

These institutions and mechanisms allow citizens to follow the actions of government on a continuous basis and allow citizens voices to be heard on an ongoing basis as well as allow citizens to pass their verdict on the fate of office holders at elections. Such mechanisms are also important to hold accountable unelected government officials and bureaucrats who make decisions in the name of the people. Accordingly, the concept of accountability has been broadened in recent discussions to include the important role of civil society in making democratic governments more responsive to the needs and voices of the people.

The independent existence of civil society organizations such as human rights monitoring groups, women and youth organizations, professional association, media organizations and the like are considered part of the vertical accountability mechanism. Smulovitz and Peruzzotti (2000) call this societal accountability and define it as

> a nonelectoral, yet vertical mechanism of control that rests on the actions of a multiple array of citizens' associations and movements and on the media, actions that aim at exposing governmental wrongdoing, bringing new issues onto the public agenda, or activating the operation of horizontal agencies (149-50).[7]

The existence of such a democratically accountable governance is to be valued not only because it is considered to be the very substance of development (as Sen 1999 cogently articulated), but also as an important instrument for achieving economic development.

This connection between democratic accountability and economic performance, as intimated earlier, is by now fully recognized beyond the academic community. In an inaugural address at a conference organized to highlight the close relationship between good governance and sustainable development, the then secretary general of the United Nations, Kofi Annan, said:

> Good governance and sustainable development are indivisible. That is the lesson of all our efforts and experiences, from Africa to Asia to Latin America. Without good governance—without the rule of law, predictable administration, legitimate power, and responsive regulation—no amount of funding, no amount of charity will set us on the path to prosperity (Annan 1997: 1).

In other words, foreign aid to poor countries, which Annan had been advocating for so long as UN secretary general, could be effective in generating long-term development only if it is complemented with good governance. Yet, what we are observing on the ground is a significant increase in foreign aid on the one hand and deterioration in democratic accountability, particularly in Africa, on the other, as well as distinct absence of development.

The reason for this incongruence between the publicly stated collective opinion of the international community and its practical policy on the ground is partly a result of the seemingly unsettled controversy within the academic community regarding the link between economic development and democratic politics. There is a large body of theoretical and empirical literature in economics and political science supporting the argument that democratization is necessary to achieve good governance, political stability, as well as economic and social development (Bhagwati 2002; Sen 1999; Stiglitz 2002; Siegel et al. 2004; Diamond 2008; Easterly 2008; Olson 1993; Mkandawire 2010). On the other hand, following the so-called Lee thesis, some argue that a soft authoritarian state that is committed to development could produce an even better economic performance than democratic regimes. In addition to the familiar "full belly thesis," which makes a minimum level of economic prosperity a necessary condition for democratic development, underlying this argument is the claim that democratic governments do not have the stomach to make the hard belt-tightening decisions that might be temporarily necessary for long-term development to occur. The fear that democratic countries succumb to populist pressures and thus will not have the discipline that is required to shield the technicians from deploying and implementing good policies is what recommends this reliance on an authoritarian developmentalist state. In this view, developing countries need a disciplined workforce more than democracy, which, according to former Singaporean Prime Minister Lee Kuan Yew, "leads to indiscipline and disorderly conduct, which are inimical to development."[8] This claim is supported by citing the experiences of China and other East Asian countries that have produced rapid economic growth and transformation under authoritarian regimes. This view has a strong following among African policymakers. Tandika Mkandawire, a passionate advocate of the "developmentalist" state in Africa, critically summarized the debate thus:

> The African literature focused on how to make authoritarian regimes stronger, more "enlightened" and more developmental. Indeed, the high economic growth rates achieved by authoritarian regimes were used to support the view that the suspension of human rights was the price one had to pay in the process of development. This was part of the "full belly thesis" ("you can't eat democracy"). African states themselves often claimed that there was a sequencing of rights, with the "right to development" taking precedence. It was this same logic about the trade-off between democracy and development that was used to justify authoritarian rule in much of Africa, because the task ahead called for sacrifices that could only be imposed by a strong state. This view was reinforced by the spectac-

ular success of some authoritarian regimes on the continent. Some achieved high rates of growth, which often concealed the fact that many other authoritarian regimes failed scandalously and that some democracies performed well. Interestingly, two of the most cited success cases were Botswana and Mauritius—both democracies (Mkandawire 2010: 70).

Even liberal supporters of democratization have indirectly endorsed this thesis, using different variants of modernization theory to claim that societies need to achieve a certain level of development to support stable democratic governance. Accordingly, poor countries should concentrate on achieving rapid economic growth. Democracy would naturally follow once the socioeconomic conditions for its survival (a sizable middle class, an educated workforce, etc.) emerge as a result of economic transformation (Lipset 1959; Huntington 1968; Lipset et.al 1993; Heliwell 1994; Gasiorowski 1995; Feng 1997; Jackman 1973).[9]

Modernization theory has also been very influential among policymakers in developed countries that determine the level of aid to poor countries. This is so despite the fact that the empirical claims of modernization theory—that higher levels of per capita income causes democratization—have been seriously questioned on empirical grounds compared to alternative explanations to the emergence of democratic politics such as the critical junctures hypothesis (Acemoglu et.al 2009). The influence of modernization theory in development policy circles, in addition to providing a modicum of respectability to dictatorships, has the added advantage of providing considerable resources to bankroll these authoritarian regimes. This is particularly so since the massive and rather effective campaign by the aid industry to "make poverty history."[10] These campaigns have been successful in pressuring developed countries to provide more resources to support the development efforts of poor countries (particularly in Africa) without asking too much on the issue of democratic accountability.

Table 1: Total ODA Flows Disbursed from All Donors (Millions of Current U.S. Dollars)

Time Period	2004	2005	2006	2007	2008	Growth Rate over Five Years (%)
Recipient(s)						
All Recipients	105,904	134,428	135,154	138,894	165,173	56
All Developing Countries	79,668	108,171	106,445	107,120	128,581	61.4
Africa (total)	29,716	35,515	43,780	39,129	44,005	48.1
Sub-Saharan Africa	26,048	32,202	40,197	34,485	38,993	49.7
Ethiopia	1,809	1,910	1,964	2,563	3,328	84

Source: OECD Data <http://stats.oecd.org/qwids/>.

As can be seen from table 1, foreign aid disbursement increased from about $106 billion in 2004 to $166 billion in 2008, an increase of 56 percent for all recipients; it increased by 61 percent for all developing countries and about 48 percent for sub-Saharan Africa.

The pressure to give to make "poverty history" has been so great that issues such as democratic accountability have been relegated to a low order priority. Some of the most prominent academic advocates of the "big push" for aid (Sachs 2005: x) have even gone to the extent of shamelessly misrepresenting the governance picture in African countries by falsely painting some of the authoritarian regimes in Africa as democratic in order to justify aid.[11]

It is not clear how much this perspective has contributed to the reversal of the democratic experiment in Africa. Whether it is from this process of what Przeworski (2004) calls "sacrificing democracy at the altar of development" or other more immediate geopolitical considerations, there is no doubt that the trend toward meaningful democratic accountability in the world that started with the collapse of Soviet communism in the 1990s has lost its momentum. Some observers even argue that there has been a significant democratic roll back or what Larry Diamond (2008) called a "slippage into a democratic recession." According to the 2010 Freedom House survey, "2009 marked the fourth consecutive year in which global freedom suffered a decline—the longest consecutive period of setbacks for freedom in the nearly 40-year history of the report. These declines were most pronounced in sub-Saharan Africa, although they also occurred in most other regions of the world."[12] Only 9 countries with 19 percent of sub-Saharan Africa's population are considered free, while 39 countries with 81 percent of the region's population are "partially free" or not free. Sixteen countries with 33 percent of the population live in a suffocating environment of unfreedom.[13]

Even where the link between democracy and development is questioned, what is not debated is the fact that political stability and accountable governance are crucial for economic development (Collier 2007; Rivera-Batiz 2002). Furthermore, given the miserable economic performance of the continent over the past four decades under all kinds of dictatorships, authoritarian rule cannot be credited for providing better economic performance. What cannot be denied is that authoritarian rule has significantly contributed to the political instability of the region and the conflicts that are raging in many countries in Africa. The practical question for Ethiopia then is whether it can achieve long-term economic development and durable political stability without a democratically accountable governance structure as the government claims.

THE ETHIOPIAN GOVERNMENT AND DEMOCRATIC ACCOUNTABILITY

Ethiopia, under what was known as the Derge regime led by Mengistu Haile Mariam, was one of the foremost client states of the Soviet Union in Africa and could not and did not survive the demise of Soviet communism. The local opposition to the Mengistu regime that finally succeeded in overthrowing the Derge in 1991 was a coalition of leftist and ethnic nationalist groups that formed the Ethiopian People's Revolutionary Democratic Front, created and led by the Tigrean People's Liberation Front (TPLF). The TPLF in turn was led by a pro-Albanian revolutionary group under the chairmanship of Ethiopia's current prime minister, Meles Zenawi, which mixed Tigrean nationalism (an ethnic group representing roughly 6 percent of the Ethiopian population) along with a radical communist ideology. With the change in the international environment and the defeat of communist ideology, the TPLF leadership quickly adjusted its ideological stance and claimed to have officially embraced some version of capitalist development along with a democratic political dispensation.

The fall of the Mengistu regime in Ethiopia brought hope that it might experience a more stable and democratically accountable governance. In 1994 Ethiopia adopted a constitution that fully accepted the United Nations Universal Human Rights Declaration as part of the country's constitution (FDRE 1994). The constitution established an ethnic-based federal government comprised of nine primarily ethnic-based regions with significant powers to decide on a variety of issues outside the purview of the federal government. The constitution established a parliamentary system with two houses. The House of Federation members equally represented the main ethnic groups in the country with smaller representation for small minority ethnic groups; this house was to decide on federal matters including the powers to interpret the federal constitution. The House of Peoples' Representatives (HPR), with 547 constituencies, was to represent the people directly as a legislative body and elect the executive branch that would run the day-to-day affairs of the government from the party that won majority of seats in that house. The constitution also promulgated that all positions of power and authority at all levels of government are to be gained only through free and fair elections. In addition to acknowledging the right of citizens to form associations for any legal purpose, the constitution explicitly declared the independence of the media and its right to obtain information from government sources. The constitution also unequivocally provided the separation of powers between the executive, the legislative, and the judiciary.

Given the relatively liberal constitution, the question of democratic accountability in Ethiopia is therefore to be measured by the extent to which it is implemented in practice. And what is observed in practice in Ethiopia is far from a democratically accountable governance. Ethiopia lacks democratic accountability in all the three areas discussed above. Vertical accountability does not exist because the government at all levels is not freely elected by the people. It is true that there have been four national (for federal and regional parliaments) and three local elections conducted since the adoption of the 1994 constitution. Pre-2005 elections were nothing but democratic pretensions as none of the conditions for a meaningful democratic dispensation were in place (Pausewang et al. 2002).

The existence of what can be considered a democratic constitution and nominal multiparty elections on the one hand, and a highly authoritarian practice that undermines the basic rights of citizens, on the other, has led some authors to characterize the regime until the 2005 elections as a hybrid regime or an electoral authoritarian state (Aalen and Tronvoll 2008).

The lack of progress toward democratization despite the regime's claims to democratic legitimacy, combined with high expectations for democratization among the population following the democratic resurgence in a number of African countries and around the world, created serious tensions within the Ethiopian body politic. The inability of the regime to address the so-called national question in a meaningful federal arrangement as declared in the constitution further aggravated the tensions by widening the gap between expectations and reality among different ethnic groups.[14]

The crack within the ruling party following the Ethiopian-Eritrean conflict in 2000 further put in doubt the ability of the regime to maintain a stable polity without some kind of democratic legitimacy. This was also recognized by the donor community, which started to put pressure on the regime to open up the political space in order to avoid serious instability in the country. Prime Minister Meles Zenawi promised a free and fair election in 2005, publicly acknowledging the undemocratic practices of his government, which he blamed on the "extremist" party leaders that he purged following the split within the executive committee of the TPLF.

The buildup to the 2005 election and the election itself were conducted in relative peace and tranquility. The massive turnout on Election Day, estimated to be over 90 percent of registered voters, was overwhelming. Furthermore, the fact that voters waited patiently for hours to cast their votes proved to any observer that Ethiopians were capable and ready to settle their political differences at the ballot box.

Unfortunately, the ending of this democratic exercise was not to be democratic. The verdict of the people was overturned and the loser was declared the winner, which, as one observer noted was "a remarkable observation to make two days after election day with little counting done" (Abbink 2006: 183).

Postelection saw a massive repression of the opposition, leading to the deaths of at least 193 peaceful demonstrators and the arrest of an estimated 30,000 to 40,000 opposition supporters in a crackdown not seen since the heydays of the red terror period of the Mengistu era.

This ended the only meaningful attempt at peaceful transition to democracy in Ethiopia. In the two elections since 2005—a local election in 2008 and the fourth national election in 2010—the political space further narrowed, making the elections totally farcical. In both elections the ruling party won over 99 percent of the votes, making a mockery out of the democratic process. The European Union election monitoring team, the only credible body to be given permission to observe the election, dismissed the election as an exercise that does not meet international norms and standards.[15]

In the absence of the vertical accountability that can be ensured through democratic elections, did Ethiopia achieve a modicum of horizontal accountability through a meaningful implementation of the checks and balances between the different branches of government as stipulated in the constitution? Unfortunately, the answer to that question is no. Parliament, which is supposed to function as an independent legislature, could not muster the institutional independence from the executive branch. Its function has simply been reduced to approving the legislative agenda provided by the council of ministers. Members of parliament owe their seats to their party bosses and vote along party lines.

The judiciary is in no better position to check the power of the executive, although Article 78(1) of the constitution provides for its independence. Independence is partly compromised by giving the prime minister the power to appoint and dismiss the judges in the absence of an independently functioning legislature. As a result, the judicial system has been turned into one more instrument of suppression since it legalizes the decisions of the executive. In fact, the judiciary has actually become an instrument of the executive that punishes its political opponents.[16] The rare judges who take their profession seriously and try to assert their independence and follow the law rather than the whims of political leaders could not only lose their job, but depending upon the political profile of the case, could face serious harm.[17]

The deficit in democratic accountability in Ethiopia has deepened since the 2005 election. The rubber-stamp parliament passed two laws dealing with the media and civil society groups. The Charities and Societies act of 2009 made it illegal for international NGOs to become involved in any way on issues related to the advancement of human and democratic rights; the promotion of equality among ethnic groups; the promotion of issues related to gender and religious equality; the promotion of the disabled and children's rights; the promotion of conflict resolution or reconciliation; or the promotion of more efficient justice and law enforcement.[18] The law also prohibits any local organization that receives more than 10 percent of its budget from foreign sources or Ethiopian citizens living abroad to engage in these activities. The result on the ground was immediate. More than half of the registered NGOs closed shop while almost all of the remaining local NGOs working in areas related to democratic accountability and empowerment changed their mandate to work in areas allowed by the government.[19]

The independent media, which is prohibited from operating an electronic media,[20] is exclusively limited to the print media, with a very small circulation relative to the size of the population. Officially there are some 19 political, economic, and social affairs newspapers with an aggregate total circulation of 82,000 per week in a country with a population of 85 million. Even then, only a few of the 19 newspapers can claim any kind of editorial independence, the rest being either direct mouthpieces of the regime or engaged in self-censorship to avoid the wrath of the government.

In 2008 the government enacted a new press law that further restricts the freedom of operation of the media and imposes severe penalty on journalists for libel.[21] The new press law, together with the Charities and Societies act and the Anti-Terrorism law, "actually criminalize[s] independent political coverage and infringes on press freedom as guaranteed by the Ethiopian Constitution."[22]

Following a speech at Colombia University on September 22, 2010, Prime Minister Zenawi was confronted by a questioner about the credibility of any election where one party wins 99.6 percent of the seats in Parliament—as happened in the most recent election in Ethiopia. Meles's answer to this question repeated the ruling party's response to similar embarrassing questions elsewhere. What he said in effect was that there should be no surprise about the electoral performance of a party that has delivered double digit growth for seven consecutive years. In other words, they won because they delivered the economic goods.[23] In other words, what we have in Ethiopia is not only a developmentalist state, but a democratic developmental state. What remains to be shown is the veracity of the regime's claim for growth.

ECONOMIC PERFORMANCE AND ACCOUNTABLE GOVERNANCE IN ETHIOPIA

The Ethiopian government claims that it has delivered rapid economic growth in the past few years, due to the good economic policies it has pursued. Government officials routinely claim that in addition to the good policies, the government's relative efficiency, its capability to implement these policies effectively, the relative absence of corruption, and its commitment to the country's development explains this good performance. In the most recent five-year plan (2010-2015) that the government unveiled following the 2010 general election, it committed itself to a gross domestic product (GDP) growth rate of between 11.6 and 15.6 percent a year compared with the average of 11.2 percent

Table 2. Ethiopia Governance Indicators Compared with Sub-Saharan Africa Average (2009)

Governance Indicator	Sources	Percentile Rank (0-100)	Regional Average, Percentile	Governance Score (-2.5 to +2.5)	Standard Error
Voice and Accountability	15	12.3	31.2	-1.26	0.12
Political Stability	7	6.1	33.5	-1.73	0.24
Government Effectiveness	10	40.5	27.3	-0.41	0.17
Regulatory Quality	10	17.6	28.9	-0.98	0.16
Rule of Law	15	23.1	28.1	-0.77	0.14
Control of Corruption	12	26.7	31.1	-0.71	0.17

Sources: Kaufmann D., A. Kraay, and M. Mastruzzi (2010); <http://info.worldbank.org/governance/wgi/sc_chart.asp#>.

per annum, in real terms, of the past decade.[24] To evaluate the veracity of this claim, we need to evaluate the credibility of the most recent growth numbers as well as the record of the government on a variety of issues, including corruption and other "good governance" indicators.

Let us first look at the claims of low levels of corruption and other good governance indicators by African standards. The government's claims are not true despite the credit some foreign institutions bestow on it.[25] A recent business attitude survey identified corruption as one of the critical obstacles for doing business in Ethiopia. In the most recent (2009) Transparency International's Corruption Perception Index, Ethiopia scored 2.7 out of 10, ranking it 120th in the world, well behind a large number of African countries.[26]

In an innovative addition to traditional mechanisms of corruption, the government created huge business organizations owned by the ruling party in order to transfer resources to itself and its cronies. These companies are involved in transport, construction, mining, tourism, banking, and insurance. The degree to which this has corrupted the overall business environment in the country is well known. In addition to siphoning off resources, these business organizations have stifled the development of an independent private sector, thus minimizing possible competition.

These inequities and unwarranted subversion of the state are confirmed by independent studies. The World Bank's comprehensive governance indicators put Ethiopia significantly behind other African countries on most measures of good governance. As can be seen from table 2, Ethiopia is well behind the average for sub-Saharan African in all but one of the six governance indicators.

According to this survey-based data set, Ethiopia was rated at more than six times on instability and more than two and half times on voice and accountability compared with the average sub-Saharan Africa (SSA) country. Ethiopia performs better only in the government effectiveness indicator which puts the country in the 40.5 percent range compared with the 27.3 percent average for SSA. In terms of control of corruption Ethiopia was 4.4 percent behind the SSA average.

Even more troubling is the deterioration in key governance indicators over time. Table 3 provides Ethiopia's score on the six governance indicators for the years 2000, 2005, and 2009. As can be seen from the table, Ethiopia's governance deteriorated in four of the six indicators. Only government effectiveness and regulatory quality showed improvement.

The deterioration was especially marked in the political stability indicator, which put the country at 6.1 percent in 2009 compared with 13 percent in 2000. The index capturing control over corruption significantly deteriorated between 2000 and 2009, dropping from close to 40 percent down to about 27 percent. These data place serious doubt on the government's claim that it is an accountable government in the sense of being able to deliver good governance. If the government's legitimacy is to be measured by its ability to deliver a relatively clean government, it is very far from achieving that. This leaves good economic performance as well as improvement in social parameters as the primary argument for the legitimacy of the current government.

Before we evaluate the economic and social performance of the country under the current regime, it is important to note that good

Table 3: Ethiopia: World Bank Governance Indicators Over Time

Governance Indicator	Sources	Year	Percentile Rank (0-100)	Governance Score (-2.5 to +2.5)	Standard Error
Voice and Accountability	15	2009	12.3	-1.26	0.12
	11	2005	14.4	-1.16	0.15
	6	2000	18.8	-0.99	0.21
Political Stability	7	2009	6.1	-1.73	0.24
	6	2005	8.2	-1.53	0.27
	4	2000	13	-1.27	0.31
Government Effectiveness	10	2009	40.5	-0.41	0.17
	8	2005	18.9	-0.94	0.16
	5	2000	14.6	-0.94	0.2
Regulatory Quality	10	2009	17.6	-0.98	0.16
	9	2005	15.1	-1.03	0.17
	6	2000	12.7	-1.22	0.24
Rule of Law	15	2009	23.1	-0.77	0.14
	12	2005	22.4	-0.86	0.16
	8	2000	25.2	-0.83	0.17
Control of Corruption	12	2009	26.7	-0.71	0.17
	10	2005	25.7	-0.77	0.17
	5	2000	39.8	-0.44	0.25

Sources: Kaufmann D., A. Kraay, and M. Mastruzzi (2010); <http://info.worldbank.org/governance/wgi/sc_chart.asp>.

economic performance by itself does not justify authoritarianism for at least two reasons. First is the obvious case that freedom and liberty are valuable in their own right without any association to economic performance. As Sen has demonstrated convincingly, freedom is valued because it is the beginning and end of development. The ultimate objective of development is the expansion of human freedom. It is therefore meaningless to justify tyranny in the name of development.

The second problem is with the claim that democracy will do worse than authoritarian regimes in relation to economic development.

If an authoritarian regime has performed well in terms of economic growth, there is nothing to indicate that a democratically accountable regime would do any worse. Rather, given all the advantages of democratic accountability, *ceteris paribus,* democracy would have performed even better under the given circumstances.

Given this caveat, let us now closely look at the validity of high growth rates the government has been claiming for the economy. The big issue here is of course the credibility of the data presented by the government in support of its claim. The first issue to note is that there is only one data source for all macroeconomic variables in Ethiopia—the Ministry of Finance and Economic Development (MoFED). MoFED collects the raw data from the Central Statistical Authority (CSA). It is this same data that is used by international financial Institutions (IFIs) such as the World Bank and the IMF.[27] While there have been questions about data inconsistency and some methodological issues largely related to the capacity limitations of the institutions, the CSA data was considered reasonably reliable and was used by researchers with some degree of confidence until recently.[28] Since approximately 2005, however, the figures used by different government institutions and the CSA have begun to raise serious concerns about their reliability. This has also, incidentally, marked the beginning of the high-growth reporting period.

Two obvious problems with the data are consistency and plausibility. To see the difference in the nature of the data reported by the government (and the international financial institutions), it is instructive to look at the data until 2005 separately from the post-2005 figures. For the purpose of comparing the data with the sub-Saharan average, I have used the World Bank data set for annual GDP growth and the growth in agricultural value added for three time periods since the current regime came to power in Ethiopia in 1991.

The first point to note from the data is that over the 19-year tenure of the government (1991-2009), average GDP growth was about 5.5 percent annually, which comes to about 2.5 percent annually in per capita terms. While this is a decent growth rate, it is not a figure that

Table 4: Average Annual Growth Rate of GDP and Agricultural Value Added

Average Annual GDP Growth Rate (%)	(1991-2004)	(2005-2009)	(1991-2009)
Sub-Saharan Africa (Developing Countries only)	2.82	5	3.39
Sub-Saharan Africa (All Income Category)	2.89	5.02	3.45
Ethiopia	3.66	10.72	5.52
Agricultural Value Added (Annual growth rate %)			
Sub-Saharan Africa (Developing Countries Only)	2.81	3.99	3.12
Sub-Saharan Africa (All Income Category)	2.81	3.99	3.12
Ethiopia	2.82	9.48	4.57

Source: World Bank, World Development Indicators Data Base <http://data.worldbank.org/data-catalog/world-development-indicators>.

supports the government's claim that the regime is a developmental state in the East Asian tradition, even though overall performance was better than the sub-Saharan African average.

The real story of the growth figures—and that raises serious doubt about its credibility—relates to the post-2005 years. During the 14 years to 2005, the growth rate of real GDP averaged 3.7 percent annually, relative to the SSA average of about 2.9 percent. In terms of growth in agricultural value added, Ethiopia's performance was essentially the same as the SSA average, at about 2.8 percent for the 14 years before 2005.

Since 2005, however, the performance of the Ethiopian economy in general as well as the agricultural sector suddenly starts to show double digit growth despite the adverse weather conditions (such as the 2006-2008 drought), which significantly impacted its performance. GDP growth averaged about 10.7 percent annually, while agricultural value added grew by about 9.5 percent per annum for Ethiopia. Reported performance for sub-Saharan Africa averaged 5 percent for GDP and 4 percent for agricultural value added during the same period.

Unfortunately, anomalies emerge following the rapid growth in agriculture, of which the most significant is the price of food.[29] A study by Gilligan et.al, reports that "the dominant economic event in Ethiopia that occurred between 2006 and 2008 was the dramatic rise in food prices." According to this household-survey-based study, "the lowest price rise is found for maize in Tigray which increases by 'only' 75.3 percent over this two-year period. The highest price rise was recorded for maize in the SNNPR [Southern Nations, Nationalities, and People's Region], which increased by 186.7 percent" (Gilligan et. al 2009: 5). To make matters worse, some of these years of "unprecedented agricultural growth" were also years of severe drought, requiring massive food aid to roughly one-sixth of the population.[30]

In a detailed and thorough study of the agriculture sector for the U.K.'s Department for International Development (DFID), Stefan Dercon and his team tried to make sense of the official data by looking at the sources of growth and concluded:

> The figures on recent agricultural performance are impressive: doubling of cereal output in the last ten years, 44 percent more land cultivated with cereals and 40 percent higher yield in the same period. In the last five years, 12 percent more cereal production *per year*, yield growth of 6 percent per year and area growth of 5 percent per year. The same data sources show no evidence of intensification of agriculture: no increase in fertilizer use per farmer or per hectare, no significantly more irrigation, and expanding but still relatively small areas under extension programme. Ethiopian yields have grown faster than recorded elsewhere, even compared to the green revolution in India, China or Vietnam. If the data are correct, this is the fastest

green revolution in history, and its mechanisms should be analyzed. If any of the data, such as the area expansion data are not correct, then this has huge implications for policy, as it would suggest that food production is considerably lower than reported (Dercon et. al 2009: 2).

The agricultural data spewed by different government agencies is so inconsistent that it is difficult to believe that they are talking about the same country. For example, the data on "land under cereal and pulses reported by the Ministry of Agriculture has been 19.5 percent higher (by 1.97 million hectares) in 2006/07 and 45 percent higher (by 2.62 million hectares) in 2005/6 than the data reported by CSA" (Adnew 2009: 12).

In fact, one of the main recommendations of the DFID-sponsored study was the need to restore confidence in the data. With characteristic understatement the researchers advised:

> In general, it would appear to be time to consider the establishment of a data auditing unit within the structures of CSA/MOFED, but with considerable independence, whose aim should be to monitor and audit the quality of data generated on key issues of economic policy making in Ethiopia by the CSA and by other institutions (Dercon et. al 2009: 8).

If one looks at more credible survey data, a decline in the productivity of agriculture will be observed for the period that the government claimed to have increased. This might partly explain the dramatic price rise in the 2006-2008 periods. An analysis of two surveys conducted in 2006 and 2008 in some 153 food insecure *woredas* (districts) indicate a significant reduction both in output and yield for the four major crops produced by the farmers. The average decline in yield, for example, was 14.4 percent for maize, 13.75 percent for wheat, 18.36 percent for barley, and 24.95 percent for teff.[31] These discrepancies are not simply errors in calculation or data collection methodology and they are not reflected on economic data alone. Given the fact that these data flows are becoming particularly prominent at a particular period following the debacle of the 2005 elections and the government's new claim to legitimacy on the basis of being a "developmentalist" state, it is not far-fetched to think that this is a result of deliberate data manipulation and massaging by government statisticians following orders from their superiors.[32]

The government-produced data has become so contentious that people closely studying the country have started to openly question the credibility of the official data, forcing the government to defend the numbers by saying that the IMF and the World Bank agree with the numbers as if they have provided an independent verification for the data.[33] But this is not persuasive since it is well known that these institutions do not have an independent mechanism of verification. In a recent article in the *Financial Times* about the betrayal of Africa's democrats by Western donors, William Wallis, the Africa editor of the paper, referring to Rwanda's and Ethiopia's recent elections, said:

> In both countries, as in much of Africa, Western donors justify continued support on the basis of their development record. In Rwanda this is exemplary. The question is whether it will be sustainable as popular frustration at the closed political environment grows. In Ethiopia, the same is almost true but with a disturbing caveat. It is an open secret that the double-digit growth of recent years is supported by dubious statistics. Yet the same figures are bandied around by development experts, who argue that a trade-off between growth and civil liberties is inevitable.[34]

The problem with data reliability is not limited to economic variables. The government's claims of achieving rapid progress on the social front, particularly in education and health, are equally contentious. If we take, for instance, the data on children vaccination in 2005, the official data provided by the Ministry of Health is higher by 60 percent compared with independent surveys at the time (Epstine 2010).[35] This data manipulation can sometimes veer into the realm of the absurd. An August 19, 2010 news report by the Ethiopian News Agency, citing regional state education authorities in the Afar region, stated that "over five million school age children in Afar State will join school in the coming academic year." But according to the most recent census, the total population of the region was only about 1.4 million.[36]

But, even when the numbers themselves are not particularly contentious, the mechanisms through which they are achieved raise troubling questions about the development prospects for the country. Nowhere is this reflected more than in the government's education policy. In its eagerness to raise enrollment numbers as part of achieving the Millennium Development Goals, the government opened schools at all levels throughout the country without providing the necessary material, financial, and human resources required to enable these schools to provide a decent education. The result is very high enrollment numbers with a disastrous decline in the quality of education. According to the most recent report by Global Campaign for Education, of the 60 worst places in the world to be a schoolchild in 2010, Ethiopia tied with Comoros at 56, scoring better than three countries only: Haiti, Eritrea, and stateless Somalia (Global Campaign for Education 2010: 6).

According to a recent study by the Forum for Social Studies using official Ministry of Education data (FSS 2009), the quality deterioration in Ethiopian higher education is a manifestation of the overall deterioration in quality. If we take the case of higher education, for instance, in seven years (from 2000 to 2007), the student population in tertiary-level public institutions doubled from about 87,400 to 176,100. By 2008, more than 50 percent of the faculty teaching in these higher education institutions were bachelor degree holders while less than 10 percent of the faculty are Ph.D. holders (FSS 2009: 44). This increase in university-level enrollment came in the wake of a significant expansion in elementary, secondary, and technical education, which grew by more than 7 times, 2 times, and 23 times, respectively, between 1994 and 2006 (FSS 2009: 140). The significant deterioration in quality is easily observed if we look at the results of the National Learning Assessment tests conducted in the years 2000, 2004, and 2007. While the official passing grade for these tests is 50 percent, the average grade for all the students was 41 percent, 39.7 percent, and 35.6 percent, respectively. (FSS 2009: 8) The situation gets even worse at the high school level. Only 7.6 percent of the students who took the high school national exam in 2007 and a meager 3 percent in 2008 were able to get the 50 percent or higher grade required to pass the exam. Forty-four percent and 58 percent of the students in 2007 and 2008, respectively, were able to get less than 25 percent, which "is equivalent to what anyone would have gotten by simply guessing the answer" (FSS 2009: 9).

What is seriously troubling about the data is the significant deterioration over time. In addition to the deterioration over time in the average scores cited above, the percentage of students getting a grade less than 25 percent in physics, math, and English increased from 96 percent, 86.3, percent and 39.6 percent, respectively, in 2007 to 99 percent, 90.1 percent, and 66.8 percent the following year. The average grade for these three subject were 14.8 percent in physics, 18.9 percent in math, and 29.3 percent in English in 2007, which was reduced to 13.3 percent, 17.9 percent, and 24.1 percent, respectively, the following year (FSS 2009: 9). What is truly bizarre and potentially very damaging to the country's future development prospects is the fact that these same students that have performed rather miserably in their assessment exams at the high school level are accepted in bulk at the public universities, further damaging the already atrocious quality of education at the tertiary level. Of the students who took the university entrance exams, 57.5 percent in 2006 and 69.6 percent in 2008 received less than 50 percent in their university entrance exams. However, the university system was forced to accept 97 percent and 88.1 percent of the students who took the exam in the ever-expanding higher education system of the country (FSS 2009: 11). Clearly, even if the rather unnatural increase in enrollment is initiated with altruistic motives, it has come at a very high cost in the quality of education, which is bound to adversely affect the country's development prospects in the long run.

If the official data on economic and social performance is questionable, what can be said about the performance of the Ethiopian economy in general and the possibility of a significant improvement in the life of the average Ethiopian to provide stability? If we go beyond the government's official GDP figures, the picture that emerges about the Ethiopian economy and the material well-being of the majority of its people is not pretty and does not show significant progress to provide political stability. Even if the growth numbers are valid, it does not necessarily ensure that the benefits of growth are distributed equitably to ensure stability in the short and medium run.

Recent reports on capital flight indicate that Ethiopia has been one of the countries in Africa where such flight has been increasing substantially.[37] According to Ndikumana and Boyce, capital flight from Ethiopia amounted to $2.4 billion in 2002 while the total stock increased to $22.4 billion in 2004. This amounts to 175 percent of GDP (Ndikumana and Boyce 2008: 41).

On the other hand, there is increasing evidence that life has gotten harder for the average person in the country. As suggested earlier, one issue that has robbed the standard of living of the average person since 2005 has been the unprecedented inflation that has plagued the country as a result of an uncontrolled increase in the money supply.[38] The level of deprivation in the country is substantial. Chronic poverty measured in terms of income in Ethiopia at a $1.25 a day level is about 39 percent, while it is 78 percent at $2 a day, according to World Bank data. When measured in terms of the more comprehensive Multidimensional Poverty Index, 90 percent of Ethiopians are MPI poor. If we use the most recent (2009) Human Development Index used by the United Nations Development Program (UNDP), Ethiopia ranks 171st out of 182 countries.[39] But according to the MPI index, which is supposed to replace the HDI in 2011, Ethiopia's rank is 103rd out of 104 countries—only higher than Niger. Recent news reports regarding the level of hunger among children in the capital Addis Ababa clearly show that the economic condition of the country among the poor is dire. Teachers in many schools in the capital are reporting an increasing number of children collapsing in class from hunger and unable to follow their lessons. Such reports about urban poverty are becoming increasingly common in the country.[40]

It is plausible that in terms of generating stability, people's expectations about the future is as much, if not more important than current conditions. Even if people's lives are not significantly improving now, they can patiently wait for a better future if they feel optimistic about the days ahead. Unfortunately for Ethiopia, there is no such hopeful expectation from the majority of the public. According to the most recent survey by Gallup and reported in the Legatum prosperity index, which put Ethiopia 107th out of 110 countries in its current and potential prosperity, significant pessimism prevails about future conditions. According to this report in Ethiopia:

> Just a third of the population is satisfied with their standard of living, a rate that places at 102nd in the Index. Economic pessimism is rife: only one out of five people believe that job market opportunities are improving, and the average citizen believes conditions are getting worse; this ranks Ethiopia in the bottom quartile of the Index with respect to economic expectations (Legatum 2010: 160).

This pessimism is not limited to economic variables. The same index reported significant displeasure among the public in relation to their health attainment and their expectation of their children's education. "Just 43 percent of the population are satisfied with the quality of their children's education, while only one-third believe their children have the opportunity to learn and grow every day." In terms of health attainment, the situation is not any better. The country's "health-adjusted life expectancy, at 41 years, places [it] in the bottom 10. Over half of the population is undernourished" (Legatum 2010: 160).

If the government is credited neither for its good governance nor for its performance in delivering better economic and social conditions for the population despite the massive amounts of aid it has received from Western donors,[41] what is going to be the basis for the future stability of the Ethiopian state? Is there any other option than establishing a democratically accountable governance system?

DEMOCRATIC ACCOUNTABILITY AS A NECESSARY CONDITION FOR A STABLE POLITY IN ETHIOPIA

Ethiopia is the second-most populous country in Africa, located in the strategic yet volatile Horn of Africa. Political stability in the country is extremely important for the country's long-term development as well as the stability of the entire region. The seemingly endless crisis in Somalia, the troubles in the now divided Sudan, the conflict between Ethiopia and Eritrea, the increasing presence of Islamic extremism in both Somalia and Yemen all have made the region one of the most dangerously unstable parts of the world. Seen from the context of the regional equation,

Ethiopia's internal political situation looks relatively more stable even if there are a number of low-intensity conflicts within the country itself. The hope that the political situation in Ethiopia can be stabilized through the establishment of a democratically accountable government that can address the country's multifaceted problems has failed to materialize with the aborted democratic experiment of 2005. Once it became clear that the ruling party was not going to live up to its own constitution and establish a democratic order, the international community seems to have settled for accepting the existing regime as a force for stability in the region, even if it has gone further away from democratizing the Ethiopian state. In fact, as the data in table 1 clearly shows, the international community (or at least Western countries) seems to be desperately trying to stabilize the regime by pumping more and more money into the country. Surely the West has indicated its displeasure with the wrong direction the country has taken since 2005 in terms of democratic accountability as the near universal condemnation of the most recent election attests. Still, the main current in Western foreign policy circles is that despite its problems, Ethiopia is the best and most stable ally that the West has in that part of the world.[42]

The concern about Ethiopia's stability is legitimate both in its own right and in its value for the stability of the region. Given the size and location of the country, serious instability in Ethiopia could have far-reaching consequences to the region's stability. To avoid a potential disaster, therefore, it will be extremely important to identify the sources of instability in Ethiopia and address these issues squarely. It is not going to be constructive in the long run to settle for what currently prevails in the country simply because as it currently stands, Ethiopia looks relatively more stable than its neighbors.

The first thing to note is that the country is not currently as stable as some analysts believe simply because of the absence of large-scale civil war. As it stands now there are a number of low-intensity conflicts taking place in different parts of the country, including in Oromia, Ogaden, Amhara, and Afar regions. Some of these conflicts are significant enough to attract international attention, as in the Ogaden. Following the raid by the Ogaden National Liberation Front (ONLF) of a Chinese-run oil exploration field killing some 74 people in April 2007, the region has remained a hotbed of rebel activity and government counterinsurgency measures that raised serious concerns about crimes against the civilian population of the region committed by the Ethiopian army.[43] According to recent reports, one of the largest oil and gas exploration companies has recently suspended its activities in the Ogaden because of security concerns.[44] The intensity of these conflicts is bound to increase as long as the underlying causes of these conflicts remain unaddressed.

One of these unresolved issues that keep festering in the country's body politics is the ethnicization of society. Ethiopia is probably the only African country that not only officially recognized ethnic-based identity but also actively discouraged citizenship-based pan-Ethiopian political discourse as a manifestation of chauvinism. In other words, Ethiopian nationalism was discouraged in favor of ethnic nationalism as official state ideology. This is rather odd for a government claiming to be a developmentalist state since the most important binding ideology for such states has always been nationalism (Mkandawire 2001).

Nine regional states were created on the basis of ethnic criteria and granted the right to secede. Children were discouraged to learn the national language in favor of their ethnic language. Although the idea of redefining politics and citizenship on the basis of ethnicity within an ethnic federal system was supposed to address historical tensions among the various ethnic groups, this has not been realized in practice as the system has "failed to accommodate grievances [while] it has powerfully promoted ethnic self-awareness among all groups" (International Crisis Group 2009: ii). Enhanced ethnic self-awareness would have been risky but tolerable if all the ethnic groups in the country felt that the system was reasonably fair and equitable for all the ethnic groups in terms of allocation of political power and distribution of economic resources. Unfortunately, there is a deep-rooted belief that a small minority elite (Tigrean) commands an inordinate amount of political power that it uses to amass economic resources for the benefit of its kith and kin. This has generated deep-rooted resentment among the larger ethnic groups (particularly Amharas and Oromos), making the situation even more volatile.

Furthermore, the changing international environment has significantly increased the awareness of the public about the ideas of liberty and representative democracy. What was observed in 2005 was, to a certain degree, a reflection of this awareness and expectation. This unfulfilled expectation particularly among the educated elite and the urban youth, combined with the failed promise of genuine self-administration for the large ethnic groups of the country, has created a potentially explosive tension within the Ethiopian body politic. The regime's exclusive concentration on staying in power by any means, especially after 2005, has created a dangerous environment that could explode to a broader armed rebellion against the regime. According to the International Crisis Group's recent study:

> After 2005, its objective has been simply to stay in power. To do so, it has established a party-state system that perpetuates its rule but frustrates large parts of the population.

Its obsession with controlling political processes from the federal to the local level reflects the former liberation fighters' paranoia and incites opposition groups to consider armed struggle their only remaining option (Crisis Group 2009: 29).

As intimated earlier, the government's attempt to bury these issues and hope to buy stability through the claimed economic growth is not going to work—not only because the rhetoric of growth and the reality of poverty on the ground do not match, but because even if this growth were real, the powerful emotional forces that are unleashed by the regime's ethnic policies are not going to be neutralized because of perceived economic benefits. As the Crisis Group study correctly observed, the link between economic performance and popular support to the regime are not strong and immediate. Accordingly, the government's hope, which is partly shared by the international community, that the country can be stabilized by generating rapid economic growth without fundamentally reforming the political system is a dangerous illusion that could generate serious instability both in Ethiopia and by extension to the volatile region of the Horn of Africa.

The only way Ethiopia can be stabilized in the long run is when the enhanced aspiration of ethnic groups for meaningful self-governance and the rising expectation of the country's youth and educated elite to live in an environment of freedom are jointly addressed. While the specific form of the political dispensation that could guarantee this within the Ethiopian context can be debated and discussed, one thing that cannot be denied is that the system that must be established is a democratically accountable state that provides citizens with a sense of ownership in the political system. In this sense accountable governance is not valuable for Ethiopia as an instrument of development and long-term prosperity, although it is needed for that too. Even more urgently, it is needed for its stability and viability as a political community. That is why the international community's indifference to the current crisis of governance in the country, or as some would say its active complicity (HRW 2010),[45] is extremely short-sighted and ill advised even from the perspective of geopolitical calculus. As the Crisis Group's study cogently concluded:

> The international community has ignored or downplayed the problems. Some donors consider food security more important than democracy in Ethiopia. In view of the mounting ethnic awareness and political tensions created by the regionalization policy, however, external actors would be well advised to take the governance problems more seriously and adopt a more principled position towards the Meles Zenawi government (Crisis Group 2009: 29).

CONCLUSION

The current regime in Ethiopia has remained in power for almost two decades, riding the wave of hatred against the Mengistu regime while at the same time promising gradual democratization in the future. It has also successfully exploited the ethnic hostility that existed in the country by declaring a new era of ethnic equality and ethnic-based federal structure that promised democratic self-government for these ethnic-based regions. Since the 2005 election debacle, it is clear that the ruling TPLF/EPRDF regime is not prepared to accept defeat at the ballot box under any circumstances. The possibility for a peaceful transition to a democratic political order is not in the cards in the foreseeable future. The ethnic equality and genuine self-government that was promised by the regime has also proved to be hollow as the senior partners in the EPRDF coalition, the Tigrean-based TPLF, made it clear that an assertive ethnic nationalism from the larger ethnic groups, such as the Oromos or the Amharas, will not be tolerated since it would undermine their dominant position in the new power structure. This was seen when they pushed the nationalist Oromo Liberation Front (OLF) out of the coalition government by force in 1992. Accordingly, the ethnic-based regional governments were established by regional parties allied to the regime with very little independence to administer their regions. Yet, the early rhetoric of democratic governance and promotion of ethnic-based identity politics have heightened ethnic awareness among the masses of the population as well as expectation of the possibility of a democratic politics among the country's educated elite. Both of these unfulfilled expectations have generated significant frustration among the population and are bound to become serious sources of political instability.

Cognizant of this frustration, the government has sought to change the political discourse from democratization and democratic accountability to development as the primary basis for the evaluation of the government's legitimacy since 2005. To this end the government has tried to position itself as a "developmentalist state" that is delivering on economic and social achievements by citing rapid economic growth as well as significant progress on social development. Interestingly, this developmentalism is also shorn of the nationalist ideology that has served as a glue to hold the state together in other countries. However, while this discourse might be buying the government support from some quarters in the international community, it is not clear that it can provide the desired political stability in the country. There is not much tangible progress in the economic well-being of the average person or optimism in his or her expectation about the future to forego the unfulfilled expectations generated by the change of regime in 1991 and the early rhetoric of liberty and equality by the new regime. In sum, at this time the Ethiopian state has no coherent and durable basis of legitimacy to enable it to avoid the dangerous instability that is observed in many parts of the region. Given the size and strategic location of the country, this should be worrisome to anyone who has a stake in the stability of the Horn of Africa region, including the international community.

Unfortunately, the government's obstinate refusal to change its direction and its continued rule with an iron fist, combined with the international community's fatigued reaction to the crisis in that part of the world, have allowed the problem of governance in Ethiopia to fester and grow increasingly intractable. In particular, the faith in modernization theory and the expectation that economic growth will solve all these problems in the long run (which is effectively exploited by the regime to shield itself from western criticism) has created a sense of resignation on the part of the international community and inhibit it from using its influence (which comes with its foreign aid money) to pressure the government for a peaceful change to a democratically accountable governance in Ethiopia. What is clear to any close observer of the Ethiopian situation, however, is that the only long-term guarantee for stable and sustainable development in Ethiopia is the establishment of a meaningful democratic state. A stable democratic Ethiopia at peace with itself is also the most durable recipe for the stability of the whole Horn of Africa Region.

NOTES
1. See the rankings of the Human Development Report at <http://hdr.undp.org/en/statistics/>.
2. For the Multidimensional Poverty Index, see Alkire and Santos (2010). They have also used the comparison between income poverty and MPI for Ethiopia in this introduction to their index.
3. This commitment to the development of the nation was not unique to Ethiopia. It is actually the common claim of postcolonial African leaders who, according to Mkandawire (2001: 296) "were deeply committed to the 'eradication of poverty, ignorance and disease' which formed an 'unholy' trinity against which nationalist swords were drawn in the post-colonial era." However, as Ake (1996: 9) noted correctly: "The ideology of development was exploited as a means of reproducing political hegemony; it got limited attention and served hardly any purpose as a framework for economic transformation."
4. This is based on the index for 2010. This index analyzes 177 countries and "rates them on 12 metrics of state decay—from refugee flows to economic implosion, human rights violations to security threats. Taken together, a country's performance on this battery of indicators tells us how stable—or unstable—it is. And unfortunately

for many of the 60 most troubled, the news from 2009 is grave. For the details about the index see <http://www.foreignpolicy.com/articles/2010/06/21/2010_failed_states_index_interactive_map_and_rankings>.

5. One of the most common refrains by Prime Minister Meles Zenawi of Ethiopia during this period was that democracy was not a luxury for Ethiopia. It was a necessity for its survival. He and his party, therefore, do not need any prodding from outsiders to be democratic.
6. Mkandawire (2001: 290) defines the ideology of a developmentalist state as one that "conceives its 'mission' as that of ensuring economic development, usually interpreted to mean high rates of accumulation and industrialization." Such a state "establishes as its principle of legitimacy its ability to promote sustained development, understanding by development the steady high rates of economic growth and structural change in the productive system, both domestically and in its relationship to the international economy."
7. Quoted in Bratton and Logan (2006: 3).
8. Cited in Bhagwati (2002: 151).
9. I have surveyed the debate on this issue in detail in another paper. See Nega (2009) for details.
10. The Make Poverty History campaign was initiated by an assortment of NGOs, charities, and celebrities in the United Kingdom and Ireland in 2005 and expanded to most rich countries in the world. It took advantage of Great Britain taking the chair of the Group of 8 (G8) under Prime Minister Tony Blair, who used the G8 meeting at Gleneagles, Scotland, to push a significant increase in aid to Africa. The campaign hopes to increase awareness in the West about poverty in developing countries and pressure rich country governments into taking actions toward relieving absolute poverty. For details about the campaign, see their official website: <http://www.makepovertyhistory.org/>.
11. It is understandable, if not justifiable, to hear politicians such as U.S. President Bill Clinton praise the "new breed of African democratic leaders" in the mid-1990s before the true nature of these regimes was revealed. It is absolutely mind boggling to hear prominent schol-

ars such as Jeffery Sachs chastise "the typical uninformed American view about Africa's governance" then praise a number of African leaders who are known for purposefully circumventing the democratic process—Kibaki of Kenya, Obasanjo of Nigeria, and Zenawi of Ethiopia, for example—as "Africa's new generation of democratic leaders" in 2005.

12. Freedom In the World 2010 Survey Release. http://www.freedomhouse.org/template.cfm?page=505
13. See Freedom House (2010).
14. For a detailed discussion on the historical roots of the so-called national question in Ethiopia and the problem it generated for establishing a liberal democratic politics in the country, see the discussion in Nega (2010).
15. For the assessment by the EU observation mission, see the mission's preliminary statement on the election. The conclusion that the election did not meet accepted international standards is echoed by both the EU and the U.S. State Department. National Security Council spokesman Mike Hammer dismissed the election whereby "an environment conducive to free and fair elections was not in place even before election day.", For the EU statement, see <http://allafrica.com/stories/201005260240.html>. For the U.S. statement, see <http://allafrica.com/stories/201005270004.html>.
16. The use of the judiciary as an instrument for exacting political vengeance by the ruling party is sufficiently documented in the case against the Coalition for Unity and Democracy (CUD) leaders in 2005, where the leaders were all sentenced to life imprisonment for alleged treason along with journalists and civil society activists. The case against the former defense minister, Seye Abreha, was another obvious case where the judiciary was used to punish a political opponent. For the CUD trials, see Amnesty International (2008). http://www.amnesty.org/en/region/ethiopia/report-2008. For the latter, see Seye Abreha's recent Amharic book *Liberty and Justice in Ethiopia* (2009).
17. One such case involves the exile of the two judges who left the country for refusing to change the findings of the enquiry commission

established by Parliament to investigate government violence against unarmed civilians following the contested 2005 election. After refusing to change their findings by the request of high-level government authorities, both were forced to flee the country and live in exile. For details about their case, see their presentation at the U.S. House of Representatives, Subcommittee on Africa <http://www.ethiomedia.com/addfile/ethiopian_inquiry_commission_briefs_congress.html>.
18. Proclamation to Provide for the Regulation and Registration of Charities and Societies, No. 621/2009 <http://www.crdaethiopia.org/Documents/Charities percent20and percent20Socities percent20Legislation percent20(Final percent20Version)-Negarit percent20Newspaper.pdf>. For a detailed analysis of the NGO law and its impact on development, see Nega and Milofsky (2009).
19. According to the most recent report by the Ministry of Justice, which is responsible for registering NGOs, out of the total of 3,522 NGOs that were registered before the country introduced the new law, only 1,655 have so far been able to reregister while the rest vanished. See *Africa News* (2010).
20. Officially there are only three independent radio stations in the country (independent of the federal or regional governments), all operating in the capital, Addis Ababa. One is owned by the ruling party and the other two are handpicked and given a permit by the authorities because of their sympathy to the ruling party.
21. For a brief analysis of the new Ethiopian media law, see Mushtaq (2008).
22. See the letter to the prime minister of Ethiopia in Committee to Protect Journalists (2009).
23. For the full presentation and the Q&A that followed Prime Minister Meles Zenawi's presentation at Columbia University's "World Leaders Forum," see <http://www.worldleaders.columbia.edu/events/prime-minister-ethiopia-meles-zenawi>.
24. For the most recent plan and the government's analysis of the previous plan, see Ministry of Finance and Economic Development (2010).

Note that the dates are according to the Ethiopian calendar, which is about eight years behind the Gregorian calendar.
25. This is actually a common refrain from foreign observers. For example, the head of the UNDP in Ethiopia, Samuel Nyambi, in an interview with *Forbes Global Magazine* states: "When I compare what I see here in terms of corruption with other African countries, I say Ethiopia is country which is exemplary in a sense." Special Country Report (1999).
26. See Transparency International (2009).
27. Other than some adjustments they make to ensure international comparability, these institutions simply take the data supplied by the government as given. They do not have their own separate or independent data collection mechanism.
28. For example, there has been significant difference between the agricultural data collected by the CSA, the Ministry of Agriculture, and the Food and Agricultural Organization, largely associated with the estimation methodology used. For these discrepancies, see, for example, the Ethiopian Economic Association (1999/2000: 157, n.3).
29. The food price inflation data during this period is contested, although everybody agrees that it was at a historically unprecedented level. For example, for 2008 it ranges from a low of about 68 percent to as high as 91.7 percent on average at the national level, while the figures are significantly higher in some regions. See for example, Loening, Durevall and Birru (2009).
30. For the food shortage and the threat of famine in 2008, see Hampson (2008).
31. Author's calculation from Gilligan et.al (2009: 12, table 1).
32. There is actually ample anecdotal evidence to corroborate this. Ministry of Agriculture representatives in rural areas, known as Development Agents (DAs), have said privately that they have been sending highly exaggerated output data to their headquarters to prove their diligence and possibly receive a promotion. These locally reported data are then added up to come up with national produc-

tion figures. In other words, there is a systematic and structural bias upward in the official reporting of output figures.

33. The data claimed by the Ethiopian government was not seriously taken by the Ethiopian public so the government usually resorts to justifying the numbers by arguing that the data is verified by the IMF and it is approved by them. For the prime minister's justification of his data by way of IMF approval, see his answer to an opposition parliamentarian's question about the incongruity of the data with the day-to-day miserable life of the people in March 2010. A portion of that answer is reported by the Voice of America radio program in Amharic on October 5, 2010 <http://www.voanews.com/mp3/voa/africa/amha/amha1800aTUE.mp3>.
34. See the article by William Wallis in the *Financial Times* (2010).
35 According to her comparison (Epstein 2010), in 2005, government officials, using Ministry of Health data, claimed that 87 percent of children had received all major vaccinations while the data from independent sources was closer to 27 percent.
36. The news article was posted on ENA's website at <http://www.ena.gov.et/EnglishNews/2010/Aug/19Aug10/119627.htm>. The news has been taken off the site since then, but no correction was posted regarding the news.
37. Philip Thornton of the *Independent,* citing a study by the New Economic Foundation, reported that foreign money deposits into British banks "had risen noticeably over the past five years, with inflows from Cameroon up 516 per cent, from Ethiopia rising 103 per cent and Nigeria up by 47 per cent" Thoornton (2006).
38. For the unprecedented increase in the money supply during this same period of inflationary pressure, see the article in a local business newspaper, *Capital* ("T-bill Auctions" 2010).
39. See UNDP, *Human Development Report,* HDI rankings, at <http://hdr.undp.org/en/statistics/>.
40. The Amharic program of Radio Deutsche Welle reports on its October 29, 2010 program about the widespread hunger in the city's schools. See <http://www.dw-world.de/dw/article/0,,6173318,00.html>.

41. According to OECD data, Ethiopia is currently the largest recipient of foreign aid money in the whole of Africa (OECD 2010).
42. A recent article in *German Foreign Policy* (October 4, 2010) regarding Germany's military and economic support to Ethiopia—despite numerous accusations of "war crimes" both in the Ogaden region of the country and in Somalia during Ethiopia's invasion of Somalia (2007-2009)—stated that "Berlin has been supporting the Ethiopian regime for years, because it has made itself useful as the West's East African proxy."*German Foreign Policy* (2010).
43. See Human Rights Watch (2008).
44. See a recent article by *Afrol News* (2010).
45. Human Rights Watch's most recent report on Ethiopia documents numerous cases where the government uses foreign aid resources to repress political dissent with full knowledge of the donor community. According to the report,

> development aid flows through, and directly supports, a virtual one-party state with a deplorable human rights record. Ethiopia's practices include jailing and silencing critics and media, enacting laws to undermine human rights activity, and hobbling the political opposition.... The government has used donor-supported programs, salaries, and training opportunities as political weapons to control the population, punish dissent, and undermine political opponents—both real and perceived. Local officials deny these people access to seeds and fertilizer, agricultural land, credit, food aid, and other resources for development.... Ethiopia's foreign donors are aware of this discrimination, but have done little to address the problem or tackle their own role in underwriting government repression. As a result, Ethiopia represents a case study of contradiction in aid policy. Donors acknowledge that aid is most effective when defined by accountability and transparency, and when programs are participatory. But, development agen-

cies have turned a blind eye to the Ethiopian government's repression of civil and political rights, even though they recognize these rights to be central to sustainable socioeconomic development (HRW, 2010:4-5).

REFERENCES

Aalen, Lovise, and Tronvoll Kjetil. "The 2008 Ethiopian Local Elections: The Return of Electoral Authoritarianism." *African Affairs* 108 (2008):111-120.

AbbInk, J. "Discomfiture of Democracy? "The 2005 Election Crisis in Ethiopia and Its Aftermath." *African Affairs* 105 (2006): 173-199.

Abouharb, Rodwan M., and Cingranell, David. *Human Rights and Structural Adjustment.* Cambridge: Cambridge University Press, 2007.

Abreha, Seye. "Liberty and Justice in Ethiopia." (In Amharic). Gaithersburg, Md.: Signature Books, 2009.

Acemoglu, Daren, Simon Johnson, James A. Robinson, and Pierre Yared. "Reevaluating the Modernization Hypothesis." *Journal of Monetary Economics* 56 (2009): 1043-1058.

Adnew, Berhanu. "The Performance of Ethiopian Agriculture: A Retrospective Study." Paper prepared as part of a study on agriculture and growth in Ethiopia. Addis Ababa, February 2009.

Africa News (July 6, 2010) <http://www.africanews.com/site/1867_NGOs_vanish_from_Ethiopia/list_messages/33257>.

———. "Multinationals Flee Ethiopia Oil Fields" (October 8, 2010) <http://www.afrol.com/articles/36734>.

Ake, Claude. "Democracy and Develoment in Africa." Washington D.C.: Brookings Institution, 1996.

Alkire, Sabina, and Maria Emma Santos. Multidimensional Poverty Index: 2010 Data. Oxford Poverty and Human Development Initiative <www.ophi.org.uk/policy/multidimensional-poverty-index/>.

Amnesty International (2008) <http://www.amnesty.org/en/region/ethiopia/report-2008>.

Annan, Kofi. Inaugural Address. International Conference on Governance for Sustainable Growth and Equity. United Nations, New York, July

28-30, 1997 <http://mirror.undp.org/magnet/icg97/ANNAN.HTM>.

Ayittey, George B. N. *Africa in Chaos.* New York: St. Martin's Griffin, 1999.

Bhagwati, Jagdish N. "Democracy and Development: Cruel Dilemma or Symbiotic Relationship? *Review of Development Economics* 6 (2002):152-162.

Bratton, Michael, and Carolyn Logan. "Voters but Not Yet Citizens: The Weak Demand for Political Accountability in Africa's Unclaimed Democracies." *Afro Barometer.* Working Paper 63 (September 2006).

Calderisi, Robert. *The Trouble With Africa: Why Foreign Aid Isn't Working.* New York: Palgrave Macmillan, 2006.

Collier, Paul. *The Bottom Billion: Why the Poorest Countries Are Failing and What Can Be Done About It.* New York: Oxford University Press, 2007.

Committee to Protect Journalists. "Anti-Terrorism Legislation Further Restricts Ethiopian Press." Washington, D.C., July 23, 2009 <http://cpj.org/2009/07/anti-terrorism-legislation-further-restricts-ethio.php>.

Dercon, Stefan, Ruth Vargas Hill, and Andrew Zeitin. "In Search of A Strategy: Rethinking Agriculture-Led Growth in Ethiopia." Paper prepared as part of a study on agriculture and Growth in Ethiopia. Addis Ababa, May 2009.

Diamond, Larry. "The Democratic Rollback: The resurgence of the Predatory State." *Foreign Affairs* 87 (March/April 2008).

Epstein, Helen. "Cruel Ethiopia." *The New York Review of Books* (May 13, 2010).

Ethiopian Economic Association. *First Annual Report on the Ethiopian Economy.* Addis Ababa, 1999/2000.

———. "Report on the Ethiopian Economy. Vol. III: Industrialization and Industrial Policy in Ethiopia." Addis Ababa, July 2004.

European Union Election Observation Mission. *Ethiopia Legislative Elections 2005: Final Report* <http://ec.europa.eu/external_relations/human_rights/election_observation/ethiopia/final_report_en.pdf>.

Federal Democratic Republic of Ethiopia. *Constitution of the Federal Democratic Republic of Ethiopia.* Addis Ababa, 1994 <http://www.erta.gov.et/pdf/Constitution.pdf>.

Feng, Yi. "Democracy, Political Stability and Economic Growth." *Journal of Political Science* 27 (1997): 391-418.

"The First 5 Year (1998-2002) Plan Implementation and the Next 5 Year (2003-2007) Growth and Transformation Plan Preparation." Paper Prepared for the Consultation Meeting of Regional and City Level Administrations. Addis Ababa: Ministry of Finance and Economic Development (July 2002). In Amharic.

Forum for Social Studies (FSS). "Quality of Higher Education in Ethiopian Public Institutions." Addis Ababa, 2009.

Freedom House. Map of Freedom: Sub-Saharan Africa, 2010 <http://www.freedomhouse.org/uploads/fiw10/FIW_2010_Map_Africa.pdf. Last visited July 21, 2010>.

Gasiorowski, Mark J. "Economic Crisis and Political Regime Change: An Event History Analysis." *American Political Science Review* 89 (1995): 882-897.

German Foreign Policy (October 4, 2010) <http://www.german-foreign-policy.com/en/fulltext/57875>.

Gilligan, D. O. et al. "An Impact Evaluation of Ethiopia's Productive Safety Nets Program." Washington, D.C.: International Food Policy Research Institute, June 30, 2009.

Global Campaign for Education. "Back To School? The Worst Places in the World to be A School Child in 2010." Saxonwold, South Africa, 2010.

Hall, Robert E., and Charles I. Jones. "Why Do Some Countries Produce So Much More Output Per Worker Than Others?" NBER Program on Economic Fluctuation and Growth, March 11, 1998 <http://elsa.berkeley.edu/~chad/pon400.pdf>.

Hampson, Rick. "Ethiopia's New Famine: A Ticking Time Bomb." *USA Today*, August 17, 2008.

Heliwell, John F. "Empirical Linkages between Democracy and Economic Growth." *British Journal of Political Science* 24 (1994): 225-248.

Human Rights Watch. "Ethiopia: Army Commits Executions, Torture, and Rape in Ogaden." New York, June 12, 2008 <http://www.hrw.org/

en/news/2008/06/12/ethiopia-army-commits-executions-torture-and-rape-ogaden>.

———. "Ethiopia, Development without Freedom: How Aid Underwrites Repression in Ethiopia." New York, 2010 <http://www.hrw.org/en/reports/2010/10/19/development-without-freedom>.

Huntington, S. *Political Order in Changing Societies.* New Haven: Yale University Press, 1968.

International Crisis Group. "Ethiopia: Ethnic Federalism and Its Discontents." *Africa Report* 153 (September 4, 2009).

Jackman, Robert. "On the Relations of Economic Development to Democratic Performance." *American Journal of Political Science* 17 (1973): 611—621.

Kaufmann, D., A. Kraay, and M. Mastruzzi. "The Worldwide Governance Indicators: Methodology and Analytical Issues." September 2010 <http://info.worldbank.org/governance/wgi/pdf/WGI.pdf>.

Legatum Institute. "The 2010 Legatum Prosperity Index" <http://www.prosperity.com/pdf/Ethiopia.pdf>.

Lipset, Seymour Martin et al. "A Comparative Analysis of the Social Requisites of Democracy." *International Social and Science Journal* 45 (1993): 155-175.

Loening, Josef L., Dick Durevall, and Yohannes Ayalew Birru. *Inflation Dynamics and Food Prices in an Agricultural Economy: The Case of Ethiopia.* Washington, D.C.: World Bank, Policy Research Working Paper Series 4969 (April 22, 2009) <http://ideas.repec.org/f/pdu207.html>.

Moss, Todd J. *African Development: Making Sense of the Issues and Actors.* Boulder, Colo.: Lynne Rienner, 2007.

Mkandawire, Tandika. "Thinking about Developmental States in Africa." *Cambridge Journal of Economics* 25 (May 2001): 289-313.

———. "From Maladjusted States to Democratic Developmental States in Africa." *Constructing a Democratic Developmental State in South Africa: Potentials and Challenges.* Ed. Omano Edigheji. Cape Town: HSRC Press, 2010.

Najum Mushtaq, "New Media Law, New Threat to Press Freedom."*Inter Press Service News Agency* (Nairobi) (July 8, 2008).

National Judicial Institute. "Independence, Transparency and Accountability in the Judiciary of Ethiopia." Prepared for the Canadian International Development Agency, October 2008 <http://www.abbaymedia.com/pdf/nij_ethiopian_judiciary_assessment.pdf>.

Ndikumana, Leonce, and Boyce, James K. "New Estimates of Capital Flight from Sub-Saharan African Countries: Linkages with External Borrowing and Policy Options." Political Economy Research Institute. Working Paper 166 (April 2008).

Nega, Berhanu. "Shortchanging the Value of Democracy for Economic Development in Africa." Paper Prepared for the Allied Social Science Conference. San Francisco, January 6-9, 2009.

———. "Identity Politics and the Struggle for Liberty and Democracy in Ethiopia." Forthcoming in the proceedings of the Oromo Studies Association 24th annual conference. Washington, D.C., Summer 2011.

Nega, Berhanu, and Carl Milofsky. "Ethiopia's Anti-NGO Law. Consequences for Development." Paper prepared for the Editorial Board Conference, *Community Development Journal*, London, September, 2009.

O'Donnell, Guillermo. "Delegative Democracy." *Journal of Democracy* 5 (January 1994): 55-69.

Olson, Mancur "Dictatorship, Democracy and Development." *American Political Science Review* 87: 3 (1993): 567-576.

Organization For Economic Cooperation and Development. "International Development Statistics (IDS) Online Databases on Aid and Other Resource Flows, 2010 <http://www.oecd.org/dataoecd/50/17/5037721.htm>.

Pausewang Siegfried, Kjetil Tronvoll, and Aalen Lovise, eds. *Ethiopia since the Derg: A Decade of Democratic Pretension and Performance*. London: Zed Books, 2002.

Przeworski, Adam. "Democracy and Development." *The Evolution of Political Knowledge: Democracy, Autonomy, and Conflict*. Eds. Edward Mansfield, and Richard Sisson. Columbus: Ohio State University Press, 2004.

Puddington, Arch. "Freedom in the World 2010: Erosion of Freedom Intensifies." *Freedom in the World 2010.* Washington, D.C., 2010.

Rivera-Batiz, Francisco L. "Democracy, Governance, and Economic Growth: Theory and Evidence." *Review of Development Economics* 6 (2002): 225-247.

Sachs, Jeffrey D. *The End of Poverty: Economic Possibilities for Our Time.* New York: Penguin Press, 2005.

Schneider, Geoffrey E. "Comparative Institutional Advantage and the Appropriate Development Model for Sub-Saharan Africa." *Forum for Social Economics* 37 (February 2008):115-124.

Sen, Amartya. *Development as Freedom.* New York: Anchor Books, 1999.

Siegle, Joseph T., et al. "Why Democracies Excel." *Foreign Affairs* 83 (Sept.-Oct. 2004).

Smulovitz, Catalina, and Enrique Peruzzotti. "Societal Accountability in Latin America." *Journal of Democracy* 11 (2000): 147-158.

Special Country Report on Ethiopia. *Forbes Global Magazine* (July 26, 1999).

Stiglitz, Joseph E. "Participation and Development: Perspectives from the Comprehensive Development Paradigm." *Review of Development Economics* 6 (2002):163-182.

———. *Globalization and Its Discontents.* New York: Norton, 2003.

"T-bill Auctions Latest Attempt to Control Liquidity." *Capital* (Addis Ababa), March 21, 2010 <http://www.capitalethiopia.com/index.php?option=com_content&view=article&id=12526:t-bill-auctions-latest-attempt-to-control-liquidity&catid=12:local-news&Itemid=4>.

Thoornton, Philip. "Cash Exodus Points to Laundering." *The Independent,* May 16, 2006.

Transparency International: Corruption Perception Index 2009 < http://www.transparency.org/policy_research/surveys_indices/cpi/2009/cpi_2009_table>.

William Wallis. "Perfidious Donors Betray Africa's Democrats." *Financial Times,* August 9, 2010.

World Bank. World Development Indicators: 2009 <http://data.worldbank.org/indicator/NY.GDP.MKTP.KD.ZG>.

social research
An International Quarterly
Vol 77 : No 4 : Winter 2010

Volume 77
Table of Contents
Index of Contributors

Contents
Vol 77 : Nos 1–4

Vol 77 : No 1
Migration Politics

v Endangered Scholars Worldwide

xi VICTORIA HATTAM AND RIVA KASTORYANO
Guest Editors' Introduction

1 KENNETH PREWITT
When Social Inequality Maps to Demographic Diversity, What Then for Liberal Democracy?

21 ROGERS M. SMITH
From the Shining City on a Hill to a Great Metropolis on a Plain? American Stories of Immigration and Peoplehood

45 SON-THIERRY LY AND PATRICK WEIL
The Antiracist Origin of the Quota System

79 RIVA KASTORYANO
Codes of Otherness

101 MARY C. WATERS AND PHILIP KASINITZ
Discrimination, Race Relations, and the Second Generation

133 VICTORIA HATTAM AND CARLOS YESCAS
From Immigration and Race to Sex and Faith: Reimagining the Politics of Opposition

163 RICHARD ALBA
Connecting the Dots between Boundary Change and Large-Scale Assimilation with Zolbergian Clues

181 SOPHIE BODY-GENDROT
European Policies of Social Control Post-9/11

205 MARTIN A. SCHAIN
Managing Difference: Immigrant Integration Policy in France, Britain, and the United States

237 ALEXANDRA DÉLANO
Immigrant Integration vs. Transnational Ties? The Role of the Sending State

269 JOHN TORPEY
A (Post-)Secular Age? Religion and the Two Exceptionalisms

297 THOMAS FAIST
Cultural Diversity and Social Inequalities

325 RICARD ZAPATA-BARRERO
Theorizing State Behavior in International Migrations: An Evaluative Ethical Framework

353 JAMES D. INGRAM AND TRIADAFILOS TRIADAFILOPOULOS
Rights, Norms, and Politics: The Case of German Citizenship Reform

Roundtable: Reflections on Aristide Zolberg's Life and Work

385 ANN SNITOW
The Joy of Memory

391 DAVID APTER
Interdisciplinary from the Start

399 COURTNEY JUNG
Professor Zolberg Goes to Africa

405 IRA KATZNELSON
Pluralism in Scholarship and Experience

411 ARISTIDE ZOLBERG
Decoding Patterns

Vol 77 : No 2
Happiness

v Endangered Scholars Worldwide

xi ARIEN MACK
Editor's Introduction

421 ALAN RYAN
Happiness and Political Philosophy

441 BO ROTHSTEIN
Happiness and the Welfare State

469 DARRIN M. MCMAHON
What Does the Ideal of Happiness Mean?

491 ALEXANDER WELSH
Living Happily However After

523 ADAM POTKAY
Narrative Possibilities of Happiness, Unhappiness, and Joy

545 SANDER L. GILMAN
Happiness and Unhappiness as a "Jewish Question"

569 MARK LARRIMORE
Religion and the Promise of Happiness

595 JON MILLER
A Distinction Regarding Happiness in Ancient Philosophy

625 FRED FELDMAN
On the Philosophical Implications of Empirical Research on Happiness

659 MORTEN L. KRINGELBACH AND KENT C. BERRIDGE
The Neuroscience of Happiness and Pleasure

679 ALOIS STUTZER AND BRUNO S. FREY
Recent Advances in the Economics of Individual Subjective Well-Being

715 CAROL GRAHAM, SOUMYA CHATTOPADHYAY, AND MARIO PICON
Adapting to Adversity: Happiness and the 2009 Economic Crisis in the United States

749 ANKE C. PLAGNOL
Subjective Well-Being over the Life Course: Conceptualizations and Evaluations

Vol 77 : No 3
Limiting Knowledge in a Democracy

v Endangered Scholars Worldwide

xiii ARIEN MACK
Editor's Introduction

Part I: Recurrence of Limits on Knowledge

769 JAMES E. MILLER
Introduction: Recurrence of Limits on Knowledge

773 DANIEL ELLSBERG
Secrecy and National Security Whistleblowing

805 DAVID T. BARSTOW
The Freedom of Information Act and the Press: Obstruction or Transparency?

811 CHRISTOPHER CAPOZZOLA
Afterburn: Knowledge and Wartime

827 GLENN GREENWALD
Limiting Democracy: The American Media's World View, and Ours

839 STEVEN AFTERGOOD
National Security Secrecy: How the Limits Change

Part II: Arguments For and Against Limits on Knowledge in a Democracy

855 DAVID Z. ALBERT
Introduction: Arguments for and against Limits on Knowledge in a Democracy

857 PHILIP KITCHER
Varieties of Freedom and Their Distribution

873 JAMEEL JAFFER
The Mosaic Theory

883 JULIE E. COHEN
The Inverse Relationship between Secrecy and Privacy

Part III: Limits on Knowledge: The Nexus of Power, Policy, and Research

901 KENNETH PREWITT
Introduction: Limits to Knowledge? No Easy Answer

905 RONALD BAYER AND AMY FAIRCHILD
When Worlds Collide: Health Surveillance, Privacy, and Public Policy

Part IV: Mechanisms of Limiting Knowledge

931 TREBOR SCHOLZ
Introduction: Points of Control

941 PETER GALISON
Secrecy in Three Acts

975 ERIC LICHTBLAU
The Obama Administration's Commitment to Transparency: A Progress Report

981 JOHN PALFREY
Four Phases of Internet Regulation

997 DANIEL SAREWITZ
Normal Science and Limits on Knowledge: What We Seek to Know, What We Choose Not to Know, What We Don't Bother Knowing

Part V: What We Have Learned about Limiting Knowledge in a Democracy: A Conversation

1013 PETER L. GALISON, VICTOR S. NAVASKY, NAOMI ORESKES, ANTHONY D. ROMERO, ARYEH NEIER

Vol 77 : No 4
From Impunity to Accountability: Africa's Development in the 21st Century

v Endangered Scholars Worldwide

xiii BEFEKADU DEGEFE AND BERHANU NEGA
Guest Editor's Introduction: Accountability for Development in Africa

1049 MARK HAUGAARD
Democracy, Political Power, and Accountability

1075 WILLIAM EASTERLY
Democratic Accountability in Development: The Double Standard

1105 PAUL COLLIER
The Political Economy of Natural Resources

1133 ROBERT H. BATES
Democracy in Africa: A Very Short History

1149 THANDIKA MKANDAWIRE
Aid, Accountability, and Democracy in Africa

1183 GEORGE B. N. AYITTEY
Traditional Institutions and the State of Accountability in Africa

1211 AGNÈS CALLAMARD
Accountability, Transparency, and Freedom of Expression in Africa

1241 CLEMENT EME ADIBE
Accountability in Africa and the International Community

1281 NICOLAS VAN DE WALLE AND KRISTIN MCKIE
An Accountable Budget Process in Sub-Saharan Africa: Problems and Prospects

1311 MUENI WA MUIU
Colonial and Postcolonial State and Development in Africa

1339 MWANGI S. KIMENYI, JOHN MUKUM MBAKU, AND NELIPHER MOYO
Reconstituting Africa's Failed States: The Case of Somalia

1367 KELECHI A. KALU
Nigeria: Learning from the Past to Meet the Challenges of the 21st Century

1401 BERHANU NEGA
No Shortcut to Stability: Democratic Accountability and Sustainable Development in Ethiopia

Comprehensive Free Access

Elsevier is proud to contribute all our journal content either free or at a very low cost to researchers in developing countries through a range of United Nations' initiatives – Hinari, AGORA and OARE.

research4life
http://www.research4life.org/

International Journal of Educational Development
Fosters critical debate about the role that education plays in development.
www.elsevier.com/locate/ijedudev

Journal of Development Economics
Publishes papers relating to all aspects of economic development - from immediate policy concerns to structural problems of underdevelopment.
www.elsevier.com/locate/devec

World Development
Multi-disciplinary journal of development studies
www.elsevier.com/locate/worlddev

Index of Contributors

1241 ADIBE, CLEMENT E. Accountability in Africa and the International Community

839 AFTERGOOD, STEVEN National Security Secrecy: How the Limits Change

163 ALBA, RICHARD Connecting the Dots between Boundary Change and Large-Scale Assimilation with Zolbergian Clues

855 ALBERT, DAVID Z. Introduction: Arguments for and against Limits on Knowledge in a Democracy

391 APTER, DAVID Interdisciplinary from the Start

1183 AYITTEY, GEORGE B. N. Traditional Institutions and the State of Accountability in Africa

805 BARSTOW, DAVID T. The Freedom of Information Act and the Press: Obstruction or Transparency?

1133 BATES, ROBERT H. Democracy in Africa: A Very Short History

905 BAYER, RONALD AND AMY FAIRCHILD When Worlds Collide: Health Surveillance, Privacy, and Public Policy

659 BERRIDGE, KENT C. AND MORTEN L. KRINGLEBACH The Neuroscience of Happiness and Pleasure

181 BODY-GENDROT, SOPHIE European Policies of Social Control Post-9/11

1211 CALLAMARD, AGNÈS Accountability, Transparency and Freedom of Expression in Africa

811 CAPOZZOLA, CHRISTOPHER Afterburn: Knowledge and Wartime

715 CHATTOPADHYAY, SOUMYA, CAROL GRAHAM AND MARIO PICON Adapting to Adversity: Happiness and the 2009 Economic Crisis in the United States

883 COHEN, JULIE E. The Inverse Relationship between Secrecy and Privacy

1105 COLLIER, PAUL The Political Economy of Natural Resources

237 DÉLANO, ALEXANDRA Immigrant Integration vs. Transnational Ties? The Role of the Sending State

xiii DEGEFE, BEFEKADU AND BERHANU NEGA Introduction: Accountability for Development in Africa

1075 EASTERLY, WILLIAM Democratic Accountability in Development: The Double Standard

773 ELLSBERG, DANIEL Secrecy and National Security Whistleblowing

905 FAIRCHILD, AMY AND RONALD BAYER When Worlds Collide: Health Surveillance, Privacy, and Public Policy

297 FAIST, THOMAS Cultural Diversity and Social Inequalities

625 FELDMAN, FRED On the Philosophical Implications of Empirical Research on Happiness

679 FREY, BRUNO S. AND ALOIS STUTZER Recent Advances in the Economics of Individual Subjective Well-Being

941 GALISON, PETER L. Secrecy in Three Acts

1013 GALISON, PETER L., VICTOR S. NAVASKY, NAOMI ORESKES, ANTHONY D. ROMERO, AND ARYEH NEIER What We Have Learned about Limiting Knowledge in a Democracy: A Conversation

545 GILMAN, SANDER L. Happiness and Unhappiness as a "Jewish Question"

715 GRAHAM, CAROL, SOUMYA CHATTOPADHYAY AND MARIO PICON Adapting to Adversity: Happiness and the 2009 Economic Crisis in the United States

827 GREENWALD, GLENN Limiting Democracy: The American Media's World View, and Ours

xi HATTAM, VICTORIA AND RIVA KASTORYANO Guest Editors' Introduction

133 HATTAM, VICTORIA AND CARLOS YESCAS From Immigration and Race to Sex and Faith: Reimagining the Politics of Opposition

1049 HAUGAARD, MARK Democracy, Political Power, and Accountability

353 INGRAM, JAMES D. AND TRIADAFILOS TRIADAFILOPOULOS Rights, Norms, and Politics: The Case of German Citizenship Reform

873 JAFFER, JAMEEL The Mosaic Theory

399 JUNG, COURTNEY Professor Zolberg Goes to Africa

1367 KALU, KELECHI A. Nigeria: Learning from the Past to Meet Challenges of the Twenty-first Century

101 KASINITZ, PHILIP AND MARY C. WATERS Discrimination, Race Relations, and the Second Generation

79 KASTORYANO, RIVA Codes of Otherness

xi KASTORYANO, RIVA AND VICTORIA HATTAM Guest Editors' Introduction

405 KATZNELSON, IRA Pluralism in Scholarship and Experience

1339 KIMENYI, MWANGI, JOHN MUKUM MBAKU, AND NELIPHER MOYO Reconstituting Africa's Failed States: The Case of Somalia

857 KITCHER, PHILLIP Varieties of Freedom and Their Distribution

659 KRINGELBACH, MORTEN L. AND KENT C. BERRIDGE The Neuroscience of Happiness and Pleasure

569 LARRIMORE, MARK Religion and the Promise of Happiness

975 LICHTBLAU, ERIC The Obama Administration's Commitment to Transparency: A Progress Report

45 LY, SON-THIERRY AND PATRICK WEIL The Antiracist Origin of the Quota System

1339 MBAKU, JOHN MUKUM, MWANGI KIMENYI, AND NELIPHER MOYO Reconstituting Africa's Failed States: The Case of Somalia

1281 MCKIE, KRISTIN AND NICOLAS VAN DE WALLE Toward an Accountable Budget Process in Sub-Saharan Africa: Problems and Prospects

469 MCMAHON, DARRIN M. What Does the Ideal of Happiness Mean?

769 MILLER, JAMES E. Introduction: Recurrence of Limits on Knowledge

595 MILLER, JON A Distinction Regarding Happiness in Ancient Philosophy

1149 MKANDAWIRE, THANDIKA Aid, Accountability and Democracy in Africa

1339 MOYO, NELIPHER, MWANGI KIMENYI, AND JOHN MUKUM MBAKU Reconstituting Africa's Failed States: The Case of Somalia

1311 MUIU, MUENI WA Colonial and Postcolonial State and Development in Africa

1013 NAVASKY, VICTOR S., PETER L. GALISON, NAOMI ORESKES, ANTHONY D. ROMERO AND ARYEH NEIER What We Have Learned about Limiting Knowledge in a Democracy: A Conversation

1401 NEGA, BERHANU No Short Cut to Stability: Democratic Accountability and Sustainable Development in Ethiopia

xiii NEGA, BERHANU AND BEFEKADU DEGEFE Introduction: Accountability for Development in Africa

1013 NEIER, ARYEH, PETER L. GALISON, VICTOR S. NAVASKY, NAOMI ORESKES, ANTHONY D. ROMERO What We Have Learned about Limiting Knowledge in a Democracy: A Conversation

1013 ORESKES, NAOMI, PETER L. GALISON, VICTOR S. NAVASKY, ANTHONY D. ROMERO AND ARYEH NEIER What We Have Learned about Limiting Knowledge in a Democracy: A Conversation

981 PALFREY, JOHN Four Phases of Internet Regulation

715 PICON, MARIO, CAROL GRAHAM, AND SOUMYA CHATTOPADHYAY Adapting to Adversity: Happiness and the 2009 Economic Crisis in the United States

749 PLAGNOL, ANKE C. Subjective Well-Being over the Life Course: Conceptualizations and Evaluations

523 POTKAY, ADAM Narrative Possibilities of Happiness, Unhappiness, and Joy

1 PREWITT, KENNETH When Social Inequality Maps to Demographic Diversity, What Then for Liberal Democracy?

901 PREWITT, KENNETH Introduction: Limits to Knowledge? No Easy Answer

1013 ROMERO, ANTHONY D., PETER L. GALISON, VICTOR S. NAVASKY, NAOMI ORESKES AND ARYEH NEIER What We Have Learned about Limiting Knowledge in a Democracy: A Conversation

441 ROTHSTEIN, BO Happiness and the Welfare State

421 RYAN, ALAN Happiness and Political Philosophy

997 SAREWITZ, DANIEL Normal Science and Limits on Knowledge: What We Seek to Know, What We Choose Not to Know, What We Don't Bother Knowing

205 SCHAIN, MARTIN A. Managing Difference: Immigrant Integration Policy in France, Britain, and the United States

931 SCHOLZ, TREBOR Introduction: Points of Control

21 SMITH, ROGERS M. From the Shining City on a Hill to a Great Metropolis on a Plain? American Stories of Immigration and Peoplehood

385 SNITOW, ANN The Joy of Memory

679 STUTZER, ALOIS AND BRUNO S. FREY Recent Advances in the Economics of Individual Subjective Well-Being

269 TORPEY, JOHN A (Post-)Secular Age? Religion and the Two Exceptionalisms

353 TRIADAFILOPOULOS, TRIADAFILOS AND JAMES D. INGRAM Rights, Norms, and Politics: The Case of German Citizenship Reform

1281 VAN DE WALLE, NICOLAS AND KRISTIN MCKIE Toward an Accountable Budget Process in Sub Saharan Africa: Problems and Prospects

101 WATERS, MARY C. AND PHILIP KASINITZ Discrimination, Race Relations, and the Second Generation

45 WEIL, PATRICK AND SON-THIERRY LY The Antiracist Origin of the Quota System

491 WELSH, ALEXANDER Living Happily However After

133 YESCAS, CARLOS AND VICTORIA HATTAM From Immigration and Race to Sex and Faith: Reimagining the Politics of Opposition

325 ZAPATA-BARRERO, RICARD Theorizing State Behavior in International Migrations: An Evaluative Ethical Framework

411 ZOLBERG, ARISTIDE Decoding Patterns

Development and Change

Celebrating over 40 years of cutting edge development research

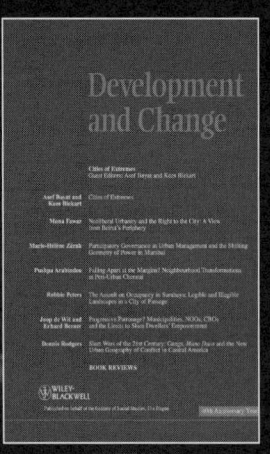

A key resource for the researcher, student, teacher and practitioner of development

- **Innovative research** in development studies and social change
- **Critical debates, intellectual legacies, topical interviews** in the FORUM issue
- **In-depth analysis** in special theme issues and book series
- **Special rates** for students and development research networks

Classic Articles

The Global Financial Crisis
Robert Wade,
interviewed by Alex Izurieta (2009)

Governing Capitol? Corporate Social Responsibility and the Limits of Regulation
Bridget O'Laughlin

From Universal Values to Millennium Development Goals: Lost in Translation
Ashwani Saith

Relocating Participation within a Radical Politics of Development
Sam Hickey and Gile Mohan

Orientalism Once More
Edward Said

The Developmet State is Dead – Long Live Social Capital?
Ben Fine

My Paradigm or Yours? Alternative Development, Post-Development, Reflexive Development
Jan Nederveen Pieterse

Daughters, Decisions and Domination: An Empirical and Conceptual Critique of Household Strategies
Diane Wolf

Conceptualizing the Household: Issues of Theory and Policy in Africa
Jane Guyer and Pauline Peters

How Agribusiness Operates in Underdeveloped Agricultures: Harvard Business School Myths and Reality
Ernest Feder

The New Generalism and the Crisis in Planning
Kurt Martin

WILEY-BLACKWELL   ISS International Institute of Social Studies

www.developmentandchange.com

JOURNAL OF THIRD WORLD STUDIES

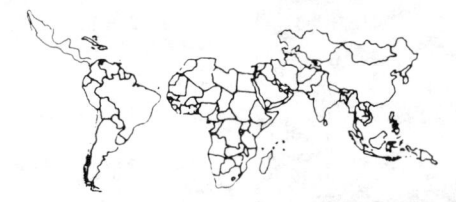

A Provocative and Scholarly Semi-Annual Periodical on Third World Developments...

FORTHCOMING ISSUES

Spring, 2010 - "Celebrating Change, Defining the Future: Social Justice, Democracy, and Cultural Renewal in the Third World."

Fall, 2010 - "Third World Problems and Issues in Historical Perspective."

Spring, 2011 - "A Confident Third World in the 21st Century: Facing the Multi-Dimensional Challenges of Transitional Periods."

Fall, 2011 - "Various Aspects of Third World Development in the Early 21st Century."

PAST CONTRIBUTORS HAVE INCLUDED:

Oscar Arias Sanchez	Paul N. Goldstene	Robert M. Maxon
A.B. Assensoh	William Head	John Mukum Mbaku
Yvette-Alex Assensoh	Harold Isaacs	J. Patrice McSherry
Michael B. Bishku	Gary Kline	Mary C. Muller
Cecil B. Currey	Thomas M. Leonard	Paul Rodell
Robert L. Curry, Jr.	Robert E. Looney	Yi Sun
Peng Deng	Paul J, Magnarella	Philip Szmedra
Nader Entessar	Rolin G. Mainuddin	Samuel Zalanga
Toyin Falola	Dorothea A.L. Martin	

YES. Please enter my one-year subscription to *Journal of Third World Studies (JTWS)*

Name _____

Address _____

_____

City/State/Zip Code _____

❑ Enclosed is my check for $60. (Make checks payable to "Association of Third World Studies, Inc."

Detach and send to: Association of Third World Studies, Inc.
P.O. Box 1232, Americus, Georgia 31709

Development Policy Review

Published on behalf of the Overseas Development Institute

Edited by: David Booth

Development Policy Review is the refereed journal that makes the crucial links between research and policy in international development. It publishes single articles and theme issues on topics at the forefront of current development policy debate. Coverage includes the latest thinking and research on poverty-reduction strategies, inequality and social exclusion, property rights and sustainable livelihoods, globalisation in trade and finance, and the reform of global governance.

Sample Articles:

- **Aid, institutions and governance: what have we learned?**
  David Booth
  Volume 29 (supplement 1) January 2011

- **Policy experiments, democratic ownership and development assistance**
  Jörg Faust
  Volume 25 (5) September 2010

- **Linking local government discretion and accountability in decentralisation**
  Serdar Yilmaz, Yakup Beris and Rodrigo Serrano-Berthet
  Volume 28 (3) May 2010

Published six times a year, ISSN: 0950-6764

To view a free online sample issue or to sign-up for our table of contents alerting service, visit:

WILEY-BLACKWELL

wileyonlinelibrary.com/journal/dpr

Comparative Politics

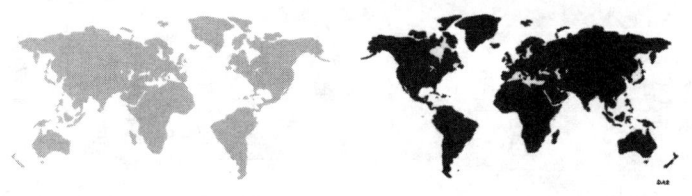

Comparative Politics is an international journal presenting articles devoted to comparative analysis of political institutions and processes. Recent issues have provided analyses of democratization, political economy, development policy, ethnic conflict, electoral institutions and practices, corruption, poverty, human rights, religion, and protest and contention. Studies have focused on all major world regions.

Comparative Politics communicates new ideas and research findings to social scientists, scholars, students, and public and NGO officials. The journal is indispensable to experts in universities, research organizations, foundations, embassies, and policymaking agencies throughout the world.

READ COMPARATIVE POLITICS ONLINE

as part of your individual or institutional subscription.

View article abstracts, place subscription orders, or purchase single articles at

WWW.INGENTACONNECT.COM/CONTENT/CUNY/CP

Recent and Forthcoming Articles:
- *David Laitin,* "American Immigration through Comparativists' Eyes"
- *Leonardo Villalón,* "From Argument to Negotiation: Constructing Democracy in African Muslim Contexts"
- *David Pion-Berlin and Harold Trinkunas,* "Civilian Praetorianism and Military Shirking During Constitutional Crises in Latin America"
- *Staffan Kumlin and Bo Rothstein,* "Questioning the New Liberal Dilemma: Immigrants, Social Trust, and the Welfare State"
- *Joshua Tucker and Grigore Pop-Eleches,* "Communism's Shadow: Post-Communist Legacies, Values, and Behavior"
- *Mona Lena Krook and Diana Z. O'Brien,* "The Politics of Group Representation: Quotas for Women and Minorities Worldwide"
- *Teresa Wright,* "State-Society Relations in Reform-Era China: A Unique Case of Postsocialist State-Led Development?"
- *Sebastián Mazzuca,* "Macrofoundations of Regime Change: State Formation and Capitalist Development"

TRACKING AFRICA'S DEVELOPMENT

AfricaRenewal

Takes you behind the headlines

Published quarterly by the United Nations, *Africa Renewal* spotlights the most important challenges facing Africa's development and the most notable African and UN initiatives to move the continent forward. From economic reform, regional integration and democratization to resource flows, trade, and the communications revolution, *Africa Renewal* provides in-depth news and analysis of a fast changing region.

Keep abreast of the ongoing debates over Africa's development stategies. Read first-hand reports from our contributors on the ground. Listen to the views of the most influential African and international analysts and policy-makers.

You can read *Africa Renewal* magazine and other Africa-related material online at:

www.un.org/AfricaRenewal

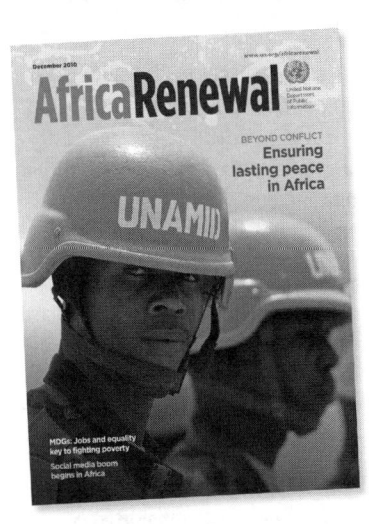

Africa Renewal is published in English and in French by the United Nations Department of Public Information.

Sign up for the print edition

Individual readers may receive a free subscription to either the English edition of *Africa Renewal* or the French version, *Afrique Renouveau* (please indicate which you would prefer) by sending your name, affiliation, and mailing address by e-mail to africarenewal@un.org or by regular mail to:

Africa Renewal, Circulation,
Room M-16031,
United Nations, NY 10017-2513, USA

Institutional and library subscriptions are also available for US$35.00, payable by international money order or by cheque in US dollars drawn on a US bank and made out to the "United Nations." Please send the mailing information and payment to the Circulation address above.

Notes on Contributors

CLEMENT EME ADIBE is Associate Professor of Political Science at Depaul University. Among his scholarly publications are *Africa in the United Nations* (2008) and *The State-Business Nexus in Nigeria* (2005).

GEORGE B. N. AYITTEY is President of the Free Africa Foundation. His books include *Africa Unchained: The Blueprint for Development* (2004), *Indigenous African Institutions* (2004), and *Africa in Chaos* (1998).

ROBERT H. BATES is Eaton Professor in the Department of Government at Harvard University and Associate Professor in the Department of Economics at the University of Toulouse. His books include *Prosperity and Violence* (2002) and *When Things Fell Apart* (2008).

AGNÈS CALLAMARD is Executive Director of ARTICLE 19, which focuses on the defense and promotion of freedom of expression and information worldwide. As Amnesty International's former Chef de Cabinet and Research Policy Coordinator, she led the organization's work on women's human rights.

PAUL COLLIER is the Director for the Center for the Study of African Economies and Professor of Economics at the University of Oxford, and Fellow of St Antony's College. His latest book is *The Plundered Planet: How to Reconcile Prosperity with Nature* (2010).

BEFEKADU DEGEFE was Research Fellow in the Department of Economics at the New School for Social Research from 2008-2010. He has served as a Senior Economic Affairs Officer with the UN Economic Commission for Africa, a Research Fellow at the International Monetary Fund, a consultant to the World Bank, and President of the Ethiopia Economic Association.

WILLIAM EASTERLY, Professor of Economics at New York University and codirector of its Development Research Institute, is the author of numerous books and articles and coeditor of the *Journal of Development Economics*. He directs and writes the Aid Watch blog.

MARK HAUGAARD is the editor of the *Journal of Power* and Senior Lecturer at the National University of Ireland, Galway. His recent publications include *The Sage Handbook of Power* (2009) and his book in progress is provisionally entitled *Rethinking Power*.